China's Rise and the Balance of Influence in Asia

THE SECURITY CONTINUUM:
GLOBAL POLITICS IN THE MODERN AGE

Series Editors: William W. Keller and Simon Reich

A series published in association with the
Matthew B. Ridgway Center for International Security
Studies and the Ford Institute for Human Security

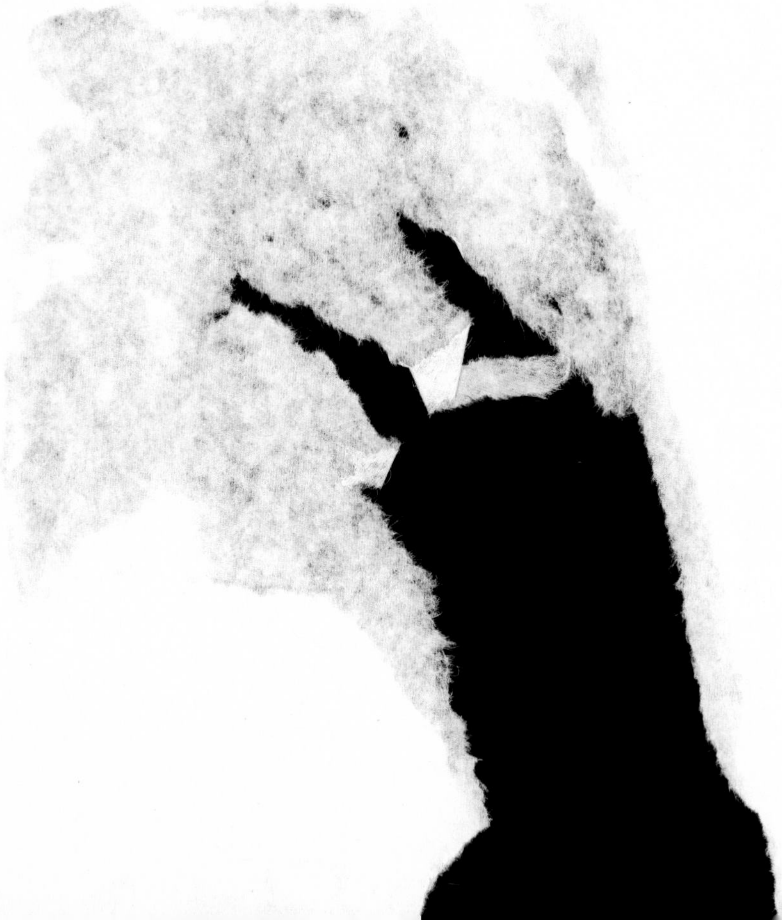

CHINA'S RISE
and the Balance of Influence in Asia

edited by WILLIAM W. KELLER
and THOMAS G. RAWSKI

University of Pittsburgh Press

Published by the University of Pittsburgh Press, Pittsburgh, Pa., 15260

Manufactured in the United States of America
Printed on acid-free paper
10 9 8 7 6 5 4 3 2 1

Library of Congress Cataloging-in-Publication Data

China's rise and the balance of influence in Asia / edited by William W. Keller and Thomas G. Rawski.

p. cm. — (The security continuum)

Includes bibliographical references and index.

ISBN-13: 978-0-8229-4312-9 (hardcover : alk. paper)

ISBN-13: 978-0-8229-5967-0 (pbk. : alk. paper)

ISBN-10: 0-8229-4312-3 (hardcover : alk. paper)

ISBN-10: 0-8229-5967-4 (pbk. : alk. paper)

1. China—Economic policy. 2. China—Foreign economic relations. 3. Asia—Economic integration. I. Keller, William W. (William Walton), 1950– II. Rawski, Thomas G., 1943–

HC427.C55985 2007

337.5105—dc22 2007006109

CONTENTS

ILLUSTRATIONS

Tables

Figures

ACKNOWLEDGMENTS

Expanding our ideas about the impact of China's long boom on the political economy of Asia into a series of conferences and finally into a book required extensive help and support. Within the University of Pittsburgh, Provost James V. Maher, Director William Brustein of the University Center for International Studies, Director Bell Yung of the Asian Studies Center, and Dean Kerry Ban of the Graduate School of Public and International Affairs provided crucial encouragement and funding. We are also grateful to the Centre for International Studies at the University of Toronto, both for funding and for the intellectual stimulation provided by its director, Louis W. Pauly, who also contributed to a chapter in this volume.

Both authors and organizers benefited from challenging and perceptive commentaries from three discussants: Robert Ross of Boston College, whom we subsequently recruited as an author, Szu-yin Ho of Taiwan's National Cheng Chi University, and Zhu Feng of Peking University. The contributors provided rapid and cheerful responses to multiple requests for revisions, clarifications, and updates. Throughout the project, we depended mightily upon members of our office staff, including Lauree Graham in Economics and A. S. M. Ali Ashraf, Beverly Brizzi, Kelly McDevitt, and Sandy Monteverde at the Matthew B. Ridgway Center for International Security Studies. Patricia Hermenault deserves special recognition for shepherding the manuscript through many revisions. Our thanks to all.

China's Rise and the Balance of Influence in Asia

PART 1

China's Rise

★1 ASIA'S SHIFTING STRATEGIC AND ECONOMIC LANDSCAPE

William W. Keller and Thomas G. Rawski

Asia's balance of influence is shifting on all fronts—economically, militarily, technologically, diplomatically, and politically. The pace of change is accelerating. From the financial disruptions of the late 1990s to the ensuing nuclear crises, first in South Asia and then on the Korean Peninsula, Asia is a land transformed and transforming. It is also a region casting off Cold War Western influence and control, ready to exert economic, political, and, potentially, military muscle in response to expressions of American hegemony.

China's economic ascendance and political transition stands out as both a major episode in the history of global political economy and as the primary driver of wide-ranging changes in Asia's economic, technological, diplomatic, and security alignments. Beginning in the late 1970s, China experienced three decades of extraordinary growth that raised every indicator of material welfare, lifted hundreds of millions from poverty, and propelled China from near autarky into regional and global prominence. These unprecedented developments have transformed China into a substantial U.S. trade and investment partner, a regional military power, and a major influence on national economies and cross-national interchange throughout the Pacific region.

China has surpassed Japan as Asia's leader in military spending and in many dimensions of international trade. China is, moreover, emerging as a voice for East Asian economic, political, and security interests.[1] Beijing's contribution to stabilizing regional markets during the Asian financial crisis beginning in 1997 and its central role in the six-power North Korea nuclear talks underscore China's growing prominence in regional and global efforts to manage contentious economic, social, and security issues. China's accession to the World Trade Organization (WTO) has accentuated these trends and may alter the balance of economic power in Asia as dynamically and dramatically as internal reform has restructured China's domestic balance between state-owned and private sector business.

We need not assume that China's high-speed growth will endure—although this is certainly possible. The dramatic multilateral impact of Japan's earlier growth spurt on trade, diplomacy, investment, technology, management, business structures, government regulation, and even national psychology demonstrates the profound consequences of economic change, even when military development remains muted. Given its far greater population, land mass, and economic potential, China's international impact during the next several decades seems likely to overshadow the global consequences of Japan's protracted growth spurt during the concluding decades of the twentieth century.

But there is a difference in kind as well. If the nations of Asia are arrayed on a techno-national versus techno-global scale, Japan and Korea seem worlds apart from China, which resembles the United States in many respects. In particular, China is more open to reciprocal trade, to foreign investment, and to trade in technology. Like the United States, China appears receptive to worldwide diffusion of technology under principles of free and open trade. These characteristics stand in stark contrast to the long-standing protectionist tendencies of official and unofficial policy in both Japan and South Korea.[2]

China's great boom already affects the regional and global alignment of power through Beijing's far-flung projection of economic, technological, and diplomatic influence. Comprehending this process, anticipating its implications, and formulating constructive responses will require new approaches that effectively integrate the often disparate worlds of economics, politics, and military strategy. Our investigation is structured to inform a U.S. policy on Asia capable of responding to dynamic change.

The central theme of this book is to examine the hypothesis that Beijing's vision of China's peaceful rise represents a practical and realistic path for the protracted and intricate global ballet to which China's vast and prolonged economic boom provides a remarkable overture.

This book analyzes the Asia-wide implications of China's rapid and largely unanticipated emergence as an economic, political, and military power and as a significant presence in both regional and global affairs. It employs a comprehensive, multidisciplinary analysis of the changing balance of influence in Asia. In this framework, the traditional notion of a balance of power is supplanted by the metaphor of a magnet, capable of causing political and economic realignment throughout Asia. One can easily envisage a world in which the rise of a single state can decisively alter long-standing patterns of military and economic relations.

An animating concern of this book is apparent U.S. disengagement from Asia at a time when China is recapturing its historical role as a great power, and positioning itself as a leading state in global affairs. This aspect of China's rise involves careful and energetic Chinese commercial diplomacy, which contrasts sharply with the tendency of recent U.S. administrations to concentrate diplomatic and military initiatives in other regions. Whether due to increased Chinese economic clout or U.S. neglect, the balance of influence is shifting in China's favor. It is past time for the United States to refocus attention on its economic and political interests in Asia.

Asia's primacy for American interests is beyond doubt. Asia has become the United States' largest economic partner: U.S. trade with Asia amounted to US$1022.3 billion in 2005 compared to US$847.6 billion of trade with Europe during the same year.[3] In the security field, Europe responded to the end of the Cold War by reducing military expenditures from US$257 billion in 1985 to US$189 billion in 2001. At the same time, Asia pursued a military buildup (both conventional and nuclear) with overall defense spending rising from US$128 billion in 1985 to US$154 billion in 2001.[4] Perhaps more telling, in 1999 and in all subsequent years, China's military budgets exceeded those of the major European powers. And in 2003, the last year for which statistics are available, China's and Japan's defense budgets reached US$56 and US$43 billion respectively, compared to US$35, US$46, and US$43 billion for Germany, France, and the United Kingdom. The Chinese and Japanese figures are notable because Chinese military expenditures have consistently exceeded those of Japan since 2001.[5]

Although divided by historical enmities, Asian nations are paradoxically rushing toward integration of trade, manufacturing, and investment, both regionally and worldwide. Trade optimists foresee a golden age of global and intra-Asian trade and investment that can raise living standards, education levels, and life prospects for Asia's billions.[6] They welcome China's new penchant for making deals rather than fomenting revolution and applaud the recent flurry of regional and bilateral free trade agreements. One analyst argues that, with the exception of the Taiwan issue, China is more open to existing international institutions and norms and even to "U.S. dominance of the international and regional power structure than at any time since 1949."[7]

Security pessimists are less sanguine. They point to China's growing military budget and extensive plans for force modernization, concomitant with the long cycle of economic expansion.[8] Some forecast the coming of a "second nuclear age" with many potential nuclear weapons states outside the West and outside the Nuclear Nonproliferation Treaty (NPT). They cite the nuclear aspirations of North Korea and Iran, the nuclear standoff between India and Pakistan, and the inability of the 2005 NPT Conference to make meaningful progress. They fear that failure to stem North Korea's nuclear ambition could stimulate other countries to follow Pyongyang's lead in withdrawing from the NPT—perhaps South Korea, Taiwan, or possibly even Japan. Several studies warn that Asian military affairs and economic relations may be far from harmonious in the future. One analyst observes that the absence of efforts to "reduce the risks of a maritime conflict in the west Pacific . . . injects major uncertainties into regional defense planning, very possibly compounding the risks in a major crisis.[9] Some raise the specter of an Asian bloodbath comparable to Europe's catastrophic twentieth-century wars.[10] Finally the U.S.-China Economic and Security Review Commission announced in its 2005 Annual Report to Congress that "on balance, the trends in the U.S.-China relationship have negative implications for the long-term economic and security interests of the United States"; it continues to maintain this position in its 2006 report.[11]

We start from the supposition that the United States, short of a declaration of war, simply does not have the ability to halt or even substantially mitigate the expansion of Chinese influence in Asia. Indeed, the movement toward intra-Asian economic integration confers few advantages on the United States compared to global integration. But, as Ellen Frost has observed, building regional ties "offers Asian leaders political and security advantages, such as engaging China peacefully in the region, [and] acquiring a stronger collective voice" for Asian governments.[12]

Some may suggest that China's policy of economic engagement and commercial diplomacy in Asia is merely tactical, a "charm offensive" designed to buy time until China is economically and militarily powerful enough to exert regional hegemony. While this possibility cannot be dismissed, it is also not a cause for action. China still faces enormous challenges and internal hurdles as it struggles to accomplish its industrial revolution and urbanization in a telescoped time frame. While these challenges are all too obvious, it would be unwise to underestimate China's political acumen or its ability to overcome adversity. The scenarios are abundant: economic setbacks could trigger political unrest; rising inequality between coastal provinces and a vast rural interior could stimulate class rivalry. The migration of many millions from farms to cities could exacerbate a housing crisis. Unemployment, environmental degradation, unfunded health and pension systems, and an aging population all may impose limitations on the Chinese growth trajectory.

Regardless of the exact outcome, the continued expansion of China's role as a regional military power and global economic player seems inevitable. As a consequence, the United States needs to rethink its approach to China and Asia in light of new realities. Unfortunately, neither the Clinton nor the George W. Bush administration has achieved significant progress in this direction. Instead, policy toward China displays a shifting sequence of compromises between cooperation and containment.

Washington's reliance on a tired mix of recycled policies in the face of rapidly shifting Asian circumstances contrasts starkly with China's patient, apparently long-term strategy of Asian engagement centered on a variety of economic and trade initiatives and backed by an expanding array of diplomatic, educational, technological, and security links. Indeed, China's policy toward its Asian neighbors is reminiscent of U.S. foreign relations following World War II. In both instances, a major power deployed a combination of bilateral and multilateral agreements, forming policy and intellectual networks that involved its allies, including former enemies, in a dense web of mutually beneficial relations. From this perspective, China's current use of trade agreements as political instruments parallels earlier U.S. reliance on security arrangements as the centerpiece of efforts to build durable and responsive alliances.

This unfortunate coincidence of U.S. neglect with concerted Chinese efforts to consolidate a new generation of economic infrastructure agreements fuels speculation that the United States is losing significant influence over the evolving balance of Asian economic and political alignments. More specifically, the balance of influence between China and the United States in Asia is shifting decidedly in China's favor. Against this background, our project seeks to provide the context for a comprehensive and integrated American policy toward Asia in light of Asia's response to a rising and vastly more powerful China.

New Approaches to Asia Are Needed

The new dynamics of Asia's political economy reflects the legacy of a remarkable interlude in which Western nuclear superiority, technological ascendancy, and overwhelming conventional forces allowed leading powers, especially the United States, to ignore or intervene in potentially destabilizing regional conflicts without endangering their own domestic economic affairs. With rich nations enjoying a simultaneous regimen of guns and butter, strategic studies diverged from political economy, the former tending to focus on power relations stripped of economic constraint, the latter concentrating on development prospects absent debilitating military disruption.[13]

Recent events have demolished the underpinnings of this disconnect between economic and strategic thinking. The debut of North Korea, an international pariah and economic weakling, as a nuclear weapons power confirms that determination alone can propel ambitious nations into the nuclear club. The spread of significant technological capabilities beyond the advanced industrial states, coupled with large-scale application of dual-use technology to military systems, will enable many countries to upgrade conventional forces and acquire the potential to develop nuclear weapons.[14]

United States military supremacy is unlikely to be challenged for many years. Even so, the inability of U.S. forces to suppress the insurgency in Iraq quickly, coupled with mounting public criticism of the human and financial toll of the U.S. occupation, demonstrates the rising costs and dangers associated with efforts by leading nations to use military means to influence events in distant lands.[15] Widespread recognition that military power alone cannot resolve the imbroglios with North Korea and Iran, for example, along with General Eric Shinseki's warning to "beware the 12-division strategy for a 10-division army,"[16] and suggestions that the U.S. military may be tied down in Iraq for several years, presage the resumption of a long-dormant national dialogue over the appropriate scale of America's military establishment.

In this geopolitical environment, isolated perspectives built on individual disciplines become increasingly unreliable. Yet disciplinary insularity remains commonplace. Highly regarded and widely cited studies of China's economy by Chinese and international scholars as well as multilateral agencies rarely mention such terms as "armaments," "defense," "military," "People's Liberation Army," "security," and "weapons," nor do they explore possible interactions among economic development, military preparedness, and regional or global security.[17] In addition, many researchers are reluctant to cross regional or national boundaries: generalists hesitate to engage with the daunting complexities of evaluating Chinese data and penetrating enigmatic Chinese institutions, while China specialists often remain cocooned within the intricacies of Chinese language materials and Chinese society and politics.

Coming to terms with a rising yet fragmented Asia will require a sustained multidisciplinary effort involving the perspectives of economics, trade and investment, politics and diplomacy, technology, and security. No single project can hope to encompass the entire range of Asian issues and nations. In this book, we have approached the task of building an integrated analysis of Asia's shifting balance of influence by assembling an interdisciplinary group to focus on the impact of one major development: China's massive and unexpected growth spurt of the past twenty-five years.

The challenge is to distill, from a wide variety of perspectives, a comprehensive and interdisciplinary analysis of the changing configurations of Chinese power and influence in Asia, with the hope that this research will contribute to devising flexible policies that respond to Asia's rapidly evolving economic, political, technological, and military landscape. This involves evaluating the feasibility of a cooperative and mutually beneficial expansion of Chinese economic and political power. In the best-case scenario, China would attain the wealth and influence appropriate to its size and achievements without inflicting unacceptable damage to the vital interests of its Asian neighbors or to those of the United States.

While such an outcome is possible and highly desirable, the realist in us suggests that it is far from assured. A cooperative response to the rise of China must build on specific attitudes and policies in China, in neighboring states, and also in the United States. Such responses may clash with the perceptions and interests of influential groups on both sides of the Pacific. Thus the global adjustment to China's rise involves not just the foreign policies of many states, but their internal politics as well.

Why Study China and the Shifting Balance of Influence in Asia?

In nearly every area of international relations and political economy, China's coming of age is stimulating dynamic change throughout Asia and beyond. This study posits prominent and continuing consequences of Chinese development in the areas of trade, investment, technology, defense, and diplomacy. In trade, for example, Chinese exports to the United States rose from 6 percent of comparable Japanese totals in 1985 to 36 percent in 1995, and surpassed Japan's U.S.-bound exports in 2002; in 2005, China's exports to the U.S. exceeded Japan's by 76 percent.[18] The pattern of export-led growth widely associated with Japan, Taiwan, South Korea, and other Asian economies adds significance to this reversal. Massive upgrading of Chinese export infrastructure will continue, bolstered both by expanding internal markets and technology-laden investment by foreign-based multinational corporations. Escalating Chinese trade and economic power exert growing influence in many Asian nations, which confront a combination of opportunity (large and growing Chinese markets) and dislocation (Chinese products supplanting local suppliers).[19]

To this must be added increasing flows of foreign direct investment (FDI), both to and from China. China's share of investment flows into eight Asian nations, for example, soared from 21 to 66 percent during the 1990s.[20] The contrast between China's unabashed promotion of investment inflows and the ambivalence of government and labor toward foreign investment in Japan, India, and especially in Korea is striking.[21] With global automakers and a broad array of Asian, European, and North American manufacturers rushing to establish and expand manufacturing facilities, China became the world's largest recipient of FDI in 2003, surpassing even the United States. We also observe the apparent beginning of a steep upward trend in outward investment from China, propelled by vigorous official support and directed toward acquisition of energy, raw materials, and manufacturing expertise. The result is an uncomfortable but potentially dynamic combination of opportunity and global economic adjustment.[22]

Foreign direct investment in China, which now extends far beyond garments, toys, and other labor-intensive sectors, surely represents the largest technology transfer in global history, eclipsing the scope and impact of Soviet technology transfers to China during the 1950s.[23] Recent investment includes massive arrivals of cutting-edge and dual-use technologies in such sectors as semiconductors, electronics, and the aerospace industry. International efforts to limit Chinese acquisition of such technologies have faded. In semiconductors, for example, interagency conflict and industry opposition have eroded U.S. export controls.[24] Independent advances in specific fields—biotechnology, pharmacology, and aerospace, among others—enrich China's technological opportunities.

In the military sphere, as in commerce and investment, China and Japan appear to be trading places, with Chinese defense spending exceeding Japan's, at least temporarily. Chinese strategists' increasingly expansive conception of their nation's defense interests extends from Beijing's growing program of manned and unmanned space exploration and the acquisition of mid-air refueling capability to aspirations to develop a blue-water navy, and the growth of military assets and capability in and around the South China Sea, the Straits of Malacca, and the Indian Ocean. The consequences of China's defense modernization ripple across Asia, from a reexamination of Japanese military posture to development of nuclear forces by India, Pakistan, and North Korea. All of China's neighbors, from Taiwan and Vietnam to more distant states like Japan and Indonesia, follow Chinese military developments with the closest attention.

But it would be a mistake to place excessive emphasis on Chinese military modernization. Strong economic ties beget diplomatic influence. This can benefit the United States—as when both America and China, sensing danger to economic links, muted confrontation over the April 2001 spy plane incident. Conversely, China's expanding trade and investment links may undercut U.S. influence, as Asian nations consider China's mounting capacity (and obvious willingness) to apply economic leverage in support of its diplomatic objectives. Australia's decision to limit official discussion of human rights issues to closed-door diplomatic sessions illustrates this outcome.[25] Economic strength reinforces Chinese diplomatic entrepreneurship, for example, in the evidently serious and well-received proposal to establish a free trade zone between China and the Association of Southeast Asian Nations (ASEAN) by 2010.

Beijing is becoming increasingly seasoned and confident in its relations with the ASEAN member states. In this context, Chinese behavior toward Taiwan may be seen as anomalous. China's hard line on Taiwan appears to have successfully engineered the political and diplomatic isolation of Taiwan from most of its Asian neighbors. For this reason, and because of booming economic ties between China and Taiwan, the Taiwan secession issue appears to be receding, despite the efforts of Taiwan's term-limited president, Chen Shui-bian.

Against this background of Chinese dynamism, the chapters in this book directly address issues surrounding China's large and growing influence throughout the Asia-Pacific region in the spheres of trade, technology, investment, commercial diplomacy, and military affairs. Crosscutting themes focus on China's changing relations with regional (and increasingly, with global) systems of manufacturing, research, trade, finance, military preparedness, and security alliances. The key issues can readily be expressed as questions: To what extent does China's rising economic power translate into political influence in the Asia Pacific region? Has China's capacity to generate innovation and to sustain technological development risen in tandem with its economy, or will Beijing continue to depend on technology imports from its trading partners and from Japanese, Korean, Taiwanese, European, and

North American multinational corporations? How does China's growing wealth and technological acumen affect its military capabilities? And how do these changes alter the way in which its neighbors and far-flung trading partners view Beijing's military and great power ambitions?

Should we expect China to replace Japan as the hub of Asia's political economy, and by extension, to become the chief source of Asia's influence on economic globalization? During the past three decades, Japan—as Asia's techno-economic powerhouse and the world's second largest economy—has clearly dominated regional economic and political interaction. But if we confine our attention to the past decade, the picture looks decidedly different. The rise of South Korea, Taiwan, and China, together with Japan's debilitating combination of economic malaise and political paralysis, makes Asia's economic and political scene appear less hierarchical and more decentralized. If we project ten years into the future, should we anticipate that China's growing global prominence will shift Asia's political and economic fulcrum from Japan and the Korean Peninsula toward Beijing and China's high-growth coastal provinces?

If the answer is yes, then we can perhaps project a more provocative scenario, one that goes beyond the economic dynamism of China. Since the end of the Second World War, the United States has been the leader and primary proponent of economic liberalism, but this may be because interdependence was always construed to be in U.S. interests. The United States could always close its borders (super 301 trade legislation, auto quotas, etc.). Now that China has become a formidable economic power, will the United States continue to champion free and open trade, unfettered capital markets, and economic interdependence? Will it do so even in the face of further expansion of Chinese manufacturing prowess, extensive outsourcing of U.S. production and services, and the rise of a massive, technically literate Chinese workforce?

There is, then, the possibility that the global economic architecture established after the Second World War, commencing with the General Agreement on Tariffs and Trade (GATT) and culminating in China's accession to the World Trade Organization (WTO), may be weakening, or at least may have to confront the stress of a rival consumer-oriented, technically astute, economic superpower coming on line. In that case, the rise of China may presage a new systems architecture for global trade and investment, one that must somehow accommodate multiple entities with insatiable appetites for energy, vast internal markets, and apparently unlimited productive capacity. If this is even suggestive of the nature of things to come, then the solution will require real and substantial interdependence, perhaps modeled on the relationship that the United States has with the European Union, involving massive two-way trade, extensive and roughly balanced penetration of foreign direct investment, intricate commercial diplomacy, and complementary if somewhat dissimilar systems of corporate governance, technology acquisition, and finance.

In such a future, the United States would not be the only economy that affects the entire world. ("When the United States sneezes, the rest of the world gets a cold.") China's economy already exerts strong influence over many international markets; it may soon acquire the critical mass to cause economic dislocation on a global scale. In such a future, lesser states would have to coexist with two huge economic systems. This may represent a fundamental challenge to the existing order.[26] The question arises: Is the United States willing to contemplate the major shifts in global systems that might be required to maintain stability as China (and India) continue their breakneck development?

China's rise, like the historical emergence of other great powers, represents a tectonic shift in the global architecture of diplomacy, security, and commerce that has the potential to unleash instability, even war. Despite such dangers, our contributors agree that existing systems are sufficiently flexible and adaptive to support peaceful accommodation to China's growing wealth and power. Although the actions of many countries will influence the outcome, the choices made by the United States are likely to be decisive. Accordingly, we place great emphasis on the need for Washington to implement a consistent and forward-looking policy that recognizes China's emergence as a regional power and global economic partner.

★2 INTERNATIONAL DIMENSIONS OF CHINA'S LONG BOOM

Loren Brandt, Thomas G. Rawski, and Xiaodong Zhu

CHINA'S LONG BOOM, which now extends beyond a quarter century, has established the People's Republic as a major trading nation, a prime destination for overseas investment, and a key link in global networks of manufacturing, capital flows, and technology transfer. What does the growth of China's economic power imply for Beijing's future foreign interactions with the United States and other nations?

Some observers view China as an economic threat and a future military rival. In the economic sphere, analysis focuses on China's rapid export expansion, its large and growing bilateral trade surplus with the United States, and the hollowing out of manufacturing in many national economies as firms shift production to Chinese plants. Highlighting China's undervalued currency, cheap labor, and disregard of intellectual property rights, this perspective portrays the People's Republic as an uncooperative partner whose interests seem destined to provoke future clashes with the United States and other major market economies.

Beijing's determination to translate some of its growing riches into military strength reinforces this interpretation. Rising defense spending may increase the likelihood that China will aggressively press its economic and political claims in Taiwan and elsewhere, again often at odds with the economic and security interests of the United States, Japan, and the European Community (EC).

This chapter evaluates these propositions and systematically reviews the international dimension of China's economic boom.[1] We build a quantitative and comparative picture of China's deepening economic ties to global markets for resources, components, final manufactures, capital, equipment, technology, management expertise, and corporate control. These links are essential components of China's past and future growth. Economic growth is essential to maintaining the legitimacy of China's present government. As China's engagement with international markets expands far beyond the boundaries of conceivable Chinese military control, pressure for Beijing to emphasize compromise and diplomacy rather than threat and conflict provides an opportunity for cooperative accommodation to China's growing power.

China's Economic Reforms

China's modern history encompasses widely varied policies toward the world economy. The Treaty of Nanking (1842) replaced policies that had largely limited trade to the southern port of Canton with a system of enforced free trade that lasted for nearly a century. After 1949, the People's Republic followed the Soviet example by establishing a plan system that restricted both the scale and the impact of foreign economic contacts. The plan system channeled all commerce through state trading companies, curtailed direct interaction between Chinese and overseas producers and consumers, and severed links between domestic and international prices.[2]

Beginning in the late 1970s, China embarked upon a series of reforms that gradually expanded economic openness. The eventual result was a system that today stands among the most open trade and investment regimes among large nations in Asia and, indeed, globally.[3] China's path toward an open economy began with modest expansion of trade and the creation of four Special Economic Zones in the southern provinces of Guangdong and Fujian. The success of the initial zones in building trade and attracting foreign investment prompted a race to extend these experiments to new locations, first along China's coast, and eventually nationwide.

Deregulation and liberalization expanded as the benefits of trade and investment multiplied. Lee Branstetter and Nicholas Lardy show that import barriers declined sharply during the 1990s.[4] Tariff revenues dropped from 16 percent to only 2.5 percent of total imports during that decade, reflecting both falling tariff rates and growing duty-free imports. Branstetter and Lardy also show that the number of firms authorized to conduct direct foreign trade increased from 12 in 1978 to 800 in 1985 and to over 35,000 by 2001, with recent totals including growing numbers of private traders. China's 2001 entry into the World Trade Organization (WTO) brought immediate reforms and promises of further liberalization, including the opening of banking, insurance, and other service industries.

These changes have transformed China's external economic relations. Commodity trade is now wide open, with low tariffs and few restrictions. Market forces predominate in domestic price determination, so that domestic prices increasingly reflect world market trends. Chinese authorities now welcome foreign participation in sectors formerly closed to private business. Liaoning Province, "one of the last bastions of the planned economy," announced in September 2005 that "international investors may take full control of almost all State-owned enterprises" except coal mine companies and firms under direct central government control.[5] Even in coal, railways, and other formerly closed sectors, foreign entry is now a realistic possibility.[6]

China's Growing Interaction with the Global Economy

This section lays out the international dimensions of China's growth, focusing on the volume and composition of trade and overseas investment. The key observation is that open-door policies have produced a vast multiplication of China's overseas ties. Linkage between the domestic economy and global markets has become broader and more intensive in China than in other large Asian economies. However, China's economy displays major regional variations, with international trade, overseas investment, and growth all concentrated along the coast.

Engagement with Global Commodity Markets

Prior to the industrial revolution, China was a major force in regional and global trade.[7] After 1800, accelerated growth of output and trade in Europe and North America pushed China to the global periphery. Beginning in 1949, three decades of socialist planning moved China in the direction of autarky, partly through choice, and partly because of a U.S.-led trade embargo dating from the Korean War.

Following the onset of reform in the late 1970s, China's international trade has grown from a trickle to a torrent. Table 2.1 and figure 2.1 summarize China's import-export surge and compare it with trends in global trade among China's East Asian neighbors.

Table 2.1 documents the extraordinary pace of trade expansion. Between

TABLE 2.1 Chinese International Trade in Regional and Global Perspective, 1913–2005

	Annual Trade Flow (US$ billion)		*Share of World Trade (percent)*			
Year	*World*	*China*	*China*	*Japan*	*Korea*	*Taiwan*
1913	39.8	0.8	1.9	1.8	0.1	0.0
1950	126.0	1.1	0.9	1.4	NA	0.1
1955	194.0	3.1	1.6	2.3	0.2	0.2
1960	267.0	5.2	2.0	3.2	0.1	0.2
1965	389.0	4.8	1.2	4.3	0.2	0.3
1970	646.0	4.6	0.7	5.9	0.4	0.5
1975	1789.0	15.6	0.9	6.4	0.7	0.6
1980	4109.0	38.0	0.9	6.6	1.0	1.0
1985	3969.0	69.6	1.8	7.8	1.5	1.3
1990	6999.0	115.4	1.6	7.5	1.9	1.7
1991	7148.0	135.7	1.9	7.7	2.1	2.0
1992	7648.0	165.5	2.2	7.5	2.1	2.0
1993	7657.0	195.7	2.6	7.9	2.2	2.1
1994	8753.0	236.6	2.7	7.7	2.3	2.1
1995	10444.0	280.9	2.7	7.5	2.5	2.1
1996	10946.0	289.9	2.6	6.9	2.6	2.0
1997	11329.0	325.2	2.9	6.7	2.5	2.1
1998	11180.0	323.9	2.9	6.0	2.0	1.9
1999	11632.0	360.6	3.1	6.3	2.3	2.0
2000	13175.0	474.3	3.6	6.5	2.5	2.2
2001	12666.0	509.7	4.0	5.9	2.3	1.8
2002	13218.0	620.8	4.7	5.7	2.4	1.9
2003	15427.0	851.0	5.5	5.5	2.4	1.8
2004	18736.0	1154.6	6.2	5.4	2.6	1.9
2005	21146.0	1422.1	6.7	5.3	2.6	1.8

Sources: Merchandise trade for 1950–2005 from World Trade Organization database, http://stat.wto.org/StatisticalProgram/WSDBViewData.aspx?Language=E. Data for 1913 are from the following sources: Antoni Estevadeordal, Brian Franz, and Alan M. Taylor, "The Rise and Fall of World Trade, 1870–1939," Working Paper w9318 (Cambridge, MA: National Bureau of Economic Research, November 2002), 36 (world); Liang-lin Hsiao, *China's Foreign Trade Statistics, 1964–1949* (Cambridge, MA: Harvard East Asian Monographs, 1974), 191, 269 (China); Kazushi Ohkawa and Henry Rosovky, *Japanese Economic Growth: Trend Acceleration in the Twentieth Century* (Stanford: Stanford University Press, 1973), 303–4 (Japan); Bank of Japan, *Hundred-Year Statistics of the Japanese Economy* (Tokyo: Bank of Japan, 1966) (Japan); Konosuke Odaka and Insang Hwang, *The Long-Term Economic Statistics of Korea, 1910–1990: An International Workshop* (Tokyo: Institute of Economic Research, Hitotsubashi University, 2000), 260–61 (Korea); Konosuke Odaka, ed., *The Long-Term Economic Statistics of Taiwan, 1905–1995: An International Workshop* (Tokyo: Institute of Economic Research, Hitotsubashi University, 1999) (Taiwan).

1980 and 2004, China's trade (measured in U.S. dollars) grew at an annual rate of 14.2 percent. By comparison, world trade grew at an annual rate of 6.3 percent. Starting from less than 1 percent of global trade in 1980, China's trade surpassed 6 percent of the 2004 global total, and in 2005 approached 7 percent. The pace of China's rise is unprecedented. In the post–World War

II period, Japan took thirty years to achieve the same growth in world trade share that China achieved in fifteen. In 2004, China's two-way trade overtook Japan's, making China the world's third-largest trading nation, behind only the United States and Germany.

Information about global commodity markets reflects China's growing impact. WTO data show, for example, that China's share of global exports of manufactures rose from 0.8 to 7.3 percent between 1985 and 2003. During the same period, Chinese exports of office and telecommunication equipment rose from 0.1 to 10.1 percent, while Chinese imports of fuel and mining products jumped from 0.6 to 5.2 percent of global totals.[8]

The impact on Chinese markets, where prices of textiles, steel, agricultural products, and many other goods formerly subject to official controls now rise and fall with global market trends, is much larger.[9] Integration even affects markets subject to official price controls. Beijing's effort to shelter domestic buyers from rising international prices for gasoline produced shortages and long lines in August 2005, evidently because China's state-owned petroleum firms, behaving like market players, diverted supplies to storage or to overseas markets for the purpose of focusing official attention on the cost squeeze arising from price caps on refined products amid rising costs for imported crude oil.[10]

Figure 2.1 examines trade trends for East Asia's high-growth economies, showing global trade shares during the initial quarter century of accelerated growth for Japan (from 1955), Taiwan (1960), South Korea (1965), and China (from 1978). During the first boom decade, growth of Chinese trade roughly tracks the patterns established by earlier growth spurts in Japan and Taiwan. Thereafter, China's share of global trade accelerates, moving well ahead of the Japanese norm after year 15 and beyond Taiwan's achievement in year 25.

Historical experience shows that large nations, which have access to extensive domestic resources and big internal markets, tend to avoid the deep involvement in international exchange typical of smaller nations.[11] Figure 2.1 points to China as a possible exception, as China's share in global trade tracks a path more like Taiwan or Korea than Japan. Information about trade ratios, which measure the combined value of imports and exports as a percentage of gross domestic product (GDP), confirms this assessment. Figure 2.2 shows long-term trends in trade ratios for the same dynamic quartet. Prior to reform, China's trade ratio is consistently low, reflecting the combined impact of self-imposed isolation and the U.S.-led embargo. During the 1980s, China's figures, while rising, roughly track Japan's, and remain far below the results for the smaller Taiwanese and Korean economies. Beginning in the early

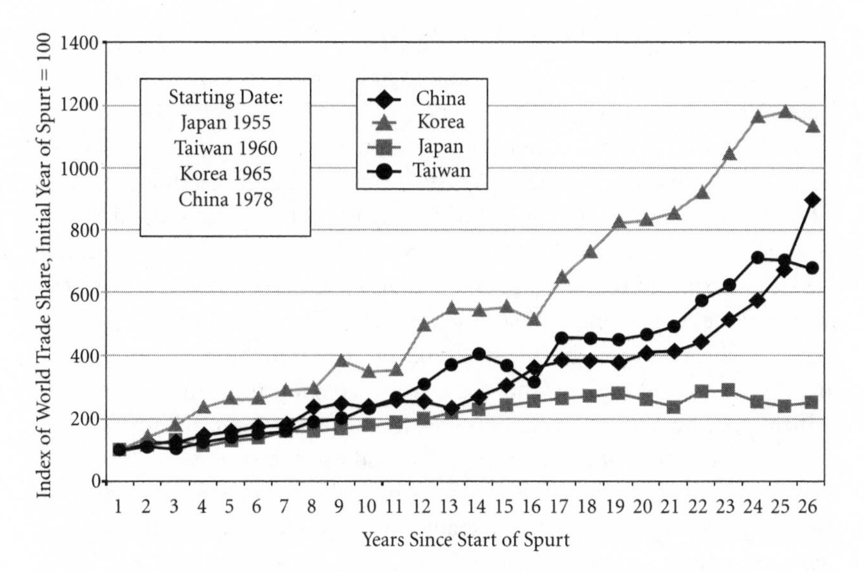

FIG. 2.1. Asian Trade Spurts: Evolution of World Trade Shares over 25 Years

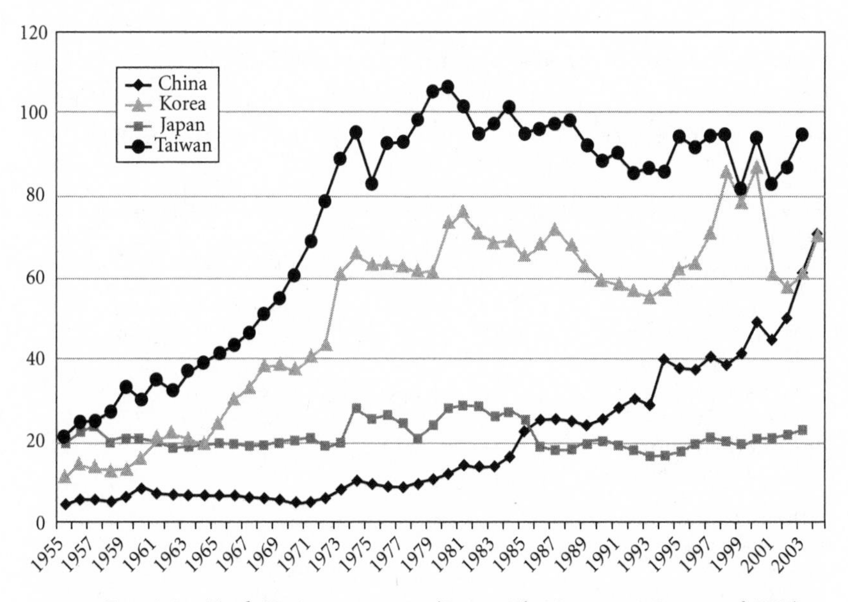

FIG. 2.2. East Asian Trade Ratios, 1955–2004 (Export Plus Import as Percent of GDP)

1990s, however, growth of China's foreign trade rapidly outpaces GDP expansion, pushing China's 2005 trade ratio to 63.9 percent, within ten percent of South Korea's 2005 trade ratio.

Trade activity, and also foreign investment (discussed below), cluster along China's eastern seaboard. Coastal provinces accounted for 92 percent of overall trade value in 2005, led by Guangdong (30.9 percent), and Shanghai and Jiangsu (combined total 29.6 percent). Guangdong, whose 91 million people contributed 11.3 percent of GDP in 2005, achieved a trade ratio of 174.5, which exceeds the comparable ratios for Ireland, Taiwan, and the Netherlands.[12] Table 2.2 highlights the stark contrast between the extreme openness of China's coastal regions and the relative isolation of western provinces, which contributed 2.7 percent of trade and 12.9 percent of GDP in 2005, implying a trade ratio of 13.2 percent, which indicates openness comparable to all China during the early 1980s. Efforts by interior provinces to expand local participation in international trade and investment by establishing one-stop service centers in Wuhan and Chongqing to facilitate granting of official permissions and approvals demonstrate the efforts of inland jurisdictions to increase their share of the stimulus associated with China's globalization.[13]

Table 2.3 summarizes trends in the composition of China's foreign trade, which has shifted markedly during the reform era. Exports, formerly dominated by raw and processed agricultural materials (including cotton textiles) and minerals (including crude oil), now consist mainly of manufactures (including chemicals and machinery), whose share of total exports jumped from

TABLE 2.2 China: Regional Differences in Development and Global Engagement, 2004

	Coast	*Central*	*West*
Regional percentage			
Population	41.8	35.1	23.1
GDP	61.2	26.7	12.0
Industrial value-added	64.6	24.9	10.5
Fixed asset spending	60.0	24.5	15.5
International trade	92.0	5.3	2.7
Trade by foreign firms	97.4	2.0	0.6
Direct foreign investment	86.6	11.6	1.8
Regional averages (National average = 100)			
GDP per person	146.4	76.1	51.9
FDI inflow per person	207.2	33.0	7.8
Foreign trade per person	220.1	15.1	11.7
Regional trade ratio	150.3	19.9	22.5

Source: Zhongguo tongji zhaiyao 2005 [China Statistical Abstract 2005], 22, 27, 29, 42, 55, 167, 170.

TABLE 2.3 Composition of China's Exports and Imports, 1985–2004

	Annual Trade Flows (US$ billion)					*Composition of Trade Flows (percent)*				
	1985	*1990*	*1995*	*2000*	*2004*	*1985*	*1990*	*1995*	*2000*	*2004*
China's Exports										
Food & live animals	2.6	6.7	9.9	12.3	18.8	12.5	10.9	6.7	4.9	3.2
Beverages & tobacco	0.0	0.3	1.4	0.7	1.2	0.2	0.6	0.9	0.3	0.2
Crude materials	2.0	3.5	4.4	4.4	5.8	9.5	5.7	2.9	1.8	1.0
Mineral fuels	6.6	5.2	5.3	7.9	14.5	31.3	8.4	3.6	3.2	2.4
Animal & vegetable oils	0.1	0.2	0.5	0.1	0.1	0.6	0.3	0.3	0.1	0.0
Chemicals	0.8	3.8	9.1	12.0	26.0	3.9	6.0	6.1	4.8	4.4
Manufactures	2.9	12.8	32.9	43.3	101.7	13.9	20.6	22.1	17.4	17.1
Machinery & transport equipment	0.5	10.8	31.4	82.5	268.2	2.2	17.4	21.1	33.1	45.2
Miscellaneous manufactures	2.3	17.5	53.7	85.5	155.8	11.0	28.2	36.1	34.3	26.3
Other	3.2	1.2	0.4	0.5	1.1	15.0	1.9	0.3	0.2	0.2
Total	21.1	62.1	148.8	249.2	593.2	100.0	100.0	100.0	100.0	100.0
China's Imports										
Food & live animals	1.3	3.5	6.1	4.7	9.1	4.6	6.5	4.6	2.1	1.6
Beverages and tobacco	0.2	0.2	0.4	0.4	0.5	0.7	0.3	0.3	0.2	0.1
Crude materials	2.6	4.1	9.9	19.7	55.2	9.2	7.7	7.5	8.8	9.8
Mineral fuels	0.2	1.3	5.2	20.8	48.4	0.6	2.4	3.9	9.2	8.6
Animal & vegetable oils	0.1	1.0	2.6	1.0	4.2	0.4	1.8	2.0	0.4	0.7
Chemicals	2.0	6.7	17.2	29.9	64.4	7.1	12.5	13.0	13.3	11.5
Manufactures	8.1	11.6	29.1	42.2	74.0	28.1	21.7	22.0	18.7	13.2
Machinery & transport equipment	11.1	21.5	52.9	92.1	253.0	38.5	40.3	40.0	40.9	45.1
Miscellaneous manufactures	0.9	3.3	8.0	12.7	50.7	3.0	6.2	6.0	5.6	9.0
Other	2.3	0.3	0.9	1.8	1.5	7.9	0.5	0.7	0.8	0.3
Total	28.7	53.4	132.1	225.1	561.0	100.0	100.0	100.0	100.0	100.0

Source: United Nations Commodity Trade Statistics Database (COMTRADE), http://comtrade.un.org/db/.

31 percent to 93 percent between 1985 and 2005. Machinery and transport equipment, previously a small component (3.2 percent of exports in 1980),[14] have emerged as the leading source of overseas sales, accounting for 46.3 percent of China's exports in 2005.

Machinery stands out as the largest import category, contributing 20 percent of imports in 1980 (ibid.), 40 percent in both 1990 and 1995, and 44 percent in 2005. In the past, these imports consisted mainly of equipment destined for domestic factories or mines. More recently, the totals for machinery imports include massive inflows of components, which have grown from a trickle during the early 1980s to approximately US$120 billion, or 29 percent of China's entire import bill, in 2003.[15] This trade in industrial components, which also involves substantial exports, reflects the growing significance of transnational production networks to the operation of China's biggest export sector. Studies of "Greater China" and "the China Circle" illuminate complex supply arrangements surrounding the manufacture of computers and electronic goods.[16] Rapid growth of two-way trade in auto parts, discussed below, provides another instance of China's growing integration into global supply chains.

Table 2.3 also highlights China's growing imports of energy and mineral products. Early in the reform period, mineral fuels, principally crude oil, ranked as China's top export category, accounting for 31.3 percent of China's exports in 1985, a figure that dropped sharply to only 2.3 percent in 2005. China's trade balance in mineral fuels and crude materials shifted from a 1985 surplus equal to 22 percent of total 1985 trade to a deficit amounting to 17 percent of overall trade in 2005.

Table 2.4 provides further detail on China's imports of energy, minerals, and other materials. Inflows of these commodities fluctuated between 9 and 20 percent of China's fast-growing import total during 1985–2005. Within the materials segment, we see a gradual shift from imports destined for domestic food, feed, and textile producers toward imports of energy and scrap metals. China's growing influence on global markets for raw materials is evident: if we calculate China's share of global imports for each of China's top ten material imports recorded in table 2.4, the average of these shares rises from 6.1 percent in 1985 to 7.7 percent in 1995, then jumps to 19.7 percent in 2004, with incomplete data showing a further increase in 2005.

Three decades of reform have moved China from economic isolation to extensive participation in global commodity markets and growing integration with them. Links with international markets have become a major feature of China's economy, particularly in the coastal provinces that dominate overseas trade flows. China's trade ratio now exceeds comparable figures for all large nations. The composition of China's imports and exports, formerly dictated by economic planners, has come to reflect comparative advantage, with thousands of producing firms and trading companies now able to buy and sell on overseas markets in response to the dictates of cost, price, and profit. In response to market signals, manufactures have replaced energy and materials as China's chief exports. Early prominence of manufactured exports built upon China's vast pool of unskilled labor has yielded to a broader mix that now includes products requiring substantial inputs of skill, technology, and capital as well as raw labor. On the import side, we see a growing dependence

TABLE 2.4 China's Top Ten Raw Materials Imports, 1985, 1995, 2004, 2005

		1985		1995		2004		2005	
SITC code	*Commodity Group*	*Rank*	*% of imports*	*Rank*	*% of imports*	*Rank*	*% of imports*	*Rank*	*% of imports*
222	Seed for "soft" fixed oil					4	1.28	5	1.21
232	Natural rubber latex	6	0.73						
233	Synthetic rubber, latex, etc.	7	0.45						
247	Other wood in the rough or roughly squared	1	4.53			9	0.50	9	0.49
251	Pulp and waste paper	5	1.17	7	0.64	6	0.94	6	0.94
263	Cotton			3	1.13	8	0.58	8	0.49
266	Synthetic fibers suitable for spinning	2	3.86	4	1.00				
267	Other man-made fibers suitable for spinning	9	0.29						
268	Wool and other animal hair	3	1.93	8	0.56				
281	Iron ore and concentrates	4	1.44	5	0.93	2	2.26	2	2.78
287	Ores and concentrates of base metals	10	0.24	6	0.76	5	1.18	4	1.59
288	Non-ferrous base metal waste and scrap			9	0.50	7	0.64	7	0.71
322	Coal, lignite, and peat	8	0.35						
333	Crude petroleum			1	1.79	1	6.04	1	7.23
334	Refined petroleum products			2	1.60	3	1.71	3	1.65
341	Gas, natural and manufactured			10	0.34	10	0.43	10	0.43
	Top ten materials' share of China's total imports (%)		14.99		9.25		15.57		17.52
	Codes 200–399 share of China's total imports (%)		15.43		11.40		17.20		20.38
	Unweighted average of top ten share of world imports (%)		6.11		7.66		19.71		25.76

Source: United Nations Commodity Trade Statistics Database (COMTRADE), http://comtrade.un.org/db/.

Note: Based on all commodities coded 200–399 in the Standard International Trade Classification, revision 2.

Note: Share of China's raw materials imports in world imports may be biased upwards because of nonreporting by some importers.

Note: Fewer nations report trade data for 2005 than for earlier years; results overstate China's actual share of world imports.

on large inflows of energy and materials. Large-scale trade in industrial components demonstrates the extent of Chinese participation in transnational supply chains. Foreign-invested firms stand out as key contributors to this process of openness and integration with foreign markets. We must therefore consider the impact on China's economy of international capital flows, chiefly foreign direct investment.

Direct Investment and Capital Flows

During China's quarter century of socialist planning, involvement with international capital flows consisted of tiny Soviet shareholdings carried over from the pre–World War II era and official Soviet lending.[17] Beginning in the late 1970s, Beijing gradually relaxed earlier prohibitions on foreign investment and participation in global capital markets. By 2005, China had become the world's leading destination for direct foreign investment, a source of modest outflows of overseas direct investment, and a significant participant in global markets for sovereign lending and portfolio investment. Our discussion focuses on direct foreign investment.

Table 2.5 summarizes annual inflows of foreign direct investment (FDI) during the period of steep increases since 1990. China surpassed the United States as the top FDI recipient in 2003; the annual inflow of FDI jumped to US$60.3 billion in 2005.

Table 2.5 also charts the sources of incoming FDI. During the early 1990s, Hong Kong sources predominated. More recently, the list has broadened to include large inflows from Japan, South Korea, Taiwan, Singapore, North America, and the European Community, among others. The regional totals in table 2.5 fall considerably short of overall inflows because of considerable sums channeled through tax havens, which reflects the recycling of funds originating in China as well as the desire of Taiwan investors to conceal financial flows from the Taipei authorities.[18]

Even though standard data overstate actual inflows of overseas investments, the officially measured inflows amount to only a small fraction of overall Chinese investment spending. Converting the 2004 FDI inflow of US$60.6 billion to renminbi at the official rate of RMB 8.28 gives a total of just over RMB 500 billion, equivalent to 7.2 percent of 2004 investment spending.[19] The concentration of FDI in manufacturing results in a much larger share of foreign funds, amounting to 18.2 percent, in that sector's 2004 investment total.[20] Like overseas trade, FDI clusters along the coast. Table 2.2 shows that 86.6 percent of 2004 inward direct investment targeted coastal regions (including

TABLE 2.5 China's Foreign Direct Investment Inflows and Outflows, 1990–2005 (US$ billion)

	1990	*1994*	*1998*	*2000*	*2001*	*2002*	*2003*	*2004*	*2005*
FDI inflow	3.48	33.94	45.46	40.71	46.88	52.74	53.50	60.63	60.32
FDI sources									
Asia			31.33	25.48	29.61	32.44	34.10	37.62	35.72
Hong Kong	1.91	19.82	18.50	15.50	16.72	17.86	17.70	19.00	17.95
Japan	0.50	2.09	3.40	2.92	4.34	4.19	5.05	5.45	6.53
Korea		0.23	1.80	1.49	2.15	2.72	4.49	6.25	5.17
Singapore	0.05	0.73	3.40	2.17	2.14	2.34	2.06	2.00	2.20
Taiwan		0.34	2.91	2.30	2.98	3.97	3.38	3.12	2.15
Europe			4.31	4.76	4.48	4.08	4.27	4.80	5.64
Germany	0.02	0.26	0.74	1.04	1.21	0.92	0.86	1.06	1.53
UK	0.01	0.69	1.17	1.16	1.05	0.57	0.72	0.79	0.96
Netherlands	0.02	0.11	0.72	0.79	0.78	0.90	0.73	0.81	1.04
North America			4.33	4.78	5.10	6.49	5.16	4.98	3.73
U.S.	0.46	2.49	3.89	4.38	4.43	5.42	4.20	3.94	3.06
Canada	0.41	0.22	0.32	0.28	0.44	0.59	0.56	0.61	0.45
FDI outflow	0.83	2.00	2.36	0.92	6.88	2.7	2.9	5.5	12.3

Sources: FDI inflow: *Zhongguo tongji nianjian* [China Statistics Yearbook], various years; *Zhongguo duiwai jingji tongji nianjian 2004* [China External Economic Statistics Yearbook 2004], 171. FDI outflow: http://stats.unctad.org/fdi/eng/TableViewer/wdsview/disviewp.asp (accessed 19 September 2005); data from 2002–2004 from http://english.sina.com/business/1/2005/0905/44731.html (accessed 10 September 2005); Jiang Wei, "Outbound FDI up 123 Percent in 2005," *China Daily*, 5 September 2006, http://www.chinadaily.com.cn/bizchina/2006-09/05/content_681592.htm (accessed 30 September 2006).

the three eastern metropolises). China's heavily publicized western development plan has not changed this geographic pattern: the share of western provinces in incoming FDI was 2.3 percent in 2003 and 1.8 percent in 2004.[21]

Asian comparisons highlight the scale of incoming FDI. China's FDI inflow during 2002–5 amounted to 4.8 times the combined total for Japan, Korea, Taiwan, and India. China's 2005 stock of foreign investment amounted to 14.9 percent of GDP, far larger than corresponding figures for South Korea (8.0), India (5.8), or Japan (2.2), nations that restricted foreign investment. With ample allowance for "round-tripping," the Chinese total approximates the figure for Taiwan (11.9 percent), which actively sought foreign participation.[22]

Not surprisingly, the impact of FDI inflows on China's economy is far larger than in these other Asian economies. Starting from less than 5 percent of China's 1985 exports, overseas sales of foreign-invested enterprises (FIEs, including wholly owned entities as well as Sino-foreign joint ventures) have shot upward to occupy a majority share of China's exports for every year beginning with 1996. Imports display a similar trend, with the share of FIEs rising from 1 percent in 1985 to 40 percent in the late 1990s and over half of total imports beginning with 2001.

Foreign investment has spread beyond early post-reform efforts to combine unskilled Chinese labor with imported materials to manufacture toys, garments, and other labor-intensive products for overseas markets. Table 2.6, compiled from a comprehensive 2002 database for industrial firms, shows that instruments and meters boast the largest accumulation of foreign investment, that electronics and telecommunications account for a larger proportion of Chinese exports than textiles and garments, and that an array of new

TABLE 2.6 Chinese Industry: Fifteen Sectors Receiving Largest FDI Inflows (percent)

Manufacturing sector	*Sector share of industry FDI*	*Export share of sector output*	*FIE share of sector exports*	*Sector share of China's industrial exports*
Instruments and meters	10.64	30.45	93.83	13.11
Electronics and telecommunications	7.88	32.16	91.12	19.01
Medical and pharmaceutical	7.03	9.11	56.34	3.42
Transportation equipment	6.50	6.55	64.03	2.78
Nonmetal mineral products	6.14	14.75	76.48	2.74
Ordinary machinery	5.56	18.82	58.13	4.66
Garments	5.07	45.93	61.40	10.63
Beverages	4.30	4.76	58.93	0.48
Textiles	3.52	27.16	50.41	5.54
Paper products	3.37	8.84	77.85	0.86
Electric equipment and machinery	3.35	16.25	81.84	2.79
Food products	3.24	23.26	60.42	2.42
Smelting/rolling of ferrous metals	3.15	7.87	49.13	2.41
Metal products	2.73	19.60	84.80	2.18
Plastics	2.18	17.30	79.19	1.44
Average	4.98	18.85	69.59	4.96
Total for top 15	74.66			74.47

Source: Chinese Industrial Microdata, database compiled by China's National Bureau of Statistics, 2002. Coverage includes the entire state sector and other firms with annual sales in excess of 5 million yuan (about US$600,000).

sectors—pharmaceuticals, transport equipment, nonmetallic minerals, and general machinery—have eclipsed textiles and garments as recipients of overseas investment.

These data highlight the lead role of FIEs in China's exports. The fifteen sectors listed in table 2.6 account for three-quarters of industrial FDI and for three-quarters of China's industrial exports. The average share of foreign-linked firms in export sales of these fifteen sectors is 69.6 percent.

Three decades of reform have propelled foreign direct investment to a central position in China's dynamic economy. As with trade, the impact of FDI remains concentrated in China's eastern coastal provinces. Even though official FDI measures include returning Chinese funds, it is evident that China has become a leading destination for global investment, and that the scale and impact of overseas investment dwarf comparable measures for Japan, Korea, Taiwan, and India. Foreign investment has generated large inflows of production technology, managerial know-how, and marketing expertise; transformed both the scale and the structure of China's foreign trade; and linked growing numbers of China-based firms to transnational supply chains, a development that promises to accelerate the penetration of valuable technological and commercial knowledge and skill.

Along with large inflows of FDI, China itself is a modest source of overseas investment. Available data, summarized in table 2.5, show that outbound FDI remains far smaller than the stock or flow of incoming foreign investment. Even so, United Nations Conference on Trade and Development (UNCTAD) now ranks China as the world's sixth largest source of outward FDI; Hiroshi Ohashi speculates that China's actual outflow of FDI may exceed officially announced totals.[23] The big jump reported for 2004–5 confirms our expectation that China's overseas FDI seems poised for rapid expansion.

Internationalization and China's Development Process

The combined impact of China's open-door policy and the accumulation of nearly three decades of market-oriented domestic reform is the primary source of both sustained economic growth and of China's expanded participation in global markets. Market-leaning domestic reforms and the liberalization of international trade and investment have encouraged growing entry of foreign and domestic producers and sellers, intensifying competition throughout the economy. The benefits of entry and competition are particularly evident in manufacturing, where they have fostered increases in both capabilities and productivity.

Despite its modest size relative to aggregate investment, FDI has played a central role in China's industrial development.[24] Financial returns among foreign-linked firms consistently exceed returns attained by domestic firms: data for 2000 and for 2003 show that FIEs achieved rates of return nearly five times that of domestic enterprises.[25] FIEs inject new products and novel manufacturing methods into China's economy, creating productivity gaps that spur reforms and upgrading among domestic firms.

Foreign participation has enabled China's auto industry to advance from isolated production of 1950-vintage autos to growing participation in the global car industry. Starting with joint ventures linking big state-owned manufacturers such as Shanghai Automotive and First and Second Auto Works with Volkswagen and Peugeot in the 1980s, the industry's global links have expanded to include China-based manufacturing operations involving every major international original equipment manufacturer (OEM) as well as Chinese auto ventures in Korea, the United Kingdom, and the Middle East. This transformation has also spread to China's auto component manufacturing, with joint ventures involving leading international parts suppliers now dominating the first-tier of China's domestic auto supply chain. China's 2005 output of vehicles (cars plus trucks) reached 5.71 million, making China one of the five largest vehicle manufacturers in the world. In the wake of these developments, we observe rapid growth in China's exports of auto parts (in excess of US$10 billion in 2005, amounting to one-sixth of auto parts production), as well as the emergence of several small but ambitious private vehicle manufacturers competing for domestic and international market share.

Elsewhere, imports, technology transfer, and FDI have been important catalysts in the remaking of entire industries. China's machine tool industry is a case in point. Precision machine tools are critical to emerging industries such as autos, trucks, shipbuilding, aircraft, electric power, and construction equipment, which demand quality components machined to exacting standards. In the 1980s, China's machine tool companies largely produced conventional lathes, and were ill-equipped to accommodate the growing demand for computerized and computer numerically controlled (CNC) products that would soon follow. This demand was largely met by imports and at the low end of the market by the manufacture of CNC machines by Chinese firms under technology licensing agreements.

In the mid- to late 1990s, several Chinese producers formed joint ventures with leading Japanese, Korean, Taiwanese, and German firms to develop CNC products. Their emergence, combined with falling import tariffs, has put considerable pressure on existing manufacturers of CNC machine tools in China. Reflecting newly elevated quality standards in the industry, a

Shenyang manufacturer has recently offered to rebuild or replace "advanced" equipment sold prior to 2000.[26] In the last five years, domestic production of CNC lathes, including that by joint ventures, has nearly tripled. These products now compete successfully in product ranges formerly served only by imports. Domestic sourcing of numerical controls, ball screws, spindles, and other key components is expanding rapidly. Although imports remain important—representing half of all CNC sales in the domestic market—they are concentrated in the increasingly advanced higher end of the market for machine tools.

New competition from domestic sales by foreign-invested firms represents only part of the FDI story. FIE activity injects international standards for design, quality control, production management, and other dimensions of business practice deep into China's industrial economy. When First Auto Works and Volkswagen initiated a joint automotive venture, the German partner provided detailed standards for automotive coatings. First Auto, which had never developed such guidelines, assigned one of its research institutes to diffuse Volkswagen's paint standards to more than twenty domestic suppliers (interview, Changchun, 28 May 1996).

Although the Chinese authorities press FIEs to expand local sourcing, market logic makes "the FIEs . . . eager to increase local content . . . because it makes good business sense."[27] A Taiwan-owned machine tool maker, for example, purchases 60 percent of the 1,000 components needed to assemble lathes from Chinese suppliers, in part to ensure that "the [final product's] price is good" (interview, Hangzhou, 14 July 2005). Sutton shows that automotive manufacturers generate massive demand for local products.[28] Although Volkswagen, Toyota, General Motors, and other global auto majors bring convoys of overseas suppliers in their wake, procurement from domestic firms remains essential. Hyundai's vehicle assembly operations, for example, benefit from the presence in China of "about one hundred" Korean auto parts producers. These firms, in turn, depend on second- and third-tier suppliers that are "mainly Chinese firms," even though local procurement amounts to "less than 20 percent" of component requirements (private communication to authors, September 2005). A Beijing-area joint-venture producer of auto seats reports sixty suppliers, including fifty domestic private enterprises (interview, Beijing, 25 July 2005).

China's open-door policy has also ramped up the participation of domestic firms in international production networks and supply chains. In the early years of reform, this took the form of processing trade (*lailiao jiagong*), in which overseas firms hired Chinese companies to process imported materials, and then reclaimed the finished products for sale abroad. More recently, the role of Chinese firms in transnational production networks has expanded dramatically, as is evident from the massive two-way trade in components mentioned earlier. The involvement of Chinese firms in international supply chains now extends to aircraft, automobiles, computers, electronics, and numerous other sectors, and has spread from manufacturing to participation in research and development (R & D) and design.

Engagement with transnational production networks deepens the exposure of formerly isolated Chinese firms to the designs, technologies, operating procedures, quality standards, and business methods practiced in world markets. These new connections, which typically accompany the arrival of overseas firms, stimulate immense flows of knowledge that multiply the domestic benefits associated with foreign investment.

FIE involvement in China's commodity trade has contributed to a modest but definite rise in the technical sophistication embodied in Chinese trade flows. We classify commodities according to their dependence on research and development using a unique survey of United States industries that specialists view as the best available measure of R & D intensity. We then apply this classification to Chinese trade flows. Although the resulting measures are not without problems, the results, which take the form of annual measures of R & D intensity for China's trade in manufactures from 1987 to 2003, provide a broadly accurate gauge of trends in the R & D intensity of China's trade flows.[29] During the late 1980s, measures of R & D intensity for China's manufactured exports cluster at the lowest levels. By 2003, the largest segment of exports has moved somewhat higher on the scale of R & D intensity. We also observe considerable growth in the export share for products ranked much higher on this scale. This outcome is entirely consistent with the observation that labor-intensive products, while still occupying a substantial share of export production, have gradually lost their dominance within China's manufactured exports.

Rankings for China's manufactured imports display similar trends but show wider transformation of the product mix, with the largest cluster of imports for 2003 located in the middle range of R & D intensity. This reflects large imports of sophisticated production equipment as well as extensive network trade in parts and components, including some (like computer chips and hard disk drives) with high levels of R & D intensity.

The new availability of Chinese partners has encouraged firms in many industries to restructure manufacturing operations by relocating final assembly work to plants in Chinese coastal cities. Office machines, telecommunication equipment, laptop computers, televisions, and many varieties of industrial machinery formerly exported from Japan, Taiwan, South Korea, or Singapore are now exported from China. The expanding presence of foreign firms in China's coastal regions, their dominant position in China's international trade, and their efforts to rearrange the geography of Asian manufacturing are critical determinants of evolving trends in China's trade balance with various world regions, including China's growing bilateral trade surplus with the United States.

Internationalization and China's Trade Patterns

Figure 2.3 displays the path of China's exports, imports, and trade balance since 1978. Exports and imports have grown steeply, with strong acceleration visible from the late 1990s. China's trade balance, however, has remained small.[30] Following several deficit years in the late 1980s, and again in 1993, China has recorded annual export surpluses beginning in 1994. During the decade ending in 2004, these modest surpluses averaged US$27.6 billion or 6.4 percent of total trade, and showed no tendency to increase. The largest surpluses are associated with periods when weakening domestic momentum

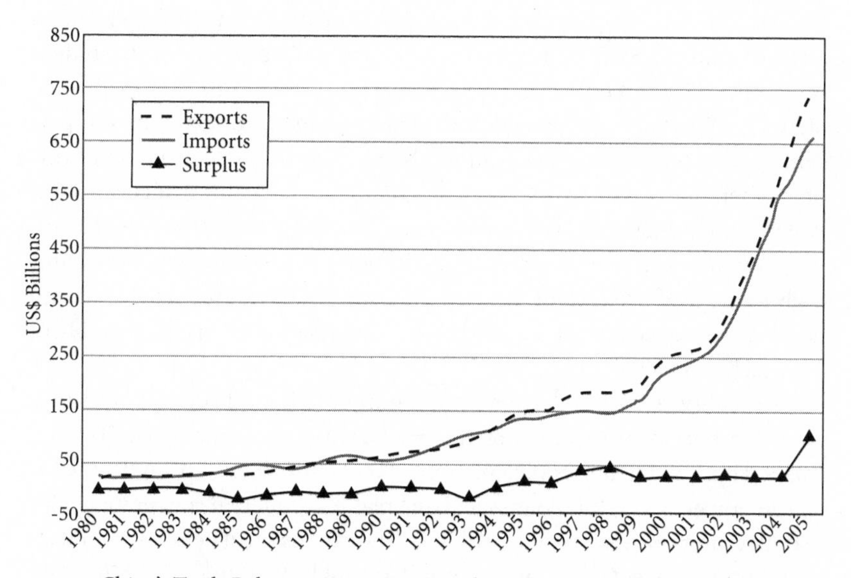

FIG. 2.3. China's Trade Balance, 1980–2005. Based on *Zhongguo tongji zhaiyao 2006* [China Statistical Abstract 2006], 161.

slowed the expansion of imports: 1997 and 1998 fall into this category. It is too early to tell whether the big increase in China's trade surplus to US$101.9 billion in 2005 and US$177.5 billion in 2006 represents a long-term trend.

This pattern of global trade balance conceals wide regional variations. Table 2.7, which explores this dimension of China's trade, reveals three distinct trends since 1990: large and growing export surpluses with Hong Kong and North America and even larger trade deficits with Asia (excluding Hong Kong). China's surplus with Hong Kong arises from shipment of Chinese goods through the former colony to overseas destinations.[31] The other trends: large Chinese deficits with Asia (excluding Hong Kong) and big surpluses with North America, are closely related. Both arise from China's growing role in transnational manufacturing networks and from the restructuring, noted above, which has brought many types of final assembly work to China. The result is big deficits in China's trade with Asian sources of materials and components, and big Chinese surpluses with importers of Asian manufactures—led by the United States.

China's large bilateral surplus with the United States, although sometimes attributed to undervaluation of China's renminbi currency and a variety of specific Chinese practices, arises from the logic of comparative costs. This conclusion emerges from table 2.8, which summarizes United States trade results for 1990, 1995, and 2000–2005. The data show China's bilateral trade surplus with the United States rocketing upward from US$11.5 billion in 1990 to US$201.6 billion in 2005. As a result, China's share of the United States' (rapidly growing) global trade deficit jumped from less than 10 percent to over one-quarter between 1990 and 2005. Public discussion of this phenomenon often blames this bilateral deficit for massive displacement of American manufactured goods and factory employment.[32] This is erroneous. As Barry Naughton emphasizes, "U.S. imports from China fit overwhelmingly into one of two categories: labor-intensive, low-tech products . . . that are no longer produced in the United States . . . and labor-intensive assembly of high-tech products."[33]

In reality, what has declined is not output of American manufactures, but the importance of U.S.-bound manufactured exports from Japan, Taiwan, Korea, Hong Kong, Singapore, and other Asian producers. This reflects China's emergence as a major manufacturing platform, often in cooperation with manufacturers located elsewhere in Asia. The expansion of network manufacturing often concentrates labor-intensive assembly operations in China. As a result, final products (for example notebook computers) manufactured cooperatively by plants in multiple jurisdictions move from China to their final

TABLE 2.7 China's Global Trade by Region, 1990–2004 (US$ billion)

	1990			*1994*			*1998*			*2004*		
	Exports	*Imports*	*X-M*	*Exports*	*Imports*	*X-M*	*Exports*	*Imports*	*X-M*	*Exports*	*Imports*	*X-M*
Total trade	62.09	53.35	8.75	121.01	115.61	5.39	183.81	140.24	43.57	593.33	561.23	32.10
Asia (excluding HK)	17.36	14.61	2.75	41.29	57.91	-16.62	59.97	77.99	-18.03	180.13	290.58	-110.45
Hong Kong	26.63	14.15	12.48	32.36	9.44	22.92	38.74	6.66	32.08	100.87	11.80	89.07
Europe	7.10	10.61	-3.52	18.60	24.66	-6.06	32.99	25.84	7.15	106.10	85.12	20.98
North America	5.61	8.03	-2.42	22.87	15.74	7.13	40.11	19.12	20.99	130.13	50.80	79.33

Source: United Nations Commodity Trade Statistics Database (COMTRADE), http://comtrade.un.org/db/.

Note: X-M refers to the trade surplus, which is the difference between exports (X) and imports (M).

TABLE 2.8 United States Trade Deficit with China and Asia, 1990–2005

United States imports (US$ billion)								
From	*1990*	*1995*	*2000*	*2001*	*2002*	*2003*	*2004*	*2005*
World	517.0	770.8	1217.9	1132.5	1202.3	1305.1	1469.7	1671.1
China	16.3	48.5	100.0	102.1	133.5	163.3	196.7	243.5
Other Asia	174.6	257.0	324.2	276.9	282.2	280.4	325.7	334.3
All Asia	190.9	305.5	424.2	379.0	415.6	443.7	522.4	577.8
Asia share (%)	36.9	39.6	34.8	33.5	34.6	34.0	35.5	34.6
United States exports (US$ billion)								
To	*1990*	*1995*	*2000*	*2001*	*2002*	*2003*	*2004*	*2005*
World	374.5	546.4	781.8	731.0	693.2	723.6	818.8	904.3
China	4.8	11.6	16.2	19.2	22.1	28.4	34.7	41.8
Other Asia	95.4	152.6	178.3	155.3	146.3	151.0	173.8	177.7
All Asia	100.2	164.2	194.5	174.5	168.4	179.5	208.6	219.5
Asia share (%)	26.7	30.1	24.9	23.9	24.3	24.8	25.5	24.3
United States trade balance (US$ billion)								
With	*1990*	*1995*	*2000*	*2001*	*2002*	*2003*	*2004*	*2005*
World	−142.4	−224.4	−436.1	−401.5	−509.1	−581.5	−650.9	−766.8
China	−11.5	−36.9	−83.8	−82.8	−111.4	−134.8	−162.0	−201.6
Other Asia	−79.3	−104.5	−145.9	−121.6	−135.8	−129.4	−151.9	−156.7
All Asia	−90.8	−141.4	−229.7	−204.5	−247.3	−264.2	−313.8	−358.3
Share of U.S. trade deficit (percent)								
With	*1990*	*1995*	*2000*	*2001*	*2002*	*2003*	*2004*	*2005*
China	8.1	16.4	19.2	20.6	21.9	23.2	24.9	26.3
Other Asia	55.7	46.6	33.4	30.3	26.7	22.3	23.3	20.4
All Asia	63.8	63.0	52.7	50.9	48.6	45.4	48.2	46.7
Non-Asia	36.3	37.0	47.3	49.1	51.4	54.6	51.8	53.3
Share of U.S. deficit with Asia (percent)								
	1990	*1995*	*2000*	*2001*	*2002*	*2003*	*2004*	*2005*
China	12.7	26.1	36.5	40.5	45.1	51.0	51.6	56.3
Other Asia	87.3	73.9	63.5	59.5	54.9	49.0	48.4	43.7

Sources: For 1990–2003 from various issues of OECD, *Monthly Statistics of Foreign Trade*, and OECD, *Monthly Statistics of International Trade*. For 2004: http://www.bea.doc.gov/bea/di/home/trade.htm (accessed 12 February 2006). For 2005: http://www.bea.gov/newsrel/tradnewsrelease.htm (accessed 12 February 2006). Disaggregated data for 2005 appear preliminary; they may exclude smaller Asian nations.

destinations, and are thus recorded as Chinese exports, even though much of the value added originates elsewhere.

Table 2.8 shows that the shifting geography of Asian factory activity has prompted a rapid decline in the share of America's trade deficit attributable to "other Asia" (i.e., excluding China). The contribution of these economies to the U.S. deficit dropped by nearly 10 percentage points between 1990 and 1995, and then plunged by a further 30 percentage points between 1995 and 2005. The drop-off in export share from "other Asia" was so steep that the combined share of all Asian nations, including China, in the U.S. trade deficit fell by 17 percentage points, from 63.8 percent to 46.7 percent, between 1990 and 2005. The rising share of non-Asian trade partners in America's trade deficit provides the clearest possible demonstration that wage levels, currency valuation, and other features of China's political economy cannot pass muster as the chief cause of structural imbalance in United States external trade.

Looking Forward

During the past three decades, rapid expansion of China's international links has moved the People's Republic from near-autarky to active participation in a large and growing array of global markets. By some measures, China's immersion in the world economy has attained unprecedented levels for large nations. We anticipate further growth of Chinese involvement in international exchanges of materials, components, final products, technology, information, management, and ownership rights.

The market forces driving China toward globalization will extend current patterns of integration. China continues to expand the scope for foreign business activity, evidently in the expectation that foreign business penetration can beneficially prod domestic participants toward improved performance, as when a vice president at China Life Insurance Company says that "bringing in foreign investors will help improve corporate governance, product development, and internal risk management."[34] Shake-ups inspired by entry of foreign products and overseas companies may be market-based, as in sectors like cars or machine tools, where the productivity and quality achievements of foreign firms create demonstration effects. Policy-directed injection of foreign ownership, as in banking and insurance, provides another option in which government encourages leading foreign firms to enter faltering domestic industries for the express purpose of injecting new standards, business methods, and management systems.

The growing domestic availability of modern logistics capabilities points to continued expansion of Chinese participation in international supply chains supporting the manufacture of goods for domestic and overseas markets.[35] Network expansion will continue to enhance domestic capabilities, as Chinese firms and also individual engineers, scientists, designers, managers, and others sharpen their skills by working in global business networks. These arrangements will continue to channel globally prevalent technologies and quality standards into domestic industries—steel and cement provide obvious and important examples.

We also observe new elements—in trade, investment, and research and development—that seem likely to multiply and intensify the sinews binding China to the global economy.

Growing Chinese Dependence on Imported Energy and Materials

China now imports one-third of its crude oil and over half of its iron ore. Worldwide efforts by Chinese companies to secure long-term access to a variety of resources reflect expectations that China's economy will become increasingly reliant on resource imports. Chinese researchers conclude:

> By 2020, China's dependence on imported crude oil will rise to 60%, and 40% for natural gas. . . . According to projections of future supply and demand, by 2020, China's domestic resources will fully supply only 9 of 45 mineral varieties. . . . In particular, crude oil, iron ore, copper, bauxite, nickel, sylvite, and other products essential to national economic security are all in long-term deficit. For example in 2003, imports of iron ore and pure iron amounted to 50% of total consumption, manganese ore imports supplied 46% of consumption, and imports of sylvite, alumina, and copper ore all rose far above their 1998 levels. Resource exhaustion intensifies day-by-day. Of 415 large and medium mines nationwide, 50% suffer crises of depleted reserves or face closure, and 47 mining cities face resource exhaustion.[36]

China as a Growing Source of Overseas Investment

Table 2.5 summarizes available information about China's outward FDI. Although the totals remain modest, UNCTAD anticipates that China may soon supplant Japan as the world's fifth largest source of overseas direct investment.[37] Backed by strong official encouragement to "go global" (*zouchuqu*), the recent jump in activity, which saw annual FDI outflows quadruple during 2003–5, probably represents the start of a steep upward climb in both annual flows and the cumulative stock of China's outward investment.

Two distinct motivations underpin this new drive to expand FDI. China's search for secure access to overseas sources of energy and raw materials, which has drawn extensive international comment, has sparked a long string of arrangements involving petroleum, natural gas, mineral ores, and timber in Australia, Brazil, Canada, Central Asia, Indonesia, Iran, Russia, Sudan, and other nations spanning every continent.

Efforts by Chinese manufacturers to expand their technical proficiency and marketing capabilities inform both overseas expansion and acquisition of overseas companies. These motives explain initiatives to develop overseas production of garments, home appliances (for example, Haier's production and research facilities in the United States), and motor vehicles. Similar objectives stand behind recent Chinese acquisitions of prominent overseas manufacturers of computers (IBM's PC operations), home appliances (Thomson), motor vehicles (Ssangyong, MG Rover), auto parts, machine tools (for example, Ikegai, Japan's oldest lathe manufacturer), chemicals (Inchon Refinery), and electronics (Hynix Semiconductor's LCD panel division).

Foreign Acquisition of Ownership Stakes in Chinese Firms

Along with continued expansion of FDI through traditional channels in which foreign companies either establish joint ventures with Chinese partners or create new, entirely foreign-owned firms, we now see a new form of foreign entry in which international firms purchase ownership stakes in established Chinese companies. International banks, including Bank of America, Citigroup, HSBC, Royal Bank of Scotland, Standard Chartered, UBS, Wing Hang Bank, and many others, have purchased stakes in Chinese banking institutions. AIG, Carlyle Group, HSBC, and Sumitomo Corporation have acquired partial ownership of Chinese insurance firms. Recent initiatives by international beer giants include a tense struggle between SABMiller and Anheuser-Busch to acquire shares in the Harbin Brewery Group. The list of prominent multinationals seeking China acquisitions includes Altria, Coca Cola, Amazon.com, Hong Kong's PCCW, and many others.

Increased Chinese Participation in Global R & D Networks

The contribution to this volume by William Keller and Louis Pauly emphasizes the success of China's education system in producing a large and growing stock of well-trained scientists and engineers. China's abundant supply of modestly priced technical expertise has attracted widespread attention from multinational enterprises, which display a growing inclination to include China in their global R & D operations. Official Chinese insistence that foreign firms include R & D activity in their investment packages has led to instances of what foreign managers dismiss as "PR & D," in which Chinese R & D entities serve to polish corporate images rather than deliver new knowledge. As with local content requirements, however, many international firms initiate or expand China-based research and design activities in the expectation that such operations will create new knowledge and boost company profits.[38] Volkswagen, for example, plans to "develop, assemble and sell a hybrid minivan in . . . cooperation with a Chinese automaker" because of "the Chinese industry's rapid advance into a complex technological area of automotive design" and because Chinese "government ministries have been heavily subsidizing research . . . into hybrid-propulsion and fuel-cell vehicles."[39] With the business press brimming with accounts of similarly expansive plans by Ericcson, General Electric, Siemens, and many other global giants, it seems evident that large-scale entry into multinational networks for research and design has begun to add a new dimension to China's international ties.

Development of Newly Competitive Industries

China is rapidly emerging as a significant player in the global market for auto parts. China's two-way trade in automotive products (including both vehicles and parts) doubled between 1995 and 2000, and then quadrupled to US$29.6 billion in 2004. Trade in auto parts rose even faster, reaching US$16.6 billion in 2004, more than five times the 2000 figure.[40] Participation has begun to expand beyond foreign-linked producers. Wanxiang, a private firm with multiple domestic and international operations, sells transmission shafts, universal joints, bearings, and braking systems to Visteon, Dana, Delphi, and other international OEMs and component suppliers (interviews, 13 August 2003 and 13 July 2005). Fuyao, "China's largest auto glass manufacturer," will export windshields for the Audi Group's car production in Europe from late 2005. Fuyao, which has sold automotive glass to Hyundai, General Motors, Mitsubishi, and Isuzu since 2003, presently occupies "50 percent of the . . . domestic OEM market and 10 percent of the automobile glass market in the United States."[41] Chinese firms are reportedly preparing to assemble vehicles in Russia, Egypt, Iran, and Malaysia and hoping to export China-made busses and cars.[42] Shipbuilding, construction machinery, telecommunications, and biotechnology, among others, show similar signs of growing internationalization.

Restructuring of Agriculture Based on International Comparative Advantage

China has relied on international markets to complement domestic food supplies since the 1960s. As urbanization reduces the supply of farmland and of agricultural labor and as north China's water supplies dwindle, we may anticipate increasing imports of cotton, soybeans, and other staple crops. China's high man-land ratio and low labor costs push farmers toward fruits, vegetables, and other labor-intensive specialty crops with strong export prospects, implying rising future dependence on grain imports. With China's farm sector "rapidly evolving in the direction of national comparative advantage . . . China's interests lie in robust liberalization of . . . market access, reduced export subsidies, and lower domestic supports" for farm products.[43]

Important segments of Chinese economic policy anticipate large-scale access to offshore resources, funds, expertise, and markets. China has adopted U.S.-style policies that encourage energy-using activities by expanding highways, limiting energy prices, and controlling ancillary costs (for example, parking fees). Such policies implicitly assume unlimited future access to imported energy. Plans to build vessels and terminals for transshipping liquid natural gas reflect similar thinking.[44] Current blueprints for the reform of China's banking and financial sectors envision major contributions of funds, expertise, and competitive pressure from overseas companies. The same observation applies to the reform of state-owned enterprises, the promotion of development in China's western regions, the expansion of modern logistics, and the improvement of China's infrastructure. Efforts to develop world-class companies in numerous industries all presume unlimited access to international markets. In shipbuilding, for example, China, already the world's third-largest producer, with exports amounting to 70 percent of current output, plans to raise its global market share from 14 to 25 percent by 2010.[45]

Summary and Policy Implications

Our analysis has documented the expansion of Chinese participation in international flows of trade, technology, and capital. Over the past three decades, this process has moved China from near-autarky to a new pattern of intensive interaction with global markets that is unusual, and perhaps unprecedented in the economic history of large nations. We anticipate the continuation of this new trend toward deeper engagement with the world economy.

China's reforms represent a giant expansion of market economics. In 1978, foreign investment and private business were largely absent from China's economy. Twelve state companies controlled China's entire foreign trade. Today, we see a transformed economy with tens of thousands of firms engaged in foreign trade, ebullient growth of private business, and accelerating penetration of multinational business and international commercial practices into most segments of China's economy. Despite the survival of the state sector and the continued importance of official intervention, reform has established market forces as a fundamental component of daily life for the quarter of humanity that makes its home in the People's Republic.

This review of China's engagement with the global economy leads to policy-related observations about the contribution of globalization to China's domestic reform process, about short-term issues surrounding bilateral trade between the United States and China, and about long-term prospects for China's integration into the global political economy.

International Engagement as a Driver of Domestic Reform

China's remarkable shift toward market economics remains far from complete. The legacy of central planning persists, especially in the management of investment and banking, the operation of state enterprises, and official strategizing for what the Chinese call "pillar industries." Chinese legal practice often falls short of international norms. Despite these and other difficulties, thousands of international firms find China's business environment sufficiently congenial to justify large and growing investments.

International involvement plays a big role in China's reform dynamic. The presence of foreign business and the prospect of future expansion of trade and investment flows drives beneficial trends: for improved laws and courts, for more extensive government-business consultation, for more transparent regulation, and for a more open and stable business environment. Foreign participation in China's economy is valued not simply for the influx of capital, technical knowledge, managerial capability, and marketing skill. Chinese reformers see rising trade volumes, growing foreign presence, and the obligations associated with China's entry into the WTO as levers that can help to overcome domestic inertia and resistance in ways that parallel the contribution of external pressure (*gaiatsu*) to breaking policy gridlock in Japan. Foreign institutions and international business practice provide inspiration and models for large and small innovations in Chinese policy, Chinese legislation, and Chinese business practice.[46]

The increased size and complexity of domestic as well as international business transactions creates a strong demand for predictable and universally applicable business arrangements. China's motorcycle industry, for example, initially developed by imitation: using "common designs" and "making economical motorcycles that were fairly similar to other domestic brands." Now, a former copycat explains that "Patented products make up an increasing portion of our product line—that's exactly what we want."[47] Steep increases in domestic and international patent activity by Chinese firms have stimulated calls to enhance the protection of intellectual property.[48] China's leaders understand that institutional changes can contribute to their goal of continued growth and modernization. Numerous initiatives—promises to treat private business on an equal footing with state firms and foreign enterprises; efforts to commercialize China's banks; expanded transparency for government operations; new arrangements for corporate governance; efforts to systematize government procurement; and many others—reflect the authorities' genuine efforts to improve the institutional underpinnings of China's economy.

Although village elections define the present limit to political democracy, China's populace has enjoyed substantial, if incomplete, expansion in many dimensions of individual rights. Progress is particularly evident in the economic sphere. Citizens now enjoy extensive (though not unlimited) opportunities to travel, to seek employment, to choose or alter their own occupations, to buy and sell, to establish private businesses, and to create or modify commercial relationships. Business associations, corporate leaders, and even foreign business executives have gained informal access to many policy processes. Scott Kennedy finds that "firms influence the policy process indirectly via their trade associations and other intermediaries, but even more common is direct lobbying by firms of their regulators."[49]

China Is Not the Source of Structural Imbalance in U.S. International Trade

China's bilateral trade surplus with the United States has risen steeply during the past fifteen years. China's share of the U.S. trade deficit now stands at over one-fourth, with further increases likely. This large and growing trade gap has sparked calls for revaluation of China's renminbi, for imposition of new tariffs and quotas on Chinese goods, and for investigation of allegedly unfair Chinese trade practices. Neither theory nor empirical evidence lends much support to such prescriptions.

Elementary macroeconomics reveals intimate links between a nation's external trade balance and the domestic balances between savings and investment and between government revenue and spending. The United States trade deficit is the mirror image of domestic fiscal and savings deficits. Substantial reduction of the U.S. trade imbalance cannot occur without fundamental and painful domestic reforms that raise domestic savings and/or reduce fiscal deficits. Furthermore, discussion of short-term remedies for the U.S. trade gap often overlooks unwelcome consequences of proposed policy changes, such as rising domestic interest rates.

Aside from theoretical considerations, the notion that China is the main cause or even one among several major factors underlying the U.S. trade deficit cannot survive a close reading of table 2.8. Although China's share of the U.S. import surplus has jumped from 8.1 percent in 1990 to 26.3 percent in 2005, much of this increase reflects growing intra-Asian trade networks that have shifted final assembly work to China. Despite the big boom in Chinese exports, Asia's share of the U.S. trade deficit has dropped sharply from a 1991 peak of 83.9 percent to less than 50 percent beginning in 2002. Since foreign-invested firms regularly account for more than half of China's exports (table 2.6), will not restrictions that somehow limit China's exports invite leading exporters to move their factories, knowledge, and expertise to other venues?

We conclude that neither near-term adjustments in Chinese and/or other Asian currencies nor protectionist measures can significantly alter important features of the United States macroeconomy. Intense focus on economic conflict arising from possible short-term adjustments has diverted attention from a broad range of common economic interests that have the potential to bring the United States and China closer together during the coming decades.

China's Reliance on Global Market Ties Enhances the Feasibility of China's Peaceful Rise

China's long boom is an unprecedented event in world history. China has rapidly emerged as a force in global markets, a regional military power, a looming influence on national economies throughout the Pacific region, and an emerging advocate for the interests of the developing world. Beijing's contributions to stabilizing regional markets during the Asian financial crisis, to promoting regional trade liberalization, and to mediating disputes surrounding North Korea's nuclear ambitions signal China's emergence as a major player in regional and global efforts to manage contentious political, economic, social, and security issues.

China's growing strength elicits deep concern, most notably in Japan and the United States, from observers who see Chinese expansion as a source of friction and possible military strife over natural resources, economic dislocation, and territorial claims. Chinese scholars counter with the notion of China's peaceful rise, meaning that China can gradually expand its role in world affairs without tearing the fabric of global stability.[50] Given the instability surrounding the rise of other great powers during the nineteenth and twentieth centuries, this idea requires careful examination.

Growing global market ties have contributed substantially to China's recent growth spurt. Chinese economic policies relating to industrial development, reform of banking and state enterprises, infrastructure expansion, overseas investment, energy consumption, and many other fields assume continued access to a vast array of global markets and resource flows.

China, like other nations, can deploy a combination of military and diplomatic tools to maintain and protect its access to international markets. Robert Ross and Adam Segal emphasize in this volume that China's military power, while expanding rapidly, does not extend far beyond its land and especially its maritime borders. Recent assessments by the United States Department of Defense (2005), the U.S.-China Economic and Security Review Commission (2004), and the Council on Foreign Relations (2003) offer similar perspectives.[51]

No conceivable expansion can enable China's armed forces to secure access to Brazil's iron ore, Canada's tar sands, Iran's crude oil, Africa's mineral wealth, or the consumer markets of North America and Western Europe. The size of China's economy and the scope of its global interactions constrain Chinese leaders from contemplating strategies that rely on military power to secure markets. China's acceptance of new U.S. and EC restrictions on textile and garment imports following the expiration of the Multi-fibre Arrangement illustrates the extent to which cooperation and diplomacy dominate Beijing's efforts to maintain access to the overseas buyers and sellers on whom China's future prosperity must build.

Beijing's astute comprehension of these realities stands behind a remarkable transformation of China's foreign policy. Revolutionary ideology and antimarket rhetoric, formerly staples of Chinese diplomacy, have faded from Beijing's agenda, now replaced by promises of contracts, investment, market access, and free-spending tourists. China's keen interest in market access may account for otherwise puzzling features of Beijing's international economic stance. Why did China quietly agree to WTO accession under conditions of unprecedented stringency? Why did the world hear no Chinese complaint that the WTO conditions "interfered in China's domestic affairs"? Why did China's leaders not insist that the United States and the European Community withdraw demands that far surpassed requirements previously applied to new signatories upon their entry into global trade agreements? Why did the Chinese not protest international demands for rapid compliance with WTO agreements? Why did Beijing not insist on the same leeway enjoyed by Japan and Korea, which flouted important provisions of multilateral trade agreements long after signing such documents? The answer to all these questions appears to rest on Beijing's early realization that such costs paled in comparison to the long-term benefits attached to WTO membership.

China's recent volley of trade liberalization initiatives has energized trade diplomacy throughout the Pacific Basin, with even protectionist stalwarts like Japan and India scrambling to join in.[52] As David Shambaugh points out, some have dismissed Beijing's activism as a "charm offensive."[53] Although Beijing's trade proposals seek to exclude Taiwan and to overshadow Japanese and American influence, we see China's espousal of open trade with ASEAN and other Pacific partners as serious policy initiatives that build on long-term economic interests.

Looking beyond short-term friction over trade balances and currency valuation, we see substantial overlap between China's economic interests and those of the United States. China is emerging as an improbable tribune for open flows of commodities and direct foreign investment, objectives long espoused by the United States. As a big importer of natural resources, China, like the United States, will benefit from and may actively seek to promote stability in the Middle East and other resource-rich regions. Ironically, it is now not China but the West, with its concern over democracy and human rights, which puts ideology ahead of commerce. We anticipate that conflicts over violations of intellectual property rights are likely to recede as growing numbers of Chinese entities "suffer . . . losses . . . [when] other enterprises began copying . . . technology without paying any royalties" and therefore join in "applying IPR [intellectual property rights] in the battle against counterfeiters."[54]

Macroeconomic policy coordination represents another potential arena for economic cooperation. Deepening links connecting short-term capital flows, exchange rates, monetary expansion, and short-term interest rates in China, Japan, the European Community, and the United States promise growing benefits from efforts to align national policies, and threaten rising costs in their absence. European and American protectionists complain that China's undervalued currency and cheap labor flood their markets with low-priced imports and demand that China (and other Asian nations) reorient their economies toward domestic rather than overseas demand. Beijing's protracted use of fiscal stimulus to boost domestic demand speaks directly to the wishes of these critics, as does China's "focus on increasing consumption demand and strengthening the role of consumption in fueling economic development."[55]

Like the United States, China faces problems of domestic structural imbalance. China's rising trade surplus is the mirror image of an excess of high domestic savings over domestic investment. Given China's extremely high investment rate and the low efficiency of domestic financial institutions in channeling savings to efficient investment projects, Beijing's policy makers are sensibly acting to curtail rather than accelerate the growth of investment outlays. On the savings side, Beijing has enlarged its own deficit spending, raised wages, extended public holidays, and increased efforts to support the rural economy—all designed to stimulate domestic consumption (which would reduce the share of household savings in total incomes). Despite these efforts, Chinese households continue to accumulate large precautionary savings to prepare for future expenses associated with retirement, illness, education, and housing. In the absence of well-funded programs for social security and health insurance, it is difficult to anticipate any substantial reduction in China's high rates of household saving.

We anticipate that high Chinese savings will continue to enlarge the global pool of savings available to international borrowers, including America—the largest borrower of all. Seeking to diversify risk and to avoid overheating of the domestic economy, China's government actively promotes a "go outward" (*zouchuqu*) policy that encourages overseas investment by a growing array of domestic companies and financial institutions (for example, insurance companies and pension funds). Here again, China stands to gain from amicable international relations and to suffer from their absence.

Our review demonstrates that growing involvement with global markets has conveyed enormous benefits to China's booming economy. Expansion of new international links involving resource imports, emergence of new industries, growing outward flows of Chinese overseas investment, participation in global R & D networks, and restructuring of Chinese agriculture will intensify the connections between international market access and China's future prosperity.

Because economic growth represents a key objective of China's present regime, Beijing's leaders will be powerfully motivated to craft cooperative strategies that can preserve Chinese access to global markets and thereby enhance China's development prospects. The centrality of growth and prosperity among China's national goals, and Beijing's resulting willingness to endorse compromise and adjustment in pursuit of economic gain, transforms the idea of China's peaceful rise into an unusual opportunity for mutually beneficial adaptation to the emergence of a newly powerful nation.

China's goals, however, encompass security, prestige, and national honor as well as economic growth. Both theory and Chinese history demonstrate that the exigencies of current rivalries and tensions can induce political leaders to abandon long-term economic benefits and embrace immediate strategies that emphasize conflict rather than cooperation. Issues surrounding the future of Taiwan, North Korea's nuclear ambitions, and growing tensions between China and Japan represent obvious arenas in which Chinese leaders could choose to reject cooperative approaches to controlling international tension. There may be others.

We conclude that China's current and future economic circumstances provide powerful leverage for advocates of international cooperation. Economics cannot guarantee that Beijing's strategists will endorse cooperation and eschew conflict. However, we do insist that the economic benefits of cooperation are immense, so that even a limited curtailment of Chinese access to global markets would threaten massive injury to the most dynamic segments of China's economy. We therefore expect China's current and future leaders to welcome efforts to resolve potential conflicts through cooperation. This economically inspired tilt toward cooperation increases the prospects of transforming "China's peaceful rise" from slogan to reality.

★3 BUILDING A TECHNOCRACY IN CHINA

Semiconductors and Security

William W. Keller and Louis W. Pauly

CHINA'S CAPACITY TO SURPRISE IS GREAT, and so too is the need for reasoned assessments of its economic, social, and political trajectory. This chapter focuses on one important aspect of China's rise and future capacity to provide regional and international leadership. The country's current leaders certainly view the expansion of the indigenous semiconductor industry as a key strategic priority. They seek the capability to design and manufacture state-of-the-art semiconductors, the microchips at the core of computers, electronics, telecommunications, weapons systems, and much more. In this light, our research concentrates on the growth of the base for applied research in this sector.[1] The building of such a base is a crucial step in the value-added innovation-production chain. In its absence, only lower-level assembly and manufacturing operations are possible; in its presence, we may catch an early glimpse of an emerging innovation system capable someday of shifting global structures of industrial power. Larger issues of interstate policy interaction inform our research. Standard theories of systemic power balancing and power transition are ill-equipped to deal with the mutually constructed perceptions of industrial leaders and official policy makers in sectors like this one.[2] The empirical evidence we present in this chapter may be interpreted in diverse ways. To be specific, as long as U.S.-China relations remain on a reasonably even keel, the building up of internal strategic resources in China can be suggestive of either a long-run strategy of balancing the power of others or of promoting the peaceful global integration of a transformed Chinese economy. In the language of international relations, our evidence cannot unambiguously suggest whether or not China is becoming a status quo power. It cannot do so because it cannot separate capabilities from intentions, and it cannot make any less thorny the intersubjective character of the intentions of China and its industrial partners and competitors. Whether China's high-technology performance contributes positively to the interdependent international economy established so painstakingly during the past half century, or whether it tips in the direction of an economic nationalism destructive of the global system, depends both on the clarification of China's intent and on official and corporate reactions abroad. What we can do in this chapter, nevertheless, is lay out the facts as they are developing in this important case, cast them in a historical and comparative light, and draw out some concluding speculations in dialogue with the other chapters of this book.

Why Study the Semiconductor Industry in China?

China's rise is transforming the regional and global foundations of the semiconductor industry. Biotechnology may be the key industry of the future, but microelectronics is arguably the key industry of the present. Certainly Chinese industrial planners see it this way, for they have assigned it their leading strategic designation. The development within China not only of a competitive manufacturing base for integrated circuits (ICs), but eventually also of a serious national system for related research and development poses new challenges for the industry globally. The evolution of an applied research base linked to now-burgeoning manufacturing operations would be an essential early step suggestive of larger national objectives. Such a base is typically contrasted with laboratories for basic research; essentially, it refers to expertise and technology most often located in or near production facilities and centered on innovative engineering at the precommercial phase of product development. A country intent on moving ahead quickly in a particular industry may be expected to concentrate efforts here, since it can generate in the near term the resources required for rapid development.

The most important factor underlying the development of China's applied research base in semiconductors is the expansion of a vast pool of engineering and, eventually, scientific talent throughout the country. Over the past decade, internally generated skills have been augmented by the migration to China of highly educated engineers, mainly from the United States and Taiwan. Many of them are of Chinese origin and are returning with industry experience. Indeed, relevant expertise has flooded into China as Chinese firms have expanded their recruiting abroad and as large-scale foreign direct investment bolstered a semiconductor industry developing to serve global and, increasingly, internal markets. Key elements of an internationally competitive semiconductor manufacturing industry in China are in place. Foreign investment in assembly operations and low-cost labor with improving skills have played a significant role. In the next decade or two, despite impediments all too obvious within China today, this will be followed by a globally competitive applied research base. Before we examine evidence suggestive of such a conclusion, some context is required.

Technology and China's Rise

In 1978, Deng Xiaoping reopened the book on China's industrial modernization. Western technology, embedded in both tools and minds, was critical. In contrast to analogous efforts preceding 1949, dependence on foreign loans would be minimized. Direct foreign investments would be conditioned on tangible technology transfers, and foreign majority control of Chinese enterprises would be carefully limited. A new resource, however, would be tapped to the fullest extent possible. Chinese business networks flourished in the diasporas that began centuries before the collapse of imperial China. Their nodes spread from Hong Kong and Taiwan to Southeast Asia, Europe, and the United States. Relinking China directly into them had both supply-push and demand-pull logic. In this light, it hardly appears surprising that overseas Chinese networks and foreign joint-venture partners would form the key building blocks for successful industrial development in the newly opening sectors of semiconductors and information technology.

China possessed hardly any integrated circuit industry at the time of Deng's policy reform. By 1985, it had imported some two dozen three-inch wafer semiconductor lines, the first from Japan's Toshiba in 1982. Ten years later, Huajing Electronics, the pioneering state-owned enterprise in this sector, followed with five-inch manufacturing-on-silicon (MOS) lines from Siemens and Lucent. In 1998, Huajing bought a six-inch line from Lucent. With technology and joint-venture capital from Motorola, NEC, STMicroelectronics, Mitsubishi, Philips, Siemens, and Toshiba, five other Chinese firms—Huawei, Shanghai Belling, Advanced Semiconductor Manufacturing Corporation, Shougang, and Huahong—did the same.[3] Given the recent pace of change in this dynamic and still high-priority sector, these relatively recent innovations seem like ancient history.[4]

By 2005, the domestic Chinese market for semiconductors had become the fastest growing in the world. If current trends continue, it will soon be the second largest after the United States. With the vast majority of China's electronics production still based on imported chips, however, the government remains committed to ambitious goals for replacement of imports with domestically produced chips. The central government's Ninth Five-Year Plan targeted large-scale indigenous chip production on six-inch wafers using an 800 nanometer (nm) design rule. Eight-inch wafers with design rules as low as 300nm and advanced packaging technology were targeted for prototyping under the government's Project 909. In 2000, Huahong-NEC produced 350nm chips on eight-inch wafers and exported 10,000 wafers (primarily memory chips) per month to Japan. By 2004, the world's leading semiconductor manufacturers were capable of mass-producing chips with a design rule of 90 nm. Chinese manufacturers hoped to match and surpass this performance in a short period of time.

The Tenth Five-Year Plan ending in 2005 specified a production goal of 20 billion integrated circuits (ICs) per year, and an import substitution goal of 30 percent of local demand growing to 50 percent by 2010. It envisaged up to four new six-inch production lines, five eight-inch 350-180nm lines, and two twelve-inch 180-130nm lines. It also targeted an array of national research and development (R & D) centers focusing on high-volume production technology and system-level semiconductors, as well as a sufficient number of IC design and computer-assisted design companies to generate annual revenues exceeding US$10 million. Finally, it promised significant assistance for selected Chinese packaging, testing, equipment, and materials companies. More directly, restrictions were reinforced on foreign investors and vendors. Although the desire for rapid technology transfer and the simultaneous acceptance of WTO obligations suggested some eventual loosening of those restrictions—especially those specifying less than 51 percent foreign control of joint ventures—industrial planners kept an eye trained on the country's historical experience of excessive reliance on foreign vendors for related cutting-edge technologies.

Rapid economic development in China continues to depend on technology transfer from abroad, as it did in the early twentieth century. But this time a basic commitment to national control in strategic industrial sectors seems firm, and the semiconductor industry is certainly one of those sectors. The delicate task of accelerating the inward transfer of technology without recapitulating the historical experience of excessive dependence on foreigners now lies at the core of a novel political experiment. That experiment combines capitalism with centralized national planning and decentralized industrial governance. It poses stark challenges for an industry that well exemplifies both the conflictual and cooperative faces of economic globalization.

Building a Technocracy in China

A range of policy debates—in the world's major semiconductor manufacturing firms, in universities, and in governments—now swirls around early evidence of China's rise in this sector. The question of when China's base for applied semiconductor research will reach internationally competitive levels is important, but virtually all close observers consider such a development to be inevitable. The more important question has to do with the character of that base when it does mature. Will it remain a net taker of technology from world markets, or will it become a more open and steady contributor?

From its earliest days, China's integrated circuit industry aimed in general at self-reliance. Korea and Japan provided the classic models for an industry organized around integrated device manufacturers (IDMs), firms that combined production capabilities from the design of microchips to the manufacture of devices for end users. This was the model for pioneering Chinese firms like Huajing and Shanghai Belling. By 2000, however, the more specialized foundry model perfected by Taiwan had clearly become dominant on the mainland, even if IDMs remained a strategic objective for the long term. (Foundries can produce chips nearer to the cutting edge, typically under contract to end-use device makers.) Burgeoning local and foreign demand for semiconductors and the promise of more rapid technology transfer provide significant reasons for the switch in near-term preferences. Even low-end Chinese chips simply could not be produced fast enough. The promise of relatively quick profits was also at work, and this certainly helped attract foreign foundries, especially from Taiwan. Table 3.1 gives an indication of China's demand for integrated circuits as well as of local production capacities.

TABLE 3.1 Total IC Demand and Production in China (billion units)

Year	*Total IC Demand*	*China's Total IC Output*	*IC Output as % of IC Demand*
2000	24.1	5.4	22
2001	22.0	4.9	22
2002	26.9	8.0	30
2003	33.0	10.4	32
2004	41.2	14.0	34
2005 (forecast)	49.5	20.0	40
2006 (forecast)	100.0	50.0	50

Source: Based on Michael Pecht and Y. C. Chan, *China's Electronics Industries* (College Park, MD: CALCE EPSC Press, 2004), 82.

During the past decade, business networks established after 1949 by overseas Chinese clearly sought opportunities to establish critical industrial nodes back in China. Taiwan's foundries—and the entrepreneurs with experience inside them—are the best example; their role in helping to build China's newest semiconductor fabrication facilities (fabs) is obvious. Of all fabs being built around the world by 2004, 33 percent were in China and 14 percent in Taiwan. Such developments were welcomed, and even endorsed by official and unofficial patronage—and for many reasons. Foundries promised municipal and provincial governments in China rapid economic growth and an expanding array of skilled jobs. They also translate into wealth for local and national elites who invest in them. Over the next decade, massive growth is forecast for China's computer components market. In 2002, a leading foundry, the Semiconductor Manufacturing International Corporation (SMIC), forecast a 21 percent compound annual growth rate.[5] In addition, China is already the world's largest market for mobile phones and is on its way to becoming the largest market for other consumer electronic products. Import substitution alone could justify the foundry strategy, even in the absence of financial incentives provided by various levels of government. (The contention that the manufacture of advanced chips in China is purely a function of value-added tax [VAT] rebates and other trade-distorting measures is therefore quite doubtful.)[6] In addition to obvious strategic factors pulling local and foreign investment into Chinese foundries, the most important long-term implication is that foundries have opened a critical avenue for the import of leading-edge manufacturing technology. This is exactly what is required to implement the stated intention of national leaders to "catch up" with the West and even to leapfrog into next-generation electronics.

Semiconductors and Talent Migration

China is now drawing heavily upon an intellectual reserve built up over the past twenty years in the Chinese diaspora. U.S. National Science Foundation data indicate that 50 percent of all science and engineering doctorates awarded to foreign students in the United States are received by Chinese, Taiwanese, South Korean, and Indian citizens (68,500 of 138,000 in 2004). Chinese students comprise the largest group; engineering and biology are the two largest fields.[7]

Since 1985, approximately 70 percent of Chinese citizens who earned their science and engineering doctorates from U.S. universities stayed in the United States for employment in postdoctoral programs.[8] If the pattern for Taiwanese who earned U.S. science and engineering doctorates holds, this will soon begin to fall. During the 1990s, these highly educated Taiwanese were lured home by a variety of enticements now commonly offered by semiconductor companies operating out of Beijing and Shanghai. Certainly official Chinese government programs are designed to reduce this brain drain. Anecdotal evidence strongly suggests that burgeoning new opportunities in Chinese electronics and other industries are beginning to work in the same direction. At the same time, as will be described and analyzed below, such efforts are complemented by a national commitment to expanding the size of the national talent pool rapidly, in both absolute and relative terms, in the sciences and, especially, engineering.

The Development of Manufacturing Technologies

The success of the foundry model in Taiwan continues to depend on a highly trained workforce. As important, however, has been the ability of the foundries to convince their customers that the intellectual property they hand over for low-cost batch-manufacturing is sacrosanct. Replicating similar assurances in China-based foundries has been challenging. Given the recent troubled history of Chinese intellectual property protection regimes, concerns among foreign customers remain, even as World Trade Organization (WTO) disciplines kick in. Nevertheless, internally generated competitive pressures among foreign chip producers—who worry about gaining a position in future Chinese electronics markets—push in the opposite direction. Here is where policy debates in the United States and elsewhere about offshoring, and especially about Chinese strategic intentionality, gain relevance.

A 2002 study of the U.S. General Accounting Office found that after ten years of explosive growth, China was only two generations behind in semiconductor manufacturing technology, and one generation behind "the commercial state of the art."[9] This was somewhat exaggerated, since it gave too much weight to innovations in the most advanced foundries, which were unlikely to soon outclass well-established foundries in Taiwan and elsewhere. China's foundries remain focused on export markets, even for lower-end chips. Nevertheless, it is increasingly clear that leading Chinese foundries intend to compete directly with the best in the world. They also intend eventually to focus more of their sales efforts on internal Chinese markets.

Security Complications and Export Controls

The prospects for open, mutual collaboration in the near future are complicated, however, by signals on the national security front emanating from China's central government and from the People's Liberation Army

(PLA). Even though Jiang Zemin finally abdicated formal political control over the military, policies he championed to compensate for China's conventional military weakness by encouraging the rapid import and absorption of microelectronics technology are likely to persist. Certainly the PLA would like to leapfrog to next-generation innovations and enhance its electronic warfare capabilities. Few Western military observers would bet on success in this regard, but the rhetoric of China's leaders is being taken seriously in defense policy circles in the United States and in Congress.[10] For their part, senior Pentagon officials assert that the PLA is already supported by a cutting-edge domestic semiconductor industry focused on "pockets of excellence." The claim is that sophisticated chips are already being produced to fit military requirements for long-range precision strike capabilities, information dominance, command and control, and integrated air defense. Pockets now being developed are said to include advanced phased-array radar, antisatellite technology, and electromagnetic pulse weapons.[11] At the same time, expert observers are aware that the hierarchical structure and risk aversion of China's military industry continue to make it difficult for the PLA to integrate sophisticated weapons systems effectively.[12] Acquiring the tools to innovate is also a serious challenge.

Export controls designed to slow the pace of semiconductor tool acquisition and/or development are fraught with complexities. The loose Wassenaar Arrangement on Export Controls for Conventional Arms and Dual-Use Goods and Technologies confronts the reality that only the United States considers the acquisition of semiconductor manufacturing equipment by China to be problematic. In 2002, the Government Accountability Office (GAO) found that under competitive pressure, European, Japanese, and even U.S. authorities were licensing the sale of tools at least two generations more advanced than specified Wassenaar thresholds.[13]

From the point of view of foreign semiconductor firms operating in China, the concerns of the U.S. military tend to be overwhelmed by now-obvious opportunities and competitive forces. If there is a long-term threat on the horizon as they see it, it is a threat to future profitability, given the possible future development of a more autonomous and less open semiconductor industry emerging in China across the whole value chain. But such a threat is ultimately a function of the development of local design capabilities.

Innovation in the Chinese Semiconductor Industry

Despite early efforts by government at various levels to stimulate design centers, design industry revenues in China do not yet exceed US$250 million per year. Most indigenous chips are application-specific integrated circuits (ASIC) or are customized for relatively inexpensive and easy-to-produce local power-management products. Few Chinese designers at this stage are able to work on sophisticated system-on-a-chip designs. Until 1995, there was little capability in either design or testing outside of Fudan, Tsinghua, and Peking universities.[14]

By 1999, however, the state-owned IC Design Center in Beijing had produced an eight-bit central processing unit for smart cards (using 800nm technology) and an MP3 decoder, with China's first complete large-scale computer-assisted design system. Within five years, the center was reported to be capable of prototype and even production testing on a small scale, and was also reported to be sharing its expertise with more recently established design centers in seven locations around the country. A similar pattern is observable in the National Engineering Center for ASIC Design, which grew out of the Microelectronics Institute of the Chinese Academy of Sciences, which concentrates on IC analysis tools. Design houses without fabrication facilities are also springing up, and by 2004, over 150 companies employing 3,000 engineers were estimated to exist. Most were located in government-sponsored centers in Shanghai, Beijing, Shenzhen, Wuxi, Chengdu, and Xi'an.[15]

Interviews—as well as personal observation at design centers in Beijing, Shanghai, and Xi'an—suggest that the industry is off to a modest start. It is important to note, however, that its future potential is already sufficient to have generated keen interest from global semiconductor tool manufacturers. Although advanced tool manufacturing in China on any serious scale remains a distant goal, Huawei in Shenzhen and others have reportedly developed a variety of relatively advanced tools.[16] In addition to Tsinghua, Peking, and Fudan, other universities have demonstrated the existence of a serious new market for tool makers.

As has been the case in other countries, there is in China an evolutionary movement in the indigenization of semiconductor production, from tools to finished microchips. Reverse engineering and process emulation lead to learning and gradual innovation. A generation ago, Japan was not expected to be in a position to support a high-level industry, and especially not an advanced tool industry. Expectations changed swiftly once Japan's national innovation system began to focus on specific targets.

China is still basically in the emulation phase of industrial development in semiconductors, but signal advances are already being made. National Jiaotung University, for example, recently developed China's first digital signal processing chip, a sixteen-bit chip produced by SMIC using a 180nm design rule, packaged and tested by local firms in Shanghai. Even though it can only compare with low-end chips sold by companies like Texas Instruments, its development in China surprised many industry observers. Recent innovations in closely related sectors, like telecommunications, also suggest that Chinese industrial planners are aggressively seeking to use the scale and scope of local markets to establish new standards.[17] Mobile telephones provided only the most obvious of targets in this regard. Even at less advanced levels of technology, associated national strategies will help local manufacturers build up the financial resources necessary to invest much more heavily in applied research and, eventually, in basic research.

Electronics Research in China

China's electronics research base was hobbled by the legacy of a Soviet-style science and technology system. During the 1980s and 1990s, rapid moves were made to jettison this legacy at the national level by following best practices in the United States and Western Europe. The Ministry of Science and Technology, the Chinese Academy of Sciences, the Chinese Academy of Engineering, a new Ministry of Information Industries, and a new National Science Foundation—together with the Ministry of Education, which funds universities—lie at the core of official reform efforts. Between the mid-1990s and the present, aggregate national R & D expenditures have risen from about 0.5 percent to over 1 percent of gross domestic product.[18] Although still much lower than the 2 to 2.5 percent registered in the most advanced industrial countries, the rate of change is staggering, particularly when China has confronted so many other pressing needs. The National Science Foundation of China (NSFC) budget doubled between 1996 and 2000, and again between 2000 and 2003. Meanwhile, undergraduate and graduate enrollments in science and engineering programs at Chinese universities and institutes increased by more than 25 percent per year in the early years of the twenty-first century.

As would be expected at this stage of China's development, the R & D intensity of Chinese firms is low in comparison with firms from advanced industrial countries. Still, patent applications by firms and research institutes rose from 83,000 in 1995 to over 170,000 five years later. And in response to financial incentives put in place by the government, China's rank in the global index of peer-reviewed and cited papers rose from seventh in the world to third.

Clearly, China's government is trying to compensate in part for the underinvestment in R & D by local companies and to lay the groundwork for a fully functioning national innovation system. Most university researchers are forced to retire early (age sixty for men, fifty-five for women) to make room for new scholars. National resources devoted to scientific research are being expanded rapidly. The Chinese Academy of Sciences (CAS) itself runs an elite graduate school, with research as its focal point. Through the Hundred Talents Program administered by the NSFC, it is trying to recruit star professors from leading foreign universities.[19] (Salaries offered are far in excess of typical academic salaries in China, a generous research allowance is provided, and a grant of RMB 200,000 is made for the purchase of a home.) When the program started in 1995, seven recruits, with an average age of thirty-four years, came from abroad. By 2001, recruiting was at the level of 130–190 per year.[20] Where Chinese universities have a difficult time differentiating between excellent and just competent performers, or among various fields of study, CAS is deliberately attempting to emulate high-level science and engineering faculties in the United States. If there is a Chinese MIT in the future, it may well be located outside conventional academic boundaries and in the elite research institutes of CAS.[21]

Two of the most prominent of those institutes are the Institute of Semiconductors and the Institute of Software. Although competition for funding is intense among all CAS institutes, these institutes and their branches across the country are flourishing. They are typically led by scholars with significant overseas research experience, and they are well known for their burgeoning links to analogous research networks in the United States. CAS scholars routinely travel abroad for conferences, although U.S. visa restrictions have slowed this activity. Anecdotes abound concerning recent difficulties that researchers have encountered.

Related organizational innovations followed the creation of the Chinese Academy of Engineering in 1994. It has a more specific mandate to provide government and firms (often spin-offs from work done in CAS institutes) with advice on the future development of engineering science and technology. Information and electronic engineering is one of the seven main divisions of the Chinese Academy of Engineering (CAE). Among other things, the division seeks to organize and promote domestic and international collaborations. Another division focuses on chemical, metallurgical, and materials engineering. Unlike CAS, the modus operandi of the CAE divisions is to work through university engineering departments. Thus far, their key partner is Tsinghua University. During the last couple of years, more prominence has been given to strengthening the management skills of engineering graduates coming out of Tsinghua and other prestigious universities.

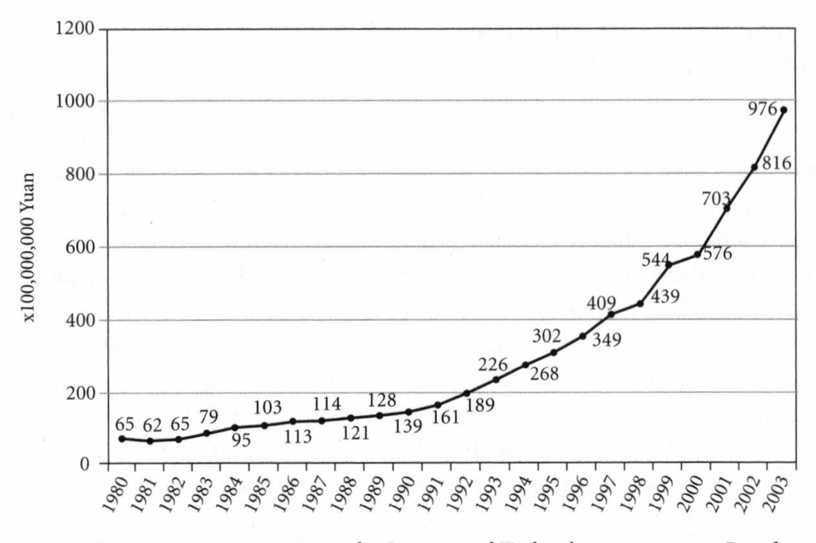

FIG. 3.1. Government Appropriation for Science and Technology, 1980–2003. Based on *China Statistical Yearbook on Science and Technology 2003* (National Bureau of Statistics, Ministry of Science and Technology), p. 3; 2004 edition, p. 4.

The National Science Foundation of China has also been more intensively promoting research of interest to China's semiconductor manufacturers, especially in life sciences and materials sciences. The foundation provides research grants on the basis of national competitions. Recently, the success rate has been approximately 16 percent of applications; a decision was made two or three years ago to concentrate resources on larger projects with the most promising prospects for near-term results. For the five-year period beginning in 1998, government funding increased by a total of 45 percent. The total NSFC budget increased from RMB 80 million in 1986 to RMB 2.6 billion by 2002; its average research grant now exceeds RMB 172,000, but key or major projects can be funded at the level of RMB 1–5 million, for up to five years. In recent years, grants in engineering and materials sciences exceeded RMB 100 million, the second largest category after life sciences.[22] A glance at figure 3.1 indicates the dramatic rise in Chinese government funding of science and technology.

Expanding the Human Resource Pool

A serious national commitment to building a solid foundation for advanced industrial production and innovation in China is evident in the rapid expansion of university-level teaching programs. Human resources are, of course, the core of any applied or basic research base in the information technology industries, including semiconductors. In this regard, careful consideration must be given to the scale and scope of what China is now accomplishing.

One broad measure of the national commitment to education is an astounding and rapidly accelerating increase in the number of Chinese students graduating over the past few years from institutions of higher learning, with about half of all degrees awarded in the fields of science and engineering. Unlike data from the U.S. National Science Foundation (NSF), the Chinese data include statistics for engineers educated at China's vast network of technical institutes in what are often two- or three-year programs. Nevertheless, even when the lower NSF figures are analyzed, as they are later in this chapter, the trend is the same, and its magnitude is still staggering.

Figure 3.2 shows the numbers of students who graduated with a bachelor's-level degree in science or engineering in China from 1994 through 2003. These figures are remarkable in themselves. But it is the slope of the increases in engineering since 2001 that bears further scrutiny. Figure 3.3 indicates the number of individuals entering bachelor's-level science and engineering programs in China during the same time period, from 1994 through 2003.

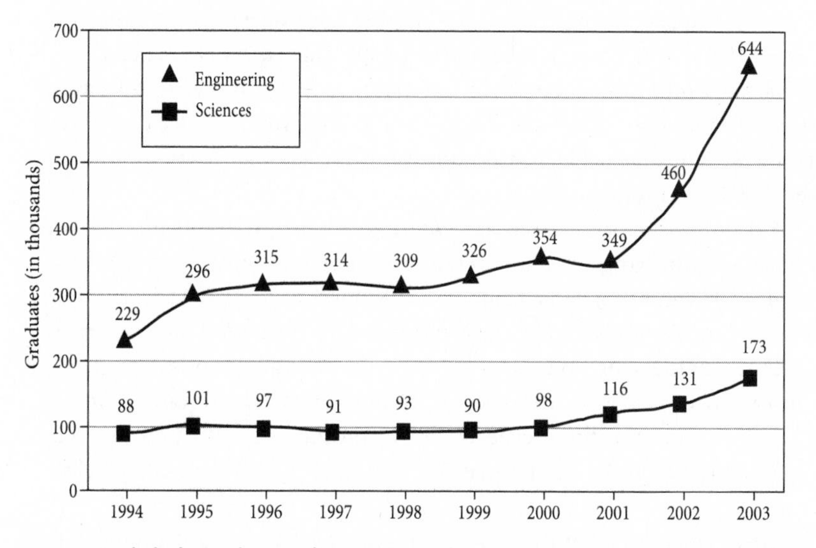

FIG. 3.2. Bachelor's Graduates of Institutions of Higher Education in China by Field of Study, 1994–2003. Based on *China Statistical Yearbook on Science and Technology 2003* (National Bureau of Statistics, Ministry of Science and Technology), p. 3; 2004 edition, p. 2.

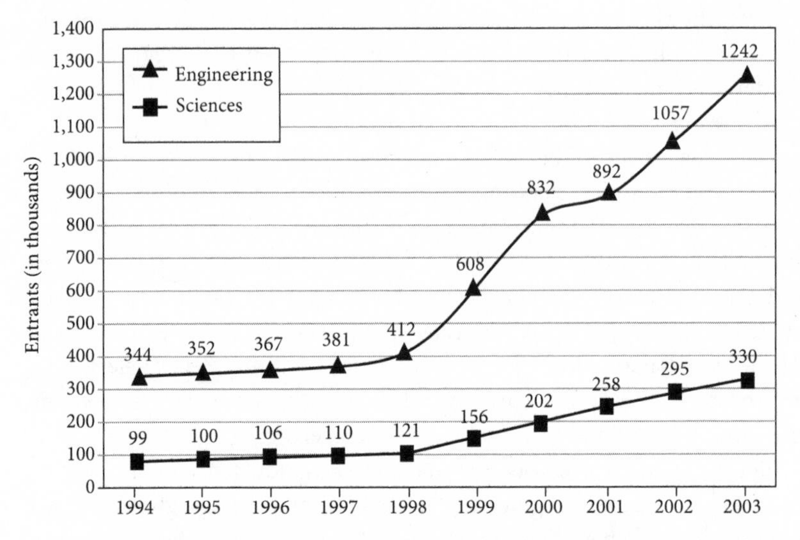

FIG. 3.3. Undergraduate Entrants in Institutions of Higher Education in China by Field of Study, 1994–2003. Based on *China Statistical Yearbook on Science and Technology 2003* (National Bureau of Statistics, Ministry of Science and Technology), p. 22.

After 1998, there is an obvious and dramatic acceleration of the numbers of young people entering higher education in both science and engineering. During the next five years, the number of students entering bachelor's-level engineering programs increased from 412,000 in 1998 to 1,242,000—an increase of more than 200 percent. During the same time period, the number of students entering science programs rose from 121,000 to 330,000—an increase of about 173 percent.

For both categories—students entering science programs and students entering engineering programs—one would expect some attrition; this is borne out in figure 3.4, which shows the numbers of scientists and engineers officially enrolled in bachelor's-level programs for the period 1994–2003.

If all engineering and science students entering in 2000 through 2003 had remained in school, the expected number of enrollees would have been 4.0 million and 1.1 million respectively. Accordingly, the attrition rate is approximately 7 percent in engineering programs and 9 percent in science programs.

These calculations provide a rough basis for projecting the numbers of bachelor's-level graduates who will be available either for entrance into the Chinese workforce or for further graduate education in science and engineering. We know the number of students entering bachelor's-level science and

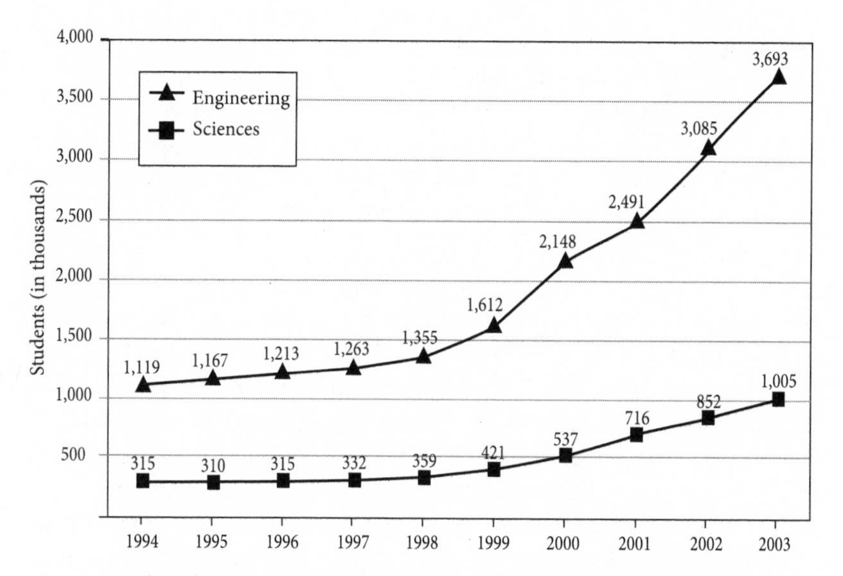

FIG. 3.4. Total Undergraduate Enrollment in Institutions of Higher Education in China by Field of Study, 1994–2003. Based on *China Statistical Yearbook on Science and Technology 2003* (National Bureau of Statistics, Ministry of Science and Technology), p. 23.

engineering programs from 1999 through 2003. If we conservatively assume an attrition rate of 10 percent, we can make an educated guess regarding the numbers of students likely to receive such degrees for the period 2004 through 2007. Table 3.2 provides a rough projection. Barring an economic meltdown in the region, military conflict involving China, or large-scale civil strife within the country, these numbers are very likely to be realized or exceeded.

There is an important debate as to whether or not the supply of talent creates its own demand. And the Chinese economy may or may not be able to shift quickly to higher-value-added work in semiconductors and other industries. A 2006 study by students at Duke University suggests that the Chinese

TABLE 3.2 Estimated Numbers of Chinese Science and Engineering Degrees Awarded at the Bachelor's Level and Above, 2004–2007 (in thousands)

Year	*Science*	*Engineering*
2004	182	749
2005	232	803
2006	266	951
2007	307	1,118

Source: Calculated from figures 3.2 through 3.4.

figures are inflated, and in effect that China educates only three times the number of scientists and engineers as does the United States.[23] Nevertheless, all available data point in the same direction: Chinese national education policy is clearly gearing up to promote a transition to a technically literate and highly capable work force. The point is reinforced by an analysis of the production of master's- and doctoral-level scientists and engineers, as documented in figure 3.5.

Based on Chinese data, figure 3.5 indicates the general trend. Although NSF calculations result in lower numbers, the Chinese report is quite consistent with the data presented in figure 3.2 (above) on bachelor's-level graduates in engineering and science. There is, once again, a remarkably steady increase in the numbers of students receiving advanced degrees in science and engineering between 1994 and 2003, the last year for which statistics are available from Chinese sources. From 1998 to 2003, the number of students graduating with master's-level degrees and above in engineering soared by nearly a factor of two. As with undergraduate engineering students, the spike for graduate students in 2003 is also quite pronounced.

Growth in the number of students earning graduate degrees in science was smooth and consistent from 1994 through 2003, increasing by about 117

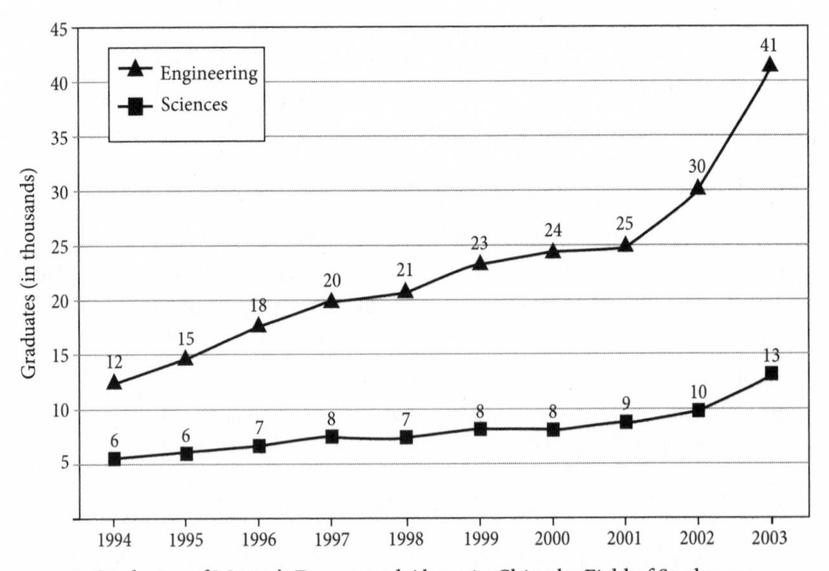

FIG. 3.5. Graduates of Master's Degree and Above in China by Field of Study, 1994–2003. Based on *China Statistical Yearbook on Science and Technology 2003* (National Bureau of Statistics, Ministry of Science and Technology), p. 3; 2004 edition, p. 2.

percent over the whole period. Interestingly, the number of science degrees granted, at both undergraduate and graduate levels, spikes in the year 2003. Nevertheless, while scientific training remains important, the real emphasis—especially after 1998—has been placed on the field of engineering. Figures 3.6 and 3.7 give these trends graphical expression.

As figure 3.6 indicates, the number of students entering graduate training programs in engineering began to increase precipitously after 1998, rising by 255 percent in six years. There was also a quite steep, if more moderate, increase in the number of science students entering graduate programs in China between 1998 and 2003, an increase of almost 209 percent—again, in only six years.

As with undergraduate enrollments in Chinese science and engineering programs, a number of insights can be gleaned from the overall numbers of students matriculating at the master's level and above. Figure 3.7 shows a strong upward swing in enrollments in both engineering and science graduate programs, again accelerating after 1998.

While it is more difficult to calculate attrition rates in graduate science and engineering programs, we can still get a rough idea of the numbers of

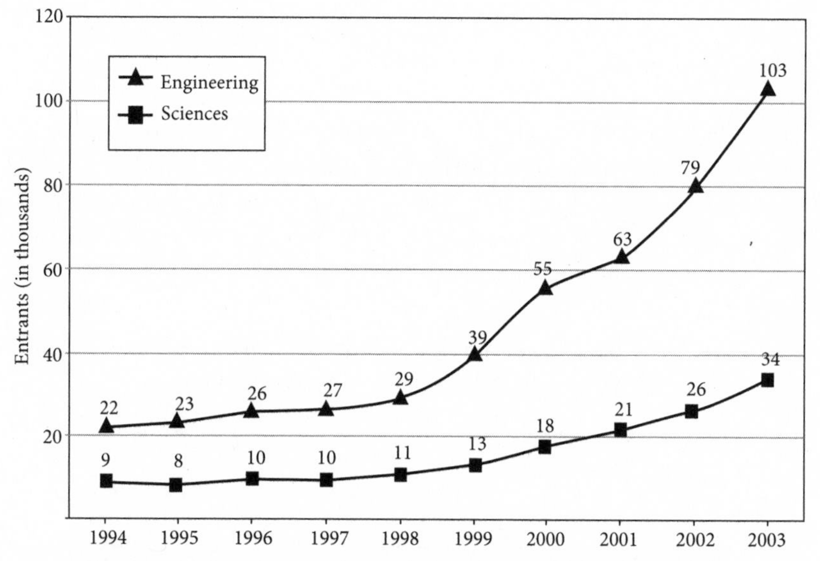

FIG. 3.6. Entrants of Master's Programs and Above in China by Field of Study, 1994–2003. Based on *China Statistical Yearbook on Science and Technology 2003* (National Bureau of Statistics, Ministry of Science and Technology), p. 3; 2004 edition, p. 2.

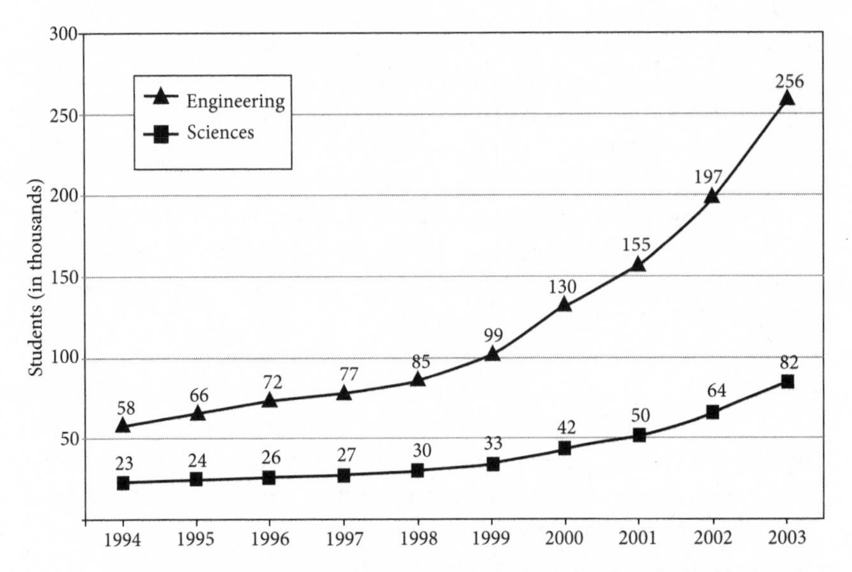

FIG. 3.7. Total Enrollment of Master's Programs and Above in China by Field of Study, 1994–2003. Based on *China Statistical Yearbook on Science and Technology 2003* (National Bureau of Statistics, Ministry of Science and Technology), p. 23.

postgraduate degrees likely to be awarded in the years immediately ahead. Like table 3.2 above, table 3.3 adapts the data and assumes an attrition rate of 10 percent.

Even if an attrition rate of 20 percent is assumed, over time the rate of growth of its science and engineering graduate labor force will place China in the first rank of technologically advanced economies. The impact is already beginning to be felt in semiconductors and in associated information technology industries, both upstream and downstream.

TABLE 3.3 Estimated Numbers of Chinese Science and Engineering Degrees Awarded at the Master's Level and Above, 2004–2007 (in thousands)

Year	*Science*	*Engineering*
2004	16.2	49.5
2005	18.9	56.7
2006	23.4	71.1
2007	30.6	92.7

Source: Calculated from figures 3.5 through 3.7.

The Prospects for High-Technology Innovation in China in Comparative Perspective

The quantity of human resources available to Chinese industry now and in the future does not necessarily translate directly into an internationally competitive labor force of high quality. One report suggests that some 30 percent of Chinese university graduates failed to find employment in 2004. It also argued that improvement in the quality of basic undergraduate engineering programs has not kept pace with rapidly expanding enrollments.[24]

Within international engineering circles, debate continues to rage on this issue. Skeptics suggest that the quantity of Chinese engineers poses little competitive threat. They contend that Chinese data overstate the numbers of engineering graduates at all levels, especially graduates capable of competing with their peers in the United States, Europe, and Japan. Indeed, they stake their claim that advanced engineering jobs in sectors like semiconductors—at comparatively high salaries—remain secure for the foreseeable future because of the vast gap in quality now evident between Chinese engineers and their counterparts elsewhere.

On the other side of this important debate are those who remind the skeptics about similar arguments made not so long ago in the case of Japan. Few close observers of the electronics industry in China, moreover, doubt that large numbers of adequately trained engineers and scientists are quite likely to compete effectively in the near future in fields where technologies are reasonably stable and most innovations are of an incremental nature. Under such conditions, advances are most likely to be made on the shop floor, so it was certainly significant that by 2005 China had become the key global producer of consumer electronics and the world's largest market for semiconductors—even if many are still imported. As the Chinese economy continues to expand, far more robust resources are likely to be made available to Chinese universities for the development of higher quality students. This would translate in the near-term into serious advances in local and national systems of innovation.

Because so much has already been accomplished in the establishment nationwide of production facilities for semiconductors, it had long been likely that one of the first such systems—for applied research—would appear in this industry. Its foundations are already apparent in key municipalities where semiconductor production is now being scaled up. Local capabilities are sure to be enhanced as that production is targeted less on export markets and more on a rapidly growing internal market, where indigenous firms are likely to retain a marketing advantage over foreign competitors.

It is important to keep this development in perspective. Not so many years ago, applied research in the United States was considered to be far less important than it is today. The lag time for comprehending its importance was even greater in Europe and Japan. It would be folly to assume that Chinese industrialists are not seeking to replicate the success of the semiconductor industry in the world's most advanced economies, partly by emulating their move up the research ladder from product development to applied research, and eventually to basic science.

Many observers were caught off guard by the rapid rise of a competitive Japanese semiconductor industry in the 1980s; others watched with incredulity as the Korean integrated device manufacturing and Taiwanese foundry models later gained significant global traction and competitiveness. The difference between these three cases and the Chinese case does not lie in relative work ethics; Chinese students are among the most able and most motivated in the world. It does not lie in ambition, for there is no doubt that China's leadership aims to return China to the global prominence it historically enjoyed. China is simply a late mover in the industry, and the key to catching up lies in the sheer volume and improving quality of the manpower available to strategic industries like semiconductors.

Semiconductor designers and manufacturers in the United States and other advanced economies cannot assume that they will be able in the near and medium term consistently to come up with leapfrog technologies that will keep leadership positions within the industry beyond the reach of China. In any event, recent history has amply demonstrated that the inventors of breakthrough technologies are not always the ones to reap the rewards. Smart follower strategies have long been evident within the industry.

In comparative data on bachelor's degrees awarded in Asia in 2002, it is easy to find discrepancies with data from Chinese sources. Some of the differences are accounted for by the fact that agricultural sciences and social/behavioral sciences data are excluded from the NSF data sets; there are many more agricultural science and engineering degrees awarded in China than in other countries. Chinese data also encompass a wider set of institutions of higher learning. Nevertheless, the latest NSF data reinforce the same broad trends highlighted above.

As figure 3.8 clearly indicates, in 2002 China had already far surpassed its East Asian neighbors in terms of the number of bachelor's degrees awarded in

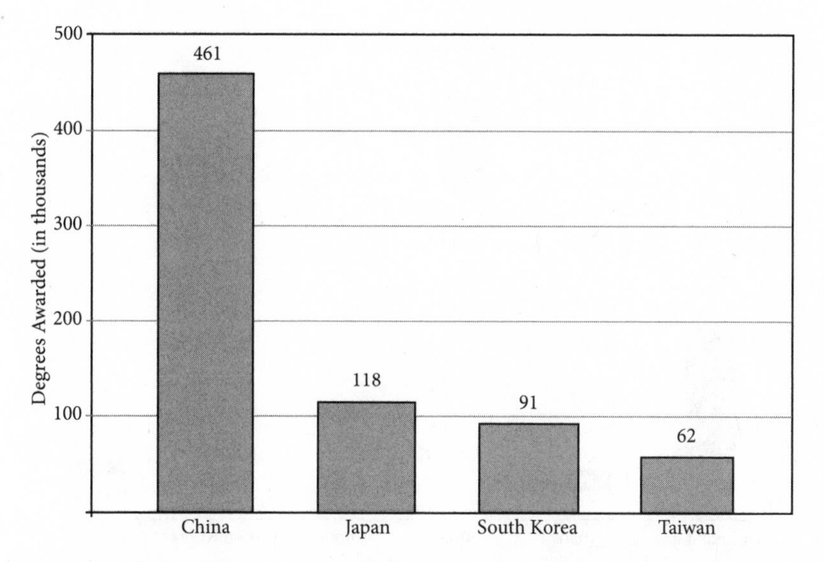

FIG. 3.8. Bachelor's Degrees Awarded in Science and Engineering in 2002, Asia. Based on United States, National Science Foundation, *Science and Engineering Indicators 2006*, appendix table 2-37. Excludes agricultural sciences and social and behavioral sciences.

science and engineering. By 2001, China had attained number one leadership status in the combined production of undergraduate science and engineering degrees, surpassing even the United States. The United States still leads the world in the number of undergraduate science degrees conferred, as shown in figure 3.9, but China dwarfs even the closest competitor in the sheer volume of engineering degrees awarded. Moreover, when U.S. undergraduate science training is excluded, China is number one on all measures, overpowering even Japan by a factor of nearly four to one. This likely foreshadows even more dramatic developments to come.

In light of concerns about outsourcing in the United States, it is worth underlining the magnitude of the differential in engineering training between China and the United States, which in recent years produced approximately 200,000 and 60,000 undergraduate engineers, respectively. Estimates vary, but one oft-cited figure indicates that hiring a "fully loaded" U.S. engineer costs between four and six times as much as his or her Chinese counterpart. It is true that persistent productivity and creativity differentials can withstand such competition, especially at the highly skilled end of the engineering labor pool.[25] But as more and better Chinese engineers come on line, and as the

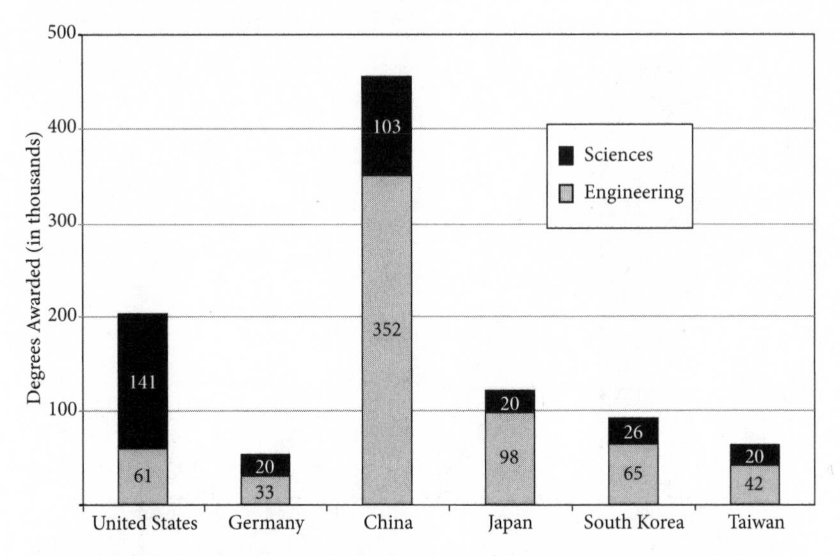

FIG. 3.9. Bachelor's Degrees Awarded in Science and Engineering in 2002, Various Countries. Based on United States, National Science Foundation, *Science and Engineering Indicators 2006*, appendix tables 2-37, 2-38. Excludes agricultural sciences and social and behavioral sciences.

global infrastructure for data transmission matures, it seems only a matter of time before even highly skilled engineering jobs move to where the labor is abundant and relatively inexpensive.

It is also significant that as many as half of the engineers currently graduating every year from U.S. universities are not American citizens. Many of these graduates are now opting or being forced by U.S. visa and immigration policies to return to their countries of origin. This is, in part, an unintended consequence of security measures taken to protect the United States in the aftermath of the 9/11 terrorist attacks. It seems very likely, however, that tighter visa policies for visiting Chinese business people and students also reflect heightened concerns in the United States over industrial espionage.[26] In any event, the overall effect is to increase the likelihood that Chinese engineers who have been trained in the United States will return to China.

Innovation in China's Semiconductor Industry and Policy Responses

Significant adjustments lie ahead for the worldwide semiconductor industry. Initially, China's rise as a key manufacturing center will have dramatic consequences on both the demand and supply sides of global markets. Based on experience elsewhere, however, the longer-term consequences are likely to be the more profound. Manufacturing still matters, and human capital is the main input in technology innovation systems. With its growing manufacturing base in semiconductors and with a rapidly expanding pool of engineers and scientists, much process innovation and applied research seems certain to migrate to China.

Eventually, as Chinese research institutes and universities improve through the efforts of a burgeoning population of trained engineers and scientists, precompetetive and eventually even basic research is likely to expand as well. In related sectors, we have already seen a willingness on the part of Chinese authorities to leverage the promise and scope of national markets to establish the kinds of technical standards that allowed leading enterprises to flourish globally.[27] Similar efforts will shape the future of a globally competitive semiconductor industry.

In line with the framework set out in chapter 1, this conclusion must be interpreted and assessed in a wider strategic and historical context. The question debated in foreign policy circles just a few years ago—whether China should be viewed as a future rival or future partner of the United States—has now become much more subtle. There is a deeper appreciation of the complexity of China's governing structure and of the social foundations of national political authority in the country. There is also a growing awareness of tensions among reformist economic elites, a traditional military establishment, and relatively autonomous provincial and local officials.

Technonationalists in China invoke memories of the experience of the early twentieth century to legitimate policies designed to accelerate technology transfer without compromising future national autonomy. This has led many observers to the conclusion that China will eventually seek to consolidate its power regionally, strive to offset or balance U.S. power within its borders, and compete more directly with the United States and other advanced countries in areas where strategic resources like petroleum are at stake.

Such a view does not necessarily portend future security conflicts, but there is certainly room for deep divisions regarding advisable foreign policy reactions by the United States and others. It is entirely plausible that a China intent on balancing U.S. power in the long run would seek to deepen and strengthen bilateral relations with the United States. Strategic realists in the United States therefore advocate a response to China characterized by caution and careful cost-benefit calculations. Although they begin with a different perspective, advocates of assertive policies aimed at promoting human rights actually come to similar conclusions. Conversely, those with a more optimistic cast of mind believe that short-term calculations are unnecessary and even counterproductive, since deeper bilateral involvement is likely to lock China into global webs of interdependence, especially in strategic industries like semiconductors.

Hard-liners in the United States have found it difficult to build a consensus in support of containing or undercutting expanding Chinese power. They confront demands on the part of both prominent businesses and leading American allies for consistent policies designed to engage China economically, to compete with European and Japanese purveyors of advanced technology, to promote gradual change in its internal governance practices, and even to acquiesce when such change is not forthcoming. In particular, American businesses directly linked to the U.S. national defense base find themselves facing the reality that they cannot achieve necessary economies of scale in new technologies if they and only they bear the brunt of export controls aimed at keeping China a generation or two behind the United States. China's current and potential human capital, together with the gradual development of its low-cost manufacturing and research base, above all in the semiconductor industry, is now building enormous pressures in the same direction. In such a context, the global movement of human and financial capital into China's semiconductor and related industries looks like a phenomenon that has only just begun.

It is still possible that nationalist impulses in both the United States and China could feed off one another and make coherent policies more difficult to craft. Mutually reinforcing perceptions of intentions, more than capabilities, are key.[28] The challenge is to find practical steps to accommodate China's rise without falling into either Panglossian dreams of inexorable harmony or self-fulfilling prophecies of future disaster. It does not take much work to find indications of a classic strategic rivalry between the United States and China. But there is no self-evident reason why competitive impulses cannot be incorporated into the arena of global capitalism. Since 1945, this has happened in most other parts of the world. Why not here? Developments in the semiconductor industry suggest just such a scenario.

Implications of China's Ascendance

Given the potential size of its internal market and the vast scale of the human and financial resources currently building up its national engineering base, China will fairly soon become a major force in process innovation and applied research in this field. But no country has been able to insulate comparable national innovation systems; even if they remain rooted in national and regional foundations, they are in fact becoming ever more deeply integrated.

Especially because the scale of investment required even for incremental breakthroughs is so high, this is particularly evident at the precompetetive level of research, where collaborative, cross-national research is a fact of life. How can China resist such a tendency, especially if the manufacturing base it is now building can only stay competitive if it learns to innovate? Can the sheer size of the rapidly developing internal market shield Chinese national champions from this necessity? Experience elsewhere would suggest not, as would the decision taken in 2006 by China's Semiconductor Industry Association to join the World Semiconductor Council, an established vehicle encouraging interfirm cooperation in the global industry.

Strategic puzzles nevertheless abound. Imagine a country where one million citizens of a competitor nation currently live inside its territory and work hard to build up its companies, companies that will compete directly with companies based in their own homeland. That is the present situation in the semiconductor industry in China and Taiwan. Now imagine some U.S. companies claiming to be recentering future corporate operations on Asia and specifically in China, while others hesitate to send or develop there any intellectual property they could not afford to lose. Which specific interests should U.S. strategists seek to defend?

It remains the case today that basic research in the semiconductor and other information technology sectors is dominated by the United States. Since 1945, a strong information technology industry has clearly remained a national strategic priority for the country, arguably a core pillar of its enduring hegemonic position within the international system.[29] As the comparative data above suggest, there evidently remains a consensus inside the United States that substantial human and financial resources should continue to be invested in the highest level of scientific research in the universities and laboratories currently at the cutting edge of semiconductor-related innovation. Given the physical limits now coming into view in the development of current technologies, this means that substantially more investment is flowing into advanced materials and biochemistry in the postsilicon era. No other country, including China, is yet behaving in a similar manner. Like China, the more typical country focuses national investments in engineering and science education clearly on the engineering side, where payoffs seem certain in the more immediate future.

Certainly from the point of view of balance-of-power theories, it remains surprising that American dominance in the natural sciences has not yet stimulated serious strategic responses. Perhaps it will someday, but something else could already be starting to temper that reality. Leading-edge science in the United States has depended not only upon substantial public and private financial investment, but also on exceptional intellectual openness to and from the rest of the world. It has sought and attracted the best brains from around the world, but it has also not strenuously impeded those brains from leaving the territorial domain of the United States. On the basis of new science, it spawns new technologies, creates new industries, and primes the pump for precompetetive collaboration by rival firms. But Americans could begin moving in the opposite direction by diverting long-term investment from human capital, or by moving to constrict the global flow of human resources in the sciences. Certainly the American semiconductor industry itself is worried that just such reversals are now under way, as mounting federal budget deficits threaten to constrain future investments and security concerns impede the flow of scientific talent to the United States. At the same time, China could seriously attempt to import and adapt foreign science and technology without allowing foreigners to benefit in any immediate sense and without reciprocating in the fullness of time.

What remains extremely difficult to imagine, however, is conscious acquiescence on the part of the American government, and American society more generally, to a secondary position in key industrial sectors like microelectronics. An American strategy of engagement with China, the only sensible strategy at the moment, could have the effect not only of forestalling overt balancing behavior by China but also by the United States itself. Serious engagement, however, does not mean simple acceptance of market facts. To the extent that it really is possible to create images of "us" and "them" that do construct the world in which we ultimately live, then serious engagement means crafting policies that both steer toward desirable outcomes and away from undesirable ones. Some political scientists use the metaphor of carrots and sticks, while others highlight the dichotomy of deterrence and reassurance. Economists speak of incentives and disincentives. But is China not inherently too big, too complex, and potentially too powerful to be steered by other countries?[30]

The ultimate objective must surely be to bring China fully into the system the United States and its key allies have built since 1945. At its core is a military alliance. Its economy rests on competing markets (still mainly national or, at most, regional) that are interdependent by design. The leading states cooperating with the United States in maintaining such a system certainly still compete with one another in the economic realm, but they are now structurally inclined to favor cooperative solutions to difficult systemic problems. China should one day be recognized as a leading state and optimists must surely cling to the belief that the system remains flexible enough to accommodate its key interests until that time. They must just as surely hope that deeper engagement will transform or marginalize those interests in China that are today threatened by the winds of change. Without naiveté concerning the forces of technonationalism at work on all sides, outside of China in sectors like semiconductors this should translate into policies that lean toward market-based competition and against market closure.

4 THE POLITICS OF ECONOMIC LIBERALIZATION

Are There Limits?

Joseph Fewsmith

A fundamental paradox lies at the center of China's post-Mao political economy. China's economic reform, whether understood in terms of marketization, expansion of international trade, privatization, or any other measure, has proceeded steadily, almost monotonically, for twenty-five years, with the result that today, living standards have improved for millions of Chinese, and China has become a major force in the global economy. Yet at each and every step along this path, reform has met with significant opposition—political, economic, and cultural. This opposition has been based in part on interests that have been threatened by reform, but also in significant part by the belief that marketization and globalization present real threats to the continued rule of the Chinese Communist Party (CCP).

How can one reconcile this sense of threat with the continuous reform of the economic system? Is it that the threat has never been that high and that those with an interest in continued economic reform have been able to brush aside concerns in the interest of economic growth? Or is it that the sense of threat has periodically obstructed and distorted the reform process, even though it has not been able to thwart it?

After two and a half decades of reform, can we now say with confidence that continued economic reform is not a threat to the CCP, and therefore that the political system is sufficiently consolidated and sure of its direction that we can expect continued reform and globalization under communist rule? Or, on the contrary, can we say that processes of institutionalization have proceeded sufficiently far that if the CCP collapsed at some point in the foreseeable future that reform would continue apace under some form of more or less consolidated democracy? In short, does the political system present an obstacle to or support for continued economic growth and reform?

These questions are of both theoretical and practical import. On a theoretical level, Kenneth Jowitt has laid out the dynamic of Leninist systems as well as anyone, but if one follows the logic of his explanation, it is difficult to explain the Chinese political system today.[1] Briefly stated, Jowitt argued that Leninist systems go through phases. As revolutionary movements, Leninist parties emphasize their exclusiveness from society. This sense of exclusivity not only enhances group solidarity within the party but also becomes a source of leverage in its revolutionary reordering of society. Rather than compromise with existing social organizations, Leninist revolutions remake society in their own image. Ideologically, their solipsistic truth claims conflict with all nonparty sources of knowledge, whether societally based social organizations (from family to religion) or those rooted in expertise (for example, science).

The difficulty for Leninist regimes comes when the revolutionary impulse is spent and economic difficulties dictate a course of reform. As Leninist parties begin to reform, they turn from their previous exclusive orientation to inclusiveness, that is, bringing in (co-opting) external social groups. The party compromises with society and indeed allows social and economic groups to develop. Ideologically, solipsistic claims to truth are compromised with admissions that there are "laws" in different realms of social experience. Rather than presenting fixed answers to all questions, Marxism becomes a methodology for trying to understand the laws of social and economic development.[2] But this more open attitude to "truth" opens the quest for understanding to those who are less knowledgeable in the classic texts of Marxism-Leninism and more adept at specialized areas of knowledge. Nowhere is this truer than in economics, which is usually the reason (and in China certainly the reason) that the regime embarks on reform. Whether looked at from a societal perspective (the growth of nonstate enterprises, the depoliticization of society) or an ideological perspective, inclusiveness undermines the organizational competence of Leninist parties, leading to their collapse.

Jowitt's theoretical perspective accords quite well with China's experience in the 1980s. The growth of the economy in the 1980s presented real problems of adjustment for such organizations as the State Planning Commission and Ministry of Finance, which were accustomed to operating in a command system. It also generated enormous controversy among economists, as they debated the relationship between the market and the plan and strategies to introduce market-oriented reforms while minimizing negative by-products.[3] The opening up of China, both domestically and internationally, also presented enormous cultural challenges as new ideas poured into China and intellectuals debated their relevance to China.[4] The Propaganda Department often took the lead in criticizing these ideas, but it is clear that the sense of threat extended well beyond the propaganda apparatus. General Secretary Hu Yaobang was purged in January 1987 for his "lax" attitude toward "bourgeois liberalization" (ideas not in conformity with orthodox interpretations of Marxism-Leninism–Mao Zedong Thought). Politically, there were very different understandings within the CCP on what the evolving economic and social situation meant for the political system. Put briefly, some felt that there should be little or no change in the traditional instruments of Leninist governance, particularly the role of the party, whereas others believed that substantial changes were needed.

Although the difficulties of economic, cultural, and political change in the 1980s can hardly be encompassed by this brief summary, the purge of Hu Yaobang in 1987 and the subsequent political meltdown of 1989 (including the ouster of then general secretary Zhao Ziyang) suggested that deepening economic reform was not compatible with Leninist institutions.[5] Indeed, some leftists in China (that is, those upholding more orthodox interpretations of Marxism-Leninism) drew the same conclusion, arguing that a reinvigoration of Leninist institutions, a reassertion of Marxist orthodoxy, and a limit on the development of private enterprises—and especially on allowing capitalists to join the CCP—were absolutely necessary for the preservation of the system.[6] Some Western observers who witnessed the backlash argued that the strengthening of political control following the crackdown would inevitably mean the stagnation of the economy. Both Chinese conservatives and Western liberals were wrong. China's economy, as other chapters in this volume detail, has done remarkably well.

In theoretical terms, in the years since the Tiananmen protests of 1989, China's experience has begun to diverge significantly from Jowitt's analysis. How has the CCP preserved both its ruling position and presided over continued economic reform, including privatization and globalization, both of which have been generally understood to present significant challenges to Leninist organization? In recent years, commentators on the Chinese political system have described it as "authoritarian" to indicate the distance it has come from the highly ideological days of Mao and even the intrusive role the party played in the era of Deng Xiaoping. But if the term "authoritarian" captures the still undemocratic nature of the party, it does not allow us to understand theoretically the tensions and dynamic of the current political system, much less the trajectory China has traversed from a traditional Leninist system to the present. More specifically, it does not address why a theoretical perspective that seemed to be congruous with the Chinese experience no longer seems useful. Has the tension between marketization and pluralization, on the one hand, and Leninist rule, on the other, simply disappeared? Is the co-optation strategy that Jowitt posited as such a threat to Leninist rule in its inclusive phase no longer the threat that it seemed to be in the late 1980s? If not, why not? Coming to grips with these questions is necessary if one is to understand the political economy of contemporary China and assess the role of the political system in the continued reform and globalization of the economy.

Changing Political Dynamic

The Tiananmen protests changed the political dynamic in China in important ways. The repression that has continued since 1989 has imposed high costs on those who seek more radical or rapid change. Liberal discourse in particular has suffered, though not entirely because of Tiananmen.[7] Nevertheless, the story of post-Tiananmen China is not simply one of repression. Two effects of Tiananmen seem particularly important. First, Tiananmen, which was followed quickly by the breakup of the Soviet Union and the collapse of socialism in Eastern Europe, changed the debate that had dominated political life through the 1980s. Whereas in the 1980s, political debate had revolved around the poles of "reform" versus "conservatism," the events associated with Tiananmen introduced a third possibility: social and political breakdown. Even reform-minded intellectuals were willing to accept the status quo if the alternative was a plunge back into social chaos and political violence. The Chinese had been too traumatized by the Cultural Revolution, not to mention the violence of twentieth-century history, to hope for (much less work toward) the collapse of the state. Chinese intellectuals who in the late 1980s had looked in envy upon Gorbachev's perestroika and glasnost, found themselves looking fondly upon incremental reform as the Soviet Union broke apart, lost its superpower status, and saw its economy and living standards decline. Whereas many intellectuals believed that China in the late 1980s stood at the brink of completing its process of "crossing the river by feeling the stones," even if what lay on the other side was only vaguely defined, by the early 1990s they had largely jettisoned their earlier romantic notions and come to accept the fact that reform was a longer, more complicated process than they had ever imagined. Incrementalism became the new mantra.[8]

The other effect of Tiananmen, though it was not immediately apparent, was that it fundamentally altered the way people thought about political reform (at least those people making policy or trying to influence it). In the 1980s, the paradigm for political reform had been the separation of the party and the government (*dangzheng fenkai*).[9] The lesson of Tiananmen, or at least the lesson that people drew from Tiananmen, was that separating the party and the government created two centers of power, exacerbated political tensions, and threatened the dominance of the party. In the years since Tiananmen, there has been a strong tendency to entwine party and state ever more tightly, though this has never been articulated as policy or elaborated theoretically. Thus, the major nonparty organizations at the top of the political system—the National People's Congress and the Chinese People's Political Consultative Congress—have been headed by members of the Politburo Standing Committee ever since Tiananmen (the State Council had always been headed by a member of the Politburo Standing Committee). Similarly, provincial party secretaries began to serve concurrently as heads of the provincial people's congresses in an effort to curb the increasing independence of those bodies. Today, more than two-thirds of provincial people's congresses are headed by provincial party secretaries.

Although some party writings still talk about the separation of party and government as desirable, at least at some point in the future, political reform efforts over the last decade and a half have been focused on local governance and intraparty reform. These have by no means solved—or even effectively curbed—abuses of power and other problems of governance, but they have laid a foundation for thinking about types of political reforms that should not be dismissed too readily. These reforms will be considered more fully below.

In 1992, China's political dynamic changed dramatically when Deng Xiaoping headed south to breathe new life into economic reform. The Fourteenth Party Congress in the same year authoritatively confirmed the direction Deng had set out, and sent a powerful message by ousting the most prominent conservative leaders of the day. For two years, the direction of China's reforms had been debated, as conservatives argued that economic reforms undermined socialism and threatened the role of the CCP (much as Jowitt would expect), and liberals argued that *without* economic reform and the legitimacy rising incomes had provided, the party would have collapsed in the face of social protest, much as other communist parties had collapsed in the Soviet Union and Eastern Europe. Deng broke the debate by weighing in heavily on the side of economic reform. There were good economic and political reasons for Deng to take this stance. Facing the need to create some eight million urban jobs a year just to meet the growth of the working-age population, and a stagnant state sector (both in terms of job provision and tax payments), China had little choice but to yield to the economic forces that the original reforms had unleashed.[10] The Dengist reforms had always been justified in terms of performance legitimacy, that is, the ability of the reforms to generate more jobs and higher incomes, but performance legitimacy had always coexisted uneasily with traditional Marxist ideological interpretations; that is what the debates in the 1980s were all about.

The reinvigoration of market-oriented reform did not mean further decentralization. On the contrary, prompted in part by the disintegration of Yugoslavia, the Chinese state made a vigorous effort to reassert its authority. The most visible manifestation of this effort was the tax reform adopted in 1994. Although this tax reform made sense on a number of economic grounds, including the simple fact that it placed revenue collection firmly in the hands of the central government for the first time in Chinese history, it also bolstered the resources available to the central government. Whereas central government revenues stood at only 10.7 percent of GDP in 1995, they rose to 18.9 percent of GDP in 2004.[11] The central state was back.[12]

With the endorsement of market-oriented reform, including the rapid expansion of the private economy and of foreign trade (including a vastly increased influx of foreign investment), the old debates about holding onto traditional understandings of Marxist ideology faded in political importance (though significant echoes could be heard in the various leftist manifestos issued in 1994–95). The implicit shift in party legitimacy in 1992 was similar to, though not as far-reaching, as that which accompanied the inauguration of reform. The party was admitting that the ideological pillars that had at least partly supported the political edifice in the 1980s were no longer adequate. New forms of legitimacy would have to be found.

This shift in political legitimacy—and the shift away from the conservative ideological agenda that party ideologues had tried to push in the period immediately following Tiananmen—was further evidenced by the consumer culture that blossomed in the mid-1990s. Family restaurants sprouted up everywhere, nightlife boomed, and popular music took off. China's emerging urban middle class took its fashion and entertainment seriously. The political system stopped worrying about pop culture (unless the lyrics were politically tinged), and people, in turn, stopped worrying so much about political life.[13] Urban culture diversified. The "zone of indifference" that the state allowed around private life grew, and as the state became less of a presence in everyday life, individuals focused less on the political and more on the private.[14] To the extent that people believed that there was nothing they could do about politics (and certainly the state encouraged such attitudes), they were more willing to acquiesce in politics and focus on issues they could (or needed to) deal with—their own employment and the raising of children.

The CCP did not collapse with this shift away from ideological orthodoxy and political control over the day-to-day lives of citizens (as Jowitt's analysis of Leninism suggests it might). This was not only because the state tolerated wider scope for private activities (and became very good at spotting and stopping potential political threats) but also because a new sense of nationalism emerged in this period. The neoconservative writers who wrote "Realistic Responses and Strategic Options for China after the Soviet Upheaval," an analysis and prescription for political action produced hastily in the days following the failed August 1991 coup attempt in the Soviet Union, argued that there were two bases of legitimacy for the CCP, the Bolshevik revolution of 1917 and the caves of Yan'an (the party's revolutionary base). With one pillar gone (though it was not gone at the time they wrote), the CCP would have to increasingly emphasize its indigenous roots. In other words, nationalism would and should become an ever more important prop to the party.[15]

Indeed, the CCP launched a "patriotic education campaign" in the early 1990s.[16] Communist propaganda, whether blatant or more subtle, has been an important part of the growth of nationalism in recent years, but it has fallen on fertile ground. Nationalism has been the leitmotif of twentieth-century Chinese politics, so it is no surprise that contemporary Chinese share their predecessors' dreams of "wealth and power," not to mention national dignity. This nationalism has indeed been an important part of government efforts to rally support (or at least neutralize dissent) since the mid-1990s, but there has always coexisted a much more populist version of nationalism—first voiced in 1996 in *Zhongguo keyi shuobu* (China Can Say No)—that has been as critical of the Chinese government as it has been an expression of xenophobic opposition to the West.[17] Nationalism has been the basis of antigovernment views and movements since Kang Youwei led 800 metropolitan examination candidates to petition against the government's acceptance of the terms of the Treaty of Shimonoseki that marked the end of the Sino-Japanese War of 1894–95.

In other words, even as the Chinese government used nationalism to bolster its legitimacy it was fully aware that nationalism was a two-edged sword that could be turned against it. Thus, the government has had to walk a tightrope, encouraging nationalism while discouraging its more populist and antigovernment expressions. This is sometimes a dangerous game to play, as the demonstrations against the U.S. bombing of the Chinese embassy in Belgrade, the strong expressions of nationalist sentiment on the Taiwan issue, and the periodic explosions of anti-Japanese sentiment suggest.

These various trends—incrementalism, statism, nationalism, and even the acceptance of consumerism—came together in a loosely articulated sense of neoconservatism. Neoconservatism had burst on the Chinese scene in the guise of neoauthoritarianism in the late 1980s as neoauthoritarians, drawing on the writings of Samuel Huntington, argued that transitional periods were inherently unstable and that a period of strong state power was necessary to carry out reform. The term "neoauthoritarianism" disappeared in the wake of Tiananmen (because it was identified with some of the people around Zhao Ziyang), but it reemerged in the early 1990s as "neoconservatism." Only a few people have been willing to identify themselves as neoconservatives, and others who are referred to as neoconservatives in intellectual circles have different emphases and beliefs, so it is difficult to call neoconservatism a coherent intellectual or ideological system of thought. Certainly no senior leader of the CCP has elaborated a neoconservative vision. Nevertheless, there was sufficient implicit acceptance of neoconservative approaches in enough circles, both governmental and nongovernmental, that we can say that neoconservatism provided an ideological prop for the CCP as Marxism-Leninism faded, plugging somewhat awkwardly the ideological hole that opened up in the wake of Tiananmen.[18] At least for the 1990s, neoconservatism sufficed to stabilize elite politics and state-society relations following the trauma of Tiananmen. It also helped focus the government's mind on the importance of economic development as well as a number of related policy matters, including the tax reform of 1994 that shored up central finances.

There was also a sociological aspect to the new order that underlay the relative social and political stability that emerged in the 1990s—namely, a growing convergence of interests among the political, economic, and intellectual elites.[19] As political leaders became more conscious of the need to regularize the political system and reduce popular resentment against familial promotions, informal limits were placed on the promotion of the children of high-ranking cadres. At the same time, the economy was growing and becoming more independent of the state, suggesting that a new economic elite might come to compete with the political elite but also providing opportunities for political families, whose legal incomes were limited, to use their family connections to secure their financial well-being. Such considerations underlay the wave of officials who "jumped into the sea" (*xiahai*) of business in the early 1990s. Years later there began a second, reverse, wave, particularly in Zhejiang, as businessmen went into politics, frequently in honorific positions in local people's congresses or Chinese People's Political Consultative Conferences, but also as political leaders.[20] Both trends illuminated the increasingly close relations between political and business leaders, as the political system found continued economic growth an important source of social stability and political legitimacy and as business leaders sought political influence and personal status.

The most surprising trend of the 1990s was the formation of increasingly close relations between much of the intellectual elite and the political establishment. Considering that only two decades earlier intellectuals had been considered the "stinking ninth category," and that most intellectuals felt alienated from the political system in the 1980s, the rise of an intellectual elite that sought to work with the state was something of a surprise. Intellectual acceptance of the state was based on an often unarticulated acceptance of nationalism and neoconservatism (which accepted that a period of strong political control was necessary in the period of transition, as the economy grew and political views diversified, before the society could move toward democracy). Much of the critical thinking that emerged in China in the 1990s supported a critique of the West, and an acceptance of Chinese values and interests as different than those of the West supported this reconciliation of state and intellectual elite.

The needs of the state and the generational change of the political elite led the state to reciprocate. The 1980s were dominated by debates over big issues—the direction in which China should move. In the 1990s, the direction was basically set; what was needed was specific advice about specific issues. A younger, more intellectually inclined political elite was more predisposed and able to communicate with the intellectual elite, while the intellectual elite often sought out opportunities to advise the government.

In short, within a few years after Tiananmen, a remarkable convergence between the political, economic, and intellectual elites emerged. This was an urbanized, wealthy, and politically connected elite that shared common interests and similar views. The core of this new elite emerged from the political elite and were able by virtue of their social position, personal connections, and education to take advantage of new opportunities. Sociologist Sun Liping has described this elite as possessing "comprehensive capital" (*zongtixing ziben*), a self-perpetuating elite that has a strong self-interest in maintaining its elite status. Although there may be long-term costs to this sociological development (see below), at present this elite provides a strong basis for political stability.

The Evolving Dynamic of State-Society Relations

The combination of neoconservatism, economic growth, and a social elite with a common interest in preserving social and political order (as well as its place in that order) has dominated China for at least the past decade and goes a long way toward explaining how the CCP has extended its existence. But neoconservatism is more of a defense of the status quo than a positive articulation of political legitimacy. Indeed, to the extent that neoconservatism is conceived of in instrumental terms—getting the political system through a period of social and economic change to an undefined future—it both undercuts the state's legitimacy as it is rooted in Marxism (because there is nothing Marxist about neoconservatism) and suggests that China will eventually move away from Marxism entirely, perhaps to democracy (as, indeed, some versions of neoconservatism hold).

Moreover, even if there is greater convergence among China's elite than there was in the 1980s, that does not mean that there is complete harmony. After all, liberal intellectuals who may have accepted the need for political stability in the 1990s become anxious and disaffected when they see the promise of incremental change dissipate into little or no change. Those concerned with social justice issues have become increasingly critical of the corruption of the wealthy and the exploitation of the poor. And economic elites who have benefited from past political arrangements do not necessarily have an interest in deepening economic reform if it means that they will face more competition, either internationally or domestically.

The most significant challenges to the status quo currently come from local society. Local society is increasingly dominated by an interlocking elite. The local party secretary, particularly at the township and county levels, is known colloquially as the *yiba shou* ("number one"), and he (it is almost always a he) controls the local political scene through appointment of his friends and relatives to critical positions. This process is depicted vividly by Li Changping, a former township party secretary, in his book *Wo xiang zongli shuo shihua* (Speaking Honestly to the Premier). Li cites numerous examples of staffs that cannot be reduced either because individuals were protected by those higher up or because cadres had paid for their positions and were not about to leave quietly. Those who were accused of malfeasance were not dismissed because they threatened to expose the problems of others. The township to which Li was assigned was some 47 million yuan in debt and owed that debt to some 6,000 people—mostly township cadres and local criminal syndicates who protected each other and their favorable position in the local political economy.[21]

This deeply embedded local corruption is reinforced by a political system that demands that local authorities attain particular targets, particularly with regard to tax collection and economic development, with the result that these local political machines exploit peasants, sometimes ruthlessly.[22] In the 1990s, the harsh collection of taxes, often well in excess of legal limits, generated increasing resistance, including violent protest, from peasants. Even as the state moved to eliminate the agricultural tax, local leaders found new ways to squeeze money out of local society. This generally takes the form of land appropriations in which local authorities take over plots of land on which to build factories while the peasants get inadequate compensation and no security for the future. Such actions have led to violent protests, such as those in Dingzhou and Taishi.[23] Overall, mass "incidents," not clearly defined, have been increasing exponentially from some 10,000 in 1993 to 58,000 in 2003, 74,000 in 2004, and 87,000 in 2005.[24] Such figures do not mean that the state is about to collapse, but they do indicate that there is a significant threat to local order and political legitimacy.

Given the extremely cautious attitude of the party toward democratic political reforms, the primary response to the *yiba shou* problem has been an intraparty response—to promulgate regulations and experiment with new procedures to govern the promotion of cadres and restrict the authority of the *yiba shou*. In 1995 the party promulgated the "Regulations on Selection and Appointment of Party and Government Leading Cadres (Trial)," which were then revised to a limited degree and promulgated in final form in 2002. The 1995 regulations were actually the first formal regulations governing cadre promotion in the history of the People's Republic, and they were intended to curb the corruption that had become associated with the promotion of officials by opening up the selection process to a limited degree. Prior to 1995, only three or four officials controlled the promotion process, and the criteria for promotion were vague. Given intense competition for promotion, opportunities for rent-seeking behavior, and the decline in public morality, the system was ripe for exploitation.

According to the regulations (both the 1995 and the 2002 regulations are identical on this point), candidates for promotion must go through four steps: "democratic recommendation" (*minzhu tuijian*), investigation (*kaocha*), preparation (*yunniang*), and discussion and decision (*taolun jueding*). The most important change introduced by the 1995 regulations was that of democratic representation. Instead of a discussion being held by the party standing committee, under the new regulations officials from a wide variety of posts, including higher and lower organizations, would participate in casting formal votes for the candidates considered most qualified for promotion. At the municipal level, perhaps 200 people might participate in this process. In short, there was an effort to make the promotion process conform to an objective set of procedures and to break up the control that a small number of officials had previously held over the promotion process. Institutionalization is an important aspect of contemporary Chinese governance, and institutionalizing the promotion system was an effort to legitimate the system for both party members (who would accept the legitimacy of others' promotions) and the public, which was assured that there were objective criteria and even a period of "public showing" (*gongshi*) in which the name of a candidate for promotion would be made public, allowing anyone with knowledge of corrupt or other disqualifying behavior to report it.[25]

As the continuing problems with local governance suggest, the regulations on selection and appointment have had limited effect at best. Indeed, opening promotion decisions to the many people involved in the democratic recommendation voting means that people who hope for promotion must cultivate a wider circle of friends than ever before. This means much wining and dining as well as outright bribery. And that requires even greater resources and energy than before, so candidates for promotion must seek the wherewithal from their subordinates. Instead of curbing corruption, the new regulations appear to have exacerbated it. Moreover, increasing the number of people involved in the decision-making process has not necessarily reduced the influence of the *yiba shou*. For instance, Li Tiecheng, the former vice chairman of the Baishan Municipal Chinese People's Political Consultative Congress in Jilin, who was sentenced to fifteen years in jail for corruption, spoke of selling offices when he was a county party secretary:

> Every time prior to the verification of cadres, I would hold a secretaries' office meeting to set a "tone." I would use the age, work experience, educational background, experience, and rank of those who had given me gifts to set a standard and demarcate a scope. I absolutely would not name anyone's name, but would let the Organization Bureau go "find people" within the "scope" I had demarcated. After they had found them, we could proceed according to procedures. On the surface, the rationale was clear and the procedures lawful, but in reality, this was

> using individuals to draw lines and using individuals to define the scope. I used this method to reward all those who had given me gifts.[26]

In the period since these regulations were formally promulgated in 2002, the party has continued to issue regulations governing party affairs, to tighten discipline inspection, and to experiment with a variety of mechanisms—short of voting—that it hopes will staunch corruption, bolster legitimacy, and limit protest.

Apart from intraparty mechanisms, the party has tried to respond to social discontent through a number of mechanisms that readjust the party's relationship to society. Zhejiang Province appears to have gone further in this regard than anywhere else in China, though there are a number of experiments going on throughout the country. One of the most interesting has been in the city of Wenling, part of Taizhou municipality, where the party has regularized what are known as "democratic consultation meetings" (*minzhu kentan hui*). Democratic consultation meetings are essentially a system of public hearings (something that has been tried out in a number of different places and in a number of different formats) to discuss issues of public interest, particularly those involving the expenditure of public monies and/or the requisition of land. Held on a quarterly basis, these meetings are particularly interesting because they are held both at the village and township levels. Whereas democratic elections have been widely held at the village level, the party has resisted pressures to move elections up to the township level. But implementation of democratic consultation meetings is a self-conscious effort to substitute procedural and participatory democracy for electoral democracy.[27] It is difficult to judge the effectiveness of such meetings in enhancing party legitimacy, but their continued institutionalization suggests some success.

As interesting as the Wenling experiment is, its applicability as a model for other parts of China appears limited. The southern Zhejiang economy is a hotbed of private sector growth, and the dispersion of wealth in the hands of local entrepreneurs and households forces cadres to deal on a more equal basis with the local population. Such conditions are not prevalent throughout China. Even in wealthy areas, much of the wealth is controlled directly or indirectly by local government, giving it less incentive to take the views of the citizenry into account. Moreover, the Wenling experiment occurs in a place that is wealthy and in which social tensions do not appear to be high. Thus, there are more resources to defuse social tensions before they become critical.

Nevertheless, the Wenling experiment illustrates the local party-state adapting to social change. In nearby Wenzhou, an area made famous by its vigorous development of the private economy, the party-state has adapted by accommodating the rapid growth of private business associations. Whereas business associations in most parts of China are heavily dominated by the government, which saps them of vitality, those in Wenzhou reflect a bottom-up dynamic that makes them effective representatives of business interests in the city. Indeed, many of them have grown up outside the auspices of the party-state. But they have not challenged the role of the party-state, and the party-state has responded by accommodating them. A cooperative relationship has worked out, to the extent that some business associations participate in the drafting of the rules governing their trades. This arrangement has not only facilitated the growth of different businesses but also the growth of the local economy and local tax revenues. As many studies have demonstrated, the growth of business in China has not challenged the political system, and the political system has been able to adjust its functioning and adapt to a marketizing, pluralizing society, one in which market forces are constantly strengthening and social interests are becoming ever more important.[28]

We see the same phenomenon in Hangzhou, the capital of Zhejiang, which has adopted a system of surveying both bureaucratic organizations and the public at large to better understand problems and issues as perceived from the bottom up. Such a mechanism does not hold the government accountable, as in democratic systems, but it does allow the party-state to understand and deal with problems in local society. Thus, in Zhejiang, we see the development of a responsive state—not a democratic state, but a state that responds, if not always quickly and efficiently, to the problems in the society. Such a state has sought to extend and bolster its legitimacy by accommodating the changing forces of local society, all the while maintaining its own monopoly on political control. If such accommodative trends prevail over the repressive trends seen in areas that have experienced rural violence, the CCP could prove viable for a considerable length of time.

China under Hu Jintao

The administration of Hu Jintao, who was named general secretary in October 2002 and became head of the powerful Central Military Commission in fall 2004, suggests two basic facts about contemporary China. First, the threats posed to Leninist organization by marketization and pluralization are real and recognized by the CCP. Second, the party-state has been able to respond to these challenges with considerable vigor. How this contest plays out remains to be seen, but those who believe that China is about to join the democratic-liberal world order are likely to be disappointed, at least in the foreseeable future.[29]

Space does not permit a detailed treatment of the Hu Jintao administration. But let us suggest that the Hu administration has moved in four somewhat contradictory directions. First, it has moved to ameliorate social tensions and accommodate social change by addressing itself to the problems of inequality and vulnerability that rapid economic growth has generated. Second, it has worked to rationalize and strengthen both party and state. Third, it has sought to reinforce Marxist ideology. And fourth, it has presided over a critique of the West that seeks to blunt the impact of Western ideas ("soft power") and to bolster the legitimacy of the party-state.

The chief criticism of the Jiang Zemin era that prevails in China today is that Jiang allowed, and indeed encouraged, the east coast to move ahead rapidly while neglecting the accumulating problems of those left behind, whether rural peasants or those laid off from state-owned enterprises (SOEs) or urban collectives in the cities. Income inequalities, which began widening again in the mid-1980s, reached dangerous levels, and certainly inequality was widely cited in public opinion surveys as a leading public concern (along with corruption and employment).[30] Some have argued that China faces a significant danger of widespread social disorder.[31] Although the Chinese government began to address these issues in the latter part of the Jiang administration, Hu Jintao and Wen Jiabao have made social justice issues central to their approach to governance. The millennium-old agricultural tax has been removed and new fiscal resources directed to the rural areas. Unemployment insurance has been stepped up, and millions have been spent to fund minimum income schemes. Although such measures remain inadequate, they are clearly aimed at reducing social conflict and winning plaudits from intellectuals. In this sense, we see the Hu Jintao administration adopting responsive measures at the macro level, just as some governments are doing at the local level.

In addition to trying to preempt serious social upheaval and win popular support by addressing the needs of those left behind, the party and government have made serious, if not altogether successful, efforts to rationalize governance and place greater emphasis on following correct procedures. In part this effort is related to generational change. As older leaders who fought in the revolution are replaced by younger leaders who did not, there is an increasing need for the political system to explain—both to the public and to those in the system—why one leader is promoted and another is not, and to win compliance by making the public policy process less capricious. Thus, as noted above, we find a greater emphasis on personal qualifications (age, education, accomplishments) in the promotion of individuals as well as the involvement of more individuals in that process, both to assure candidates that procedures have been followed and to assure the public that the most qualified candidate was chosen (even if that is not the case). Similarly, we find efforts to downsize and rationalize government, place greater emphasis on law, create regulatory bodies, and make governance more transparent (including the promotion of "e-government").[32]

Efforts to bolster legitimacy, however, have not been limited to adopting populist themes, ameliorating the hardships faced by the worst off in society, and rationalizing the functioning of government. On the contrary, and in contrast to the de-emphasis on ideology that many predicted, the Hu administration has placed a great deal of weight on ideology as well as its Siamese twin, media control. Indeed, the attention that the Hu Jintao administration has paid to ideological issues provides strong evidence that the people who rule China do not believe that economic growth, administrative rationalization, policy adjustment, and local adaptation are sufficient to maintain the legitimacy and stability of the party-state. Many writers throughout the years have argued that Chinese government (and perhaps any government) must have a belief system that can provide a "congealing force" (*ningjuli*) to hold together the otherwise centrifugal forces of society.[33] Jiang Zemin attempted to do this by promoting his "Three Represents" (that the party represents the advanced forces of production, advanced culture, and the fundamental interests of the vast majority of the people), which had the virtue of making a realistic concession to the growth of the nonstate economy by allowing private entrepreneurs to join the CCP (which they were already doing in any case). As necessary as that step was, it did nothing for the party's claim to represent some version of Marxism.

Since being named general secretary, Hu has emphasized the third of the "Three Represents" and emphasized that the party "serves the public interest and governs for the people" (*lidang weigong, zhizheng weimin*). Striking a populist note, Hu and Wen have tried to identify themselves with the people, particularly those most vulnerable. Sometimes this effort has been dramatic, as when Hu Jintao traveled to Guangdong in the midst of the SARS crisis (at a time when Jiang Zemin was reportedly in Shanghai) or when Wen publicly embraced an AIDS sufferer.

At the same time, Hu has worked to bolster Marxism and undermine the legitimacy of Western economics. Perhaps surprisingly, the effort to criticize "neoliberal" economics began at a time when the SARS crisis was still ongoing. In the summer of 2003, the Chinese Academy of Social Sciences established, with support from the "center," a group to criticize neoliberal economics. A year later, the group produced a book called *Xinziyou zhuyi pingxi* (Neoliberalism: Criticism and Analysis). Gathering together a group of leftist and "New Left" economists, the book criticized a wide range of Western economists, from Adam Smith on.

It was shortly after this publication that the Larry Lang incident burst on the scene. Larry Lang (Lang Xianping) is a Western-trained economist teaching at the Chinese University of Hong Kong. Lang sharply criticized several well-known Chinese enterprises that had carried out management buyouts in dubious ways, allegedly causing a significant loss of state assets. The charge that SOEs were being privatized at the expense of the state had long been a staple of New Left criticism, but Larry Lang's Western training and careful research gave the charges new credibility. Soon China's Internet was reverberating with arguments that went well beyond the charge that specific enterprises had engaged in wrongdoing to a broad critique of privatization and Westernization.[34] The fact that Gu Chujun, chairman of Kelon (Greencool), one of the entrepreneurs Lang had charged with wrongdoing, was subsequently arrested seemed to vindicate the New Left critique.[35]

By late 2005 and early 2006, the debate over the course of China's reforms was widespread and vigorous. Intellectuals called it the third great debate in the course of China's reforms, the first being over "practice as the sole criterion of truth" that inaugurated reform, and the second being over the role of the planned economy in the wake of Tiananmen. The debate became so heated that Hu Jintao and Wen Jiabao both made statements at the National People's Congress (NPC) meeting in March 2006 intended to tamp down discussion. Hu said, "We should unswervingly adhere to the reform orientation, further strengthen our determination and confidence in the reforms, repeatedly perfect the socialist market economic structure, and fully exercise the basic role of the market in the allocation of resources."[36] Similarly, Wen Jiabao told reporters, "we should unswervingly push forward the reform and opening up. . . . Although in our way ahead there will be difficulties we cannot stop, retrogression offers no way out."[37] Although Hu and Wen strongly affirmed reform, it seems certain that their version of reform will attach more importance to social justice issues than did previous efforts at reform. Indeed, social fairness was a major theme of the Eleventh Five-Year Program approved by the Fifth Plenary Session of the Sixteenth Central Committee in October 2005 and adopted by the NPC meeting in 2006.

These ideological initiatives and debates were accompanied by a harsher ideological atmosphere, directed primarily at liberal intellectuals. According to Hong Kong's *Kaifang* magazine, Hu Jintao, addressing the Fourth Plenary Session of the Sixteenth Central Committee on September 19, gave a speech, which has not been publicly disseminated, in which he allegedly said, "For some time, enemy forces abroad have wantonly attacked our leadership and political system. And our domestic media has upheld the flag of political structural reform to propagate Western-style parliamentary democracy, human rights, [and] journalistic freedom. . . . Enemy forces inevitably take public opinion to be their point of attack. . . . The [former] Soviet Union disintegrated under the assault of their 'Westernization' and 'bourgeois liberalization.' This is the fundamental reason why problems appeared internally in the Soviet Union."[38]

It was just before Hu Jintao allegedly made these remarks that a new crackdown on China's media began. On 2 September 2004, Xiao Weibi, editor of the liberal, Guangdong-based *Tongzhou gongjin* (Moving Forward on a Single Ship), was dismissed for publishing a no-holds-barred interview with Ren Zhongyi, the liberal former Guangdong party secretary who voiced strong criticisms in the years before his death in 2005. Shortly thereafter, Jiao Guobiao, a journalism professor at Beijing University who had created a sensation with his hard-hitting Internet piece harshly criticizing the Propaganda Department, was suspended (and subsequently dismissed) from teaching. The popular bulletin board service at Beijing University, *Yitahutu*, was closed down, as was the serious but occasionally controversial journal *Zhanlue yu guanli* (Strategy and Management), apparently because it published an article critical of North Korea. Wang Guangze, a journalist at the *21st-Century Economic Report*, was dismissed after he gave a speech in the United States called "The Development and Possible Evolution of Political Ecology in China in the Age of the Internet." "Public intellectuals" also came under assault.[39]

Hu Jintao's effort to revive Marxism in China has been quite consistent. In January 2004, the Politburo Standing Committee approved "Opinions on the Further Flourishing of Philosophy and Social Sciences" (Document No. 3), which said that in order to "deal with the mutual agitation of various sorts of ideologies and cultures in the world" it was necessary to "consolidate the guiding status of Marxism in ideological fields and vigorously carry forward and cultivate the national spirit."[40] On the 112th anniversary of the birth of Mao Zedong, the Chinese Academy of Social Sciences formally inaugurated a new Research Academy on Marxism, the establishment of which had been approved by the Politburo Standing Committee the previous May. Projected to include some 200 researchers, the new academy was established because "the current international situation is rapidly changing, the hostile forces of the West are stepping up their efforts to Westernize and divide us, the ideological struggles are intense and complicated, and Marxism is faced with harsh challenges from all sides."[41] Two and a half decades after inaugurating reform, the CCP, while still vigorously supporting economic reform—including privatization and globalization—still views market forces and Western thinking, including thinking on economics, as a threat to the party. What is remarkable is how well the party, believing that marketization is dangerous, has nevertheless been able to maintain its political position while riding the tiger of reform.

It is unclear at this point how this renewed emphasis on Marxism will develop, but the party has called for more innovation and sinicization. This call suggests that this movement is not a simple revival of orthodoxy, as was seen in the early 1990s, but rather an effort to combine China's historical traditions (the day in which Marxism-Leninism was seen as being opposed to China's "feudal" traditions has passed), its sense of the country's uniqueness (its "national conditions" or *guoqing*), nationalism, social justice (which will uneasily coexist with great disparities of wealth for a long time to come), and resistance to Western ideas, whether conceived of in economic (neoliberal) or political (liberal democracy) terms. Such a cocktail of ideas may not satisfy the needs of intellectuals for consistency, but it could prove sufficient to legitimate CCP rule for some time to come. It should not be surprising that the Chinese state is not abandoning the ideational realm; it never has.

Conclusion

Two and a half decades of economic reform have generated constant tension between the demands of marketization and globalization on the one hand and Leninist organization and legitimacy claims on the other. The debates of the 1980s and the eventual crisis of 1989 reflected these tensions, just as writings on Leninist political systems would suggest. Political tension has lessened in the 1990s and since, even as economic reform has continued to deepen. How has the Chinese party-state been able to survive the challenges of marketization and pluralization? Can we assume that the party-state is now able to forge ahead with an agenda of economic reform without regard to the sorts of legitimacy issues that plagued it in the 1980s?

This chapter has argued that the party-state made palpable adjustments, particularly after the immediate trauma of Tiananmen had passed and Deng Xiaoping made his journey to the south. There are three basic facets of this argument. First, that in accepting the inevitability and even desirability of continued economic reform, including privatization and globalization, the party-state gave up some traditional understandings of Marxism-Leninism in favor of expanding its legitimacy claims through continued economic growth and provision of employment, something that was not possible through SOEs as they then existed and the planning system that they were still attached to. The party-state has also worked to rationalize its own structures and procedures and to accept, at least in some places, new structures that allow citizens and organized business interests some role in the governing process, thus working to increase procedural and participatory legitimacy rather than electoral democracy.

Second, although these adaptive changes have proven viable for the short term and seem likely to stave off challenges to party authority for the foreseeable future, assuming adjustments of various sorts continue to be made, certain sociological and political changes are generating new sources of resistance to the party-state. Governance by cronyism and the evident economic competition between the local elite and the local populace has increased tensions at the local level. These problems have stimulated policy change, such as the elimination of the agricultural tax, and are likely to continue to do so, but the area of contention is so large and the number of people involved so great that social order problems will certainly persist, and perhaps get worse, for a long time to come. At the same time, the convergence among China's political, economic, and intellectual elites has reduced political tension, increased the willingness to pursue market-oriented reform, and provided a degree of social acceptance. This "ruling elite" could provide the party-state with a substantial lease on life, as it is in the interests of this elite to maintain stability. But it also raises substantial difficulties. To the extent that social mobility rates decrease, this elite could be perceived as closed, generating hostility from those excluded.[42] Also, because economic and political elites benefit from such close cooperation, there is a strong tendency for elites to resist further economic reform; beneficiaries of cooperative relationships often dislike open, competitive, legally based social organization.[43]

Finally, the party-state's own actions in bolstering Marxist ideology, criticizing the West, and tightening controls over the media provide strong evidence that the party-state continues to see certain types of reform as threatening—especially those that accept a fully free, competitive economic system; critical public opinion; and certain types of integration into the international community.[44] It may turn out that the tightening we have seen recently is just a phase that will soon be followed by renewed liberalization, as has often happened in the past. But the consistent emphasis since Tiananmen on ideological control suggests that the CCP is trying to feel its way toward a nonliberal political order. The effort to tout a "Beijing consensus" that emphasizes the uniqueness of China's development experience and the need for different policies than those embodied in the "Washington consensus" suggests that there are certain political limitations on economic reform.[45] It also suggests that the tension between marketization and Leninism has not disappeared entirely, despite the adaptability that the party-state has shown.

In short, the Chinese political system has avoided the collapse predicted by Jowitt's understanding of Leninism by moving away from traditional understandings of Marxism-Leninism, by incorporating newly emerging socioeconomic forces into the political system, rationalizing party and state structures, forging a social coalition of political, economic, and intellectual elites, and by repressing the emergence of opposition forces, but also by vigorously asserting the ruling position of the party-state, continuing to emphasize ideological control, and working to delegitimize ideological challenges—such as neoliberal economics—that undermine its authority. Such a state has been able to pursue economic development (indeed, the interests of its elites are very much tied up with economic growth) without losing authority. The track record over the past two and a half decades, and especially over the last decade, suggests that the CCP will continue to adjust to the needs of a marketizing and pluralizing society, and thus support economic reforms, but that it will do so in ways that are consistent with the continued rule of the party. And that means that the party-state will continue to play a very large role, both at the central level in defining loan policies and developmental strategies, and at the local level where the state is often a direct player in the economy. It also means that as new institutions emerge, they will remain dependent on the state for the foreseeable future. We can expect continued tension as the state yields as little as possible to the demands of a marketizing society. Within this authoritarian framework, tensions with the CCP's Leninist roots will remain, and these tensions are likely to distort China's patterns of economic growth by favoring the interests of remaining SOEs and well-connected economic elites, as the party-state continues to protect its own interests.[46]

★5

CHINA'S COMMERCIAL DIPLOMACY IN ASIA

Promise or Threat?

Ellen L. Frost

TWO RECENT TRENDS ARE REDEFINING the balance of power in Asia, shifting its fulcrum from security only to a subtle mixture of security and economics. First, the drive toward closer regional integration has gained momentum, giving rise to a burst of preferential trade arrangements. Loosely known as free trade agreements (FTAs), these arrangements symbolize closer political ties as well as commercial opportunity. Second, China has taken advantage of this new regionalism and has become a skilled practitioner of commercial diplomacy. This chapter describes these trends and analyzes the strategic opportunities and risks that such a combination poses for the United States.

Commercial diplomacy is by no means the only mode of expression of the drive toward closer integration, but it has become its most visible glue. It has erected a structured, organized, cooperative political framework in a part of the world where governments cling fiercely to national sovereignty and resist both formal institutions and enforceable rule-making. Intra-Asian FTAs in particular have assumed a role akin to that of security alliances, serving as expressions of political and security ties as well as harbingers of trade and investment. FTAs do not affect the military balance of power, but they alter and redefine the balance of influence, perceptions of security, and political alignments.

The Chinese government has adapted skillfully to this new environment. A key turning point was the Asian financial crisis of 1997–98. As the crisis gathered force, China took credit for not devaluing its currency and then announced a series of trade-related relief measures. The most visible symbol of Beijing's foray into commercial diplomacy occurred in 2000, when China floated the idea of an FTA between China and the Association of Southeast Asian Nations (ASEAN). Two years later, Chinese and ASEAN leaders formally announced a decision to start negotiations aimed at establishing such an FTA within ten years. The initial phase of this agreement is in effect, but many details—governing exceptions for "sensitive" sectors, phase-in periods, and other significant provisions—remain to be worked out.

If present trends continue, Beijing's new commercial-diplomatic embeddedness bodes well for regional peace and prosperity and is broadly consistent with U.S. interests—provided, and it is a crucial proviso, that the United States stays engaged in the region. But many things can go wrong. In addition to U.S. engagement in the region, a positive outcome from a U.S. perspective depends heavily on the constructive management of Sino-American relations. Here, I list a number of possible crises of a political-economic nature that could sharply escalate Sino-American tensions, raise the likelihood of conflict, polarize governments in the region, and derail Asia's potential prosperity—at considerable cost to the United States. These setbacks are by no means inevitable, and I end by suggesting several changes in American behavior, attitude, and style of decision-making to help ensure a peaceful and prosperous future.

Commercial Diplomacy and Asia's New Political Geography

Commercial diplomacy is a relatively new component of strategic analysis. What distinguishes it from ordinary commercial ties is the direct involvement of governments. One definition refers to the process and conduct of negotiations designed to influence foreign government policy and regulatory decisions affecting trade and investment. The issue at hand may be tariffs, quotas, standards, services, subsidies, agricultural support, competition policy, privatization, a major procurement deal benefiting a particular firm, or anything else affecting international commerce. Since these practices are shaped by domestic politics, commercial diplomacy necessarily targets political decision makers and those who exercise political influence.[1]

Another definition, more relevant to this analysis, encompasses the use of commercial power such as market access or technology transfer to influence noncommercial decisions in the political or even the security realm. In addition to trade agreements, it often targets large and visible infrastructure projects such as bridges, ports, and highways. Support for these large projects is popular with recipient governments because they come without the usual environmental and other strings attached to loans from the World Bank and other multilateral institutions. This version of commercial diplomacy illustrates with particular clarity the linkage between economics and security.

The exercise of commercial diplomacy relies on "positive-sum" economic incentives rather than "zero-sum" military buildups. It provides a fluid and flexible medium that both reinvigorates bilateral rivalries and channels them in peaceful and synergistic directions. It is "softening" the politics of the region because it puts a premium on the balance of power in the form of influence rather than the balance of power defined as potential force.

Commercial diplomacy molds Asian security relationships in subtle but tangible ways. For China, it opens up new opportunities for influencing political and security developments in its most important neighborhood. The sheer size and dynamism of China's economy may make explicit diplomatic intervention unnecessary. For non-Chinese Asians, commercial diplomacy is a key tool in a conscious geopolitical and security strategy aimed at embedding a rising China in a web of peaceful relationships. For Japan, the various meetings associated with it constitute a safe, unpublicized neutral ground on which the government can hold bilateral discussions on sensitive topics behind the scenes. This is particularly important for Japan's relations with China, which are frequently prickly. From Tokyo's perspective, the new prominence of commercial diplomacy also reminds Asians that while China's domestic market is huge, Japan's economy is enormous and its assets—including business, banking, technology, and a highly educated workforce—are considerable. For India and Russia, commercial diplomacy provides a means of expanding their political presence in East Asia, broadcasting their peaceful intent, soliciting investment, and competing with China for influence. Moreover, India is a beneficiary of commercial diplomacy initiatives on the part of Japan and Singapore.

Commercial diplomacy is also altering the political geography of Asia. It is forging a north-south bridge linking two quite different subregions, Northeast Asia and Southeast Asia. China, currently assigned to Northeast Asia because of its Confucian heritage, actually overlaps substantially with parts of Southeast Asia (and Central Asia) as well. This overlap stems partly from geography; Hong Kong and Hainan Island are on roughly the same latitude as Indochina and Myanmar. It also arises from China-related commercial activities on the part of both non-Han ethnic groups spanning China's borders and Chinese minorities in neighboring countries and elsewhere in Asia.[2]

The expansion of trade and investment sparked by trade-liberalizing agreements is revitalizing maritime Asia. The slow but steady reduction of barriers to cross-border business is linking coastal cities and their surrounding regions and permitting communities long divided by colonial-era boundaries to trade freely again. At the same time, the concentration of trade and investment along or near this chain is widening the gap between coastal regions and ocean-accessible cities, on the one hand, and poorer interior regions, on the other. This gap draws huge numbers of people to the cities in search of jobs and threatens to overwhelm the limited infrastructure of urban localities. These problems are particularly acute in China, where cities are overcrowded and polluted and the gap between rich and poor has risen sharply within certain provinces.

Furthermore, commercial diplomacy in Asia is knitting together the "spokes" of the U.S.-centered hub-and-spoke security-alliance system and connecting them more closely with governments less friendly to Washington. This thickening of ties among Asian nations is patchy and uneven, however. At China's insistence, Taiwan is left out, and Hong Kong lacks a separate voice, even though both are members of the Asia-Pacific Economic Cooperation forum (APEC). Three members of the web—Myanmar, Laos, and Cambodia—lag so far behind the rest of ASEAN politically and economically that their governments have little interest in economic integration. Mongolia is ignored. Australia sends a higher percentage of its exports to Asia than any of the so-called "ASEAN + 3" countries but is grouped, along with New Zealand, in a separate "+ 2" category.[3] Canberra was not on the original invitee list for the December 2005 East Asian Summit (EAS) but was eventually invited, along with New Zealand, after both governments agreed to sign ASEAN's Treaty of Amity and Cooperation. Despite these anomalies, ASEAN + 3 provides the only ongoing, multilevel framework within which East Asians can consult regularly and freely. The ASEAN Regional Forum, for instance, includes the United States, Russia, and the European Union, among others.

A web of new agreements has motivated India to enter the game of commercial diplomacy, thus expanding the geographic boundaries of Asian economic integration. Reinvigorating its "Look East" policy, New Delhi has greatly improved its relations with Beijing as well as other Asian governments. But Indian officials remain suspicious of China's intentions and hope to track and if possible match its initiatives. (A current example is Myanmar, where both governments are courting the military regime.) The Indian government has negotiated a framework agreement with ASEAN whose ambition and scope resemble the China-ASEAN agreement. It has also negotiated an economic cooperation agreement with Singapore, which could be a launching pad of sorts for an India-ASEAN FTA. An FTA with Thailand is also joining the list. Thanks to these and other diplomatic efforts, New Delhi now holds its own annual summit meeting with ASEAN in an "ASEAN + 1" arrangement, and India was included in the December 2005 East Asian Summit.[4]

This logical and long overdue move is strategically significant. India already fields a powerful military force, including nuclear weapons and a blue-water navy. Anyone who has visited the great monuments and ruins of Southeast Asia sees carvings and inscriptions reflecting the vast historical sweep of India's cultural and religious influence. But decades of inward-looking and protectionist policies reduced India's economic role in the regional and global economy to a level lower than at the time of independence. India's infrastructure is decrepit, and its regulatory inertia calls to mind Dickens's Department of Circumlocution. Latching on to East Asia's dynamic growth is one way for India to escape its poverty-ridden neighborhoods, tap the Indian diaspora, and stimulate reform and domestic competition, especially in coastal cities and outward-looking southern states.

The Emergence of ASEAN + 3

Asia's new political geography and the driving role of ASEAN + 3 demonstrate that U.S. initiatives undertaken in one part of the world may have unintended consequences in another. A major catalyst in the early 1990s was the domino effect of regional trade agreements in the Americas and the widening and deepening of the European single market. These moves stimulated Asians to launch their own regional initiative for fear of being left behind in the competition for trade and investment. It is doubtful that the Americans who negotiated the North American Free Trade Agreement (NAFTA) or the Europeans who hammered out a single European market gave much thought to the possibility of a collective and defensive Asian response. To the extent that they thought about Asia at all, the designers of NAFTA believed that Asians would be content to be members of APEC, which includes the United States and spans a much bigger market.[5]

There are many reasons to be skeptical about economic integration in Asia. Many Asian governments won their independence relatively recently and cling fast to national sovereignty. The societies, cultures, religions, and languages of Asia are extraordinarily diverse. And from an economic viewpoint, the use of FTAs to bolster the drive toward regional economic integration in Asia is distinctly "third best." Every serious economic study shows that global free trade and investment would reap far more benefits for participants than narrowly regional or bilateral arrangements would. Second best would be liberalization within the vast Asia-Pacific market, including North America, Australia, New Zealand, and Taiwan.[6]

For a while it looked as if this second-best option would win out. In 1993, the newly elected Clinton administration announced that it was carrying forward a three-track trade strategy (global, regional, and bilateral) and placed trade high on its agenda. It concluded both the Uruguay Round of global trade talks and the North American Free Trade Agreement (NAFTA) and proposed the Free Trade Area of the Americas. Its Asia trade strategy found expression in the Asia-Pacific Economic Cooperation forum (APEC), which includes Taiwan, Hong Kong, Australia, and New Zealand as well as China. In a highly successful 1993 summit in Seattle, hosted by President Clinton, APEC's leaders committed themselves to "free and open trade and investment." In the following year, in Indonesia, they made this commitment meaningful by attaching a deadline of 2010 (2020 for developing countries).

By the mid- to late 1990s, however, APEC had lost steam and the WTO process had stalled. Seeking to whittle down European protectionism and add structure to an important relationship, ASEAN began a series of dialogues with the European Union known as the Asia-Europe Meeting (ASEM).[7] The European Union, which is excluded from APEC, saw a chance to expand its market share in Asia and add a layer of political visibility to the global reach of European companies and banks.[8]

The first ASEM meeting took place in Bangkok in February 1996. It was at that time that ASEAN + 3 began to crystallize from an informal grouping to a structured body. Championed by Malaysian prime minister Dr. Mahathir Mohamed, it gained significant momentum as a result of the Asian financial crisis of 1997–98. The crisis began in Thailand, but the ensuing financial contagion convinced Asian leaders that Northeast Asia and Southeast Asia are linked and that Asians cannot count on outsiders to help with similar crises in the future. Ever since then, ASEAN + 3 has been the main vehicle of incipient East Asian integration. Its members have proposed—and in some cases negotiated—mostly bilateral trade agreements between themselves (as well as with others outside of the region).[9]

ASEAN + 3 has also taken on institutional characteristics. There is now an ASEAN + 3 unit within the ASEAN secretariat in Jakarta. ASEAN + 3 governments and associated private-sector and academic groups hold regular meetings, establish working groups, and commission research and advice from outside experts. There is a flourishing "Track 2" (nongovernment) process, which some call "Track 1.5" because some of the participants have close ties to their governments.[10]

Building on the ASEAN + 3 process, in December 2005 the Malaysian government hosted an East Asian Summit (EAS) to which India, Australia, and New Zealand were also invited. The most visible public results of the meeting were to establish the EAS as an annual forum for dialogue as an "integral part of the evolving regional architecture" and to proclaim an undefined "East Asian community" (with a small "c") as a long-term goal.

The first effort to establish an East Asia grouping, spearheaded in the early 1990s by former Malaysian prime minister Mahathir, aroused fears of a closed, protectionist, and implicitly anti-American bloc. By contrast, Asian leaders are presenting the current drive as a fluid, benign effort to address common challenges based on an emerging, outward-oriented, cosmopolitan East Asian identity.[11] Chinese officials have echoed these themes.[12]

Dimensions and Limitations of China's Expanding Commercial Profile

Commercial diplomacy is an obvious tool for China. No other nation has ever expanded its role in international trade and investment on the scale that China has. The volume of its exports and imports has expanded at an average rate of 15 percent each year since 1979, compared to a global expansion of 7 percent. Its share in world trade jumped from less than 1 percent in 1979 to about 7 percent in 2005.[13] China is now the world's third largest merchandise exporter, accounting for more than 7 percent of world totals. It manufactures about 70 percent of the world's toys and about 10 percent of office telecommunications equipment. But an estimated 60–70 percent of China's exports stem from foreign companies (known as "foreign-invested enterprises") or joint ventures between Chinese and foreigners.

China is also the world's second-largest importer. Imports of energy and raw materials are contributing to an upsurge in world prices. China consumes about a third of the world's iron ore and two-fifths of the world's copper. Its burgeoning manufactured exports consist in large part of imported components, undercutting the accuracy of the label "Made in China."

In the area of foreign direct investment (FDI), China also breaks records. By the end of the 1990s, China's total stock of FDI was almost a third of cumulative foreign direct investment in all developing countries. As noted in this volume by Loren Brandt, Thomas G. Rawski, and Xiaodong Zhu, China surpassed the United States as the top FDI recipient in 2003.

The combination of China's large size and release of pent-up demand is creating a huge market for China's trading partners. China is already the world's largest market for cell phones (269 million in 2003).[14] United Parcel Service, the world's largest package delivery company, has announced plans to build sixty warehouses covering 200 Chinese cities.[15] China's demand for energy is a bonanza for vast numbers of companies specializing in energy-related exploration, extraction, refining, infrastructure, and transportation. Similarly, outbound tourism is exploding. At a signing ceremony in February 2004, China granted twelve EU member countries the status of "approved destinations," heralding a growth rate in outbound tourism likely to be three times the rate in the rest of the world. By 2020, according to the World Tourism Organization, China will be the fourth largest source of outbound tourism in the world, with travelers expected to spend a whopping US$1,200 (at today's prices) per person.[16]

The impact of all this activity on the rest of Asia is complex. On the one hand, it is a bonanza. As a percentage of China's total imports, imports from Asia have jumped from 15 percent in 1980 to over 50 percent in 2000.[17] In some years imports from Asia in dollar terms have been increasing by as much as one-third, compared to roughly 20 percent from Europe and 10–15 percent or less from the United States.[18] China is now the number one customer for Japan and South Korea. Specific industries have benefited enormously. In 2003, for example, a 30 percent increase in China's oil imports helped feed a doubling of ship orders in South Korea.[19] Incoming travel has been a boon for the aviation, travel, and tourism industries. For example, there are now direct flights from Seoul to 24 Chinese cities. About 35,000 South Korean students are studying in China. More and more Asian students are learning Mandarin, studying in China, and watching Chinese films and cultural performances.

If fully implemented, the China-ASEAN FTA would create an economic area with a population of 1.7 billion, a combined GDP of over US$2 trillion, and a total trade volume of US$1.23 trillion.[20] Despite the likely loopholes and shortcomings of the agreement, the very prospect of such a large market is already beaming a positive signal to traders and investors as businessmen in the region step up their activities in anticipation of more commercial opportunities.

On the other hand, as John Ravenhill's chapter in this volume demonstrates, China's explosive growth challenges other Asian governments, particularly those whose domestic policies fail to meet the demands of global competition. With respect to both the manufacturing sector and the ability to attract foreign investment, Indonesia's post-crisis record is particularly weak, but no country can rest on its laurels. As illustrated by William W. Keller and

Louis W. Pauly in this volume, the Chinese are moving rapidly up the technology ladder, forcing other Asian governments and private entities to undertake painful and difficult structural changes. Time is pressing; China's export base has diversified away from textiles and light manufacturing in a relatively short period. For example, the proportion of China's exports represented by machinery, transport, and electronics increased from 17 percent in 1993 to over 40 percent in 2003. China's dynamism is contributing to a high degree of specialization of production within an Asia-wide production network, particularly in the field of information technology.[21]

Offsetting China's huge economic assets are various limitations on China's potential weight in the balance of influence. Known weaknesses in the banking system and widespread intellectual property violations have a dampening effect, and corruption is a serious problem. None of the world's "fifty most admired companies" is Chinese, and China's biggest companies still lumber along under state control or state influence.[22] Japan, Asia's number one aid donor, still wields great economic power. One economist has calculated that a Japan–South Korea FTA could match China's status as a hub.[23] China may be the leader in low-cost manufacturing, but Japan is way ahead in technology; Singapore, Hong Kong, and Australia lead in high-end services; India has shown a flair for software design and English-language services; and Americans are geniuses at inventing popular new services and products that people didn't know they needed, and delivering them rapidly and efficiently.

Moreover, for decades to come, Beijing will not be able to provide public security and economic welfare benefits comparable to those offered by the United States. The Chinese are hoping to build a blue-water navy but have a long way to go. Nor has China acquired much appeal as a society beyond its economic and commercial attractions. In previous centuries traditional Chinese culture and governance were widely admired and emulated in the region, whereas today's China draws mixed reviews. Although forced modernization driven by an authoritarian government appeals to some, democratic governments and their supporters in Asia look askance at curbs on press freedom, the harsh treatment of dissidents, and the effort to contain democracy in Hong Kong. China's one-party political system is increasingly archaic. Chinese leaders themselves are seeking different models and talking openly of the need for more democracy.

Whether or not China can sustain its booming economic growth is a matter of debate. But for purposes of this analysis, it suffices to say that China's growth is a magnet for other Asians. And like other magnets, it changes the alignment of objects lying in its field.

Beijing's New Activism

Along with China's galloping growth has come a new willingness to embrace commercial diplomacy. This shift was initially reactive in nature. In the early and mid-1990s China was a wary and reluctant novice in the field of commercial diplomacy. Its trade priorities were concentrated on gaining membership in the World Trade Organization (WTO). Although it took part in APEC meetings, it did so gingerly. Chinese leaders mistrusted global and regional institutions, believing that they were dominated by the United States or otherwise shaped to satisfy U.S. interests. Likewise, Beijing's security posture in Asia was unsettling; in 1995, China seized an unoccupied reef in the disputed Spratly Islands claimed by the Philippines. A year later, its military forces engaged in major saber rattling vis-à-vis Taiwan, which caused President Clinton to send U.S. naval vessels toward the Taiwan Strait.

During these same years, however, China's policy in Asia was evidently undergoing a strategic shift.[24] There was a growing realization that economic modernization required peace and prosperity in Asia, deeper economic engagement with Asia and other important regions, market-oriented economic policies, and better relations with the United States. As Joseph Fewsmith's chapter points out, those whose interests are harmed by international market forces ("reform losers") could threaten this consensus, but so far it appears to be holding.

The devastating Asian financial crisis of 1997–98 presented China with an unprecedented opportunity to carry out this shift toward engagement in Asia and reap good will at the same time. To some extent the financial crisis gave the Chinese the chance to just "walk in" to a situation created mainly by other Asians and downplayed or ignored by American policy makers. Largely unaffected by the crisis because of controls on its capital market, China nevertheless took an active part in post-crisis agreements initiated by Japan. Known as the Chiang Mai Initiative, the heart of these agreements is a network of bilateral currency swap arrangements.[25] Beijing also lowered or eliminated tariffs on selected products from ASEAN countries and added the ASEAN countries to the list of approved destinations for which Chinese tourists would no longer require an exit visa.

Nevertheless, Chinese officials stopped short of offering a full-blown FTA to the region and continued to express caution about the trend. What evidently tipped the balance in the minds of China's top leaders was the need to keep pace with Japan and South Korea, both of which had taken the lead in proposing bilateral trade initiatives. Chinese negotiators complained privately that Japan and Singapore were considering a bilateral FTA at a time when China was wholly preoccupied with WTO accession. Finally, in November 2000, Premier Zhu Rongji proposed to set up an expert group to study how economic cooperation and free trade relations between ASEAN and China could be deepened. The proposal to establish a China-ASEAN FTA followed soon thereafter.[26]

Asian Reactions to Chinese Engagement

Asian leaders have by no means shed their wariness about China's intentions in the region. Most of them are old enough to remember the Maoist era, when Chinese leaders whipped young people into a destructive frenzy and sought to manipulate overseas Chinese minorities to foment instability. But they encourage and applaud China's engagement in the region for at least five sound reasons.

First, China is a rising power with the potential to become a threat. But in Asian eyes, containment is not an option because it would be counterproductive. They do not wish to be forced to choose between Beijing and Washington. The integration initiative with its commercial diplomacy arm is consciously designed to embed China in a web of interdependence. Most Asian leaders believe that integration promotes security by building trust, facilitating confidence-building measures, and raising the cost of war. It also provides a peaceful and constructive forum for political rivalry between China, Japan, and increasingly India in ways that benefit Asia as a whole.

Second, Asian governments believe that their countries are competing with China for investment, and China is winning. The drive to achieve a more integrated Asian market is a practical effort to ride China's economic coattails instead of being "hollowed out." ASEAN leaders in particular are convinced that they have no choice but to agree to a more integrated market with China in order to expand their own exports and especially to make their economies more appealing to foreign investors.[27] If investors can export freely to China, they will not be tempted to pull up stakes in other parts of Asia.

Third, affected Asian governments appreciated Beijing's nimble and seemingly generous response to the Asian financial crisis of 1997–98, which included loans to several Southeast Asian countries. Unwisely, the United States turned its back on Thailand when its currency collapsed, triggering the crisis, even though Washington had extended help to Mexico when the peso crashed in 1994. This contrasting behavior seriously undermined confidence in the United States and convinced Asians that no non-Asian power or institution can be counted on to help. Although ASEAN as a collective body was also on the sidelines, Malaysia and Singapore, along with Japan and Australia, offered assistance to hardest-hit Indonesia, and Japan proposed an Asian Monetary Fund (subsequently vetoed by the United States). ASEAN + 3, which includes Japan as well as China, was a logical place to discuss measures to prevent or mitigate future crises.

Fourth, outward-looking governments with competitive economies, such as Singapore, are frustrated by the slow pace of global trade liberalization and the unwieldy nature of APEC. The WTO's Uruguay Round of trade negotiations took seven years to complete (1986–93). The WTO's current round, euphemistically called the "Doha Development Agenda," has been equally time-consuming, and its final results (if any) are likely to be disappointing. Regional and bilateral free trade agreements seem attractive because they can usually be negotiated much more quickly and because they stimulate competitive liberalization elsewhere. Asia's corporate leaders have become lobbyists for measures facilitating cross-border business, including FTAs. The big prize is access to the Chinese market.

Finally, Asian leaders need China's cooperation to address a wide range of nonmilitary threats. In the criminal category are terrorism, piracy, drug smuggling, human trafficking, money laundering, fraud, the illegal plundering of endangered species, and other crimes. Many if not most of these have been around for a long time, but globalization and advanced technology have empowered their perpetrators. Other threats include depletion of water and other natural resources, treatment of contagious disease, and illegal cross-border pollution.

Japan, a member of ASEAN + 3, shares these perspectives but views both Asian regionalism and China with considerable concern. Loyal to the WTO and reliant on global trade rules, Tokyo was initially reluctant to go along with the ASEAN + 3 initiative and still prefers to involve the United States, Australia, and New Zealand. But trade officials, already stung by their exclusion from the NAFTA and seeking an offsetting economic stimulus, joined forces with foreign ministry officials and the business community. Along with South Korea, Japan was the first to initiate bilateral agreements with Asian neighbors and others.[28]

Japan's residual protectionism, its resistance to large-scale immigration, and the clubby nature of its business culture act as a drag on Japanese influence in the region. Given the size of its economy, Japan punches below its weight. But rivalry with China is jarring entrenched habits. The announcement of a China-ASEAN FTA gave a particular jolt to Japan, loosening—at least to a small extent—the grip of agricultural protectionists. Tokyo's FTA with Mexico was considered a breakthrough because when fully implemented it will permit the import into Japan of at least small volumes of orange juice and pork. This "camel's nose" breakthrough could eventually open the tent to similar concessions to ASEAN and South Korea, but only if the prime minister lends his personal support.[29] (Thus far the camel is still out in the cold.) The more Japan becomes a "normal" trading partner, able to sign full-blown FTAs, the more it will achieve its goal of being perceived as a "normal" country.

Japan has also shifted its aid priorities. Seeing a strategic opportunity and reluctant to feed a giant competitor, the Japanese government has channeled its aid loans away from China and towards India. Tokyo has already slashed its soft yen loans to China by 50 percent since 2001, while India will become the prime recipient of such loans for the first time. Loans to India will be concentrated in the infrastructure sector, particularly power generation and transport, where serious weaknesses hobble India's competitiveness.[30]

Although the Japanese proposal to establish an Asian Monetary Fund was defeated, Japan retains a competitive advantage in finance. Taking diplomatic advantage of the depth and sophistication of Japan's financial sector, Japan's Ministry of Finance and the Asian Development Bank have launched studies analyzing the feasibility of a regional bond market. Known as the Asian Bond Market Initiative, the idea is to mobilize Asia's considerable domestic savings and make them available for domestic investment without channeling them through foreign markets. Other goals include broadening the investor base, reducing foreign exchange risks, and strengthening the credit ratings of the issuers by enhancing the capability of local bond rating agencies. Bonds would be issued in local currencies (and eventually in a basket of Asian currencies) by multilateral development banks, foreign government agencies, and Asia-based multinational corporations.[31] To assist other governments in financial matters, Tokyo has established the Japan Financial Technical Assistance program ("JAFTA").[32]

To summarize what has been described thus far, China has taken advantage of the new regionalism to enhance its position in Asia through skillful use of commercial diplomacy. A workable and largely constructive balance of influence is evolving within Asia, with a prospering China, a lagging but still wealthy and resourceful Japan, a new suitor in the form of India, an active role for Australia despite its perceived outsider status, and a group of smaller ASEAN countries that actively invite the new jockeying while carefully hedging their bets. This mixture is dynamic but stable, fostering continued economic growth. The rest of this analysis describes the advantages of these trends for the United States—and then lists some of the many things that could go wrong.

Benefits and Risks for the United States

On balance, the United States has much to gain and little if anything to lose from the marriage of Asian regionalism and commercial diplomacy. All major members of ASEAN + 3, including China, insist that the effort to form a more integrated community in Asia is in no way directed against the United States. Japan, South Korea, and various ASEAN governments have told the Chinese and others that they have no intention of relinquishing their alliances with Washington. Smaller Asian nations have made plain that they see the United States as a stabilizing, constructive counterweight to China (as well as to India and Japan). A supranational Asian Union comparable to the European Union has no place in Asian plans. Asia's huge stake in global markets rules out a protectionist "Fortress Asia"—even if one or two countries unfriendly to the United States might favor erecting one.

From an economic point of view, the evolving Asian landscape is dotted with encouraging trends. Competition in trade and services sprouting from cross-border trade and investment is raising standards of quality and customer satisfaction and allocating resources more efficiently. Competition for foreign investment is putting pressure on governments to slash excessive regulations and reduce corruption. Improvements in transparency and accountability are undermining entrenched elites and improving investor confidence. Weaker members of ASEAN + 3 are receiving at least limited amounts of aid and technical assistance from richer neighbors. All governments are under pressure to lower barriers to trade and investment, streamline customs, slash red tape, crack down on corruption, and improve education.

The combination of regional integration and commercial diplomacy also works in favor of good governance and social opportunity. The need for contract enforcement, banking supervision, stable and predictable taxation systems, bankruptcy laws, intellectual property protection, and other features of a business-friendly environment puts pressure on governments to strengthen the rule of law. In countries ruled by authoritarian or semiauthoritarian regimes, the expansion of commercial opportunities and the availability of Internet services are nudging the authorities to permit more open information and institute more transparency and accountability. Restless and unemployed young people, at least those with technical and language skills, are finding jobs.

Two large and separate sets of risks threaten the future of this rosy picture, however. The first consists of disasters and cross-border threats that all sides have an interest in controlling or eliminating. These include disease, pollution, natural disasters, piracy, smuggling, human trafficking, money-laundering, financial crises, and additional spikes in the price of energy and raw materials. Many of these threats are already the focus of pan-Asian, Asia-Pacific, or global working groups. Lessons from the outbreak of Sudden Acute Respiratory Syndrome (SARS), improvements in the handling of avian flu, and the rapid response to the 2004 tsunami suggest that governments can make a difference if they work together, but in many areas there is a very long way to go.

The other set of risks lie more or less within the control of national governments. They include the dangers posed by the North Korean regime, China's desire to regain control of Taiwan, unresolved territorial disputes in the South China and East China seas, and local flare-ups in border regions (southern Thailand, for instance, from which Muslim insurgents and others fled to Malaysia and sought refugee status, triggering a sharp exchange of views). Handling them successfully requires communication, cooperation, and willingness to compromise on the part of all the governments concerned. But the most crucial variable is the state of relations between Beijing and Washington. As one influential Chinese analyst puts it, "The emergence of Chinese power and influence in Asia is an almost indisputable reality. . . . However, the most prominent factor in shaping geostrategic trends remains the China-U.S. relationship."[33] Although the current U.S.-China relationship is quite stable, high-level U.S. policy makers and politicians have indulged in on-again, off-again diplomacy with China, alternatively excoriating and cultivating its leadership. The Chinese government, too, has been volatile and harbors a number of "hawks" who resent American "hegemony" and the U.S. presence in Asia. Thanks in part to years of indoctrination, a single episode can ignite strong anti-Americanism on the part of the Chinese public.

The major threat to cooperative U.S.-China ties is the possible use of force to settle the status of Taiwan. An unexpected event such as the shooting down of another U.S. reconnaissance plane or the U.S. bombing of the Chinese Embassy in Belgrade could also roil the relationship. In addition, one can imagine a number of crisis scenarios that might embitter or inflame Sino-American relations and polarize or destabilize Asia. In line with the theme of this chapter, all of the following hypothetical illustrations are political-economic rather than military in their origin, but they quickly flag security concerns. They center on disputes over such issues as trade, investment, finance, technology transfer, economic reconstruction, economic sanctions, export controls, and energy. They are fictional, but they all have a basis in current facts.

Hypothetical Political-Economic Crisis Scenarios

North Korea

In a first fictional scenario, North Korea presses on with nuclear weapons and explodes a test weapon. The remaining five powers in the six-power group split. The United States and Japan favor sanctions or other punitive action. China sides with South Korea in opposing them. Russia plays both sides. American anger at Beijing mounts.

Alternatively, North Korea implodes as the colonels surrounding Kim Jong Il stage a palace coup. They try to govern in his name, but word spreads. Soldiers at the DMZ begin to lay down their arms, key officials seek to flee the country, and hungry refugees begin streaming north into China and south into South Korea. China's first priority is stability. Chinese border police treat North Korean refugees brutally. South Korea refuses to talk about outside assistance and blocks American C-130s from delivering rice; China backs Seoul. The six-power group, once considered an incipient security framework, collapses, leaving the U.S.-Japan alliance intact but strained as Tokyo is forced to choose sides. Sino-American and Sino-Japanese tensions increase sharply.

Iran

Iran has publicly renounced nuclear weapons and claims to be pursuing peaceful nuclear power only, but it has not given up its right to acquire the bomb. In a fictional future scenario, Tehran announces that Iran has successfully tested its first bomb. Iranian crowds greet the announcement with pride and rejoicing. The United States proposes to tighten sanctions, but China's vast stake in Iranian energy leads Beijing to block U.S. moves in the UN Security Council. Russia, a long-standing provider of assistance to Iran, follows suit. Seeing that their efforts failed, the members of the European negotiating group (France, Germany, and the UK) begin to ignore existing sanctions, urging the United States to adjust to Iran's nuclear capability as it has to Indian and Pakistani bombs. The United States, isolated, feels betrayed.

Meanwhile, the United States continues to advocate market-oriented solutions to energy shortages. But contrary to its own rhetoric, it continues to exert strong pressure to block oil and gas pipelines transiting Iran. China sides with Iran and helps finance these pipelines, providing credits and technology. Fortified by such support from China and others, Iran steps up its support for violent groups in Iraq and elsewhere in the Middle East.

Energy Security

Fueling China's explosive growth requires huge amounts of energy. China's coal is dirty and its mines are unsafe, but shutting down the industry or refitting coal-fired power plants are not yet viable options. Oil is central to Beijing's energy strategy. China produces oil but became a net importer in 1993 and currently relies on imports for about a third of its supplies. It has become the world's second largest oil consumer after the United States and the fifth largest importer. In the last few years China has tripled its purchases of oil from the unstable Middle East, which now accounts for more than half of China's oil imports; by 2015 that share is expected to rise to 70 percent. Imports of liquefied natural gas are expected to begin in 2007.[34]

Energy has not been a topic of commercial diplomacy because Beijing takes a somewhat mercantilist approach to world energy markets. Its energy policy is founded on a lingering distrust of markets and a preference to lock up supplies.

Four hypothetical examples show how China's relentless quest for energy security might prompt congressional hearings and exacerbate U.S.-China tensions. In one scenario, China's state-owned or state-influenced oil companies form strategic alliances with Middle Eastern and African governments to lock up supplies. Oil-for-arms deals are rumored. A second scenario takes place in Myanmar, where China's plan to build a pipeline from the Bay of Bengal to Kunming prompts Beijing to shower aid and support on the country's repressive government. Beijing ignores the government's criminal activities and human rights violations and refuses to cooperate with U.S.-backed efforts to halt money laundering and narcotics trafficking.

In a third possible development, Sudan is on the point of splitting into two regions as the Sudanese government continues to refuse to take responsibility for the slaughter in Darfur. But Sudan is a major source of oil for China (and India). In the UN Security Council, China backs the government and vetoes a resolution that would have divided the country.

A fourth hypothetical episode centers on the South China Sea, where China abandons its current restraint and presses its claim that a disputed Japanese-held island is merely a "rock" in order to deprive Japan of claims to oil in territorial waters. Seeking maximum stockpiles, Beijing rejects a proposal to establish a regional energy-sharing scheme similar to the one that covers Western countries and Japan.

Trade and Finance

U.S. "neorealists" already worry that as Asians become dependent on the Chinese economy, China will become an exclusive hegemon, drawing investment away from U.S. allies and elbowing out the United States. The U.S.-China Security Review Commission, established by Congress when normal trade relations were extended permanently to China, issued a report that describes the shifting balance of power in traditional zero-sum terms. It warned that China's economic integration with its neighbors raises the prospects of an "Asia[n] economic area dominated or significantly influenced by China." China's gain, the commission implied, would be America's loss.[35] According to another view, Asia may be reverting to a kind of China-centered hierarchy broadly comparable to the premodern tribute system.[36]

Meanwhile, in language reminiscent of the Japan scare of the 1980s, some companies and labor unions are predicting the demise of American competitiveness and the collapse of American manufacturing. China's undervalued currency compounds this complaint.

It is not difficult to construct a dismal scenario. China continues to refuse to revalue the renminbi to any significant degree. The U.S. trade deficit with China continues to swell to unprecedented levels. Beijing reveals that it will henceforth peg its currency to a mixed basket of currencies. Currency traders speculate, not necessarily correctly, that China intends to diversify its foreign-currency holdings and reduce its dollar holdings. This move causes the dollar to tumble further and raises U.S. interest rates. The Treasury Department finally names China as a currency manipulator. Members of Congress vow retaliation for this "currency war" and pass legislation hiking tariffs on imports from China to 30 percent. The president vetoes the bill.

In another fictional political drama, reminiscent of events leading to the Plaza Accord of 1985 when Japan revalued the yen, the U.S. trade authorities reverse themselves and agree to accept a petition charging that China's pegged currency is the equivalent of an illegal export subsidy. This move temporarily pacifies the Congress. But China wins the subsequent case in the World Trade Organization, reviving congressional calls to withdraw from the organization. The conflict undermines supporters of free trade and encourages U.S. hard-liners and protectionists, who push through a 15 percent tariff on Chinese imports by a veto-proof majority. Seeking to mobilize the U.S. business community, the Chinese government suspends further purchases of U.S. telecommunications and aerospace exports and invites European companies to resubmit their bids.

Another possible scenario centers on money laundering. Terrorists are known to acquire money both legitimately and criminally generated.[37] The Financial Action Task Force on Money Laundering (FATF), established by the Group of 7 (G-7) in 1989 and housed at the OECD, has listed China among the countries of "primary concern." China supports the goals of FATF but is not yet a member.

In another future episode, publicity focusses on U.S. investigators who trace a source of terrorist financing to a bank in Kunming already known to harbor cross-border criminal operations. Fearing that greater transparency would invite U.S.-led sanctions and trigger a loss of confidence in the banking system, the Chinese government refuses to divulge the bank's financial records. Invoking national sovereignty, it declines a World Bank/IMF request to submit a report on compliance with FATF standards.

Investment and Technology Transfer

The state-owned China National Offshore Oil Corporation (CNOOC) recently attempted to purchase the U.S. oil company Unocal but subsequently retracted the move in the face of congressional opposition. While the bidding was under way, other potential buyers reportedly hesitated to enter the bidding process for fear of offending the Chinese government. The episode illustrated China's new weight in the balance of influence.[38]

In a possible future scenario, China tries again, targeting a high-technology company. Opponents of the sale, fearing China's acquisition of U.S. assets, demand a review by the interagency Committee on Foreign Investment in the United States. Several damaging leaks compound the controversy. It is revealed that a branch of this U.S. company illegally transferred state-of-the-art dual-use technology to China. As if on cue, newspapers report that the FBI has cracked a major industrial espionage ring and traced it back to China. Chinese officials react badly to the accusations and suspend several large and visible deals in the aerospace, energy, and transportation sectors, singling out U.S. companies for punishment. Washington accuses Beijing of violating WTO commitments.

Military Discontent at Home

A fictional insurgency in western China intensifies as rebels demand independence for "East Turkmenistan." China suppresses the rebellion harshly.

Russia, seeing a "Chinese Chechnya," supports Beijing. Meanwhile, the Chinese government uses the rebellion as an excuse to clamp down on militant Islam and intensifies the repression of other threatening spiritual or religious movements, including evangelical Christianity. Conservative Christian groups in the United States take up the cause. Charging treason, the Chinese government executes a dissident known and supported in Western religious circles. Adopting an "I told you so" attitude, military hard-liners on each side see an opportunity to launch provocative or aggressive actions against the other. The Chinese generals gain support from corrupt senior Party members, who fear that privatization, investor-led demands for public accountability, and greater freedom of the press will expose their illegal assets and preclude further bribery.

Meanwhile, China accelerates the modernization of its navy, citing the need to protect commercial vessels and oil tankers. Hard-liners in Washington see this as a direct challenge to U.S. control of the sea lanes. An incident at sea brings this tension to the public eye when Chinese refusal to cooperate with a U.S. naval vessel in a search-and-rescue operation leads to unnecessary deaths. Beijing urges other Asians to withdraw from joint exercises with U.S. forces in the region, such as RIMPAC and Cobra Gold. The Pentagon orders ships to head toward the Taiwan Strait.

Some Concluding Observations on U.S. Policy

As long as Asia remains peaceful, trust and communication among those who deal with these various problems should continue to improve, but the risks are substantial. As long as China is not fully democratic, the basic questions must remain unanswered. Is China's commercial diplomacy merely a tactical move, a mask concealing an attempt to dominate the rest of Asia and eject all but a token U.S. presence? This author thinks not, but no one can say for sure. Even if those are China's current goals, after ten or twenty years a new generation of Chinese leaders may see them as irrelevant and counterproductive.

The great question about China's future is how and in what ways will the slow, wrenching, and enriching process of engagement in the global economy and polity temper and transform the coming generation of Chinese leadership, whether or not China becomes significantly more democratic?

Seen in that light, the combination of Asian regionalism and China's skillful use of commercial diplomacy poses a challenge for the United States—a constructive one, but a challenge all the same. American policy makers often propose regional initiatives, or suggest that others do so. In this case, Asians are marching ahead with a set of initiatives from which the United States is excluded. China is among those in the lead.

So far, there have been only two substantive but relatively narrow U.S. responses to the new commercial-diplomatic momentum in East Asia. In 2002, President Bush announced an "Enterprise for ASEAN Initiative," offering bilateral FTAs to individual ASEAN nations subject to certain conditions.[39] This offer was eminently respectable as a matter of trade policy, fully consistent with WTO obligations, and more tangible and immediate in trade terms than a vague "U.S.-ASEAN" proposal. But the initiative was not backed up by high-level strategic attention to the region and did not capture Asian imagination in the way that China's more ambitious proposal did.

Until 2005, Washington's response to East Asian regionalism and the strategic use of commercial diplomacy was "benign neglect." In June 2004, for example, Assistant Secretary of State James Kelly expressed this view in less than a paragraph. In congressional testimony, he declared that regional cooperation and integration in East Asia is part of an encouraging set of trends that includes democracy, the rejection of radical Islam, globalization, economic development, and peace. Then he moved on to antiterrorism and nonproliferation.[40] The few public pronouncements about Asia's emerging regionalism have subtly warned against a protectionist economic bloc. The joint statement issued at the time of Indonesian president Yudhoyono's visit to the White House in May 2005, for example, contains typical language: the two presidents "welcomed the development in the Asia-Pacific region of an *open and inclusive* institutional architecture that . . . contributes to economic development and prosperity."[41] Shortly thereafter Secretary of State Condoleezza Rice failed to attend the annual meeting of the ASEAN Regional Forum, a decision greeted with dismay in many capitals.

The second initiative, announced by the United States and ASEAN in November 2005, was the ASEAN-U.S. Enhanced Partnership. Described as "comprehensive, action-oriented, and forward-looking," it encompasses co-operation in political and security affairs, economic and social affairs, and development.[42] A "Plan of Action" covered topics ranging from traditional and nontraditional security concerns to energy, agriculture, tourism, environment, education, and many other subjects.[43]

To date there has been no U.S.-ASEAN summit. In the eyes of U.S. policy makers, such a gathering would legitimize Myanmar's repressive government.[44] Moreover, no U.S. president likes to travel without a clear purpose, and other issues seem far more pressing. Unfortunately, many Asian leaders and elites interpret this lack of interest as a sign that Washington only cares about antiterrorism, Taiwan, and North Korea and not about the rest of Asia. The Plan of Action to implement the ASEAN-U.S. Enhanced Partnership contained commitments to "explore the possibility" of a U.S.-ASEAN summit and to convene a meeting of U.S. and ASEAN leaders on the sidelines of the 2006 APEC meeting, which conveniently excludes Myanmar.

The two recent U.S. initiatives are helpful, but they have not dispelled a widespread impression that America is indifferent to the changing balance of influence in Asia. The war in Iraq compounds that impression. This is unfortunate. All major governments in the region, including China's, want the United States not only to retain a sizable military presence in Asia for the foreseeable future, but also to engage actively with the region. Non-Chinese Asians welcome China's new role, but they have no desire to be dominated by China—or by Japan or India, for that matter. They see an actively engaged United States as a balancing and stabilizing presence that expands their room to maneuver and their freedom to choose.

The risk is not that the United States is in danger of being shut out from East Asian markets or forced to withdraw its military forces, but rather that its voice will be slowly drained of influence. If this happens, it will be not so much because of what Beijing is doing or hoping to do as what Washington is not doing. Preoccupied with antiterrorism and nonproliferation and fixated on "homeland security," the Bush administration is taking only limited steps to avoid being left behind.

If current and future U.S. foreign-policy makers compound this risk by mismanaging the Sino-American relationship, prosperity and stability in the entire Asia-Pacific region will suffer. As Adam Segal's chapter points out, Chinese objectives overlap with many U.S. security concerns and are not necessarily threats. Beijing and Washington have launched a low-key, ongoing strategic dialogue, but it is not yet clear whether its content will include anticipating and heading off potential crises of the sort sketched above. Nor is it settled whether the two sides will consciously strive to identify and reinforce common goals and interests, share information, and establish coordinated crisis-management measures.

It is a law of human nature that someone who is treated like an enemy is more likely to behave like an enemy. The same is true of governments. As the first chapter in this book makes clear, the United States has neither the political will nor the power to halt or even change substantially the expansion of China's political-economic influence in Asia. Beijing's commercial diplomacy is a tool of that influence. The U.S. government should recognize the harm caused by its on-again, off-again attention span and restore sustained, open-minded, high-level involvement with what is going on in Asia.

Finally, politicians and policy makers should break their shortsighted habit of alternately demonizing and embracing China's leaders. While not ignoring China's poor human rights record, they should get the U.S. economic house in order and work with the Chinese and others to stabilize the global economy. They will find their task easier if they approach China with the respect due to a great civilization that has emerged from war, domestic turmoil, and humiliation to become both a major commercial actor and a rapidly emerging regional power.

PART 2
The Balance of Influence in Asia

★6

BALANCE OF POWER POLITICS AND THE RISE OF CHINA

Accomodation and Balancing in East Asia

Robert S. Ross

REALISTS, WHETHER THEY ARE TRADITIONAL realists or structural realists, agree that great powers balance the military strength of rising powers. But there is debate regarding secondary state responses to rising powers. Some realist scholars, including Kenneth Waltz and Hans Morgenthau, argue that secondary states' preferences are situationally determined.[1] Other scholars argue that anarchic structures promote balancing on the part of all but the very weakest states.[2] Opinion also differs regarding the importance of economic and military factors in secondary state alignment. The balance of power literature universally ignores the role of economic dependence in secondary state alignments, focusing simply on military power, while the realist political economy literature ignores the role of military capabilities, focusing on economic power.[3]

Scholars have argued that state alignments are not necessarily determined by realist variables, but can also reflect historical experiences or cultural influences. According to Samuel Huntington, a common East Asian civilization promotes regionwide accommodation with China, including by Japan, so that the United States should accommodate the rise of China.[4] In David Kang's view, balance of power politics is a European process, whereas in East Asia a cultural predisposition toward hierarchy encourages accommodation with China.[5] An apparent consensus exists among security specialists that the rise of China will lead to either a costly U.S.-China strategic rivalry or to regionwide accommodation of Chinese power. Scholars have argued that the rise of China will enable Beijing to coerce U.S. allies and contest U.S. military power throughout East Asia, leading to an "open and intense geopolitical rivalry." Alternatively, China will be the "center" of a "new power arrangement" throughout Asia.[6]

This chapter uses the term "accommodation" to capture the process of secondary state alignment with rising powers. Although "bandwagoning" is often the preferred term for this process, it can be misleading. The term is most commonly associated with domestic politics, in which political actors voluntarily flock to the stronger side for gain, rather than out of strategic imperative to maintain security. In this respect, as Randall Schweller has observed, bandwagoning in international politics is best characterized as "bandwagoning for profit," the preferred behavior of revisionist secondary powers. Furthermore, as Robert Kaufman has argued, bandwagoning suggests an either/all alignment, in which cooperation with a threatening great power precludes all cooperation with its great power rival. Yet, such submission or capitulation is the behavior of the truly "weak state." Finally, while bandwagoning suggests an immediate or short-term process, alignment can take place over decades, in response to gradual and unequal rates of change among the great powers. During the transition period, a state's alignment policy may exhibit considerable ambiguity.[7]

Here, following Waltz and Morgenthau, I argue that secondary state behavior is sensitive to local variation in the great power capabilities and that secondary states tend to accommodate rather than balance rising powers. Through examining the role of military power and economic power as independent factors affecting secondary state alignment, I conclude that economic capabilities alone are insufficient to generate accommodation. East Asian secondary state alignments establish that there is nothing sui generis or culturally determined in East Asian international politics and that realism explains alignment behavior of East Asian as much as European states. This realist analysis of East Asian great power relations challenges assumptions of an emerging Chinese regional hegemony or of a costly regionwide U.S.-China competition.

Secondary Power Alignment Strategies

Waltz's argument that "secondary states, if they are free to choose, flock to the weaker side" follows the traditional literature of international politics. Robert Rothstein's definition of a "Small Power" is similar to Waltz's definition of a secondary power. Rothstein differentiates between a great power, one that can fight wars against any country, and a small power, one that "can not obtain security primarily by use of its own capabilities."[8] Whereas great powers make alignment decisions with regard to threats to systemic balances, small powers' behavior is contingent; a secondary state will ally "in terms of a threat to its local balance" and "the range of options open to Small Powers will be related to the specific nature" of its international setting.[9] Morgenthau similarly suggests that a local power's alignment is determined by the shifting balance of great powers in its immediate vicinity. He examines Korea's periodic adjustment to the shifting fortunes of Chinese and Japanese power in Northeast Asia to illustrate his approach to secondary state alignments.[10] George Liska emphasizes that vulnerability to great power capabilities constrains the abilities of secondary states to balance against a great power, unless a local equilibrium is created by the counterpressure of another great power.[11] Thus, for all but the great powers, a state's response to a rising power will depend on how the status quo great powers respond to the rising power and on the implications for the distribution of power in the immediate vicinity of the secondary state.

In contrast to realist authors who stress the indeterminancy of secondary state alignment, Stephen Walt has argued that only the behavior of "weak states" is situationally determined; all other states balance against rising powers, reflecting the enduring and consistent systemic effect of anarchy.[12] Walt's analysis of the behavior of such secondary states as Egypt and Iraq suggests that his structural assumption of balancing not only encompasses the behavior of larger secondary states, such as France and Japan, but also many smaller states traditionally assumed to be the subjects of great power competition. The concept of "weak states" thus applies only to a very limited subset, such as Myanmar and Bhutan, which have traditionally submitted to their larger neighbors.

The balance of power literature argues that military power determines secondary state alignments. But the realist political economy literature argues that a secondary state's alignment pattern may simply reflect economic vulnerability. An economic great power develops political power from the secondary state's dependence on its market for exports, which promote economic growth, employment, and political stability. Economic dependence reflects a state's vulnerability to interruption of trade by its trading partner. For a small power, this can be a decisive element in its alignment policy. Hirschman observed that "the power to interrupt commercial or financial relations . . . is the root cause of the . . . power position which a country acquires in countries, just as it is the root cause of dependence."[13] As in security relations, dependence is maximized to the extent that the secondary state cannot redirect trade to another economic partner, that it cannot find a "balancing" economic relationship.

Large economies can also develop political power when they are targets of a secondary state's economic investment. As in trade, investment dependence will reflect the degree that the smaller economy's foreign investments are concentrated in the larger target economy. Secondary state dependence on foreign investment enables a larger economy to threaten appropriation of the secondary state's investments and thus yields its influence over the latter's alignment policy. Dependence from both trade and investment can also reflect the role of a dependent influential sector of a secondary state's economy on decision making. As Hirschman observes, "vested interests" can become an influential "commercial fifth column" that can affect security policy.[14]

The importance of economic dependence in secondary state alignment decisions is ignored by both the traditional and structural realist literature on secondary state alignment preferences.[15] Similarly, the realist political economy literature overlooks the role of military power, suggesting that an economic great power possessing only secondary-level military capabilities can exercise sufficient influence to determine the alignment preferences of an economically dependent state.[16] Yet sensitivity to the two potential sources of secondary state alignment necessarily draws attention to multiple kinds of great powers—those with great military capabilities, those with superior economic capabilities, and those with both great military and economic capabilities. Thus, analysis of the impact of the rise of China on the East Asia order requires attention to the multiple sources of Chinese influence and to the spatial variation of its influence, that is, attention to both the "domain" and "scope" of Chinese capabilities.[17]

To assess the alignment preferences of secondary states, working measures of alignment are required. A traditional measure of alignment is alliance policy. But only in highly polarized systems do secondary states formally ally with one great power while engaging in heightened and belligerent conflict with another.[18] More often, secondary states have cooperative relations with multiple great powers even as they take sides in competition between them. Such was the case in Europe during much of the nineteenth century and is the case in international politics in the early twenty-first century. A more sensitive indicator of alignment during periods of "normal" politics is a secondary state's position on issues of war and peace. A secondary state's ability to defy a great power on such an issue reflects balancing with another great power, whereas an emerging compromise on such an issue reflects accommodation. Traditional measures of alignment thus include a secondary state's policy toward such issues as a great power's strategic interests vis-à-vis third parties, arms imports, defense planning, and provision of military facilities to a great power.[19] In addition, societal developments in secondary states reflecting attitudes toward conflict and cooperation with the great powers can suggest emerging alignment trends. The development or erosion of "soft power" following the development of "hard power" can be an indicator of long-term accommodation or balancing.[20]

Analysis of the rise of China also requires a working definition of power. Military power can reflect varied capabilities, depending on the particular requirements of military operations in any given theater, so that neither gross economic and demographic indicators of power nor a focus on a specific military capability (for example, ground forces, air power, naval power, nuclear weaponry, or information technologies) can capture a rising power's capabilities in a particular theater and in relation to any particular secondary state. There is no all-purpose measure of power that enables predictions of interstate behavior in varied historical and distinct geographic settings; therefore I adopt different measures of military capability to evaluate improved Chinese military capability and its impact on secondary state alignments on the Korean Peninsula, in the Taiwan Strait, and in maritime East Asia.

China's Military Rise

The military rise of China and the corresponding decline of U.S. military power vis-à-vis third countries is not a uniform development across the region. Rather, the growth of Chinese power reflects the character of China's developing military capabilities in each of the East Asian subsystem balances of power.

Chinese Military Modernization and Change in Mainland Theaters

The most important change in relative Chinese military capabilities has occurred on mainland Asia. Once the Soviet Union withdrew from Indochina beginning in the late 1980s, China emerged as the sole great power in that region. Since then, as China's economic and military reforms have developed, Chinese superiority over its immediate neighbors has widened. Thus, since 1989, Chinese capabilities vis-à-vis Vietnam, Myanmar, and Mongolia, for example, have improved considerably, and despite fear and even animosity toward China, these countries have accommodated Chinese interests.

Similarly, over the last fifteen years as Russian capabilities have declined and China's have grown, Chinese power relative to the Soviet successor states on China's border in Central Asia has expanded.[21] An outlier in this trend had been Chinese military capabilities compared with those of South Korea. Reflecting the ongoing development of Seoul's economy and independent military power, Seoul's alliance with the United States and the presence of North Korea between China and South Korea have blunted Chinese power in the area. Yet in recent years the growth of Chinese influence has extended to the Korean Peninsula. This change reflects the combination of improvements in Chinese ground forces, political change in China, and the expectation of political change on the Korean Peninsula.

The modernization of Chinese ground forces reflects low-cost yet effective reforms. First, because of the demobilization of soldiers engaged in business activities and the transfer of soldiers to either the militia or to the People's Armed Police (PAP), China's domestic security force, the People's Liberation Army (PLA), is now comprised of more effective war-fighting forces. Even modest increases in the ground force's acquisitions budget have had a great impact on resources for training and acquisitions and thus on war-fighting capability.[22] Second, during the 1990s Beijing created units with advanced capabilities. Rapid Reaction Units (RRUs) are combined-arms units that train to mobilize and respond to a crisis within twenty-four to forty-eight hours. Altogether there may be 100,000 soldiers in the RRUs. Beijing has created special units for emergency border defense, which are estimated to have 300,000 soldiers. China has also modernized its Special Operations Forces, which focus on destruction of key enemy C^4I to C^4ISR (command, control, communications, computers, intelligence, surveillance, and reconnaissance); airfields; and air defense.[23] Third, elite forces receive priority funding for training and are the first to receive new weapons, including imports from Russia and advanced tanks, artillery, ground-transport vehicles, and heavy-lift helicopters. They also benefit from the modernization of China's C^4I infrastructure. New communication satellites, military-dedicated fiber-optic cables, and microwave technologies have resulted in a "dramatic improvement of transmission capacity, as well as communications and operation security" and a substantial increase in overall C^4I capabilities.[24]

Since the PLA has not fought a war since 1979, the effect of these reforms on China's war-fighting capability remains untested. Nevertheless, the improved capabilities of the Chinese military should enable the PLA to better contend with United States forces anywhere on the East Asian mainland, including the Korean Peninsula, than was the case fifteen years ago following the 1991 Gulf War. The PLA can now wage a high-intensity and modern high-tech conflict near its territory, even against U.S. forces.[25] As one expert has observed, its capability will continue to improve and "adds great risks and costs for potential opponents in China's near periphery."[26]

Reinforcing these trends in Chinese ground force capabilities is the prospect of continued Chinese economic and political stability and thus continued military growth. South Korea assumes that China's current economic and military trajectory is an enduring trend that will continue to transform its security environment. Furthermore, in recent years Seoul has increasingly focused on the likelihood of Korean unification, which would remove the North Korean buffer separating South Korea from China and expose Seoul to the direct threat of Chinese military power. As Taeho Kim has observed, contemporary South Korean foreign policy is fundamentally shaped by the long-term growth in Chinese military power, by the geographic proximity of China, and by the need to chart a post-unification Sino-Korean relationship.[27]

PLA Modernization and the Changing Military Balance in the Taiwan Strait

Chinese relative military power is also improving in the immediate vicinity of the Taiwan Strait. But in the Taiwan theater, rather than rely on its ground forces, Beijing relies on air power to alter the military balance and challenge U.S. ability to provide for Taiwan's security.

Since Taiwan's leader Lee Teng-hui visited Cornell University in 1995 and escalated Taiwan's independence activities, China has deployed between fifty and one hundred short-range M-9 ballistic missiles per year across from Taiwan.[28] By 2000 it had deployed approximately three hundred of these missiles. These are relatively low-technology missiles, yet they provide China with an effective and credible capability to inflict high costs on Taiwanese society in a war over Taiwan independence. Moreover, since 1995 the accuracy of these missiles has steadily improved. And because they are mobile, they are secure from preemptive strikes and thus threaten assured retaliation. By 2005 Beijing had deployed as many as six hundred of these missiles.[29] Equally significant, Beijing is making progress in the development of cruise missiles.

Complementing China's development of missile power is its acquisition of modern Russian military aircraft, including Su-27s and Su-30s. Thus far it has agreed to purchase at least two hundred of these aircraft. Over the next five years, as China acquires and puts into operation more Russian aircraft, it will end Taiwan's air superiority across the Taiwan Strait.[30] Although the PLA

Air Force will not be able to challenge U.S. air superiority over the Taiwan Strait, its growing capability vis-à-vis Taiwan contributes to its ability to inflict high costs on Taiwan in a cross-strait war.

China cannot contend with U.S. naval power throughout the western Pacific. But the PLA can now reach across the Taiwan Strait and target Taiwan's civilian and military centers. It can critically undermine the Taiwan economy and its democracy, regardless of the level of U.S. military intervention.[31]

The Limits to China's Rise: The Enduring Military Status Quo in Maritime Theaters

Whereas in the past five years China has developed greater military power on the Korean Peninsula and in the Taiwan Strait, China has yet to enhance its relative military presence in the maritime regions of East Asia, outside the range of its land-based capabilities. The result is a stable post–Cold War balance of power in the East Asian maritime region.

Maritime power depends on force protection. But the Chinese Navy has no aircraft carriers and has not begun construction of one.[32] The U.S. Navy possesses eleven aircraft carriers, two of which can operate simultaneously in the region: one based in Japan and one in Singapore. It also continues to modernize its carrier force, with the launching of the *Harry S. Truman* and the *Ronald Reagan*. Moreover, U.S. interceptor aircraft based at Kadena in Japan provide significant coverage of the Western Pacific. The 2006 Quadrennial Defense Review (QDR) also calls for the United States to deploy 60 percent of its submarine force in Asia. Thus, whereas U.S. naval force projection capabilities in East Asia are secure from a Chinese air attack, Chinese surface vessels, both those at sea in blue waters and those that remain in port, are vulnerable to U.S. air power. Indeed, once PRC surface vessels leave the range of Chinese land-based aircraft, they are vulnerable to the air power of even the smaller regional states, such as Singapore, Malaysia, and Thailand.

The only element of Chinese modernization that might eventually affect this situation is PRC access-denial capability. PRC acquisition of Russian Kilo-class submarines could serve this purpose, compelling U.S. surface vessels to maintain greater distance from the region during crises and war. But access denial offers neither coercive capability nor even deterrent capability against a much superior navy. Moreover, until China develops situational awareness capability and can degrade U.S. countersurveillance technologies, possession of advanced submarines will be insufficient to provide it with a credible access-denial capability, even should it master the skills necessary for maintenance and operation of the Kilo submarines.[33]

As in the past, the United States possesses absolute military superiority in maritime East Asia. Thus, the modernization of the Chinese military has not affected the immediate U.S.-China force-on-force balance in the vicinity of the insular countries of East Asia. Japan, the Philippines, Indonesia, Singapore, and Malaysia all remain within a stable U.S. military region.

China's Economic Rise: Emerging Trends In U.S.-China Relative Power

The growth of the Chinese economy has had a major global impact. As an engine of growth, it has contributed to the prosperity of many countries. But coinciding with the absolute economic gains that China has contributed to other countries' economies, China has also developed its own relative economic power. As in the development of Chinese military gains, Chinese economic gains have occurred at U.S. expense, because increased third-party dependence on the Chinese economy has caused a relative reduction in their dependence on the U.S. economy. But the scope of Chinese economic power does not coincide with the scope of its military power, creating regional complexities that result in secondary power alignment decisions that are not amenable to easy generalizations.

China as the Dominant Economic Power: South Korea and Taiwan

During the past four years, China has become the dominant source of economic growth for both South Korea and Taiwan. The result is that their dependence on the Chinese economy is increasingly greater than their dependence on the U.S. economy.

In 2002 the combined China–Hong Kong market became South Korea's largest export market.[34] For the first time since World War II, Seoul was not primarily dependent on the United States for economic growth. Moreover, South Korean annual exports to China increased nearly 50 percent from 2001 to 2003. Between 2002 and 2003, South Korean exports to the United States, in contrast, increased by less than 1 percent. In 2003, more than 31 per cent of South Korean exports went to China. In contrast, Chinese exports to Korea amounted to only 5 percent of Chinese exports.

Beijing underscored South Korean dependence on the Chinese market during the China–South Korea "garlic war" in 2000. While ostensibly a dispute over a minor Chinese export product, it was an exercise in Chinese economic signaling. In retaliation against South Korean tariffs on Chinese garlic, Beijing imposed massive tariffs on South Korean polyethylene and mobile phone equipment, causing losses of nearly US$100 million to South Korean companies. Faced with intense pressure from its domestic industries, South

Korean leaders compromised, agreeing to an increased market share for Chinese garlic. Faced with credible threats of a costly trade war it would surely lose, Seoul compromised.[35]

South Korea has also increased its investments in China. By 2001 China had become South Korea's number one target of foreign direct investment (FDI).[36] By early 2004 there were more than 22,000 South Korean companies with production facilities in China, with an average of twelve new investments daily. Similarly, in 2003, nearly 50 percent of all South Korean foreign direct investment was destined for China. In contrast, whereas the United States was once South Korea's primary target for Korean foreign investment, in 2003 the United States absorbed only 15 percent of total South Korean FDI. South Korea plans to increase its investment in China by more than 50 percent by 2006.[37]

The Chinese market has just as rapidly been engaging the Taiwan economy. In 2001 the combined China–Hong Kong market surpassed the U.S. market as Taiwan's most important export market. In 2002 and in 2003, Taiwan's exports to the mainland increased by more than 25 percent, while Taiwan's exports to the United States declined. And in 2003, more than 35 percent of Taiwan's exports went to the China–Hong Kong market, while Chinese exports to Taiwan amounted to only 6.4 percent of total Chinese exports.[38] Moreover, Taiwan has not been able to develop alternative economic partners to diversify its economic relationships. Even should Taiwan reach a free trade agreement with the United States, for example, there would be only a small impact on Taiwan's exports and its economy.[39]

Cross-strait investment trends are equally significant for Taiwan dependence on the mainland. In 2001 the mainland became the leading target of Taiwan foreign investment, and in 2002 it became the leading production center of overseas Taiwan investors. Approximately 60 percent of Taiwan overseas investment is now located on the mainland, and Taiwan's largest and most advanced industries, including high-technology semiconductor manufacturers, are moving production to the mainland. By 2004 Taiwan firms had invested up to US$160 billion in approximately 70,000 projects. Overall, total investment on the mainland is equivalent to nearly 50 percent of the Taiwan GDP. More than 30,000 Taiwan companies have manufacturing facilities on the mainland.[40] The Taiwan government tried to restrict high-technology investment on the mainland and to encourage Taiwan businesses to invest in Southeast Asia, but as in trade relations, the lure of the China market has been irresistible.[41]

Because South Korea and Taiwan are now dependent on China for prosperity, they are highly vulnerable to the disruption of trade, and they do not have the option of diversifying their economic relations with other economic powers. These are the characteristics Hirschman identified as critical to the development of politically important economic dependence. Moreover, these trends will likely endure for at least the next few decades. Given the small size of the South Korean and Taiwan economies relative to the Chinese economy, their full integration into the larger Chinese economy is all but inevitable.

China and the Japanese Economy

Since the onset of China's economic reforms in December 1978, the Chinese economy has grown more than 9 percent per year. In contrast, during the 1990s, Japan's economy grew less than 1.5 percent per year. Although in recent years the growth rate of the Japanese economy has begun to increase, it cannot compare to the rate of growth of the Chinese economy. These developments have affected relative Chinese and Japanese GDP. By 1995, measured in terms of the World Bank's purchasing power parity methodology, the Chinese economy was already larger than the Japanese economy. Using market exchange rates to convert GDP totals to U.S. dollars, Japan's 2005 GDP was twice as large as China's. But in 1978, when Chinese reforms began, Japan's GDP was seven times larger than China's. China's faster growth rate has quickly narrowed the gap, and the trend suggests that China's GDP will soon be larger than Japan's.[42] Although there is no direct link between economic size and military capability, relative economic size does contribute to strategic potential. Accordingly, prolonged Chinese success and Japanese difficulty have contributed to each side's assessment of relative capabilities.[43]

The growth of the Chinese economy has also affected Japan's foreign economic relationships. Japanese exports to China increased by more than 50 percent between 2000 and 2002 and by another 25 percent in 2003. During this same three-year period, Japanese exports to the United States declined by approximately 1.5 percent. In 2002 there would have been no growth in the Japanese economy were it not for exports to China. By 2003 the value of Japanese exports to China and Hong Kong combined was more than 75 percent of the value of its exports to the United States. By 2006 the Chinese market will be larger and more important to long-term Japanese economic growth than the American market.[44]

After Beijing waged the "garlic war" with Seoul in 2000, it waged the "tatami mat war" with Tokyo. In June 2001 Tokyo imposed temporary safeguards on imports of Chinese leeks, shiitake mushrooms, and reeds used in the making of tatami mats. Beijing retaliated with 100 percent duties on Japanese automobiles, cell phones, and air conditioners. The value of the Chinese sanctions on the Japanese goods was seven times the value of the Japanese sanctions on the Chinese goods and threatened the Japanese automobile industry with 420 billion yen in lost sales. Japan quickly agreed to lift the tariffs on Chinese goods and to put off consideration of tariffs on other Chinese imports.[45] Since then, Japanese economic interest groups have become increasingly vocal in opposition to government policy that challenges Sino-Japanese cooperation. In 2004, leaders of Japan's major business associations, including the Keidanren, emerged as vocal critics of Japan's resistance to Beijing's complaints regarding attitudes toward Japanese military activities in China during World War II.[46]

Trends in Japanese direct foreign investment are also important. From 2000 to 2002, annual Japanese investment in the United States declined by 35 percent, but during this same period Japanese investment in China increased by nearly 35 percent per year. In 2002, for the first time there were more cases of new Japanese investment in China than in the United States, and this trend continued in 2003.[47] Even as the U.S. economy recovered from two and a half years of recession and experienced 3–4 percent growth from 2003 to 2004, these trade and investment trends have continued. Because of China's proximity to Japan, its nearly inexhaustible supply of inexpensive labor, and its large domestic market, it will continue to present Japan with more attractive investment opportunities than the United States.

China's economic rise will not eliminate the importance of the U.S economy to Japanese economic development. The large size of Japan's domestic market will also limit Japanese dependence on the Chinese economy. Thus, unlike China's economic relationship with South Korea and Taiwan, China will not quickly become a dominant economic power vis-à-vis Japan. Nonetheless, the importance of the U.S. economy for Japan will continue to decline as China gradually shares with and in some instances overtakes the United States as a critical international partner determining Japanese economic growth and prosperity.

The Chinese Economy and the ASEAN Countries

Significant changes are also under way in China's economic relationship with the major ASEAN countries aligned with the United States. The November 2002 ASEAN-China free trade agreement was an important development in China's transition to a global economic power. The agreement is reminiscent of the 1947 General Agreement on Tariffs and Trade (GATT), in which Western Europe enjoyed preferential access to the U.S. market for certain commodities. The result was the development of the post–World War II liberal trade order, but equally significant, the GATT contributed to the expansion of relative U.S. global market power. The ASEAN-China free trade agreement reflects a similar economic expansion strategy for China. Beijing has granted preferential access to its economy to the ASEAN countries, thus promoting their exports to the Chinese market. But as these countries expand their exports to China, their economies will increasingly depend on China.[48] China is also negotiating more expansive bilateral trade agreements with the ASEAN countries, such as with Singapore.

As John Ravenhill discusses in this volume, the redirection of ASEAN exports from the United States to China is already under way. From 1998 to 2001, Malaysian and Indonesian exports to China more than doubled. Philippine exports to China nearly doubled from 2003 to 2004, while its exports to the United States declined by over 10 percent. From 2002 to 2003, combined exports from all of the ASEAN states to China grew by 51.7 percent, and by mid-2004 China had become the region's leading trade partner, surpassing the United States. Singapore is the lead state in this trend. By the end of 2003 Singapore's exports to China were nearly one-third larger than the value of its exports to the United States. Moreover, over the next few years the China-ASEAN Free Trade Agreement will use complementarity in China-ASEAN agricultural products to encourage further trade expansion. Its "Early Harvest" program allows ASEAN agricultural products initial preferential access to the Chinese market.[49]

Despite Washington's free trade agreement with Singapore and its effort to reach agreements with other Southeast Asian states, the ASEAN countries will increasingly become vulnerable to Chinese economic power. China's market may well become the anchor of an East Asian free trade area, just as the U.S. market anchors the North American Free Trade Agreement. Since 2001, the proportion of exports by East Asian nations that stayed within the region has steadily increased, reaching a high of 44 percent, suggesting that a regional trade system may be emerging. Much of this increase reflects the growth of exports to China.[50] The 2004 China-ASEAN agreement aims for a regionwide free trade area by 2010, suggesting that China wants to use its growing market to become the anchor of an East Asian free trade association.[51]

Accommodating and Balancing in East Asia

The complexity of the rise of China is matched by the complexity of state alignment decisions. There is no uniform East Asian response to Chinese power. Rather, among East Asia's secondary powers there are accommodators as well as balancers, reflecting trends in the scope and domain of relative Chinese and American power.

The Accommodators: South Korea and Taiwan

South Korea and Taiwan, the two East Asian actors most vulnerable to the rise of Chinese military power, are accommodating China by resolving conflicts with Beijing and adjusting their defense ties with the United States. Simultaneously, Beijing is penetrating South Korean and Taiwanese societies by developing soft power, reflecting trends in Chinese hard power.

China's rise has affected South Korea most notably in terms of Seoul's response to the North Korean threat. Whereas during the 1994 nuclear crisis Seoul supported U.S. policies that threatened war, in 2003 it publicly and dramatically distanced itself from U.S. policy.[52] Following North Korea's admission in October 2002 that it had resumed work on a proscribed nuclear reactor, the United States threatened war. In February the United States placed B-1 and B-52 bombers on alert for deployment to Guam and positioned equipment enabling launches of precision-guided missiles near North Korea. In March, it deployed its bombers to Guam, just following President George W. Bush's warning that he was prepared to use force to end North Korea's nuclear program. In addition, U.S. and South Korean forces carried out large-scale war exercises, with F-117 Stealth fighters participating for the first time in seven years. Afterwards, these fighters remained deployed in South Korea. During the exercises, U.S. forces also increased aerial and naval reconnaissance of North Korea. According to North Korean sources, in March the United States carried out more than 220 surveillance flights against North Korea. Then, in the aftermath of the invasion of Iraq, Washington transited three aircraft carriers from the Iraq theater to the Pacific theater, so that in April it had four carriers deployed in range of the Korean Peninsula. Two of the carriers returned to the United States, but two remained in the region within range of North Korea.[53] Then, in May, Washington deployed a Stryker Brigade Combat Team to South Korea, facilitating rapid and flexible application of U.S. medium and heavy weaponry. It also announced that it would deploy Apache military helicopters and PAC-3 missiles in Korea.[54]

As Washington moved closer to war with North Korea, South Korea distanced itself from the United States. It held senior-level meetings with the North Korean leadership and continued to offer North Korea food shipments in return for minor quid pro quos. When President Bush threatened economic sanctions against North Korea, South Korea's president publicly opposed sanctions.[55] Indeed, South Korea's policy toward North Korea was closer to China's policy than to U.S. policy. Frequent high-level consultations between Beijing and Seoul revealed that at the height of the crisis the South Korean leadership was far more comfortable working with Chinese leaders than with U.S. leaders.

South Korean accommodation of the rise of China is also reflected in Seoul's resistance to post–Cold War defense cooperation with the United States. The United States is adjusting its defense planning to stress "strategic flexibility," in which U.S. forces abroad are deployed not for a single contingency but for whatever contingency may arise. In this context, the Pentagon envisions that U.S. forces in South Korea can be deployed anywhere in East Asia, which suggests planning for conflict with China. Seoul has resisted cooperating with U.S. defense policy insofar as it implies that South Korean territory could be used by the United States against China. Thus, in 2005 President Roh Moo-hyun declared that South Korean facilities could not be used by U.S. forces in a Taiwan conflict, and the United States has been unable to reach agreement with Seoul to enable U.S. use of its South Korean bases for regional contingencies.[56]

These trends in South Korean defense policy also explain Seoul's increasingly sanguine response to U.S. plans to withdraw its troops from between Seoul and the demilitarized zone, and to reduce the overall number of U.S. troops in South Korea. In 1977 Seoul resisted President Jimmy Carter's plan to reduce U.S. troops in Korea. The origin of "Koreagate," in which South Korea bribed members of the U.S. Congress, was Seoul's anxiety over fears of abandonment by the United States.[57] In contrast, when Secretary of Defense Donald Rumsfeld, at the height of U.S. preparations for war against North Korea, proposed removal of U.S. troops from the demilitarized zone and a reduction of U.S. military presence on the peninsula, Seoul merely questioned the timing of the proposal and then entered into negotiations regarding the schedule for U.S. redeployments. In 2004, when the U.S. announced that it would transfer 4,000 troops from South Korea to Iraq and it would reduce its forces in South Korea by one-third in 2005, Seoul was not alarmed.[58] In the context of South Korean accommodation of the rise of China, U.S. military presence was becoming less relevant to South Korean security. South Korean defense minister Yoon Kwang-ung explained that South Korea planned to be less dependent on its alliance with the United States and that it would increasingly cooperate with Russia and China as it developed a balancer role in Northeast Asia.[59] Although President Roh criticized the North Korean ballistic missile tests in June 2006, he criticized Japan's response to the tests as the more dangerous threat to regional stability.[60]

In a case of soft power following hard power, the rise of China has led to socioeconomic changes in South Korea's relationship with China. There are now direct flights between seven South Korean cities and twenty-four Chinese cities, and more than 200,000 South Koreans have residences in China. More than 30,000 South Koreans are studying Chinese in China, more than any other group of foreign students in China. In mid-2003 there were approximately 300,000 South Koreans studying Chinese in South Korea; there is a shortage of South Koreans who can teach Chinese in South Korean schools.[61] Since 1997, South Korean attitudes toward China have steadily improved, largely at the expense of America's standing in South Korea. In 2001 73 percent of South Koreans had a favorable attitude toward China, while only 66 percent held a favorable attitude toward the United States.[62]

The rise of China has also affected U.S. policy toward North Korea. U.S. agreement to hold the meetings on the North Korean nuclear program in Beijing and to work through Beijing to control North Korea's nuclear program revealed Washington's inability to manage the North Korean threat without Chinese cooperation. Moreover, its ultimate search for a diplomatic solution to the crisis reflected growing U.S. isolation on the Korean Peninsula. Coercion of North Korea cannot be effective when China and South Korea cooperate against U.S. policy.

Furthermore, Chinese relative gains explain Beijing's willingness to pressure North Korea to give up its nuclear weapons program and to make concessions regarding its participation in multilateral negotiations with the United States and its allies. In 1994 China's veiled threat to refrain from vetoing a U.N. Security Council vote on sanctions against North Korea was considered a major concession to the U.S. position.[63] In contrast, in 2002–3 China called for Pyongyang to maintain a nuclear-free Korean Peninsula and cooperated with South Korea in opposition to North Korea's nuclear program. It also significantly reduced its aid for North Korea. In 2002 Chinese fuel shipments to North Korea declined by approximately 30 percent and its grain exports declined by approximately 15 percent. In 2003 China suspended fuel shipments to North Korea for three days. In 2006 it reduced fuel shipments to North Korea in response to Pyongyang's July missile tests. In 2006 China also cooperated with the United States in sanctioning North Korea for counterfeiting foreign currencies.[64] Whereas China had once been dependent on its close relationship with North Korea to ensure its security in Northeast Asia, its increasingly close relationship with Seoul enables it to distance itself from North Korean foreign policy. Chinese policy analysts now openly call for Beijing to cancel China's treaty commitment to defend North Korea.[65]

Taiwan's Accommodation of Rising Chinese Power

The rise of Chinese economic and military power also explains recent developments in Taiwan's defense and foreign policies. From the early 1970s to the late 1990s, Taiwan made annual requests for American advanced weaponry, only to be disappointed by U.S. restraint. Then, in early 2001, the Bush administration agreed to sell Taiwan diesel submarines, *Kidd*-class destroyers, and antisubmarine reconnaissance aircraft. It has also licensed for export to Taiwan the Patriot III missile, a key ingredient in a Taiwan missile defense system. But then Taiwan became the reluctant party. It required more than two years to purchase four 1970s-generation *Kidd*-class destroyers and, despite considerable U.S. pressure, Taiwan's legislature has yet to consider a supplementary budget for acquisition of these weapons.

In part, Taiwan's acquisitions policy reflects democratic politics and the resultant demands for increased social spending. Nonetheless, Taiwan's reluctance to purchase U.S. weapons also reflects its increasing accommodation to Chinese power. In a recent public opinion poll, approximately 55 percent of the respondents believed that advanced U.S. weaponry could not make Taiwan secure. Only 37 percent of the respondents supported the acquisition plan. Another poll reported that nearly 60 percent of the public believed that Taiwan could not defend itself in a war with the mainland.[66] Taiwan's ministry of defense concurs. In 2004 it concluded that the mainland will gain military superiority over Taiwan in 2006. Because it would require up to a decade to complete the acquisition of the U.S. weaponry, arms acquisitions from the United States will not make Taiwan more secure because the mainland will continue to upgrade its capabilities.[67] Moreover, Taiwan's 2003 regular defense budget was the lowest since 1996, and the 2004 defense budget was 20 percent lower than the 2003 figure, despite a growing Taiwan economy and increased government revenues.[68]

Until the late 1990s the combination of Taiwan capabilities and U.S. intervention could provide an effective defense against the mainland military, but by 2000 Taiwan had become vulnerable to assured PRC economic and military punishment of its economy and democracy. Indeed, Taiwan's dependence on the mainland means that Beijing will not need to contend with the U.S. Navy to deploy an effective blockade against Taiwan's economy. The mere loss of the mainland market or mainland "nationalization" of Taiwan investments would undermine economic, political, and social stability in Taiwan. Moreover, should there be hostilities between the mainland and Taiwan, Taiwan's other major trading partners, including U.S. businesses, would likely suspend trade with Taiwan, preferring to maintain economic cooperation with Beijing.[69] In early 1996, when China massed troops and carried out military exercises in the vicinity of Taiwan, the Taiwan stock market fell by 25 percent. Loss of confidence in the Taiwan dollar and panic buying of the U.S. dollar required the Taiwan government to intervene in capital markets.[70] The continued rise of Chinese economic power guarantees that Taiwan will suffer far greater and unacceptable costs in a future war.

Taiwan's vulnerability to the mainland is also reflected in political trends suggesting accommodation to Chinese interests regarding de jure independence for Taiwan. Taiwan polling consistently reveals that less than 10 percent of the population supports an immediate declaration of independence. Eighty percent oppose changing the name of the island from "Republic of China." Moreover, nearly 65 percent would favor a fifty-year "peace treaty" with the mainland that would preserve the status quo, in which the mainland does not use force against Taiwan and Taiwan does not declare independence.[71] Similar prudence is reflected in attitudes toward Chen Shui-bian's March 2004 initiative for a "defensive referendum" regarding Taiwan's mainland policy. Public opinion polls conducted by a wide range of media outlets revealed that a majority believed that the referendum was at best unnecessary and at worst provocative. Despite his ultimate electoral victory, Chen's political advisors acknowledged that the referendum initiative had reduced voter support for his candidacy. Even Chen's party colleagues worry about his policies. Some party leaders have publicly advised Chen to rethink his plans to seek a new constitution and possibly alter Taiwan's legal relationship with the mainland.[72]

The majority vote for Chen Shui-bian in the March 2004 presidential election was not a vote for independence. It reflected the effect of an alleged assassination attempt against Chen the day before the election. Prior to the shooting, despite a lackluster campaign led by Lien Chan, the Kuomintang (KMT) was well ahead of the Democratic Progressive Party (DPP) in almost all opinion polls.[73] Indeed, despite his many advantages, Chen secured only 50.1 percent of the vote.[74] Then, in the December 2004 legislative elections, the DPP failed to gain control of the Taiwan legislature. In March 2005, Beijing issued its "Anti-Secession Law" and inflamed Taiwan public opinion. Nonetheless, in April, KMT chairman Lien Chan traveled to Beijing, met with Chinese Communist Party leader Hu Jintao, declared the KMT's opposition to Taiwan independence, and gave an emotional speech at Peking University that advocated cross-strait cooperation. Fifty-six percent of the Taiwan people supported his visit. A poll conducted shortly after Lien's visit reported that 46 percent of the voters saw the KMT as most capable of handling cross-strait relations, while only 9.4 percent believed that the DPP was most capable. Taiwan's "accommodationist" trend continued through the December 2005 election for city mayors and county-level magistrates. The DPP suffered a major defeat, securing only six of the twenty-three open posts. Following the election, Chen's popularity rating fell to 10 percent. Meanwhile, Ma Ying-jeou, the KMT's candidate for the 2008 presidential election, who is also mayor of Taipei and the new KMT chairman, received an 80 percent approval rating. In a clear sign of accommodation, Ma publicly opposes independence and supports opening of the "three links" across the Taiwan Strait, which would eliminate the requirement that shipping and flights pass through Hong Kong before entering the mainland. The Taiwan electorate has spoken and rejected independence; the risk is simply too high. This trend of accommodation to Chinese power is irreversible, insofar as the mainland's military power will continue to grow, and its stranglehold over the Taiwan economy will deepen.

These trends have also affected the policy preferences of the Taiwan business community. Reflecting Taiwan's economic dependence on the mainland, support from large businesses for the pro-independence DPP has declined in recent years, and during the 2004 presidential election many refused to support Chen Shui-bian. Their political migration to the KMT has increasingly reflected opposition to Chen's focus on independence, and their preference for pragmatic policies promotes cross-strait stability and economic opportunities. These businesses also pressure the government to open direct air and sea transportation links to expand trade with the mainland, despite the implications for Taiwan's security. Seventy-five percent of the business community support liberalized trade relations with the mainland, despite the consequences this would have for Taiwan's dependence on the mainland economy. In May 2006 pro-DPP business leaders, frustrated by Chen's mainland policy, traveled to Beijing with an opposition party delegation and made a direct appeal to Hu Jintao to smooth cross-strait business relations.[75] In apparent response to such pressure, Chen Shui-bian took the first step in June 2006 toward direct trade with the mainland by allowing cross-strait cargo flights on a case-by-case basis.[76] Taiwan's business community has become what Hirschman called a "commercial fifth column."

As in Chinese-South Korean relations, China's soft power vis-à-vis Taiwan has followed the rise of its hard power. More than one million Taiwanese now have residences on the mainland, where they have established separate Taiwan communities with elementary schools. More than 500,000 Taiwanese live in the Shanghai area alone. Taiwan tourism on the mainland continues to expand. In 1988 approximately 450,000 Taiwan tourists visited mainland

China; in 2003 the number was nearly 3 million. According to Taiwan's statistics, by the end of 2004 there were more than 250,000 "cross-strait marriages" in Taiwan, amounting to over 20 percent of all Taiwan marriages. In early 2004, there were 5,000 students from Taiwan studying for degrees in Chinese universities, even though Chinese degrees are not recognized by Taiwan.[77] Change in cross-strait relations is also reflected in subtle shifts in identity among the Taiwan electorate. The younger the generation, the less likely it is that voters consider themselves Taiwanese and more likely that they consider themselves Taiwanese and Chinese. Taiwan voters who did not experience the harsh rule of the mainland KMT government from the 1950s to the 1970s but who have been exposed to contemporary mainland China and benefit from cross-strait relations possess greater affinity for mainland China.[78]

The Balancers: Japan and the ASEAN States

Elsewhere in East Asia, China is a rising economic power but not a rising military power; the military balance in maritime East Asia is stable, insofar as the United States remains the dominant military power. But despite these states' growing economic dependence on China and the development of domestic economic interest groups promoting more cooperative policies, U.S. military supremacy provides these secondary powers the opportunity to balance with the United States.

Japan began balancing the rise of Chinese power in the mid-1990s, just as China was experiencing its second post-Mao economic boom.[79] In 1995 Tokyo agreed to revised guidelines for the U.S.-Japan alliance. The guidelines called for closer wartime coordination between the Japanese and U.S. militaries, including U.S. use of Japanese territory and logistical services in case of war with a third country.[80] Since then, Japan has become the most active U.S. partner in the development of missile defense technologies. In 2004 it agreed to a five-year plan for U.S.-Japan joint production of a missile defense system and committed one billion dollars for construction of missile defense hardware; it plans to spend ten billion dollars by the end of the decade.[81] In late 2005 Japan formally agreed for the first time to base a U.S. nuclear-powered aircraft carrier at the U.S. naval base at Yokosuka; later that year Japan and the United States announced that they would hold the first joint military exercise simulating defense of a small Japanese island, with China the implicit adversary.[82] Moreover, after many years of U.S. encouragement, in 2005 Tokyo agreed to a U.S.-Japan joint statement on Taiwan expressing mutual interest in the "peaceful resolution" of the Taiwan conflict.[83] Defense cooperation with the United States has also eroded Japan's reluctance to deploy forces overseas. In the 1990s Japanese participation in UN peacekeeping operations in Cambodia was a major development. In 2001 Japan passed legislation allowing the Japanese military to provide noncombat support to U.S. antiterrorist operations, and then sent its navy to join in the search for Al Qaeda forces in the waters off Pakistan and Iran. That same year Japan passed legislation allowing Japan to deploy ground troops in support of U.S. operations in Iraq.[84] Japanese forces have participated in the war in Iraq since 2003.

Japanese national defense policy is also changing to reflect the possibility of war with China. In 2004 the Japanese Defense Agency publicly referred to a potential Chinese challenge to Japanese security for the first time. The next year the Japanese foreign minister Taro Aso followed up with the assertion that growing Chinese military power and increased defense spending posed a "threat" to Japan.[85] Moreover, Tokyo has adopted a more assertive posture on islands and territorial waters claimed by both China and Japan. In late 2005 officials said that Tokyo would increase the number of ships and planes patrolling gas and oil fields claimed by both Japan and China. Tokyo has decided to develop a surface-to-surface missile, reportedly to defend disputed islands from other claimants. It will build a radar facility on the islands, and has begun allocating gas exploration in the disputed waters.[86]

Japanese balancing of Chinese power is also reflected in changes in Japanese public opinion regarding use of force. Leaders of the ruling Liberal Democratic Party have called for revision of article 9 of the Japanese constitution, which prohibits Japanese participation in collective defense; a 2003 poll found that 42 percent of the public supported its revision. In late 2005 the Liberal Democratic Party issued a draft revision of the Japanese constitution that would permit Japanese military participation in collective defense.[87] There is also a growing debate in Japan over possession of nuclear weapons. Senior government officials have argued that possession of nuclear weapons would not violate the Japanese constitution.[88] Japan is leaving behind its "pacifist" past and is on its way to becoming a "normal" country. It took the rise of China to start this process.

The rise of China and Japanese balancing coincides with socioeconomic changes in Japan and the erosion of Chinese soft power. The percentage of Japanese reporting a positive attitude toward China has steadily declined following the 1989 Tiananmen incident, China's nuclear tests, and its 1996 show of force against Taiwan. According to Japanese government surveys, in 2001, for the first time, Japanese who held no affinity for China outnumbered Japanese who did feel such an affinity.[89] In this domestic context, Japanese politicians no longer anguish over whether to pay tribute to World War II soldiers at the Yasukuni Shrine. Rather, they warn that Chinese opposition to the visits could inflame anti-Chinese attitudes in Japan. There is also declining support for economic assistance to China. Japanese had long considered aid to China as an obligation, tantamount to reparations for World War II. But according to a December 2004 poll, less than one-third of the public supports continued aid for China. Since fiscal year 2000, Tokyo has reduced its aid by over half, and in 2004 China ranked only third as a recipient of Japanese aid, behind India and Indonesia.[90]

As in Japan, the rise of China has not diminished U.S. dominance in the South China Sea or U.S. ability to determine the security of Southeast Asia's maritime states. Thus in this theater the rise of China is limited to this region's growing economic dependence on the Chinese economy. In these strategic circumstances, the secondary states are consolidating defense cooperation with the United States.

Since 1995 countries throughout maritime Southeast Asia have conducted annual Cooperation Afloat Readiness and Training (CARAT) bilateral military exercises with the U.S. Navy. Indonesia's accommodation of superior U.S. capabilities was especially pronounced in 1999, when it acquiesced to the secession of East Timor from Indonesia. When the United States and its allies deployed significant military forces in the South China Sea in support of East Timor independence, and in the absence of countervailing great power capabilities, Indonesia cooperated with U.S. power.[91] Indonesia continued to participate in the CARAT exercises despite the U.S. military embargo imposed on Indonesia following the East Timor issue. Since then, it has been increasingly active in these exercises. In 2002 it resumed security cooperation talks with Washington, and it has purchased more U.S. military equipment.[92] Malaysia is improving defense ties with Washington. About fifteen to twenty U.S. Navy vessels visit Malaysian ports each year. U.S. Army and Navy Seals conduct training in Malaysia each year, and Malaysia provides jungle warfare training for U.S. military personnel. U.S. aircraft carriers often berth at Port Klang in the Strait of Malacca.[93]

Singapore and the Philippines have been particularly active in cooperation with the U.S. military, including basing, defense planning, and arms acquisitions. In 2000 Singapore began annual participation in the U.S. Cobra Gold military exercises. In 2001 it completed construction of its Changi port facility, designed to accommodate a U.S. aircraft carrier, and in March 2001 it hosted the first visit of the USS *Kitty Hawk*. As the Singapore defense minister explained, "It is no secret that Singapore believes that the presence of the U.S. military . . . contributes to the peace and stability of the region. To that extent, we have facilitated the presence of U.S. military forces."[94] There are approximately one hundred U.S. naval ship visits to Singapore each year. In 2005 Singapore and the United States signed the Singapore-U.S. Strategic Framework Agreement, which consolidates defense and security ties and enables greater cooperation in joint exercises. Singapore also relies on the United States for acquisition of advanced weaponry. It has joined in the U.S. program for development of the Lockheed Martin Joint Strike Fighter.[95]

In 1999 the Philippines reached a Visiting Forces Agreement with the United States, permitting U.S. forces to hold exercises with Philippine forces in the Philippines. Since then the size of U.S. participation in joint exercises has steadily expanded, doubling from 2003 to 2004. In addition, the focus has expanded beyond antiterrorist activities to include U.S. Navy participation in amphibious exercises in the vicinity of the Spratly Islands, which both Beijing and Manila claim as their territory, suggesting that the exercises possess a regional focus. In late 2004 the U.S. and Philippine air forces conducted joint air exercises using the former U.S. base at the Clark Airfield.[96] Since 2001 annual U.S. military assistance to the Philippines has increased from US$1.9 million to a projected US$126 million in 2005, and the Philippines is now the largest recipient of U.S. military assistance in East Asia. Manila is also planning to purchase U.S. fighter planes. Whereas for most of the 1990s the Philippines was hostile to the U.S. military, it is now a "major non-NATO ally" with an expanding U.S. presence on its territory.[97]

The Emerging East Asian Balance of Power

China's rise is uneven in its scope and domain. Economic dependence on China is growing throughout the region while economic dependence on the United States lessens. But the rise of Chinese military power is less uniform. China is balancing U.S. power in distinct theaters rather than throughout the region.

Where the relative rise of Chinese economic and military power correspond and China is altering the U.S.-China balance of power, secondary states are accommodating Chinese interests. This is the case on the Korean Peninsula, where there has been a gradual yet fundamental repositioning of South Korean foreign and defense policies toward alignment with China. This has also been the case regarding Taiwan's mainland policy. Remnant Taiwan resistance to Chinese pressure regarding sovereignty reflects the countervailing influence of a risk-acceptant leader seeking a nationalistic objective rather than a concerted strategic effort to balance Chinese power.[98]

Where the scope and domain of the rise of Chinese power is less consistent, secondary state alignment patterns are very different. This is the case in the rest of East Asia, where the United States has retained its military dominance and the rise of Chinese power is limited to relative gains in economic capabilities. In this region, the secondary states, despite their growing and in some cases significant dependence on the Chinese economy, are balancing Chinese power by strengthening security cooperation with the United States. This trend is clear not only in Japan, but also in Singapore and the Philippines. The trend is less pronounced but nonetheless evident in Malaysian and Indonesian defense policies.

Alignment patterns in East Asia indicate that economic dependence is insufficient to alter strategic alignments and compel accommodation by secondary states. Moreover, as suggested by the dominant approach in the realist balance of power literature, including the works of Waltz, Morgenthau, and other traditional realists, the East Asian response to the rise of China indicates that secondary states accommodate rather than balance improved relative military capabilities of rising great powers, in contrast to the expected balancing behavior of the great powers. In the presence of shifting capabilities of the great powers in the immediate vicinity, accommodation is not only the policy of the very weakest states in international politics but is the policy of all but the handful of the most powerful states—the great powers.

The East Asian response to the rise of China further establishes that realism and traditional balance of power theory are as appropriate for understanding alignment policies in East Asia as in any other region of international politics, including Europe. Predictions of general East Asian accommodation of the rise of China, contrary to realist expectations, were premised on assumptions of pan-Asian cultural predispositions that are not supported by empirical research. Even within the "Confucian world" there is considerable variation, as South Korea and Taiwan are accommodating Chinese power and Japan and Singapore have consolidated security cooperation with the United States. More generally, the pattern of accommodation and balancing strategies in East Asia suggests that secondary state alignment choices are not the result of particular historical experiences or of shared cultural traits, but reflect cross-cultural and timeless determinants of foreign policy choices.

Equally important, variation in East Asian alignment policies in response to the rise of China reveals that predictions of regionwide accommodation to Chinese power are as misleading as theoretical propositions of uniform tendencies of secondary states toward balancing or accommodation. Even in the absence of costly U.S. balancing efforts and intensified U.S.-China strategic competition, East Asia is experiencing not Chinese hegemony but the consolidation of bipolarity, as some secondary states increasingly align with China, and others remain aligned with the United States.

The United States' role in East Asia will increasingly coincide with Secretary of State Dean Acheson's 1950 definition of the U.S. "defense perimeter" in East Asia, which excluded mainland East Asia. By 1950 the United States had withdrawn its forces from Korea, reflecting its understanding that the peninsula was not a strategic priority. And in 1949 the National Security Council, based on the findings of the Joint Chiefs of Staff, concluded that Taiwan was not a vital U.S. security interest. Acheson later observed to members of Congress that even should the mainland occupy Taiwan, it would only add forty miles to Chinese power projection toward Guam.[99] Credibility to resist communist armed expansion, not material interests, drove American intervention in the Korea conflict and the Chinese civil war. Since then, U.S. policy has sought peaceful resolution of these conflicts, reflecting its interest in the process of change rather than the outcome. Well into the twenty-first century China will lack the advanced technologies and the funds to develop the power projection capability necessary to challenge U.S. military dominance in maritime East Asia.[100] If the United States remains committed to maintaining its forward presence in East Asia, it can be assured of maritime supremacy, the ability to manage the rise of China at acceptable costs, and a stable East Asian balance of power.

7 CHINESE ECONOMIC STATECRAFT AND THE POLITICAL ECONOMY OF ASIAN SECURITY

Adam Segal

China's rise is expected to reshape Asian security in at least two ways. First, economic growth will fund the development of national military power. China's rising prosperity makes it possible for the government to devote more resources to all of its domestic programs, including spending on military modernization, which rose throughout the 1990s. Moreover, trade, investment, and technology provided by the United States, Japan, and Europe could make China militarily more powerful than it would otherwise be. Foreign investment—total utilized investment totaled US$61 billion in 2004[1]—and a positive trade balance allow China to accumulate significant foreign reserves (over US$700 billion as of 2004), some of which have been used to purchase advanced weapon systems from Russia, Israel, and other foreign suppliers. Senator Paul Sarbanes may have summed up the argument best: "It is difficult to escape the conclusion that the large bilateral trade surplus that China runs with the United States is used, at least in part, to bolster and support the Chinese military establishment."[2]

Second, China is expected to use its new diplomatic and economic power to influence the regional security order. As the Chinese economy continues to develop, the countries of the region are becoming increasingly dependent on China for trade and investment. Growing trade ties have expanded Beijing's political and diplomatic influence.[3] Although Washington still plays a large role in the region, changing trade patterns might in the future marginalize the United States as an economic and political partner. Without a strong Japan to act as a counterweight, the countries of Southeast Asia might become more dependent on trade ties to China and thus more sensitive to PRC preferences. Similarly, in Northeast Asia, Korea might distance itself from the United States. Even Japan may decide that it is unwilling or unable to balance against China's rising power. A political shift toward Beijing could deprive the United States of the regional allies and access to bases required to pursue American security objectives.

Much of the literature on the political economy of Asian security has focused on China's economic growth, regionalism, and economic interdependence, and how these trends either increase or dampen the possibility of military conflict.[4] While these developments define the environment in which the regional actors interact, the focus of this chapter is China's attempts to coordinate the building of national military power with the use of influence through economic statecraft—the employment of economics as an instrument of power.[5]

For Beijing, there is currently an overlap between security and economic concerns. In most assumptions of realist political economy, states are willing to sacrifice economic gains in order to ensure security.[6] Power wins out over plenty. By contrast, liberal institutional approaches suggest that the pursuit of economic objectives (and participation in multilateral institutions) may eventually moderate or modify a state's security objectives. The increased interaction that accompanies trade and foreign direct investment encourages communication, fosters cooperation, and promotes a collective sense of security.

In addition, since conflict risks jeopardizing very real gains from trade, public officials and private businesses dependent on trade have a strong interest in maintaining stable relations. In the case of China, Paul P. Papayoanou and Scott Kastner argue that engagement "empowers more cooperative economic internationalists in China."[7]

Beijing at present does not have to choose between strategic and economic objectives, and so can pursue both power and plenty. China's security concerns are addressed by closer economic relations with its neighbors. Conversely, the pursuit of economic goals does not mean that Beijing has abandoned or modified its security objectives, or that it is necessarily any less likely to employ military or other coercive measures to achieve core strategic goals, especially in the case of a potential Taiwan conflict. Focused on domestic issues—economic growth, regime stability, and leadership succession—the Chinese government's primary foreign policy goal is creating the stable international environment necessary to address these challenges at home. For China, the central objective is fostering a peaceful international environment that lacks a balancing coalition. Beijing's promotion of regional multilateral institutions, its offer to enter into free trade agreements with ASEAN, and its promotion of direct investment in regional economies all have both a strategic and an economic logic. They foster economic development while lowering suspicion in neighboring countries about China's growing power, making it more difficult for the United States and its allies to contain Beijing.

This overlap between economic and security objectives—what some observers call "enlightened self-interest"—raises two interrelated questions. Will Beijing have the necessary institutional, political, and economic capacity to maintain the unity between "high" and "low" politics, between security and foreign economic policy? In the next five to fifteen years, it will not be easy to maintain a coherent economic and security strategy. A unified vision must be maintained within the leadership core, and the central leadership must have the ability to insulate the policy from economic and political disruptions, as well as compensate losers within the domestic economy.

Even if Beijing has the ability, will it have the desire to continue to coordinate economic and political objectives? Once Beijing attains what it sees as an adequate level of power and stability, could it simply decide that there are goals that could best be achieved through swift military action? Simple self-interest would replace "enlightened" self-interest. Or are there political crises that could abruptly end Beijing's reliance on diplomacy, influence, and other instruments of soft power? Beijing has made it clear that it will sacrifice immediate economic gains if core security interests are threatened, at either a domestic or regional level and especially in the case of Taiwan. There may also be resistance from China's neighbors—they may be unwilling to accept assurances from China that economic ties do in fact ensure Beijing's peaceful intentions. Although China is now Japan's largest trade partner and Japanese investment in China is at record levels, China and Japan have recently clashed over control of the Senkaku/Diaoyu Islands, the portrayal of history in textbooks, the incursion of a Chinese submarine into Japanese waters, continued visits to Yasukuni Shrine, new National Defense Program Guidelines highlighting China's military modernization, and a joint U.S.-Japan declaration on Taiwan. Despite close economic ties, Korea and China recently clashed over the historical lineage of the Goguryeo dynasty.

Coercion and Influence

Much policy analysis of China's potential economic statecraft draws heavily on Albert Hirschman's discussion of foreign trade as an instrument of national power.[8] In *National Power and the Structure of Foreign Trade*, Hirschman uses Nazi Germany's trade relations to illustrate how asymmetric trade relations create political gains for the larger state. Since trade makes up a smaller percentage of the larger nation's total trade and may make up to 50 percent of the smaller state's total, threats of interruption affect smaller states disproportionately. Implicit or explicit threats to break commercial relations thus give the larger state coercive power. In Hirschman's view, the ability to threaten to interrupt trade with another state is "an effective weapon in the struggle for power."[9]

In addition to coercive power, as Rawi Abdelal and Jonathan Kirshner note, Hirschman also describes an influence effect.[10] Commerce affects the domestic politics in the smaller state, shaping politics and definitions of national interest. Firms and sectors form political coalitions, create vested interests in target states, and reshape governmental policies in different ways than if they had been affected by domestic pressures alone.[11] This happens in all economic relations but is especially true in asymmetric relations where the effects are visible and almost wholly found in the smaller country in the trade relationship.

Mainland China's economic policy toward Taiwan best exemplifies the political relationships—and the uses of coercion and influence—that Hirschman describes. China displaced the United States as Taiwan's largest export market in 2001; in 2004, 37 percent of Taiwan's total exports were to mainland China, Macao, and Hong Kong. Taiwan sent 25 percent of its total exports to China in 2001, and accepted 7.3 percent of its total imports from China. In 2004 exports to China had increased to 36 percent, while imports from China increased to 11 percent. China plays a similarly large role in shares of Taiwan's outward foreign direct investment. In 2003 Taiwan invested US$5.68 billion abroad, US$3.38 billion of that in China, making China the recipient of 59.5 percent of Taiwan's total FDI. In 2003 cumulative Taiwanese investment in China totaled more than US$24.72 billion.[12]

From the beginning of economic contact between the two sides, Chinese policy makers have had a clear view of the political objectives of cross-strait trade. As an internal 1990 Chinese document explained, expanding trade with Taiwan would break through the "three no's" policy, contain separatist trends, and help "interest groups involved closely with the mainland emerge in Taiwan's politics in the future and facilitate peaceful unification."[13] Chinese president Yang Shangkun noted at a December 1990 National Conference on Taiwan Work that the "emphasis should be placed on economic and other exchanges in order to use business to press politics [*yi shang wei zheng*] and use the public to pressure the official [*yi min bi guan*]."[14]

Taiwanese politicians have been equally clear about how they perceive the politics of economic integration. Under former president Lee Teng-hui, the Taiwanese government refused to negotiate the opening of the "three links" (trade, transport, and communication between China and Taiwan) and limited exchange through a conservative policy of investment, "no haste, be patient" (*jieji yongren*). The Chen Shui-bian administration replaced "no haste" with "active opening, effective management" (*jiji kaifang, youxiao guanli*) and opened direct contacts between Taiwan's Jinmen (Kinmen) and Mazu (Matzu) islands and the mainland (the "three mini links"), but has placed a ceiling on Taiwanese investments on the mainland, proposed a "national technology protection law" to regulate the flow of high-tech products, and attempted to lure Taiwanese- and foreign-invested firms back to Taiwan by offering preferential tax exemptions and other incentives.[15] Taiwan has tried to reduce its dependence on China by promoting investment in Southeast Asia and by calling for the creation of free trade agreements with the United States and Japan.[16] Speaking to a group of Taiwanese businessmen in July 2002, President Chen Shui-bian warned that Taiwan should not become too reliant on the Chinese market: "It's good to create fortunes overseas, however, Taiwan's national security should be considered a priority and the public interest must be put first. We should not have any illusions about seeking peace by stooping to compromise with China. If our country is not secure, making more money does not mean anything."[17]

From the beginning of renewed trade, China has attempted to use the Taiwanese business community to influence policy, especially to push for the three links. Members of the Kuomintang (KMT), People First Party, and Chamber of Taiwan Businessmen in China have been invited to meet with central leaders in Beijing to facilitate political and business exchanges across the strait. Faced with the Chen administration's refusal to negotiate over the three links, Chen Yunlin, director of the Taiwan Affairs Office, proposed in 2002 that Taiwan send business leaders, preferably tycoon Wang Yung-ching and food baron Kao Chin-yen, to negotiate the issue of direct transport, postal, and trade links. The head of Taiwan's Mainland Affairs Council Tsai Ing-wen responded that China cannot "appoint people on our behalf," but it is clear that flexibility by China plays into the hands of Taiwanese business.[18] In April 2005 China hosted a visit by KMT Party Chairman Lien Chan, followed in May by People First Party Chairman James Soong.

China has also tried to drive a wedge between the business community and Chen Shui-bian. Several papers in Hong Kong sympathetic to the mainland ran editorials in 2002 that emphasized how Chen Shui-bian's agenda is to "cheat Taiwan businessmen." One noted that Chen Shui-bian's refusal to establish direct links is "making the business circles . . . in Taiwan feel greatly indignant."[19]

Always lurking behind the attempts at influence was the threat of economic coercion, although it played a largely supporting role in Beijing's overall strategy from the 1980s to the mid-1990s. During the 1995–96 Taiwan Strait crisis China sent its message through military exercises and public pronouncements harshly criticizing Lee Teng-hui and other "separatist" influences, not through economic policy. Political coercion, however, had severe economic costs. For example, during the second half of 1995, the Taipei stock market dropped 20 percent, and the New Taiwan dollar depreciated 10 percent. Taiwan's Central Economic Research Institute estimated that the 1995 tensions cost Taipei NT$23.7 billion to stabilize foreign exchange markets and restore public confidence.[20] The political efficacy of the measures was mixed. On one hand, the threats imposed huge costs on Beijing's friends in the business community. On the other, it successfully demonstrated to Taiwan's populace the fragility of the economy and the need for good relations across the strait.

In the run-up to the 1999 Taiwanese elections and in their immediate aftermath, targeted, directed economic coercion played a larger role in Beijing's strategy. A message was sent to specific businesses with strong political ties to Chen Shui-bian, to the Democratic Progressive Party (DPP), or to others seen to "favor independence." On 16 March, two days before the presidential elections, the vice chairman of the Association for Relations across the Taiwan Straits Tang Shubei stated that if the "forces of Taiwanese independence won," economic relations between the two sides would be seriously impaired. As a result, the stock market fell 4.5 percent, and the Taiwanese government injected NT$1.5 billion. By mid-March the Taiwanese government was estimated to have spent NT$3.4 billion to shore up the Taipei index.[21]

Economic pressure continued after the election. Li Bingcai, deputy director of China's Taiwan Affairs Office of the State Council and Taiwan Work Office of the Central Committee of the Chinese Communist Party, stated that Taiwan's industrial and commercial leaders would not be allowed to advocate the "Lee Teng-hui line" while engaging in business and economic operations in China.[22] Beijing warned that individual Taiwanese companies could be barred from business if they promoted independence.

After Chen Shui-bian assumed Taiwan's presidency, his ties with Acer Co. president Stan Shih may have exposed Acer to harassment on the mainland. Acer products apparently disappeared from the shelves of many stores and the company was more or less forced to introduce a new brand name to sell its products. During the dispute, Shih made a trip to Beijing to restate his support for reunification.[23]

Taiwanese businesses with strong links to either the DPP or Chen Shui-bian faced similar concerns in 2001. For example, state-owned enterprises (SOEs) were ordered not to do business with the petroleum conglomerate Chi Mei Group, whose operations on the mainland faced constant scrutiny from zealous tax inspectors.[24] In response to a question about Hsu Wen-lung, chairman of Chi Mei and the first leading businessmen to support Chen Shui-bian's presidential campaign, the head of the Ministry of Foreign Economic Relations, Shi Guangsheng, declared "We will not allow Taiwanese businessmen to make political capital at home by supporting independence and make economic profits in the mainland."[25]

The pattern of coercion suggests a limited sanction policy directed at those with close ties to Chen and the DPP and those who have actively engaged in political support for independence. In fact, Chinese leaders tried to reassure the majority of Taiwanese businesses that they would not be affected. In December 2002, for example, Vice Premier Qian Qichen traveled around Guangdong inspecting Taiwan-invested enterprises and holding meetings with Taiwan businesspeople to discuss cross-strait trade. In his conversations, Qian stated that "In the last decade, exchange across the strait, especially economic exchange, has seen very great progress. Under any circumstances, the mainland's policy of welcoming Taiwan compatriots to carry out economic activities on the mainland will not change, and so Taiwan compatriots can feel completely assured."[26]

Trade and Power

Trade and investment are essential elements of power politics, strengthening ties among countries that have similar defense and military orientations. Because trade creates security externalities—trade releases economic resources for potential military use—adherence to a policy of free trade may not make the most sense in an anarchic system. Rather, trade should be used to bind potential allies closer together, and free trade is more likely to emerge across political-military alliances.[27]

China is not creating an alliance system in Asia, but Beijing does use commercial relations to bolster the position of its friends. During the Vietnamese invasion of Cambodia, China provided guns, tanks, armored personnel carriers, and antiaircraft guns to Thailand at "friendship" prices. In the 1980s, China and Thailand signed a Strategic Partnership arrangement, which has included a regular exchange of military personnel and exercises. Today, Cambodia and Myanmar both receive economic and military assistance from Beijing. In 1999 Cambodia obtained US$18.3 million in foreign assistance guarantees and US$200 million in no-interest loans for infrastructure projects. China has supplied substantial official development assistance to Myanmar, with much of it going to improve the road system in the upper reaches of the country and to support the building of a navigable waterway down the Irrawaddy River, projects which could have commercial and possibly military applications. In addition, Beijing is the major supplier of arms to the Myanmar regime—some estimates of the value of the supplies exceed US$2 billion.

For the majority of the countries in East Asia, China's increasing economic and political standing in the region creates a new type of influence—the need to consult with Beijing before making major decisions. U.S. naval officials report that requests to increase port calls to Vietnam from one to two a year are met with the response: "we must first gauge reaction in China." In Malaysia, according to political analyst Abdul Razak Baginda, "there is now this feeling that we have to consult the Chinese. We have to accept some degree of Chinese leadership, particularly in light of the lack of leadership elsewhere."[28]

In addition, China may use trade policy to indicate intentions, signal commitments, or project overall foreign policy orientations.[29] Besides the economic benefits that may accrue from any future cooperation, China's recent push for a free trade agreement with ASEAN sends a number of important messages: China is now a status quo power in Asia, more engaged in multilateral diplomacy, supportive of free trade, and committed to the development of the region. Avery Goldstein argues that the decision not to devalue the yuan during the Asian financial crisis in 1997 reflected in part Beijing's desire to substitute the image of a responsible power for its reputation as an "irredentist, revisionist, rising power" that it acquired in 1995–96.[30]

Furthermore, as Ellen Frost argues in this volume, "Intra-Asian FTAs [free trade agreements] in particular have assumed a role akin to that of security alliances, serving as an expression of political and security ties as well as a harbinger of trade and investment. FTAs do not affect the military balance of power, but they alter and redefine the balance of influence, perceptions of security, and new political alignments." Frost notes that trade negotiations and FTAs in particular open new avenues for influence throughout the region.

How Successful Can Economic Statecraft Be?

Despite Beijing's widespread efforts to cultivate political sway through economic relations, converting trade and investment into influence is not a simple linear process. Beijing's attempts to build regional influence appear to depend on the size and level of development in its own market, the nature of the interests (regional, subregional, global) at stake, and the degree of threat the smaller economies perceive in China's rise.[31]

In the case of trade, a large, developing economy may be less able to exert influence in the region than a large developed nation (such as Japan or the United States). Pursuing political objectives at the cost of shorter-term economic goals requires a fairly stable and mature economy as well as the ability to balance the demands of competing domestic interests. Serious economic dislocation would put pressure on Beijing to adjust trade or investment patterns, undermining the political coherence of economic and security policies. Faced with rising unemployment and social instability, Beijing may be less willing to run trade deficits with and open domestic markets to its neighbors. Even in the absence of a serious downturn, the center would have to be able to compensate the industrial sectors or geographical regions that lost as a result of trade concessions made in pursuit of political goals.

Beijing will also have to convince its trading partners that it can follow through and implement its trade commitments. Without political transparency and accountability, China's proposals on trade risk becoming good public relations with little substance.[32] The highly touted China-ASEAN free trade pact signed in November 2004 is an example. Close observers note that the more than one hundred exceptions in the agreement, which would eliminate tariffs between China and the members of ASEAN by 2015, render it far less substantial than has been advertised.

There may also be a mismatch between what the Chinese economy can offer and what other developing economies need. The Chinese and Southeast Asian economies may be competitive rather than complementary. The rather widespread belief that the FDI available to the region has been largely diverted to China is not supported by the data, according to John Ravenhill's chapter in this volume. Ravenhill argues that diversion of FDI to China is almost certainly overstated, and fails "to take into account the substantial 'round-tripping' of mainland funds in China's FDI inflows, and peculiarities in China's reporting of inward FDI." On the trade side, however, while Beijing portrays itself as a new export market, Chinese goods could flood global export markets at the expense of the region's smaller or less developed members (and to some degree, they already do). Ravenhill's chapter, for example, shows ASEAN producers losing market shares and value in office machinery, footwear, apparel, and electrical machinery.

Strong economic ties may also coexist with strained political relations, diminishing Beijing's ability to influence domestic politics in the target state. Here my analytical framework differs from that applied by Robert Ross in his chapter in this volume. For Ross, the response of states along China's periphery is essentially explained by the balance of power and geography. Over the last decade, China has greatly improved its ability to project power across land borders against smaller countries. As a result, Thailand, Vietnam, and Korea have essentially accepted the conclusion that they will not be able to balance against China and have so realigned their politics toward Beijing. States that can rely on the ocean to provide defense in depth have more leeway, since PLA power projection capabilities remain limited, especially over the sea. Although the Taiwan Strait separates China from Taiwan, 700 short-range missiles and a growing fleet of destroyers and attack submarines make Taiwan's future more like that of Korea and other countries that share land borders with China than like maritime Southeast Asia.

Domestic politics and national identity play a larger role than geography in explaining the response of nations of China's periphery to China's rise. Geography is a constant and defining condition, but it is important to remember that exerting influence is a political process that requires domestic mediators. Beijing's influence is in the end expressed through military threat and domestic politics in the target states. These politics help define the threat and are contingent; they can be remade by shifting alliances within the target state. In the case of China's bilateral relations, political battles over national identity and history can have a large impact on the perception of threat.

In 2004 China replaced the United States as Japan's top trade partner, with total trade of US$167.9 billion. Japanese investment in China totaled almost US$5.5 billion. But even as the two economies grow increasingly interdependent, analysts characterize the current bifurcation of Sino-Japanese relations as "cold politics; hot economics."[33] In the recent past, Tokyo and Beijing have clashed over the exploration of natural gas in the East China Sea; the presence of a Chinese submarine off Okinawa; Japanese politicians' visits to Yasukuni Shrine; the granting of a visa to Lee Teng-hui; the new National Defense Program Guideline, which specifically refers to a threat from China; and a joint U.S.-Japan declaration identifying stability in the Taiwan Strait as a common strategic objective.

The trick for Beijing (and in some part Tokyo) is to balance nationalist public sentiment—feelings that are often nurtured by government propaganda—with the need to maintain stable economic relations. In the past, Erica Strecker Downs and Phillip Saunders argue, China's "government proved willing to incur significant damage to its nationalist credentials by following restrained policies and cooperating with the Japanese government to prevent the territorial disputes from harming bilateral relations."[34] Chinese leaders were relatively successful in preventing anti-Japanese nationalism from influencing foreign policy decisions in the 1980s and 1990s. The April 2005 protests against Japanese textbooks as well as subsequent attacks on the Japanese embassy and commercial entities in Beijing, Shanghai, Chengdu, Shenzhen, and Chongqing certainly suggest that technological and generational change may be weakening the ability, or willingness, of Chinese leaders to insulate these decisions from public opinion As a result of the protests, the percentage of Japan's population holding positive views of China has decreased dramatically, as has the influence of the "China school" in the foreign ministry. Japan's pursuit of "normal nation" status, a goal that seems to be held across party lines, is likely to promote continued friction.[35]

Although nowhere close to reaching the level of vitriol that exists in Sino-Japanese relations, Sino-Korean relations have also deteriorated. Since normalization of relations between Seoul and Beijing in 1992, commercial relations exploded, and China surpassed the United States to become South Korea's number one trade partner and investment destination in 2003. For much of the 1990s, Korea was swept by "China fever"; Chinatowns emerged in cities throughout South Korea, language schools reported surging demand for Chinese lessons, and South Korean students came to dominate classrooms in Chinese language programs at the top Chinese universities. Many analysts were surprised when former president Kim Dae Jung referred to the "special relationship" between South Korea and China, an expression usually reserved for Seoul's ties with Washington.[36] While differences between the United States and South Korea over the handling of the North Korean nuclear program are helping push Seoul closer to Beijing, Korea's desire to benefit from the opening of the Chinese markets is also playing a role.

Even though there is optimism about export opportunities to China, Korean producers are increasingly worried about competition from low-cost

Chinese manufacturers and the hollowing out of Korean industry. If the rate of growth in bilateral trade slows, it will become more difficult to ignore potential trade conflict. Scott Snyder argues that with the loss of momentum in the economic relationship, "there will also be less excuse to gloss over political disputes between South Korea and China over refugees, historical issues, or other disagreements in the relationship."[37] China's claim in 2004 to the ancient Goguryeo Kingdom appears to have cooled some of the fervor that gripped South Korea, injecting a greater degree of suspicion into South Korean thinking about China's motives and methods.

The degree of threat perceived by the smaller actor plays a large, and perhaps defining, role in determining Beijing's success in actually converting asymmetric trade relations into political influence. The Chinese have been unable to convert economic dependence into political influence in Taiwan. Increased trade clearly created interest groups in Taiwan who pushed for even greater economic integration. From the first businesspeople who funneled money illegally through Hong Kong to invest on the mainland to the industrial leaders claiming to be too restricted by the "Go Slow, Be Patient" policy, Taiwanese businesses have continually pushed the pace of economic integration. For example, in a 1998 survey, 70 percent of Taiwanese businesses had investments in China, and 50 percent hoped for greater relaxation of restrictions on investments.[38] Industries with direct interest in trade such as shipping lines and computer manufacturers have taken the lead in the campaign for cross-strait shipping ties. Taiwan Semiconductor chairman Morris Chang, for example, protested against the Taiwanese government's "blatant interference" in investments on the mainland.

Yet, for the most part, these organized interests have pushed for greater economic, not political, integration. There have been some limited cases of calls for political concessions, but these remain at the margins.[39] In the end, it appears that economic integration has polarized Taiwanese domestic politics, creating one pole around Lee Teng-hui and Chen Shui-bian, and another around the business community. Chen Ming-chi argues that economic losers in cross-strait integration tend to be concentrated in central and southern Taiwan and that these groups tend to identify with the DPP.[40] In addition, the more dependent the economy has become on the mainland and the greater the perceived vulnerability of Taiwan to China, the greater the political pressure on Chen to expand and tighten ties with the United States and to continue to promote the development of a separate Taiwanese national identity.

The larger problem is that the goal Beijing is trying to achieve through influence—essentially to convince the Taiwanese to give up de facto sovereignty—appears incompatible with the use of threat. Since the mid-1990s, one of the central goals of military modernization has been to pose a credible threat to Taiwan in order to influence Taiwan's choices about its political future; or, failing that, to prevent Taiwan from achieving political independence.[41] The most visible sign of this coercive ability has been the deployment of over 700 short-range missiles opposite Taiwan. In addition, China's arsenal includes major weapon systems purchases from Russia like the Kilo class submarine, Sovremenny class destroyer, and Su-27 and Su-30 aircraft as well as the comprehensive transformation of PLA tactics, doctrine, and training. Beijing has also adopted an increasingly inflexible position toward Taiwan, defining sovereignty narrowly and rejecting any diplomatic space for Taiwan in international institutions like the World Health Organization. In this political context, the objects of influence—the business associations and the Pan-Blue Coalition (the coalition among the KMT, People First Party, and the New Party—more willing to accept the status quo across the strait)—have little political room to maneuver. Beijing's threats delegitimize accommodation with Beijing; concrete suggestions about working with the mainland present an appearance of selling Taiwan out.

How Long Will Beijing's Interest in Economic Statecraft Last?

Beijing's commitment to economic statecraft and to the uses of influence in particular will continue only as long as the policy is seen to be effective. China could quickly shift its emphasis to coercion if Taiwan crosses one of Beijing's "red lines" in a move toward formal independence. Under such circumstances, the high economic costs of military conflict—in the disruption of trade and investment as well as possible sanctions from the United States, Japan, and the European Union—might not persuade China's leaders to maintain the current emphasis on international cooperation. Chinese scholars note that Beijing came to Pyongyang's assistance during the Korean War, though this meant facing a much more technologically advanced enemy while it was still engaging in economic reconstruction after the end of World War II and the civil war. "If China could make such huge national sacrifice at the cost of national construction to aid another country, then it will definitely go to war to achieve territorial integrity and national reunification."[42]

The balance between influence and coercion is already a source of debate in Beijing. Some analysts have argued that the focus on economic integration may have in part convinced Taiwanese politicians to pursue separatist policies more aggressively. Taiwan has moved closer to independence "not because the response was too strong but rather because the response was insufficiently strong."[43] The focus on peaceful reunification and economic integration reduced the credibility of Chinese deterrence. To prevent further erosion of China's current position, Beijing must make Taiwan, and the United States, recognize that it is "willing to pay any price" to contain Taiwanese independence.

The pursuit of influence and attempts to reassure neighbors is also based in a particular view of Sino-U.S. relations. In the late 1990s Chinese foreign policy analysts and policy makers began to believe that U.S. preponderance was likely to continue at least for the next several decades. Belligerence toward the United States, and toward the region as a whole, was counterproductive.[44] At the Sixteenth Party Congress in November 2002 Jiang Zemin described the first twenty years of the twenty-first century as a "period of important strategic opportunity," a period during which Beijing could cooperate with other powers. Hu Jintao and Wen Jiabao have continued this policy line, working to establish long-term stable relations with the United States that will be conducive to China's modernization drive.

A breakdown in this consensus view of the world—caused by an increased sense of threat or internal struggle among different policy factions—could shift the balance between economics and security. A greater sense of encirclement by the United States might prompt greater defense spending and/or an effort to formalize alliance relationships. Chinese efforts to balance the United States might provoke counterbalancing from ASEAN, to the detriment of economic cooperation with China.

Can the United States Accommodate China?

While the increasing confidence of Chinese diplomacy in the region has often been cast as a zero-sum competition with the United States, the end results may be less disruptive and adversarial than predicted, for at least two reasons.[45] First, the other states of the region are not passive players, but are also involved in shaping and reacting to China's rise. Much depends on how we perceive the behavior of the states on China's periphery, and if we see them as balancing, bandwagoning, or hedging against the rise of China. For example, Amitav Acharya describes the states of ASEAN as unwilling to rely on either Beijing or Washington for their security and therefore engaged in "double binding"—efforts to enmesh China and the United State in regional institutions.[46] These institutions have so far proven surprisingly flexible and durable in supporting regional stability. There has been a tendency to see rising economic cooperation as a sign of bandwagoning. But the smaller states of Southeast Asia may be engaged in a strategy that mirrors Beijing's own efforts to reassure the region, using economic ties to reduce threat perception while improving defense coordination with the United States. As Lyall Breckon argues, "U.S. trade and security involvement in Southeast Asia, and improved U.S.-China relations overall, may be necessary conditions for the climate of confidence in which China has achieved its striking gains in Southeast Asia."[47]

Furthermore, in many respects, China's current use of economic statecraft overlaps with many U.S. security concerns in the region. As Frost notes in her chapter: "Beijing's new commercial-diplomatic 'embedded-ness' bodes well for regional peace and prosperity and is broadly consistent with U.S. interests—provided, and it is a crucial proviso, that the United States stays engaged in the region." For example, Chinese plans for market-oriented regional integration complement rather than oppose U.S. interests.[48] As Iain Johnston has noted, the evidence supporting Beijing's drive for regional hegemony is not clear-cut.[49] China's increasing military weight in the region could constrain American security capabilities. Even before the war in Iraq and the nuclear standoff with North Korea, U.S. military planners were thinking about how to use a greater maritime emphasis and long-distance strike capabilities to compensate for fewer U.S. bases and lack of infrastructure in the region.[50] But there is little evidence that China is actively using economic ties to try and separate the United States from its regional allies. In fact there is mixed evidence that China continues to see the U.S.–South Korea and U.S.–Japan alliance as the basis of regional stability.

As chapters 1 and 9 note, the overlap of Chinese and American interests is not a given and in large part depends on the attitudes, behaviors, and responses to the rise of China by North and Southeast Asia, the United States, and the Chinese themselves. The United States must in particular hedge against two future possibilities. First, the primary focus on international stability and internal development may not prevent the use of coercion, despite the best intentions of China's current leaders. As Thomas Christensen notes, even if the pursuit of economic growth is Beijing's main policy goal, unease "about domestic stability and national integrity, and the need for military might and nationalistic posturing, often make the straightforward pursuit of national wealth an impossibility for the CCP."[51] A legitimacy crisis, provoked by either domestic disturbance or external threats to territorial integrity and national sovereignty, could derail the mainly status quo orientation of Beijing's current foreign policy.

Moreover, cooperative behavior from Beijing now may not ensure responsible action in the future. Economic development may generate domestic expectations about continued growth and empower social forces in China that inhibit the flexibility of Beijing (much as U.S. business interests influence Washington). But it is also possible that Beijing has chosen to rely on influence because it does not yet have the ability to follow through on coercive threats. Without the ability to project power and sustain a military presence in maritime East Asia, military threats would be more than counterproductive. They would expose Beijing's weakness.

Given the uncertainty about Chinese intentions (and the inability to block Beijing's rising influence), this chapter reinforces the point made in this volume by Keller and Rawski, Frost, and others: to maintain at the least the possibility of China's peaceful rise, the United States must actively reengage with Asia. China has benefited from the perception that it is now the status quo power in Asia—in contrast to what Breckon describes as a regional perception of the United States as "unilateralist, given to preemptive military action, and insistent in pushing an agenda that ignored Southeast Asian interests in favor of counterterrorism and non-proliferation."[52] The United States must renew its interest in developing multilateral trade agreements and institutions in the region, while at the same time strengthening bilateral cooperation with Japan and India. The key for Washington is to realize that both the bilateral and multilateral paths must be pursued in order to counter Beijing's rapidly deepening multilateral engagement with Asia.[53] In effect, a policy that responds to the rise of China should pay as much attention to the larger Asian framework as it does to China.

★8 CHINA'S "PEACEFUL DEVELOPMENT" AND SOUTHEAST ASIA

A Positive Sum Game?

John Ravenhill

THE ECONOMIC GROWTH UNDERPINNING China's peaceful development has caused as much alarm among its Southeast Asian neighbors as has the growth of its military prowess. Politicians and academics alike in Southeast Asia have expressed concern that the sustained expansion of the Chinese economy will have a negative impact on ASEAN's economic prospects through diverting investment and displacing Southeast Asian goods in foreign markets. Typical of such sentiments were the views of (then) Singaporean deputy prime minister Lee Hsien Loong, who commented in November 2002 that "Southeast Asian countries are under intense competitive pressure, as their former activities, especially labor-intensive manufacturing, migrate to China. One indicator of this massive shift is the fact that Southeast Asia used to attract twice as much foreign direct investment as Northeast Asia, but the ratio is [now] reversed."[1]

Such populist expressions of potentially zero-sum competition between China and ASEAN states for markets and for foreign investment, reminiscent of Ross Perot's predictions on the impact of NAFTA on the U.S. economy, would not normally be expected to find resonance in the views of mainstream economics. A series of studies by the World Bank in the years leading up to China's accession to the WTO concluded, however, that the lower-income ASEAN economies were the ones most likely to be adversely affected by

China's WTO membership, particularly after the country quotas associated with the Multi-fibre Arrangement were removed at the end of 2004. Several other studies using a variety of methodologies reached similar conclusions about the potentially negative impact of China's export-oriented growth on ASEAN.[2]

What has been the actual impact on Southeast Asian economies of China's sustained economic growth? Has the surge of foreign direct investment (FDI) into China come at the expense of ASEAN? Has the improved access to foreign markets that Chinese exports have enjoyed since the country's WTO accession amplified the trend toward displacement of Southeast Asian goods? None of the studies listed in the previous endnote had data available to them for the period after China joined the WTO: their conclusions rested instead on projections drawn from computer modeling. Data on investment and trade have now been published for the four years following China's accession to the WTO; these enable us to observe for the first time the impact that China's WTO membership has had on ASEAN. In this chapter, we use these data to explore trends in FDI and the impact of China's growth on ASEAN's exports.

Foreign Direct Investment

A dramatic increase in China's receipts of foreign direct investment has seen it emerge as the largest single recipient of FDI in the global economy. The rapid growth in China's FDI receipts in the last years of the twentieth century occurred at a time when many Southeast Asian countries were experiencing a downturn in investment inflows. China now receives a substantial majority of the foreign investment that is recorded as flowing into East Asia as a whole, a fact that some commentators perceive as evidence that China is capturing a disproportionate share of such flows. The contrast in performance between ASEAN and China led some observers to assert that the growth of inflows into China came at the expense of Southeast Asian states. For John Wong and Sarah Chan, the experience suggested that "much of regional FDI [has been] diverted from ASEAN in favor of China."[3]

While the fears that underlie such statements are entirely understandable, they reflect a number of logical fallacies. These include mistaking correlation for causation, a misrepresentation of foreign direct investment as constituting a fixed sum and a consequent fallacy that competition for foreign direct investment is inevitably a zero-sum game, and implicit unwarranted assumptions about what an appropriate level of FDI for China might be.

Alarm that China's receipts of FDI have come at the expense of ASEAN is often based on a cursory review of data on FDI flows, particularly those in the five years following the East Asian financial crises of 1997–98. Figure 8.1 shows the source of the concern: even though China was already receiving substantially larger inflows of FDI than ASEAN economies on average in the years 1992–97, the trends diverged spectacularly after 1999.[4] Whereas in 2002 China's FDI inflows increased to over US$50 billion per year, FDI inflows into ASEAN fell substantially (by 2002 they were half the level of 1999). When viewed in terms of shares in all inflows to China, Hong Kong, and ASEAN combined, the apparent diversion to China is even more graphic: whereas ASEAN gained an average of 40 percent of all inflows to the region in the years 1992–97, its share of FDI inflows from 2000 onward was nearly halved to slightly over 20 percent (figure 8.2).

Even if one accepts that these data suggest a strong negative correlation between FDI flows to ASEAN and those to China (and as we will see, this is a questionable conclusion to draw, given various complications with the figures), correlation does not necessarily equate with causation. The reasons for Southeast Asia's relatively poor aggregate performance as a recipient of FDI around the turn of the new millennium have much to do with the aftermath of the financial crises in the region and subsequent political instability. Of particular note here is the failure of the Indonesian economy to make a rapid

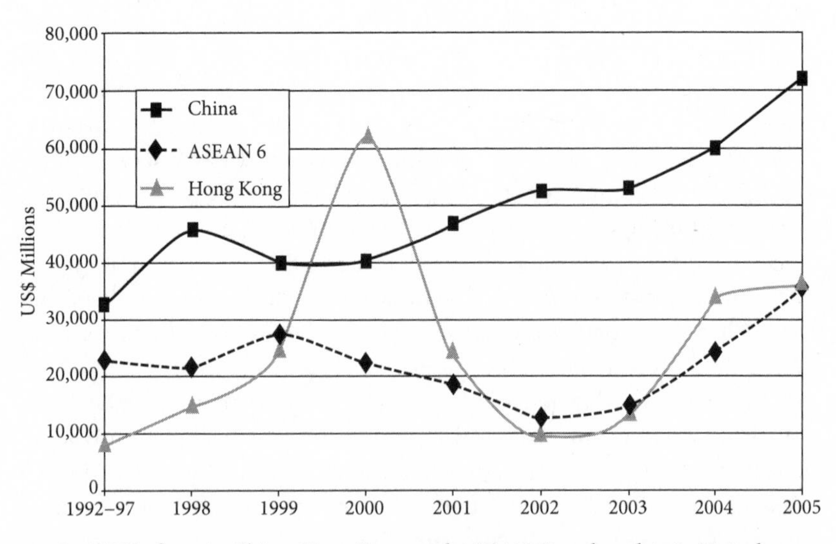

FIG. 8.1. FDI Inflows in China, Hong Kong, and ASEAN. Based on data in United Nations Conference on Trade and Development (UNCTAD), *World Investment Report 2005*

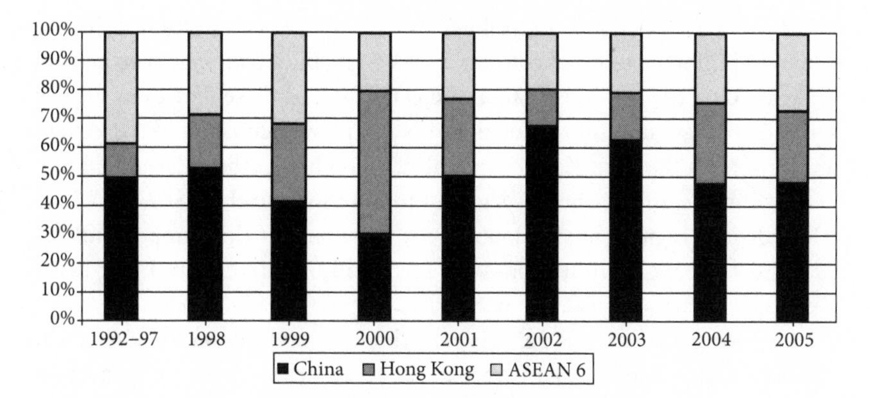

FIG. 8.2. Shares in East Asian FDI Inflows. Based on data from figure 8.1.

recovery from the shocks of 1997, and the response of Western investors to Malaysia's imposition of capital controls in 1998. Political uncertainty in these countries and in Thailand in the first years of the new century further weakened the investment climate. Indonesia experienced net outflows of FDI in every year between 1998 and 2003; for Malaysia, FDI inflows in 2005 were still one-third lower than in the peak year of 1996. Similarly, Thailand's annual inflows for the period 2002–4 were less than the average in the decade from 1985–95.

ASEAN's performance in attracting new inflows of FDI has been poor, with the exception of Singapore. But can this be attributed to investment being diverted to China? A fundamental problem with the argument that increased FDI flows to China have come at the expense of ASEAN is the implicit assumption that the total amount of FDI in the global economy at any given time is fixed. Analysis that compares ASEAN and Chinese shares in FDI going to the ASEAN-China region as a whole (as presented in figure 8.2) encourages a zero-sum perspective. Yet even a cursory glance at the variability in annual flows of FDI (even to this region let alone globally) would point to the fallacy that underlies such perspectives.

Global FDI increased substantially in the last years of the twentieth century, a reflection of a massive increase in merger and acquisition activities (primarily among industrialized economies but with some substantial LDC participation as well) during the dot-com boom. FDI flows to developing economies rose from an annual average of US$118.6 billion over the years 1992–97 to a peak of US$252.5 billion in 2000. The bursting of the dot-com bubble in combination with the events of September 11, 2001, led to a steep decline in global FDI flows. Inflows to developing economies declined to US$157.6 billion in 2002 but rebounded to US$233 billion in 2004, a 40 percent increase over the previous year. There is nothing in these figures to suggest that the overall amount of global FDI is in any way constant. An excellent example from the countries under consideration here is the bulge in FDI into Hong Kong in 2000 (when its share of total inflows to the ASEAN-China–Hong Kong "region" nearly doubled). A large part of this jump in inflows was due to a single acquisition—the US$12 billion purchase of Hong Kong Telecom by Pacific Century Cyberworks.

As Geng Xiao argues persuasively, there is good reason to believe that a substantial portion of FDI is endogenously determined (that is, generated by investment opportunities and by the profits of firms already operating in the recipient economy).[5] He suggests that one way to interpret the recent surge of FDI into China is that it is a reflection of the capacity of the Chinese economy to create new profits and new capital. A portion of the new FDI inflow recorded by China is simply Chinese flight capital returning home or foreign investors reinvesting in China some of the profits that they have made there. Looked at from this perspective, the key challenge for less-developed economies (especially China's competitors in Southeast Asia) is to undertake the domestic reforms necessary to enhance their economies' capacity to generate new investment opportunities and new capital. This is the principal arena for competition rather than over a fixed amount of global FDI flows.

To suggest that increased FDI flows to China have caused a loss of jobs in Southeast Asia is to make some heroic inferences from the data. Only careful, on-the-ground investigation can establish where a direct transfer of production from Southeast Asia to China has occurred (and some evidence of such transfers has been discovered in the closure of electronic plants in Penang and the transfer of their responsibilities to subsidiaries in China).[6] But correlations of (highly variable) aggregate FDI flows in themselves are not sufficient to establish such trends.

Does China Receive a Disproportionate Share of FDI Inflows?

Some of the commentary on China's recent FDI inflows appears to assume that there is a natural level of FDI that is appropriate for an economy and that China has exceeded this level in the volume of investment it has attracted. In reality, China, despite currently benefiting from the largest volume of FDI inflows in the world, receives a small to medium amount of FDI relative to the size of its population and its GDP. During the 1990s, China went from underperforming grossly as a recipient of foreign direct investment to becoming a medium-ranked player in terms of the inflows it receives relative to its GDP. This relationship is captured by UNCTAD's "Inward FDI Performance Index," calculated as the ratio of a country's share in global FDI flows to its share in global GDP (see table 8.1). A ratio greater than one indicates that the country attracts more GDP than one would anticipate from its economic size; a ratio of less than one indicates underperformance in terms of economic size.

China's performance on the FDI Index has improved substantially in the last fifteen years. But in a world in which openness to FDI has generally increased, its rank of 45 among 140 developing economies on this index in 2002–4 was essentially unchanged from 1988–90 (46th). This suggests that despite the surge of foreign investment since the mid-1990s, China has not attracted FDI inflows disproportionate to its size, and that the increase in foreign investment has merely kept pace with the growth of the economy.[7]

The key contrast in table 8.1 comes not from an improvement in China's ranking but from deterioration in rankings of the ASEAN economies. None of the ASEAN members is ranked higher in the 2002–4 period than it was in the years 1988–90. (Vietnam, having advanced at the turn of the century, has fallen back in the most recent ranking.) Other ASEAN economies have slipped badly: Indonesia (already below China in 1988–90) is now in the bottom five performers of the 140 countries on the UNCTAD list. The Philippines, ranked above China in 1988–90, has also fallen badly. Perhaps more surprising is the poor performance of two of the ASEAN economies generally considered most open to foreign investment: Malaysia and Thailand. Malaysia has dropped from a top-five ranking to close to the midway point on the UNCTAD table. And Thailand has performed particularly poorly, a substantial drop in its ratio

TABLE 8.1 China and ASEAN on UNCTAD's FDI Performance Index

	FDI Performance Index				*FDI Performance Rank*			
Countries	*1988–1990*	*1998–2000*	*2001–2003*	*2002–2004*	*1988–1990*	*1998–2000*	*2001–2003*	*2002–2004*
China	0.9	1.2	2.0	2.1	46	47	37	45
Indonesia	0.8	−0.6	−0.3	0.05	56	138	139	136
Malaysia	4.4	1.2	1.1	1.8	4	50	75	56
Philippines	1.7	0.6	0.7	0.6	39	89	96	100
Singapore	13.8	2.2	6.0	6.1	1	6	6	8
Thailand	2.6	1.3	0.9	0.5	17	44	87	106
Vietnam	1.0	1.5	1.9	2.0	47	36	39	50

Sources: UNCTAD, *World Investment Report*, various years; UNCTAD, "Inward FDI Performance Index 2001–2003," http://www.unctad.org/sections/dite_dir/docs/Performance_Index_2001-2003_en.pdf; "Inward FDI Performance Index 2002–2004," http://www.unctad.org/sections/dite_dir/docs/Performance_Index_2002-2004_en.pdf.

of FDI share to global GDP share being reflected in a plunge in the UNCTAD rankings from the top twenty in 1988–90 to 106 in the most recent period. It now ranks substantially below Vietnam as well as China.

Only Singapore among the ASEAN economies has maintained its stellar FDI performance, although even Singapore's ratio and ranking slipped at the end of the 1990s. While these data suggest that China's performance is not extraordinary by international standards, in recent years it has surpassed that of any ASEAN country with the exception of Singapore. The UNCTAD data indicate that most ASEAN economies have not only done poorly since the mid-1990s in relation to China but also in comparison with many other developing countries. While data for individual years may be misleading, the sustained trend recorded for ASEAN economies is not promising.

Flows vs. Stocks of FDI

While the picture for most ASEAN countries in terms of FDI inflows is far from reassuring, analysis of FDI data from other perspectives is less gloomy and arguably provides the basis for a more accurate assessment of the relationship between the rise of China and the FDI record of ASEAN economies. First, consider data on FDI stocks rather than flows.

For many analysts of foreign investment, stocks data present a more accurate picture of trends in foreign ownership in an economy than do data on flows. The principal reason is that stocks data include investments these corporations make that are financed with locally raised funds and from reinvested earnings. When a subsidiary has been established for some time, the majority of its additional investments may be funded by local borrowings or reinvested earnings, rather than from money raised from the parent corporation. Data on FDI inflows (collected by host governments for balance of payments statistics) consequently may considerably understate the influence of foreign ownership in economies where the foreign presence is long established.[8] The data for the Philippines provide an excellent example of how these different measures can lead to alternative judgments on FDI performance. According to the U.S. Bureau of International Economic Analysis, in 2002 the Philippines incurred a net outflow of American FDI of US$669 million. But for the same year the bureau reported that stocks of American FDI in the Philippines rose by US$560 million.[9]

Looking at FDI stocks, the picture for ASEAN is less grim than that portrayed by data on flows. Although China's FDI inflows surpassed those to ASEAN economies after 1995, the trend in FDI stocks in ASEAN continued upward even in the immediate aftermath of the financial crisis (see figure 8.3).

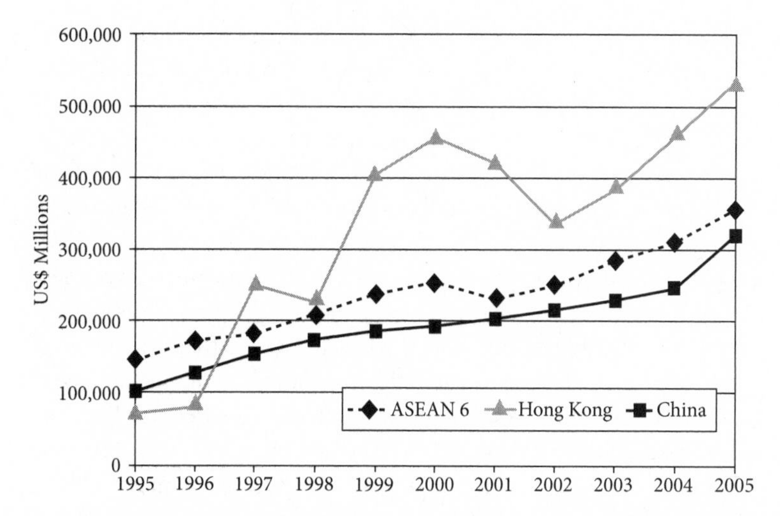

FIG. 8.3. FDI Stocks in China, Hong Kong, and ASEAN. Based on data in United Nations Conference on Trade and Development (UNCTAD), *World Investment Report 2006.*

The stock data give no suggestion of a zero-sum relationship between China and ASEAN. Between 1995 and 2005, the value of FDI stocks in ASEAN increased by more than 150 percent. Even in 2004, FDI stocks in ASEAN remained substantially (20 percent) above the level of those in China. A note of caution has to be sounded about the aggregation of the data, however. Singapore accounted for a large share (85 percent) of the growth in FDI stocks in the ASEAN region. Nonetheless, stocks of FDI also grew strongly in Thailand and Vietnam, presenting a very different picture from the data on flows or UNCTAD's flows-based performance index.

Overstatement of China's FDI Inflows

Another reason why ASEAN's FDI performance vis-à-vis that of China may not be as bad as the data on flows seem to suggest is because China's total inflows of foreign capital may be considerably overstated. There are two principal factors underlying such overstatement: the manner in which China's inflows are calculated; and the significant proportion of inflows that may be "round-tripping" investment, that is, investment that originates within China and is sent out of the country to be reinvested in China.

Most countries have adopted OECD standards for the measurement of FDI inflows: in essence, under the OECD guidelines, foreign investment is counted as part of FDI inflows only where investment by foreigners gives them control of at least 10 percent of the shares of a company. China does not apply this minimum limit. Any foreign investment is included in China's FDI inflow data, inevitably overstating China's receipts of FDI compared to home countries' data on outflows (and other recipients' data on inflows, too). Moreover, as Geng Xiao notes, since local government departments in charge of FDI promotion in China are responsible for collecting and reporting data on investment inflows, they have a powerful incentive to inflate these figures.[10]

A far more significant source of overstatement of China's FDI inflows, however, is that a large percentage of supposed foreign direct investment originates within China itself, a phenomenon known as "round-tripping." The principal reason why Chinese investors might seek to send their capital out of the country for ultimate reinvestment in the mainland is to take advantage of benefits available only to foreign-invested enterprises. The People's Republic of China provides a variety of incentives to attract foreign capital, including preferential tax treatment; preferential property rights, particularly relating to land; and preferential access to financial services. Because of ongoing ambiguity over the status of property rights and their enforcement, private enterprises in the PRC often operate in an atmosphere of uncertainty. Property rights for foreign-invested enterprises are somewhat better enforced, and domestic investors certainly covet this preferential treatment. They also seek the tax advantages afforded foreign investors.

The short life span of many foreign-invested enterprises in China itself reflects the desire of investors to exploit the tax benefits gained from an initial grant of this status. Geng Xiao quotes data that suggest that at the end of 2002, 48 percent of the cumulative total of 424,196 foreign-invested enterprises that had been registered in China had closed.[11] Many were shut down by their owners so that they could start new foreign-invested enterprises to take advantage once again of the preferential tax treatment that enterprises receive during their first five years of operation.

Round-tripping is also encouraged by investors' worries about possible exchange rate realignments (an increasing concern in recent years). With intensified conjecture about the likelihood of a revaluation of the renminbi, domestic investors have a powerful incentive to engage in speculative transborder movement of their capital. Finally, round-tripping may be undertaken with the objective of taking advantage of the expertise in financial services available in Hong Kong and to list on Hong Kong's stock market.[12]

An initial indication that round-tripping is a significant issue in China's FDI inflows is seen in the country's sources of inward FDI. The three big players (the "Triad") in global FDI—the United States, the EU, and Japan—together account for only one-quarter of China's FDI inflows (table 8.2). In contrast, Hong Kong (43 percent) and offshore financial centers (British Virgin Islands, Cayman Islands, Pacific Islands, Western Samoa, Mauritius, Bermuda, and Panama) (9 percent) account for more than one-half of all PRC inflows. Considered together, inflows from the offshore financial centers exceed the flows of FDI from the EU, Japan, or the United States.[13]

Estimating the extent of round-tripping is inevitably complex, not least because the activity under investigation is illegal. Early work by the World Bank suggested that round-tripping might account for as much as one-quarter of all China's FDI inflows.[14] In its *Global Development Finance* report for 2002, the World Bank commented that the share of total flows that originated within the mainland had actually increased in the last years of the twentieth century.[15] Geng Xiao provides the most comprehensive investigation of this issue to date.[16] Based on a careful comparison of China's own data on FDI inflows with that of its major FDI partners on outflows to China, he estimates that "unverifiable" FDI, most likely round-tripping capital, constitutes as much as 46.5 percent of China's recorded inflows, with a range (allowing for possible statistical error equivalent to one standard deviation) of between 34.9 percent and 58.1 percent. To reduce the volume of inflows of FDI to China reflected in figure 8.1 by 46 percent would present a dramatically different basis for comparison of China's recent performance with that of ASEAN—including China's relative standing on UNCTAD's FDI Performance Index.

Further evidence pointing to the likelihood that round-tripping capital constitutes a significant portion of China's recorded FDI inflows comes from estimations of capital flight from China. In a careful study of the various

TABLE 8.2 Sources of Foreign Direct Investment into China, 1994–2002 (US$ billion current)

	1994	*1995*	*1996*	*1997*	*1998*	*1999*	*2000*	*2001*	*2002*	*Total*	*Share 1994–2002*
Hong Kong	19.7	20.1	20.7	20.6	18.5	16.4	15.5	16.7	17.9	166.0	43.2%
Offshore Financial Centers*	0.3	0.9	1.8	2.5	9	3.8	5.5	7.9	9.3	34.4	8.9%
Taiwan	3.4	3.2	3.5	3.3	2.9	2.6	2.3	3	4.0	28.1	7.3%
Korea	0.7	1.4	1.4	2.1	1.8	1.3	1.5	2.2	2.8	14.7	3.8%
Singapore	1.2	1.9	2.2	2.6	3.4	2.6	2.2	2.1	2.3	20.6	5.4%
USA	2.5	3.1	3.4	3.2	3.9	4.2	4.4	4.4	4.4	33.6	8.8%
Japan	2.1	3.1	3.7	4.3	3.4	3	2.9	4.3	4.2	31.0	8.1%
EU	1.5	2.1	2.7	4.2	4	4.5	4.5	4.2	3.8	31.4	8.2%
TOTAL	33.8	37.5	41.7	45.3	45.5	40.3	40.7	46.9	52.7	384.4	

Sources: Data from *Zhongguo duiwai jingji tongji nianjian 2003* [China Foreign Economic Statistics Yearbook] (Beijing: Zhongguo tongji chubanshe, 2003).

*British Virgin Islands, Cayman Islands, Pacific Islands, Western Samoa, Mauritius, Bermuda, and Panama.

elements of capital flight, the most significant of which is incorrect trade invoicing, Frank Gunter estimates that capital flight from the PRC amounted to over US$100 billion a year between 1997 and 2000, and that a total of about US$900 billion had fled the PRC since 1984.[17] These sums are substantially in excess of China's annual FDI inflows: it is not unreasonable to assume that sizeable amounts of this capital returned to China in the form of round-tripping investment.

Home Country Data

Because China's data on inward FDI inflows are suspect, and because of the round-tripping phenomenon, it is important in attempting to evaluate the relative performance of China in attracting FDI to seek alternative sources of data. The most obvious alternative is to examine national data from source countries. Figure 8.4 uses U.S. data to calculate the shares of ASEAN, Hong Kong, and China in FDI outflows from the United States to this region. Here the picture is very different than that presented by UNCTAD data on FDI inflows (which are usually sourced from host country central banks). Although U.S. investment into ASEAN slumped in the aftermath of the financial crisis, 1998 was the only year in which U.S. FDI flows to China exceeded those to the ASEAN region.[18] By 2002, ASEAN countries were again receiving two-thirds of all U.S. FDI into ASEAN, China, and Hong Kong combined: China's share

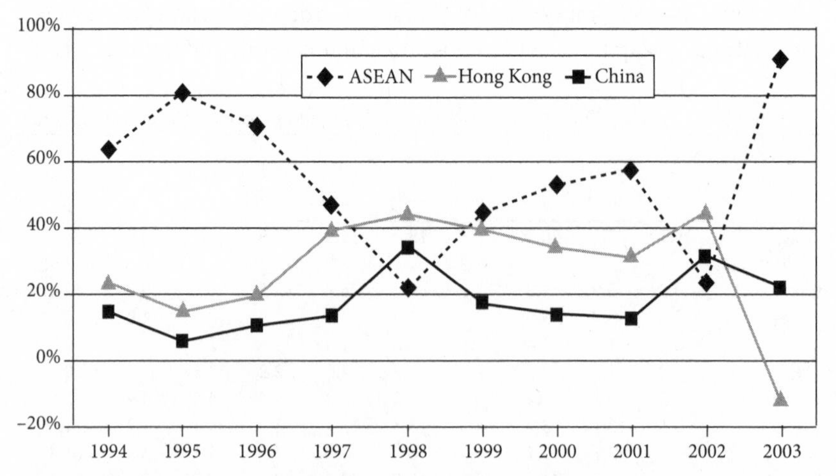

FIG. 8.4. Shares in U.S. FDI Outflows. Based on U.S. Bureau of Economic Analysis, International Economic Accounts, http://www.bea.gov/international/ii_web/timeseries7-2.cfm

of U.S. FDI flows languished at less than 20 percent. Even allowing for the possibility that a portion of the flows to Hong Kong ended up in the mainland, China's share of FDI from the United States remained remarkably small.

The data from the EU for FDI flows to ASEAN, China, and Hong Kong (figure 8.5) show enormous volatility (the chart excludes data for 2000, which reflect a negative inflow [net outflow] of US$3.8 billion from Hong Kong, a spike that takes the percentage figures well beyond the limits of the graph). Despite the volatility in flows, there is only one year (1998) in which China's share of EU FDI flows exceeds that of ASEAN. Again, the data from one of the world's major sources of foreign investment do not match those for the inflows recorded by the Chinese authorities.

Data on shares in U.S. FDI stocks in ASEAN, China, and Hong Kong (figure 8.6) also do not suggest a precipitous drop in ASEAN shares of U.S. FDI stocks in the region (which have actually remained remarkably constant over the ten-year period). ASEAN's share did fall from 1994 to 2005 but only from two-thirds to 60 percent of the U.S. total. China's share in U.S. FDI stocks in the region remains at only slightly over 10 percent. Finally, equivalent data (figure 8.7) for the EU again show more volatility than those for the United States. China's share of EU FDI stocks in the region was experiencing a steady

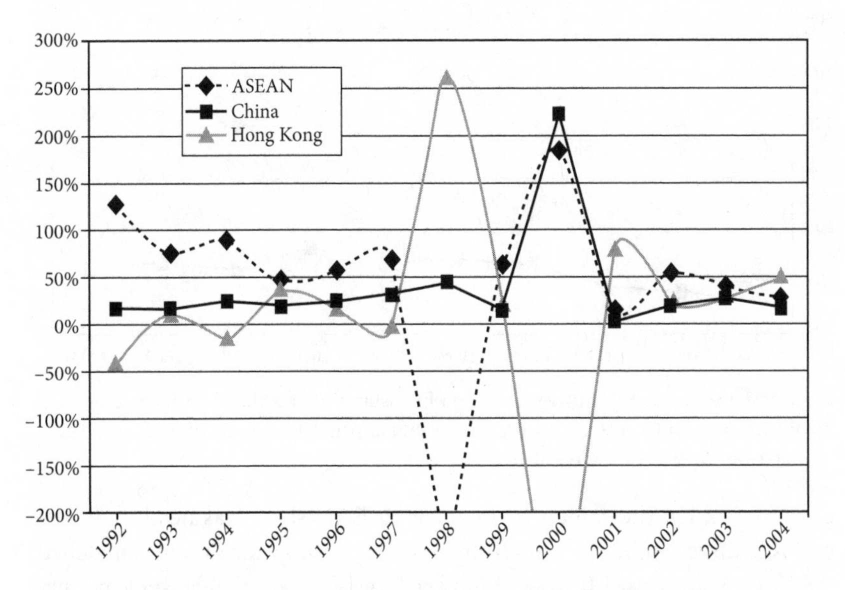

FIG. 8.5. Shares in EU 15 FDI Outflows. Based on Eurostat, Data for the Eurostat Yearbook, http://europa.eu.int/comm/eurostat/.

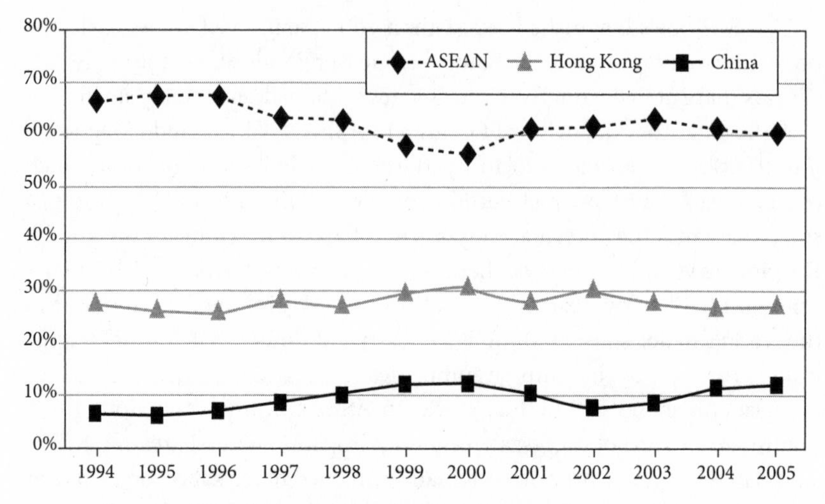

FIG. 8.6. Shares in U.S. FDI Stocks. Based on U.S. Bureau of Economic Analysis, International Economic Accounts, http://bea.gov/bea/di1.htm.

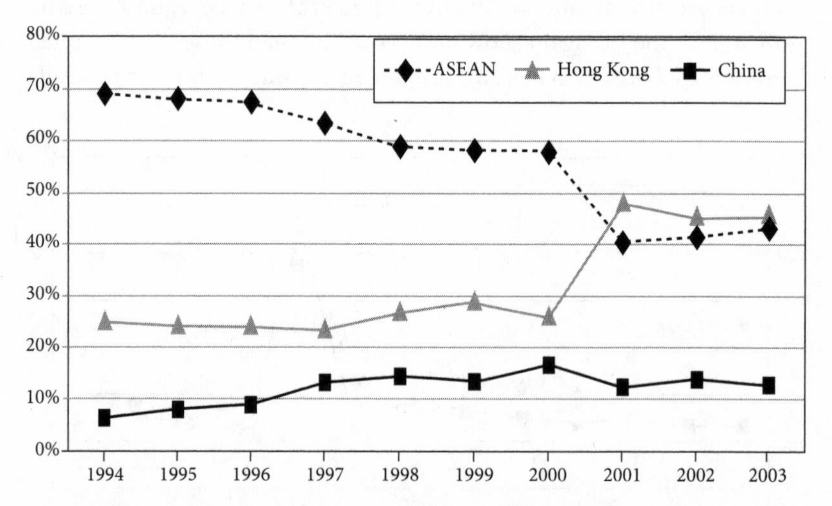

FIG. 8.7. Shares in EU FDI Stocks. Based on Eurostat, Data for the Eurostat Yearbook, http://europa.eu.int/comm/eurostat/. At the end of August 2006 the most recent data available on the Eurostat Web site was for 2003.

upward trend at the same time that the ASEAN share was heading in the opposite direction in the years from 1994 to 2000 (at which point it matched the Hong Kong share). In 2000, however, largely as a result of a single merger and acquisition in the telecommunications industry in Hong Kong, the Hong Kong share in EU FDI stocks soared. The distortion caused by this single acquisition again points to the dangers of reading too much into short-term trends in foreign direct investment.

FDI in ASEAN and China: A Zero-Sum or Positive Sum Game?

The performance of most ASEAN countries since the mid-1990s in attracting new inflows of FDI has been poor (Singapore, the ASEAN economy facing the least competition from China, remains the notable exception). Even though the data on FDI stocks are more encouraging than those on flows, indicating that ASEAN economies have benefited from significant new investment by existing subsidiaries of foreign corporations, little in the analysis above will provide much comfort to governments of ASEAN countries. The decline in the relative attractiveness of Malaysia and Thailand as hosts to new foreign investment inflows is particularly notable. Whether this poor performance can be largely attributed to the new competition from the PRC for investment funds is questionable. The source of the relatively poor record is more likely to lie in domestic policies and performance, influenced in part by the difficulties of coping with the financial crisis. The recent upturn in aggregate flows to Southeast Asia (which in 2005 reached a new record of 36 billion) suggests that post-crisis recovery has seen a revival of FDI. (Care must once again be exercised, however, in drawing conclusions from the aggregated data, because Singapore accounted for 56 percent of the region's inflows in 2005.)

In the years after 2000 when FDI flows to developing economies fell substantially, if a sizeable portion of inflows to China was in fact round-tripping capital (and thus to a considerable extent "captive"), China might reasonably have been expected to increase its share in overall flows to less-developed countries. There is no reason to believe that ASEAN countries were competing in any way for such round-tripping funds. Even if one accepts that the recent record of ASEAN countries in attracting FDI is poor relative to that of China, this does not necessarily indicate a zero-sum competition for capital flows. The variability of FDI flows over the last decade suggests that no fixed sum of investment capital exists over which countries inevitably must compete.

Moreover, several studies have suggested that inflows of FDI into China have actually had a positive effect on ASEAN's FDI receipts. Using a panel regression approach in a series of papers, Busakorn Chantasasawat, K. E. Fung, Hitomi Iizaka, and Alan Liu estimate that a 10 percent increase in FDI inflows to China raises the level of FDI inflows to East and Southeast Asian countries by approximately 5 percent to 6 percent, depending on how the model is specified.[19] Yuping Zhou and Sanjaya Lall, using a similar methodology, report that FDI into China had a positive impact on investment flows into Southeast Asia after 1992.[20] And Barry Eichengreen and Hui Tong, using a gravity model, also find that FDI inflows into China are complementary with FDI flows to other Asian countries.[21]

While the variability in the data examined earlier in this paper and the problems involved in measuring FDI suggest that conclusions from the application of regression analysis to the FDI data should be treated with a great deal of caution, these studies cast further doubt on arguments that the increase in FDI into China has come at the expense of ASEAN. As Chantasasawat et al. argue, the emergence of China as the "workshop of the world" can have both investment-diversion and investment-creation effects. Public discussion and much academic commentary have focused almost exclusively on potential investment diversion—the possibility that multinational companies will choose to locate in China rather than in other East Asian countries in order to take advantage not only of its relatively inexpensive unskilled and skilled labor but good infrastructure and huge domestic market.

However, China's stunning economic growth may also generate an investment creation effect. As China's industrialization proceeds apace, China's appetite for minerals and raw materials grows, spurring inflows of FDI into countries with the resources to feed this appetite. Of greater interest to governments that have concerns that China will displace their manufactured exports in the global marketplace is another possible source of investment creation: the establishment of an increasingly sophisticated regional division of labor based on transborder production networks that facilitate trade in components and their ultimate assembly. China's accession to the WTO, with the consequent removal of Trade-Related Investment Measures such as local-content requirements, may facilitate multinationals' construction of such regional networks. In such circumstances, an increase in FDI in China, for instance, for the purpose of assembly of components, may stimulate complementary investments in manufacturing elsewhere in the region. It is to the new division of labor in the region that we now turn.

Trade

Much of the conjecture about the negative impact on ASEAN of China's integration into the global economy rests on analysis of data for the period before China joined the WTO. Data are now available (from the UN's COMTRADE database) that cover the first four years following China's WTO entry, which for the first time permits observation of the impact of China's WTO entry on ASEAN trade.

Here I look at the evolution of ASEAN and China's position in the markets of Japan and the United States for five major categories of exports (aggregated at the two-digit level of the Standard International Trade Classification [SITC] Revision 3): office machinery; electrical machinery; telecommunications and sound equipment; clothing; and footwear. The last two of these sectors feature relatively unsophisticated, labor-intensive manufactures. In both of these, China's share of the U.S. and Japanese markets already exceeded that of ASEAN by 1995. The other three product sectors comprise relatively sophisticated manufactures. In all three of these in 1995, exports from ASEAN had a substantially larger share of the U.S. and Japanese markets than did those from China. These five commodity groups, combined, accounted in 2003 for 71 percent of all ASEAN manufactured exports to the world (81 percent of all manufactured exports from ASEAN to the United States; 62 percent of the total of ASEAN manufactured exports to Japan).

Office Machinery (SITC 75)

China's exports of office machinery (a category that includes computers) to the U.S. market were less than one-fifth of the value of those from ASEAN in 1995 (figure 8.8).[22] The value of China's exports expanded rapidly after China's accession to the WTO in 2001, surpassing the value of those from ASEAN in 2003. China appears to account for much of the expansion in U.S. imports in the last four years, testimony to its increasing competitiveness in higher-value-added goods. In contrast, not only have ASEAN countries lost market share but the absolute value of their exports of office machinery (a product category that accounts for nearly one-third of all ASEAN manufactured exports to the United States) has also not matched the peaks reached at the end of the 1990s.

A similar pattern holds in the Japanese market, although there, the decline in the ASEAN share and the increase in the Chinese share are even more pronounced (figure 8.9). ASEAN accounted for one-third of all of Japan's imports of office machinery in 1995, its exports amounting to nearly six times the value of those of China. In 2002, the value of Japanese imports of office machinery from China exceeded that of imports from ASEAN. By 2005 China accounted for more than one-half of Japan's imports of these products, the value of imports from China being substantially more than double those from ASEAN. Again, this is an instance where ASEAN countries not only lost market share, but the absolute value of their exports also fell substantially from its peak in 2000.

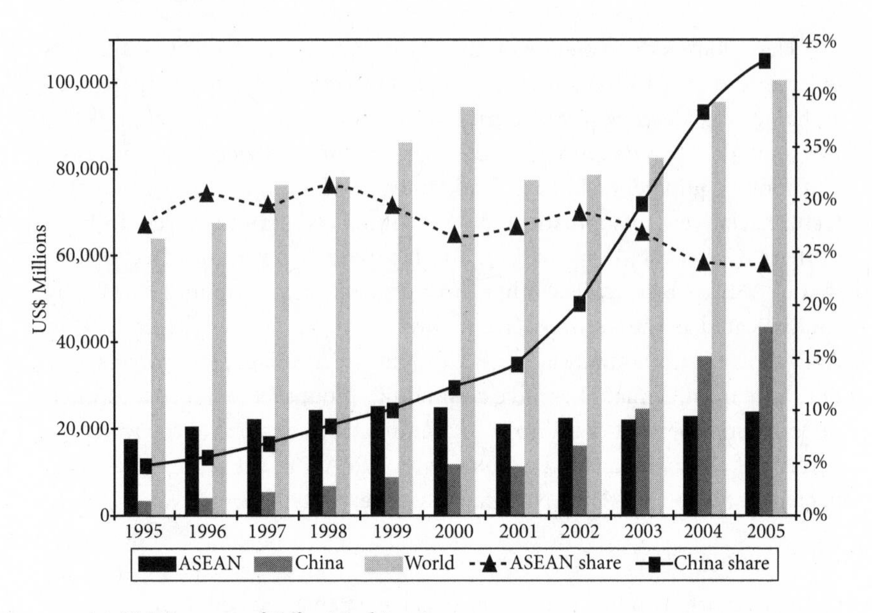

FIG. 8.8. U.S. Imports of Office Machinery

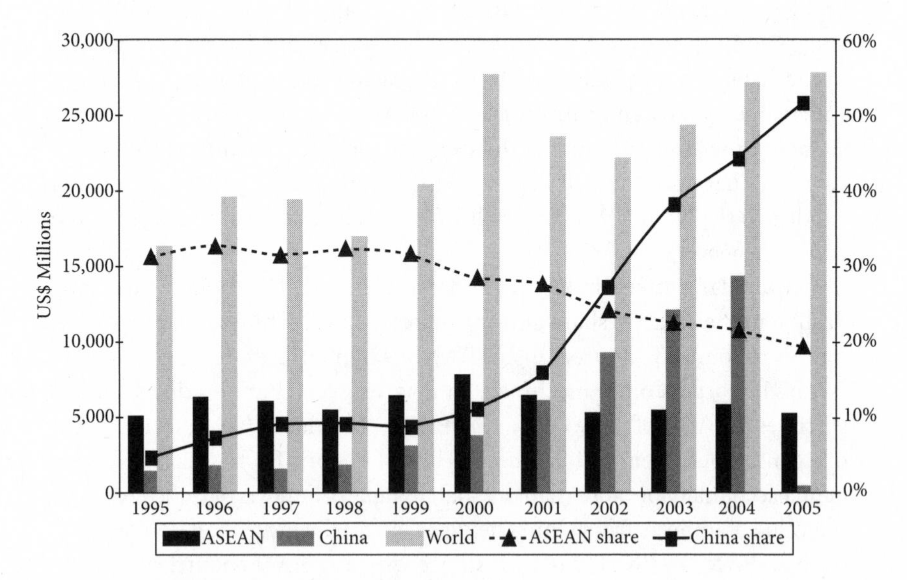

FIG. 8.9. Japan's Imports of Office Machinery

Electrical Machinery (SITC 77)

This is the only sector (one that includes semiconductors, electrical switching machinery, cathode ray tubes, and household electrical equipment) where ASEAN kept pace with China in the Japanese market (until the very last year in the period covered by this study). In the Japanese market, the value of imports from ASEAN in this sector rose substantially over the 1995–2003 period, probably testimony to the growing significance of "reverse exports" from Japanese subsidiaries in Southeast Asia. By 2004 the value of imports from ASEAN was more than three times that of 1995. Electrical machinery contributed one-third of the value of all ASEAN manufactured exports to Japan (figure 8.10). In 2004, however, the growth trend trailed off so that by the following year, imports from China had overtaken those from ASEAN. The value of imports from China quadrupled over the period. China's share rose from 7.1 percent in 1995 to 25 percent in 2005. This is one of the few instances in the commodities investigated in this study where both ASEAN and China over the decade after 1995 increased their shares in a significant export market.

In the U.S. market, in contrast, imports from ASEAN peaked in 2000 (figure 8.11). By 2003 imports from China exceeded those from ASEAN. Imports from ASEAN had fallen to less than their value in 1995, and by 2005 ASEAN's share of U.S. imports of this product category fell to under 12 percent, a particularly poor performance in a product group that contributed close to a quarter of the value of all ASEAN exports to the United States. The value of imports from China, in contrast, increased fivefold in the period 1995–2005 to capture a 19 percent share of all imports by the latter date.

Telecommunications and Sound Recording Equipment (SITC 76)

The value of U.S. imports of telecommunications and sound recording equipment (TVs, radios, VCRs, DVD players) from ASEAN more than doubled over the years 1999–2005 (figure 8.12). This growth, however, was insufficient to maintain ASEAN's share of U.S. imports of this category (which accounts for 14 percent of all ASEAN manufactured exports to the United States). ASEAN's share of the U.S. market fell from 22 percent in 1995 to 15 percent by 2005. Imports from ASEAN were 75 percent above the value of those from China in 1995: in 1998, the value of imports from China exceeded those from ASEAN for the first time. By the end of the period, the value of imports from China was more than double that from ASEAN; China accounted for more than a third of the U.S. market by 2005.

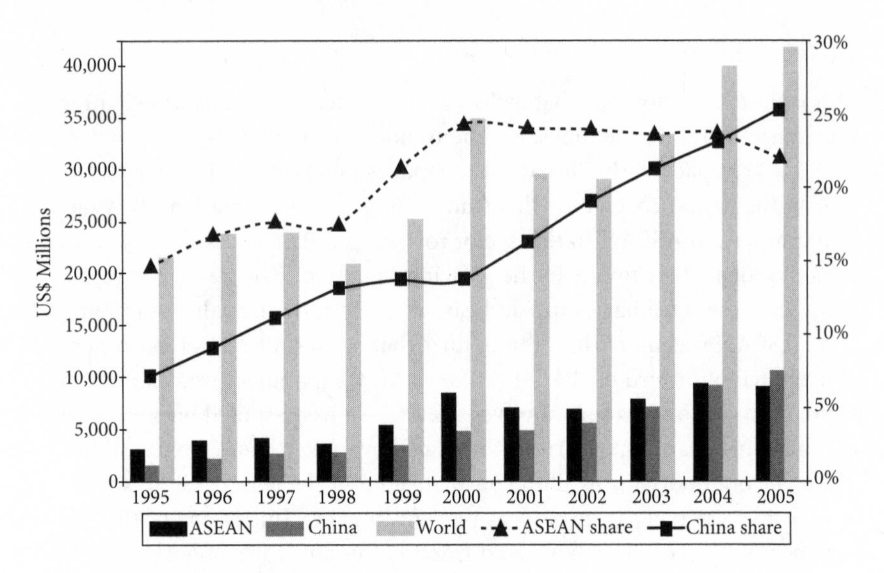

FIG. 8.10. Japan's Imports of Electrical Machinery

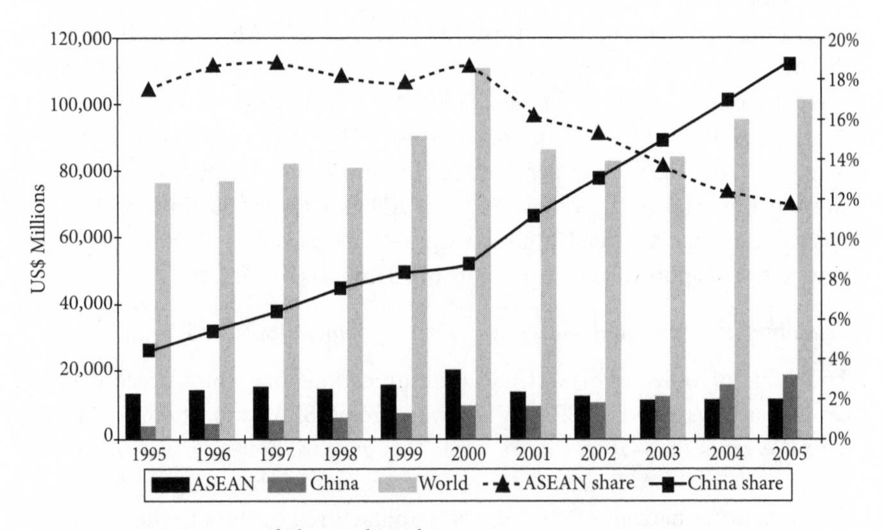

FIG. 8.11. U.S. Imports of Electrical Machinery

A similar situation prevailed in Japan, where the value of imports in this sector from China surpassed those from ASEAN in 2002 (figure 8.13). By 2004, the value of imports from ASEAN had recovered to be 5% higher than its previous peak in 2001. The value of imports from China increased sixfold over the period 1995–2005: China's share in Japan's total imports in this sector

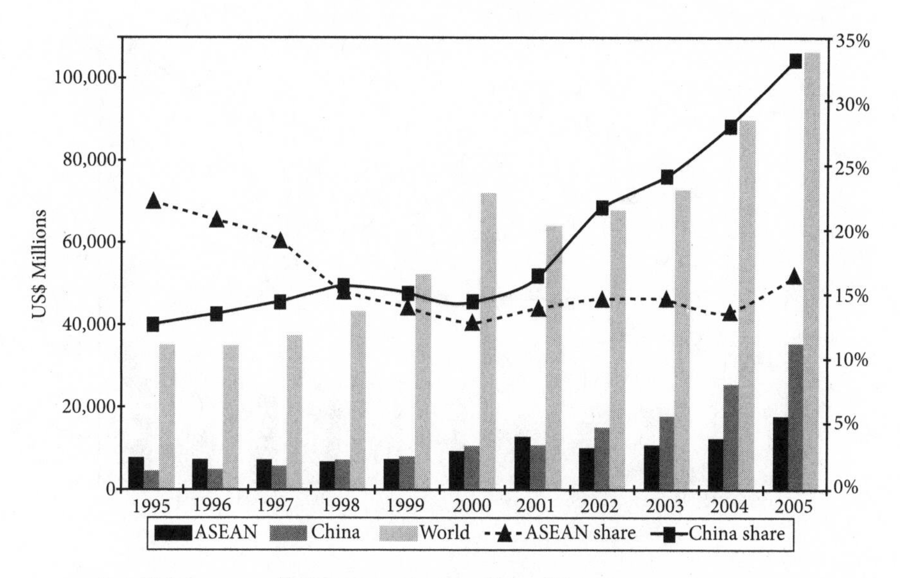

FIG. 8.12. U.S. Imports of Telecommunications/Sound Equipment

rose from 14.4 percent to close to one-half, whereas ASEAN's share decreased from 35 percent to 24 percent.

Clothing and Apparel (SITC 84)

In contrast to the three sectors considered above, clothing and footwear are two relatively labor-intensive sectors where China was a major source of imports for Japan and the United States even before its accession to the WTO.

This is the sector where new exports from China were expected to have the most negative impact on ASEAN economies. The full impact of China's competitiveness in this sector would not be felt, however, until after the abolition of the Multi-fibre Arrangement quota system from 1 January 2005, and the phasing out of the transitional arrangements that accompanied China's accession to the WTO. For the period for which data are available, country quotas continued to constrain access to the U.S. market. Here we see the effects of quotas in operation, with similar market shares and similar increases in the value of imports from ASEAN and those from China occurring until 2001 (figure 8.14). From 2001, however, when the United States began to relax some quotas, imports from China began to expand at a more rapid pace than those from ASEAN.

The situation in the Japanese market was entirely different (figure 8.15).

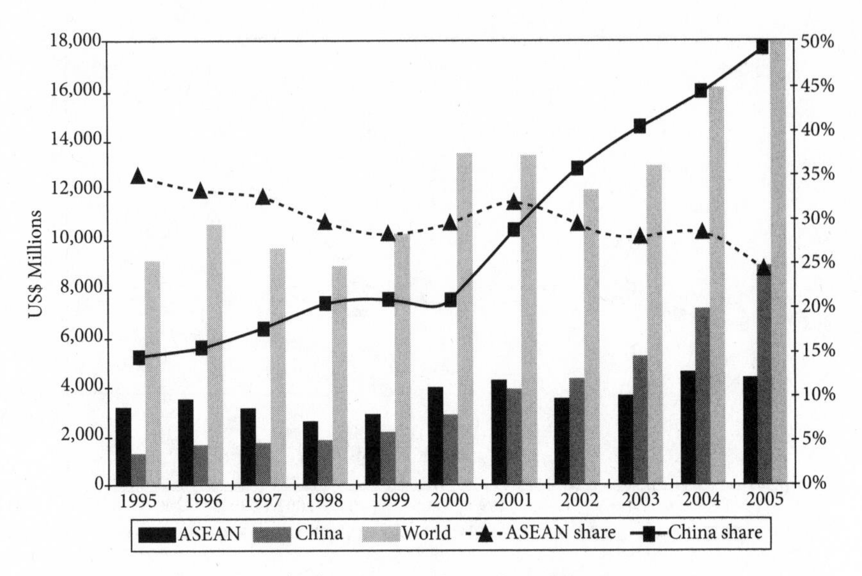

FIG. 8.13. Japan's Imports of Telecommunications/Sound Equipment

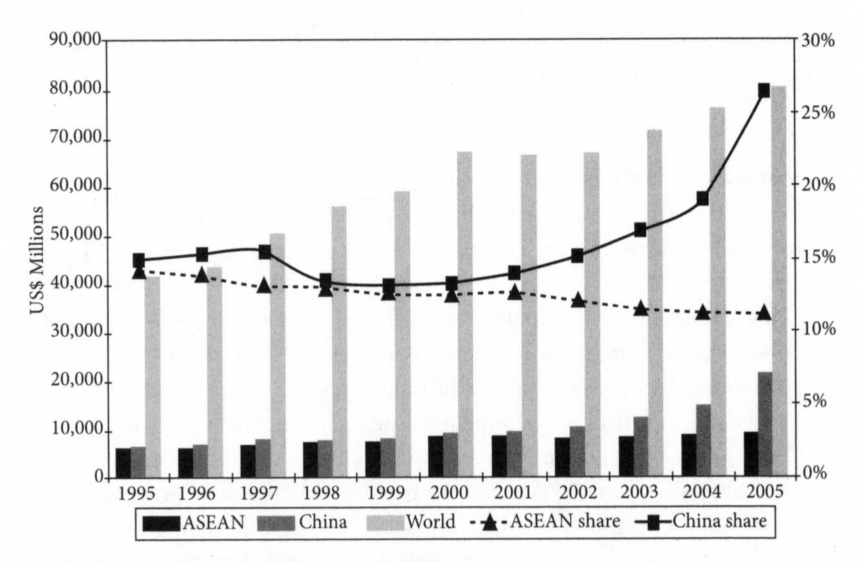

FIG. 8.14. U.S. Imports of Apparel and Clothing

The Japanese market was not subject to country quotas for clothing and textiles; it therefore provides a possible signpost to how world markets will look once industrialized countries completely remove the MFA restrictions. Whereas apparel and clothing constituted 13 percent of the total value of

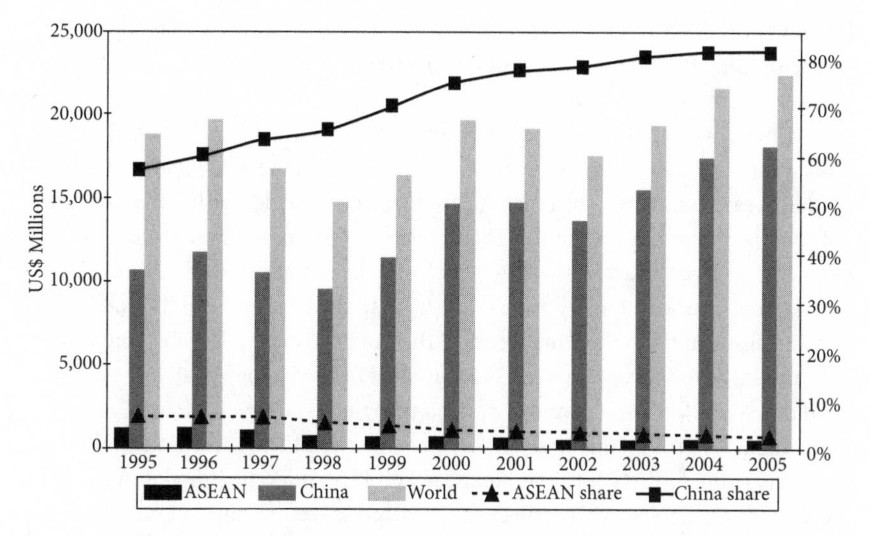

FIG. 8.15. Japan's Imports of Apparel and Clothing

ASEAN's manufactured exports to the United States in 2003, they contributed only 2 percent of such exports to Japan. By 1995 China was already by far the dominant player in Japan's market for apparel and clothing, contributing 56 percent of the total value of Japan's imports in this sector. Between 1995 and 2005 the value of imports of clothing from China into the Japanese market increased by more than 80 percent, and China's share of overall Japanese imports of clothing grew to 80 percent. In contrast, the value of imports of clothing from ASEAN fell by nearly one-half during the period. The share of ASEAN in Japan's imports of clothing fell from 6.5 percent to under 3.0 percent.

Footwear (SITC 85)

Footwear was the other labor-intensive sector where ASEAN countries were expected to experience significant difficulties because of the growth of exports from China. Data for the United States show that China in 1995 was already a much more significant source of imports than was ASEAN, accounting for more than four times the value of imports from Southeast Asia (figure 8.16). The gap between the two has widened considerably since then. Whereas imports from China have more than kept pace with the growth of global imports of this sector into the United States, China's share of the U.S. market rising from under one-half to more than 70 percent from 1995 to 2005,

ASEAN's market share has fallen from 12 percent to under 5 percent in the same period. The absolute value of imports from ASEAN has also fallen by 50 percent from its peak in 1997.

China was also a more significant source than ASEAN of imported footwear for Japan by 1995 (figure 8.17). Again, the data show Japan's imports of footwear from China mirroring those from the world, with China's share of total Japanese imports in this sector rising from under one-half to close to 70 percent. In contrast to the situation in the U.S. market, ASEAN's share of the Japanese market had by 2002 come back to the level enjoyed in 1998, after declining abruptly in the worst years of the financial crises. The absolute value of imports of footwear from ASEAN remains below its 1997 peak but by 2003 had climbed to 50 percent above its 1999 trough.

Table 8.3 provides a summary of the changes in the value and shares of imports from ASEAN into the Japanese and U.S. markets. It makes for grim reading from the ASEAN perspective. In only one sector/country combination (electrical machinery in Japan) did both the value of imports and the share of ASEAN countries in total imports increase over the period 1995–2005 (and even here ASEAN's share of the market fell substantially in 2005). The value of imports from ASEAN increased in only one other sector, telecommunications, in both the Japanese and U.S. markets, although ASEAN lost market share in both countries while that of China increased. For clothing, still governed in

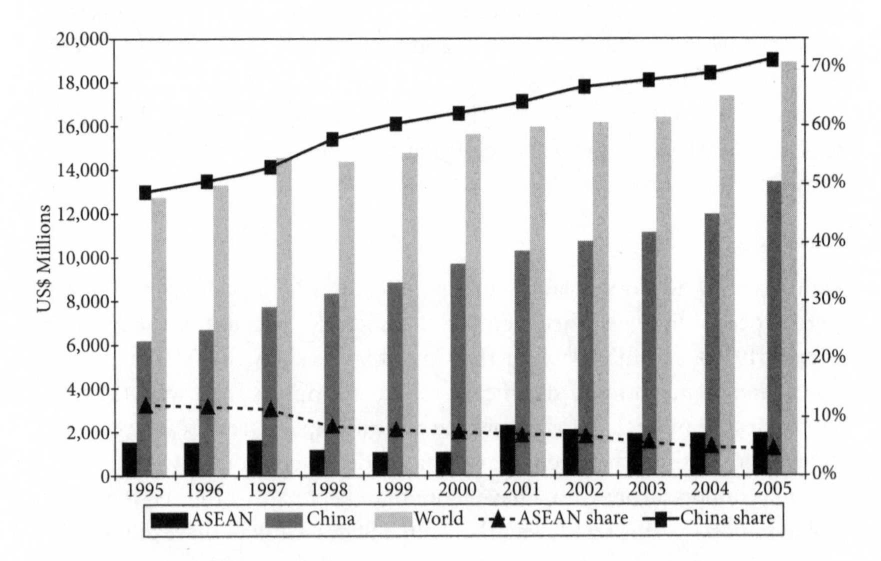

FIG. 8.16. U.S. Imports of Footwear

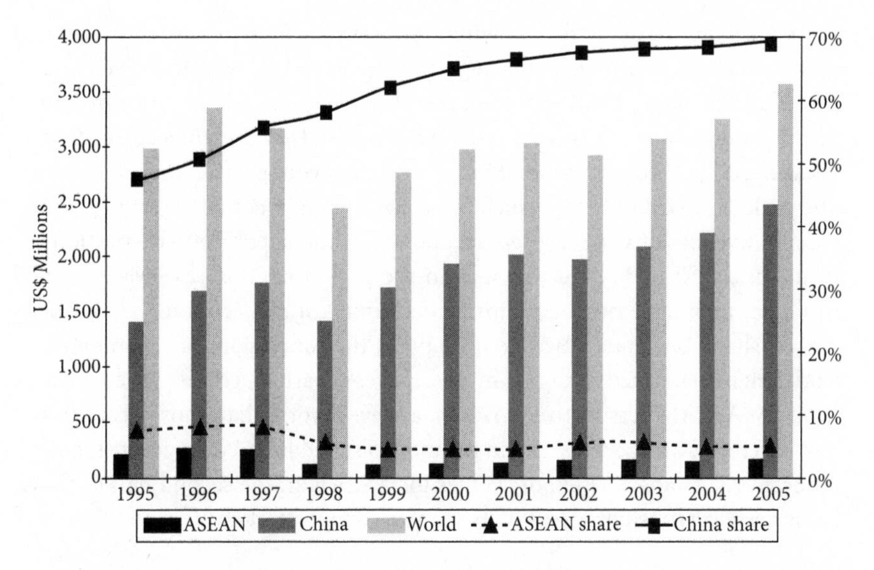

FIG. 8.17. Japan's Imports of Footwear

TABLE 8.3 Summary of Changes in ASEAN Shares of the Japanese and U.S. Markets

Value Up, Market Share Up Electrical Machinery (Japan)	*Value Up, Market Share Down* Telecommunications (Japan, U.S.) Apparel and Clothing (U.S.)
Value Down, Market Share Up	*Value Down, Market Share Down* Office Machinery (U.S., Japan) Footwear (U.S., Japan) Apparel and Clothing (Japan) Electrical Machinery (U.S.)

the United States by the country quotas of the MFA, the value of ASEAN imports increased but its market share decreased. For all the other sector and country combinations, including the higher-value-added sectors of office machinery in both the Japanese and U.S. markets, and electrical machinery in the U.S. market, ASEAN economies suffered not only an erosion of their share of the import market but an absolute decline in the value of their exports.

Care must be exercised in drawing any inferences from the descriptive data presented above. They are highly aggregated (at the SITC two-digit level) and across all the major ASEAN economies, obscuring variance in performance across products and across countries. And, at best, they present a correlation between ASEAN loss of market share and simultaneous gains in that of China. The underlying factor behind such a correlation might not necessarily be the competitiveness of Chinese exports, however; the supply-side disruptions in the crisis-hit ASEAN economies in the period from 1997 onwards, for instance, may have been a factor underlying ASEAN economies' loss of market share. The data, however, do support the conclusions of econometric work that has analyzed changing market shares in earlier periods.[23] The results from the ASEAN perspective, however, are even worse than those of studies that covered earlier periods. David Roland Holst and John Weiss, for instance, reported rising absolute export values for ASEAN in the second half of the 1990s despite a substantial loss of its share in foreign markets.[24]

ASEAN's Integration into Regional Production Networks

While developments in recent years in ASEAN's two principal export markets—Japan and the United States—appear to confirm fears about the damaging impact that China's growth would have on ASEAN exports, to look only at competition in third-country markets is to ignore another potentially significant stimulus to ASEAN trade: growth in China itself and in China's exports of assembled products to the world.

The emergence of China as "workshop to the world" (or at least its assembly plant) has caused dramatic changes in the patterns and composition of trade within East Asia. The trade triangles that had developed in the late 1980s following the G7 Plaza Accord currency realignments, in which components were shipped from Northeast Asia for assembly in Southeast Asia for export to world markets, have been largely superseded by new trade triangles in which components from other East Asian economies are being shipped to China primarily for assembly and export to industrialized countries' markets. One consequence has been a significant growth in the overall importance of intraregional trade in East Asia. Although this still lags behind that of Europe, it now constitutes more than half of the total trade of countries in the region.[25] China has grown rapidly in significance as an export market for other East Asian states—not least Korea, for which it is now the single most important export market.

These new trade triangles reflect dramatic changes in the composition of intra-regional trade in East Asia and the Asia-Pacific region more generally.

Economic complementarity in the Asia-Pacific region has frequently been discussed in terms of patterns that characterized global trade before 1945—the exchange of raw materials for manufactures. Complementarity was seen, for instance, in the exchange of Australian and Indonesian raw materials for Japanese manufactures.[26] Such a static view of economic complementarity informs Wong and Chan's assessment of the potential for an ASEAN-China Free Trade Agreement:

> The lack of complementarity between the Chinese and ASEAN economies limits the capacity that each can absorb of the other's products. This obstructs to a certain degree the economic integration and interdependence of China and the ASEAN countries.... Mutually competitive, rather than complementary, structures of China and ASEAN prevented significant growth in trade, with the possible exception of China and Singapore.... In the area of traditional labor-intensive industries like textiles, clothing, and footwear, China's gains have come at the expense of ASEAN's.... China's emergence as a global manufacturing base has apparently also resulted in most ASEAN economies experiencing a severe hollowing out of their industries.[27]

Postwar trade, however, increasingly was dominated by intra-industry trade among the industrialized economies, a development that with FDI-driven globalization of production has spread rapidly to trade between industrialized and middle-income developing economies, and increasingly among developing economies themselves. The growth of international production networks facilitated this intra-industry trade, a phenomenon that accelerated in the Asia-Pacific region following the currency realignments of the Plaza Accord.[28] Rather than static complementarities, the globalized economy is driven by a dynamic and rapidly evolving division of labor. China's recent rapid economic growth in large part reflects its incorporation into this new division of labor through a further extension of production networks. Despite the growth of intra-regional trade in East Asia, the region as a whole remains dependent on extra-regional markets for sales of finished manufactures. The difference over the past decade is that a larger percentage of finished goods exports to Europe and the United States are being sourced from China, displacing goods previously exported from Japan, Taiwan, Korea, and ASEAN.

Intra-industry trade has been a major source of the growth in East Asia's intra-regional trade in the last decade: Harm Zebregs estimates that three-quarters of the growth of trade among East Asian economies in the period

1996–2000 was attributable to intra-industry trade.[29] As early as 1995, one-third of intra-regional trade was estimated to consist of intermediate goods that are processed further and then exported to countries outside the region.[30] The share has probably increased in the subsequent decade. Studies estimate that exports of processed components contribute between 60 percent and 80 percent of the value of all Chinese exports. In turn, components for processing constitute more than 50 percent of the total value of Chinese imports. Most of the components for processing in China come from Northeast Asian economies, however. Hong Kong, Japan, Korea, and Taiwan supply close to two-thirds of the inputs for China's processing activities; these components account for 40 percent of Japan's exports to China, and 60 percent of the exports of the other three economies.[31] To what extent have Southeast Asian economies also been integrated into these new trade triangles?

ASEAN and China have become more important economic partners for one another in the last decade. From 1995 to 2004 China's share in ASEAN's total exports increased almost threefold, from 2.6 percent to 7.5 percent. In line with a general trend of China drawing an increasing share of its overall imports from developing economies, ASEAN's share of China's market increased in the same period from 7 percent to nearly 11 percent. Some ASEAN economies have benefited significantly from China's need for imported raw materials to fuel industrialization. But ultimately, given their emphasis on economic upgrading, most governments are interested in the opportunities that China will offer for sale of their manufactures. Here, China's accession to the WTO has assisted them: China's average tariff level was halved to an average of 12.7 percent in the years from 1997 to 2002 and was scheduled to fall to 9.4 percent in 2005.

Table 8.4 examines the changing composition of ASEAN exports to China. It shows that a dramatic transformation in ASEAN exports to China occurred from the second half of the 1990s (with the notable exception of Indonesia, whose exports continue to be dominated by energy products). The share of manufactures grew rapidly so that by 1998 they constituted more than half of the value of total exports. The share has continued to increase (in an era when the prices of some of ASEAN's commodity exports have risen substantially) so that by 2005, manufactures constituted more than two-thirds of the value of ASEAN's merchandise exports to China.

A more detailed breakdown of exchanges between ASEAN and China finds significant growth in intra-industry trade. The share of parts and components in Malaysia's exports of manufactures to China, for instance, rose from 6.4 percent in 1992 to 16.1 percent in 1996 to 50.6 percent in 2000;

TABLE 8.4 Share of Manufactures in China's Imports from ASEAN

	1990	1995	1996	1997	1998	1999	2000	2001	2002	2003	2004
Indonesia	54.4	29.2	22.5	23.5	34.1	29.0	25.3	27.0	25.0	22.4	22.3
Malaysia	11.9	41.0	48.3	40.9	41.9	49.4	54.5	62.1	54.5	50.8	50.2
Philippines	1.8	6.5	18.6	24.1	45.6	58.4	59.9	69.2	79.3	81.0	92.5
Singapore	28.6	48.5	48.2	50.9	60.5	68.1	66.5	67.1	66.0	66.6	68.4
Thailand	10.4	14.5	21.5	31.7	47.7	45.2	44.5	45.9	53.3	46.7	59.7
ASEAN (weighted) average	31.1	34.9	36.5	39.1	49.2	52.2	51.7	56.0	56.1	54.1	55.5

Source: UN Commodity Trade Statistics Database (COMTRADE), http://unstats.un.org/unsd/comtrade/.
Note: Manufactures defined as Standard International Trade Classification 6, 7, and 8 less categories 67 and 68.

for Singapore the respective figures were 23.1 percent, 41.9 percent, and 50.3 percent; for Thailand 6.8 percent, 29.2 percent, and 54.0 percent.[32] ASEAN's share of China's burgeoning imports of components increased from 0.9 percent in 1992 to 19.3 percent in 2004.[33] China's rapid industrialization is fostering a new division of labor in East Asia, including the ASEAN economies, and a significant expansion of intra-industry trade.

While the composition of ASEAN exports has been transformed over the past decade because of the rapid growth of exports of manufactures, imports of manufactures from China have grown even more rapidly, generating a deteriorating trade balance in manufactures from the perspective of the ASEAN economies. This has been true for Indonesia, Malaysia, Singapore, Thailand, and Vietnam. The one exception has been the Philippines, which has tripled the value of its manufactured exports (primarily electrical circuits) to China since 2001, and has enjoyed a positive balance of trade in manufactures with China throughout the period. Only Indonesia, because of its burgeoning exports of raw materials, has consistently run balance-of-trade surpluses with China over the years 1995–2004. (Brunei has also done so in the years from 2000 onwards.) For most other ASEAN economies, however, the balance of trade in nonmanufactured merchandise has at least partially offset imbalances in manufactures trade. And these data do not include trade in services, which would be expected to generate a healthy surplus, at least in the case of Singapore. From the viewpoint of economic theory, bilateral trade balances are largely meaningless. But, as has been all too evident from the perennial concerns of the U.S. Congress, economic and political logics do not always coincide. No doubt ASEAN governments will be looking at their bilateral trade balances with China as a litmus test of the commitment of China to a good neighbor policy.

To what extent has the growth of the Chinese market offset the losses that ASEAN economies have suffered in the Japanese and U.S. markets? A first point to note is that the aggregated position for ASEAN manufactured exports in the Japanese market is largely unchanged; losses in market shares in office machinery and telecommunications and sound equipment are offset by gains in the market share for electrical machinery. The question here then is reduced to asking to what extent gains in China have offset aggregate losses in the U.S. market. If ASEAN had maintained its peak shares of U.S. imports of the three categories of advanced manufactures included in this study—electrical machinery, office machinery, and telecommunications/sound equipment—its total exports of these products would have been worth approximately an additional US$21 billion in 2005 (a loss of about US$7 billion in each of the product categories). In the Chinese market, however, ASEAN countries have increased their sales of these products by approximately US$34 billion since 2000 (table 8.5).

The principal gains have come in electrical machinery, where exports increased more than sixfold from 2000 to 2005—primarily from Malaysia and the Philippines. Substantial increases also occurred in office machinery, with the value of exports up more than 300 percent. The single most important supplier for this product is Thailand. Again, one must bear in mind various caveats in considering these data; the level of aggregation means that gains in one product sector and/or market may not necessarily offset losses in another for individual countries, let alone individual companies. Significant adjustment costs may have been incurred as exports shifted primarily from finished products to the manufacture of components. But they do point to an emerging regional division of labor that is incorporating ASEAN states to a greater extent than some anticipated, to growing dynamic complementarities, and to the stimulus that China's growth has provided to some manufacturing sectors in some ASEAN economies.

TABLE 8.5 China's Imports of Office Machinery, Telecommunications Equipment, and Electrical Machinery from ASEAN (US$ millions current)

	1997	*1998*	*1999*	*2000*	*2001*	*2002*	*2003*	*2004*	*2005*
Office machinery	1,356	2,113	1,921	2,866	3,092	3,990	6,935	8,283	10,692
Telecommunications, sound equipment	305	369	411	692	735	815	1,184	2,127	2,799
Electrical machinery	934	1,309	2,384	4,498	5,509	9,086	15,365	21,765	28,489

Source: United Nations Commodity Trade Statistics Database (COMTRADE), http://comtrade.un.org/db.

A New Complementarity?

China's rapid economic growth presents an enormous challenge to other economies, not least its neighbors in East Asia that have export structures similar to those of the mainland. How economies will fare in the face of the new competition will depend in large part on how successfully governments manage the process of domestic adjustment. This will involve, inter alia, investments for upgrading local skills and infrastructure and improvements in governance structures and in institutional performance.

The evidence presented in this chapter suggests that the pessimism of analysts who conceive of the China-ASEAN relationship primarily in zero-sum terms is misplaced. While ASEAN did not do well in attracting new inflows of foreign direct investment in the period from 1998 to 2003, there is little reason to believe that the primary cause of this relatively poor performance was competition from China. China's data overstate the magnitude of *foreign* investment inflows. Moreover, data on FDI stocks demonstrate that ASEAN remains a significant host of investment from the United States and the European Union. And the most recent data on FDI inflows to ASEAN, which increase in the years 2004–5, suggest that much of the concern of ASEAN's leaders regarding the China threat may have been misplaced.

The picture for ASEAN countries' exports to their traditional markets of Japan and the United States at first sight seems to sustain alarmist scenarios regarding the "China threat." For the five major export sectors and two markets for which this chapter presents data, in only one sector in one market—electrical machinery in the Japanese market—did ASEAN countries increase both the value and their share of imports. In other products, ASEAN economies lost market shares in both Japan and the United States. The success in increasing exports of clothing to the United States is likely to be short-lived unless Washington maintains administrative intervention in the market. And contrary to some expectations that ASEAN would at least be able to increase the overall value of its exports even if it lost market share to China, there was only one other product sector where this occurred—telecommunications and sound equipment.

Despite these findings, the recent data suggest that ASEAN economies are beginning to participate in a significant way in the new trade triangles that have accompanied China's rapid industrialization. Rather than a decline in ASEAN exports of manufactured goods to China, as the zero-sum scenarios would suggest, substantial increases in exports of components to

China have occurred since its accession to the WTO. To a considerable extent, the increases in exports of components to China have offset losses in exports to the U.S. market of products in the same SITC classifications, and have transformed the composition of ASEAN exports to China.[34]

What implications might these trends have for relations between ASEAN and China? The concerns that Southeast Asian countries voiced about the economic threat from China prior to China's accession to the WTO underscore the tactical brilliance of Beijing in proposing a free trade agreement to ASEAN, especially one that contained "early harvest" provisions for immediate gains for its Southeast Asian neighbors (see Ellen Frost's chapter in this volume). Regardless of the overall economic value of the China-ASEAN agreement—and, given that many of Southeast Asia's exports would enter the Chinese market duty-free either because they are raw materials or components for assembly for export, the actual benefits from the agreement may be limited—it was a diplomatic masterstroke both for its effects in assuaging ASEAN concerns about China's peaceful rise and in putting Tokyo on the defensive.

China, however, remains a far less significant market for ASEAN economies than it is for Japan, Korea, and Taiwan. Whereas China in 2004 absorbed close to 20 percent of Korea's and Taiwan's exports, and 13 percent of Japan's, for no ASEAN country did China account for more than 9 percent of total exports.[35] Despite the rapid growth in exports to China, it is nowhere close to becoming the largest single market for any of the Southeast Asian economies. Nonetheless, Southeast Asian states are worried about future dependence on China and potential economic as well as military vulnerability: they have no desire to place all their eggs in one basket. They can be expected, therefore, not only to maintain their commitment to their own preferential trade scheme, the ASEAN Free Trade Area, but to continue to seek preferential trade arrangements with countries from outside the region—hence the enthusiasm not just from Singapore but also from Thailand and Malaysia for negotiating a free trade agreement with Washington.

CHINA'S PEACEFUL RISE

Road Map or Fantasy?

William W. Keller and Thomas G. Rawski

THIS BOOK ANALYZES THE ASIA-WIDE implications of China's rapid and unanticipated emergence as an economic, political, and military power and as a significant, expanding presence in regional and global affairs. China has recently surpassed Japan as Asia's leader in terms of import-export trade and military spending. According to some measures, China's economy is now larger than Japan's.[1]

Our central mission is to examine the theme of China's peaceful rise associated with President Hu Jintao. This optimistic perspective holds out the prospect of a smooth and peaceful adjustment to China's emergence as a regional power and major player in global economic and political affairs. The rise of the United States in the late nineteenth and early twentieth centuries demonstrates that peaceful emergence of new powers can occur, as did the rise of Japan in the concluding decades of the twentieth century.

But this felicitous outcome is only one possibility. The history of regional and global adjustment to the ascent of new powers has as often been punctuated by large-scale military conquest and attendant political and economic disruption. When one thinks of the Napoleonic wars, Japan's colonization of East Asia, or the world wars of the twentieth century, it is tempting to conclude that armed conflict on a grand scale is the more typical backdrop to the emergence of newly powerful states.

Two factors have tended to limit large-scale warfare in recent decades.

The first is nuclear deterrence, the development of significant, survivable nuclear weapons forces capable of wreaking unimaginable damage on adversaries, who have striven mightily to secure their own second strike or retaliatory nuclear options. The second is global economic interdependence. No two nuclear forces have engaged militarily to date. Instead, the nuclear powers, excluding North Korea and Pakistan, have engaged both nuclear and nonnuclear states in a thickening web of trade, investment, technology transfer, and commercial diplomacy. Membership in multilateral political and economic organizations and broad-based economic integration through trade, unfettered capital markets, and networks of multinational corporations all militate against conflict.

These innovations highlight the possibility that the dynamic adjustments associated with China's economic and political rise could proceed without massive strife. Our objective is to examine the feasibility of this result, to test the hypothesis that China's peaceful rise represents a realistic outcome following China's unexpected dash from poverty and backwardness into an era of dynamic growth and rapid technological development. Can existing systems of global trade, finance, and overall economic relations accommodate the extraordinary system-wide stress that Chinese competition will surely engender? In the foregoing essays, a group of talented and accomplished researchers examined this issue from multiple disciplinary vantage points. To our surprise, two years of discussion and debate produced considerable agreement.

China's New Trajectory of Growth and Openness Will Continue

The growth and internationalization of China's economy represent long-term shifts that we expect to survive the volatility of business cycles and the uncertainty surrounding China's elite politics. Three decades of unprecedented economic expansion and market opening have injected an enormous array of knowledge and skills into every level of China's economy. Future growth can build on accumulated expertise; thousands of Chinese firms and millions of managers, engineers, and entrepreneurs have mastered the art of expanding and deepening the economic, industrial, and technological capabilities on which international competitiveness rests. In addition to such decentralized processes, economic growth is firmly entrenched as a central objective of China's political system.

China's political economy rests on a grand but unspoken bargain between the Communist Party and the Chinese public. The party delivers economic growth and promotes China's global standing in return for public acquiescence to its autocratic rule and anachronistic ideology. The primacy of economic advance among the objectives of Chinese leaders at every level encourages our confidence that Beijing's pro-growth stance does not depend on the continuation of Communist rule. At the same time, the economic liberalization that has brought unprecedented wealth and economic freedom could generate pressures for political reform that might endanger the regime's stability. Such pressures certainly exist: William Keller and Louis Pauly found restrictions on free speech to be the number one complaint among U.S.-educated returnees in China's semiconductor industry.

China faces a veritable litany of internal challenges and impediments as it navigates the path toward parity with the advanced industrial states. Rising inequality between city dwellers and villagers, between educated and unskilled, and between residents of the coastal provinces and the vast rural interior could ignite political or economic disruption. China is in the midst of a great migration, with many millions moving to the cities each year. China's one-child policy has led to a significant gender imbalance and a rapidly aging population. Unfunded pension systems and inadequate health care will pose major hurdles. Unrestrained economic growth has exacerbated environmental degradation. While these and other difficulties could obstruct future growth, it would be unwise to underestimate the capacity of China's leadership or its populace to overcome adversity. We have no reason to expect that China's twenty-first century economy has lost its twentieth-century capacity to shrug off the impact of repeated setbacks arising from invasion, warfare, embargo, natural disaster, and policy blunders.

The opening of China's economy is as dramatic as its growth. China's trade ratio (the combined value of exports and imports as a percentage of GDP) has jumped from pre-reform levels reflecting North Korea–style isolation to heights that no large nation has ever achieved. China's 2005 trade ratio of 63.9 percent is far higher than comparable figures for the United States, Russia, India, Brazil, or Japan. At 95.5 percent, the trade ratio for China's coastal region, a vast economy of nearly 550 million people, exceeds comparable figures for the larger EU nations like Great Britain (54.5), France (51.9), Germany (71.3), and Italy (51.6).[2] In tandem with China's new status as the world's leading recipient of foreign direct investment, this shift has catapulted China to a level of economic openness unprecedented among large nations.

The contrasting history of major crises before and since China's economic reform illustrates the extent and impact of China's integration into global markets. Accounts of the oil shocks that roiled the global economy during the 1970s hardly mention China. Nor do reviews of China's pre-reform economy allude to the OPEC embargoes. The reason is clear: at that time, connections between global markets and China's semi-autarkic economy were so thin that neither steep rises in global oil prices nor the ensuing global recession exerted a substantial impact on China's economy. The effect of Chinese internal developments on world markets was equally slight.

The contrast with more recent episodes is stark. China's maintenance of the fixed parity between the renminbi and the U.S. dollar is widely credited with softening the impact of the 1997–98 Asian financial crisis by preventing a downward spiral of competitive currency devaluations. Following the September 2001 attacks on the World Trade Center towers in New York, the phrase "9-11" entered the quotidian vocabulary of Chinese analysts describing circumstances in their own economy. Today China figures prominently in discussions of the American trade deficit, of the development paths for autos, textiles, garments, semiconductors, steel, consumer electronics, shipbuilding, and many other industries; as well as price trends in global commodity markets, among them energy, iron ore, scrap steel, and even used cardboard.

Finally, China looms large in recent debates on offshore outsourcing. With "Made in China" labels visible everywhere and U.S. manufacturing employment continuing its long decline, many observers complain that businesses are relocating jobs from the United States (and other nations) to China. These claims, whatever their merit, illustrate the tensions emanating from accelerated growth in China (and India, among other countries). The combination of ongoing changes in product design, management systems, and information technology with accelerated growth of technical and engineering skills in China (and India) encourages multinational firms to add R & D, design, and back-office operations to the manufacturing operations already under way in the People's Republic.

New opportunities associated with the evolution of overseas investment in China, along with the benefits that Beijing anticipates from growing offshore investment by Chinese firms, allow us to anticipate that China's open-door policies will continue despite an undercurrent of chauvinism that has sparked nationalistic resistance to foreign takeovers—for example in China's construction equipment and cookware industries.

Chinese Military Ambitions Are Limited in Scope

The economic, diplomatic, and technological transformation chronicled in the chapters of this book is proceeding hand in hand with a major upgrading of Chinese military capabilities. Large expenditures aimed at force modernization should come as no surprise. The "Four Modernizations" program of the late 1970s highlighted national goals for defense together with industry, agriculture, and technology. Conversion of economic prosperity into military strength fulfills Chinese ambitions that date back to late-nineteenth-century "self-strengthening" efforts designed to eradicate the humiliation of successive "unequal treaties," beginning with the 1842 Nanking agreement that ended the first Opium War. These objectives echo Japanese ambitions captured in the "Rich Nation, Strong Army" slogan that inspired Japan's economic growth and consequent military expansion beginning in the late nineteenth century.[3]

But here the parallel could easily be drawn too closely. China's current military ambitions target local objectives, rather than global force projection. Both the history of Chinese military activity since 1949 and the recent military buildup focus on protecting China's borders, controlling regions (including Taiwan and Tibet) that Beijing has consistently identified as part of its national territory, and expanding power projection within what might be described as China's "near abroad." Thus the United States Department of Defense, in its 2003 annual report on Chinese military power, observes that "Preparing for a potential conflict in the Taiwan Strait is the primary driver for China's military modernization."[4] Three years later, the Pentagon's 2006 report describes a "process of long-term transformation from a mass army designed for protracted wars of attrition on its territory to a more modern force capable of fighting short duration, high intensity conflicts against high-tech adversaries," but also notes that "China's ability to sustain military power at a distance is limited."[5] In a similar vein, one analyst observes that "the foundation of Beijing's security policy is a high-tech armed force that is capable of winning 'local wars'—a posture it calls 'active defense.'"[6] A white paper on China's national defense published in late 2006 is broadly consistent with the twin concerns of protecting China's borders and containing separatist ambitions in Taiwan.[7]

China's dramatic advances in engineering education and in semiconductors and other defense-related areas of electronics and information technology will continue to translate into more sophisticated weaponry. The infusion of digital technology into Chinese military platforms will advance as China's high technology sectors aggressively compete for global market share with their commercial counterparts in the United States, the European Union, and Japan.

Although the U.S. Quadrennial Defense Review describes China's "potential to compete militarily with the United States and field disruptive military technologies that could over time offset traditional U.S. military advantages absent U.S. counter strategies," China shows no sign of initiating an arms race with the United States. We emphasize that realization of "China's peaceful rise" does not require perfect harmony between Beijing and its partners in trade and diplomacy any more than today's global balance rests on complete agreement between the United States and leading European nations on the invasion and occupation of Iraq, the war on terror, or the Kyoto Protocols. From this perspective, the apparent absence of Chinese plans to overcome United States leadership in nuclear weapons, long-range delivery systems and countermeasures, space-based military assets, or control of the high seas indicates that Beijing's present military trajectory does not conflict with the objective of China's peaceful rise.

China's military operates within the context of current and likely future economic realities. China's economic expansion rests on extensive participation in global markets for energy and mineral resources, manufacturing and farm products, capital, technology, ownership rights, and business acumen. Interdependence is broad and deep. China's dynamic coastal provinces represent a classic instance of export-led growth. Companies with part or full foreign ownership contribute more than half of China's exports and imports. Exports depend not only on overseas markets and on China-based foreign-owned manufacturers, but also on massive imports of components and raw materials.

Discussions surrounding Chinese economic policy and future plans assume continued large-scale expansion of China's involvement with global markets, as Chinese firms scour the globe in search of oil, raw materials, export markets, investment opportunities, and business partners. Chinese companies initiate high-profile takeover bids in pursuit of established brand names and technology resources, such as Lenovo's acquisition of IBM's PC business. Occasional dissent suggesting that China should limit its global involvement and economic ambitions falls on deaf ears at home.[8]

This burgeoning web of economic interactions extends far beyond the limits of Chinese military ambition. No military planner in Beijing can imagine that Chinese forces could control the trade routes linking China with Middle East oil and gas, Australian and Brazilian iron ore, or Canada's tar sands. During the early twentieth century, Japan attempted to secure its economic future by establishing the Greater East Asia Co-prosperity Sphere to exert control over key raw materials and export outlets, but the scale of China's economy, the scope of its current and future raw material imports, and the sweep of its export markets preclude China's leaders from contemplating a similar effort.

Let any analyst or military planner identify regions of the globe over which China might gain dominion within the next ten, twenty, or thirty years. Whatever the outcome, the indicated territory cannot provide China with the resources that it now absorbs or with the markets on which its exporters currently depend, not to mention future absorption or sales outlets.

These realities militate against the advent of what might be termed a Second Cold War with China. Doubtless, there are scenarios in which internal political developments might lead to a more aggressive Chinese military posture, but the commercial and diplomatic cost to China would be very steep. China's leaders understand these dynamics. They also understand that continued Communist Party rule depends on sustained growth in Chinese living standards.

The contributors to this volume generally agree that China's future economic security will rest more on international cooperation and commercial diplomacy than on military strength or force projection capabilities. China continues to expand its military power in order to protect its borders, to support its claim to great power status, and above all, to strengthen its leverage over Taiwan's political future. Neither recent military modernization nor feasible increments to China's armed forces can provide significant protection against the most likely external threats to continued Chinese growth: disruption of global trade in energy and other raw materials, global recession, or reversal of recent trends toward liberalization of international trade and investment flows.

Under these circumstances, China's push to join the World Trade Organization, followed by multiple initiatives to reduce barriers to intra-Asian economic linkages (dismissed in some quarters as a temporary "charm offensive") appears firmly rooted in China's long-term national interests. In joining the WTO, China's leaders quietly agreed to uniquely onerous conditions. Complaints of unfairness, of discrimination, of interference in domestic affairs, although surely justified, were never aired, in all probability because China's top leaders viewed WTO membership as the only viable strategy to sustain their high-growth economy.

We observe that China's behavior in the international economic arena bears similarities to U.S. actions in the immediate aftermath of World War II. Beijing now takes the lead in proposing sweeping reductions in trade barriers—for example through its plan for a free trade arrangement with the ASEAN states—and in offering immediate unilateral concessions, specifically in the form of "early harvest" tariff reductions, to assuage the concerns of reluctant partner nations. China's active commercial diplomacy has spawned a surge of trade negotiations as Japan, Korea, and India scramble to modify traditional protectionism in favor of new options for bilateral and multilateral trade opening. In this context, it seems entirely possible that China will emerge as a leading advocate, perhaps the leading advocate, of large-scale liberalization of trade and investment flows over the coming decade. The question, which would have been unthinkable even a few years ago, is whether China's major trading partners will contemplate putting on the brakes.

Asia's Response to the Rise of China Is Multiplex and Diverse

The international consequences of China's growing economic power and military strength are separate and may be quite distinct. In this volume, Robert Ross argues that the combined impact of China's economic and military power is gradually shifting the political orientation of both Taiwan and the Republic of Korea from Washington toward Beijing. Recent developments reinforce this view. For example, President George W. Bush's public demand in 2005 for restraint on the part of Taiwan's leaders, delivered on global television with Chinese premier Wen Jiabao at the president's side, underlined the weakness of Taiwan's military and diplomatic position.[9]

China's growing military power and far-flung web of commercial interactions reduces the likelihood that a future U.S. leader would opt to replicate President Clinton's dispatch of aircraft carrier battle groups to the Taiwan Strait in advance of Taiwan's 1996 elections. In their chapters, Ross and Adam Segal argue that strong mainland economic links have inspired elements of Taiwan's business community to oppose the independence-oriented policies of Taiwan's ruling party. Popular approval of opposition politicians' highly publicized visits to the People's Republic during the spring of 2005 has obliged Taiwan president Chen Shui-bian to adopt an uncharacteristically accommodating stance toward Beijing. Thus Beijing's astute diplomacy has at least temporarily transformed Taiwan's democracy from an obstacle to China's goal of unification into a check on the behavior of Taiwan's independence-minded leader.

While Ross argues that Taiwan and Korea have entered a transition process that will gradually bring them under some form of Chinese dominion, his chapter, and those of Ellen Frost, Segal, and John Ravenhill demonstrate that China's growing strength has inspired very different responses in Japan and in the nations of Southeast Asia, with economic outcomes diverging sharply from security trends. These states have eagerly embraced the economic opportunities associated with China's extended boom. China has become Japan's largest trade partner, and its share in the trade of ASEAN nations has risen steeply. But the magnetic attraction of China's dynamic coastal provinces has exercised no comparable influence on the security side. U.S. military ties with Japan, Indonesia, Singapore, the Philippines, and India have strengthened markedly in the past decade, while (or perhaps, as Segal suggests, because) China's military capabilities have expanded relative to those of its Asian neighbors.

There is ambivalence as well to the rise of China in the business community. As Keller and Pauly argue in chapter 3, China is now educating more engineers each year than the rest of the world combined. This unprecedented talent pool will facilitate China's transformation from an agrarian to a technocratic society. In time, this development will catapult Chinese industry and productive capability into the most technologically advanced sectors of the global economy. One side effect will be a protracted debate regarding the terms and conditions of competition and cooperation in the international arena, as local industries everywhere feel the pressure of Chinese high-technology wage competition, and businesses increasingly opt to outsource segments of high-end manufacturing and even research and development operations to China.

This process is already under way. Expertise is flooding into China, as Chinese firms expand their recruiting abroad, and as foreign direct investment bolsters a semiconductor industry (and its corresponding electronics sector) expanding to serve both global and internal markets. An internationally competitive high-technology manufacturing sector in China will fully establish itself in the near term; in the medium term, the emergence of a globally competitive research base will create new generations of opportunities for cross-national research collaboration and investment.

Envisaging China's Peaceful Rise

The contributors to this volume see China's peaceful rise as a plausible outcome that is well worth pursuing in a world where economic, political, and military realignments are likely to characterize international relations for some time to come. Notwithstanding President Franklin Roosevelt's admonition not to "let so-called facts or figures lead you to believe that any Western civilization's action can ever affect the people of China very deeply,"[10] U.S. foreign and economic policy will certainly cast a long shadow over Asia for the foreseeable future. Indeed it may be determinative.

The assumptions underlying U.S. foreign policy are likely to define opportunities both for bilateral diplomacy and for doing business with China, and may also exert a marked directionality on the rise of China itself.

Lack of continuity within and across recent U.S. administrations makes it difficult to characterize America's China policy. In part, this reflects changing circumstances: the rise of new economic challenges, the unexpected demise of the Soviet threat and new security challenges associated with transnational terrorist organizations. Nevertheless, from an Asian perspective, U.S. foreign policy must appear volatile, unstable, reactive, and increasingly difficult to read, much less to predict. At a macro policy level, three basic worldviews now compete for ascendance in Washington, each emphasizing different aspects of twenty-first century American global presence: America as hyperpower (neoconservatism); a return to Cold War realism (ideological confrontation); and economic interdependence (liberalism).

Because American foreign policy will exert a strong influence on the ultimate configuration of Chinese power in the twenty-first century, each of these views can contribute some insight to our understanding of the road ahead. In the neoconservative view, the United States emerged victorious from the Cold War as the only remaining superpower, or hyperpower, as the French describe it. This perspective emphasizes the opportunity for U.S. foreign policy to embrace global leadership. Advocates view lone superpower status as a perishable commodity, which leads them to propose expeditious consolidation of America's international primacy. Above all, in this view, the United States must prevent the rise of a peer competitor. Military power and agile force projection are key ingredients, along with the presumption that unilateral action is a viable diplomatic and military tool. In the neoconservative lexicon, the United States must "shape" the twenty-first century to its advantage. In this policy universe, China, with its rapidly expanding economic, diplomatic, technological, and military power, is the only plausible peer competitor. This position, prominent in the first administration of President George W. Bush, is widely seen as undergirding the U.S. invasion and occupation of Iraq.[11]

A second formulation of American foreign policy envisages a new Cold War, this time with China. It proceeds from the traditional realist view that the international system is an inherently anarchic and dangerous realm where states compete for power, first to survive and later to dominate. In this worldview, states' security concerns control national policies. States may achieve equilibrium of military power though "balancing" or "bandwagoning," or through the mutual assured destruction of bilateral deterrence. But as John Steinbrenner has noted, realism requires the "continuous presentation of an active threat."[12] This is the essential logic of the Cold War, and those who espouse it in the twenty-first century may go so far as to posit that a second

Cold War may be necessary to contain what they see as China's superpower ambitions.

A third option emphasizes the mutual benefits of economic interdependence. Here, authority is distributed or decentralized locally, regionally, and globally. In recent decades, the deterrent capabilities of nuclear weapons and the benefits of expanded trade and financial relationships have progressively lessened the concern of leading states with security issues, most notably in Western Europe. Economic interdependence gives states common goals, principally economic growth and expanded social security. National policies shift from confrontation toward more orderly systems of free markets and open trade on the theory that a rising tide lifts all boats. Multinational corporations figure prominently in the spread of prosperity and the transnational organization of production, research, and capital flows.

China represents a huge national entity—huge in terms of demography, economy, and, eventually, military strength. History demonstrates that the absorption of newly risen giants into preexisting structures of regional and global trade, security, and order is always difficult, and often punctuated with catastrophic armed conflict. Despite this daunting background, the authors of this volume are inclined to believe that the idea of China's peaceful rise is more than wishful thinking, provided that U.S. foreign policy is constructed along liberal lines that encourage economic integration rather than the other dimensions described above.

Peaceful absorption of a greatly strengthened China into regional and global nation state structures is feasible because accommodation to China's growing power need not threaten the fundamental interests of potential rivals, especially the United States. What will China demand of the world community in recognition of its enlarged power and influence? We see Beijing's key concerns as including the integrity and security of territory now under Beijing's control; prevention of formal independence for Taiwan to allow scope for Beijing's continued efforts to secure mutually agreed reunification; the removal or prevention of potentially hostile forces in China's "near abroad"; and continued access to international markets for resources and technology and to global outlets for China's exports and capital.

In the absence of a neoconservative backlash or a reassertion of containment, protectionism, or isolationist tendencies that could arise in response to outsourcing or structural economic adjustments, these requirements raise no deep conflict with the United States, with other industrial powers, or with China's neighbors. The collapse of the Soviet Union eliminated the only threat to China's territorial integrity. No nation, with the possible exception of the United States, possesses the capacity or the desire to concentrate military assets near China's borders. It is increasingly unlikely that Taiwan's elected leaders will precipitate a crisis with a bold independence initiative. And Beijing's consummate commercial diplomacy only increases China's access to markets, intermediate inputs, foreign investment, and raw materials.

What are the minimal conditions that would alleviate U.S. concerns about the rise of China? From the American perspective, the essential conditions for acceptance of China's new status would appear to be: Chinese reliance on persuasion rather than force in its efforts to regain control of Taiwan; Chinese avoidance of any challenge to U.S. strategic dominance and control of the high seas; continued vigorous implementation of Beijing's WTO commitments to pursue market opening and respect intellectual property rights; and avoidance of the non-tariff barriers to inward trade and investment that characterized Japanese and Korean foreign economic policy in the last decades of the twentieth century. Here again, we see no clash with China's fundamental interests.

Even a Peaceful Rise of China Will Impose Significant Costs

To say that the peaceful absorption of a greatly strengthened Chinese nation and economy into existing structures of trade and global finance as well as multinational networks of research, production, and distribution is feasible does not mean that the process of accommodating China's new power will advance smoothly. Success presupposes the recognition and acceptance of unpleasant realities on all sides.

For China, a peaceful rise necessitates acceptance of protracted delay in achieving its quest to regain Taiwan. This could prove difficult, particularly if a major economic slowdown or demands for greater political freedom were to cause growing numbers of Chinese to question the legitimacy of the ruling Communist Party. For Taiwan, the peaceful rise of China will doom the quest for independence, an objective cherished by a substantial fraction of the island's citizenry.

For the United States and the European powers, the greatest difficulties cluster on the economic side. Asian dynamism will continue to reduce America's and Europe's relative economic strength; Asia's oil consumption, for example, overtook North America's in 2005.[13] This gradual shift of economic weight may compel Washington to back away from its long-standing insistence that other nations bear the brunt of adjustment to economic change, as in the dollar shortage of the 1950s, when the United States expected the deficit nations to make needed adjustments; or today, when the United States, burdened with massive trade deficits, calls for China and other surplus nations to revalue their currencies.

The most profound economic consequences of China's rise involve the restructuring of specific industries. The historical experience of Japan's impact on global manufacturing structures shows that accommodation to new economic power is painful and controversial at best, as increasingly competitive firms domiciled in the new player shatter long-established industrial structures. (This can be seen, for example, in the impact of Japanese competition on U.S. steel and auto industries.)

China's economy, while far smaller than Japan's in terms of nominal output (converted to U.S. dollars using current exchange rates), now exceeds Japan's current economic size if GDP is measured at purchasing power parity. China's demographic mass—more than ten times Japan's—and low level of per capita income and consumption underscore the growth potential of Chinese industries, which already rank first in global output of coal, steel, textiles, televisions, cement, and many other products. As noted earlier, continued expansion of China's higher education system will surely expand the array of sectors and activities in which China-based producers develop formidable capabilities.

We anticipate that the eventual impact of China's growth on global economic structures will be far larger than Japan's. Recent developments illustrate what this will mean. Rising Chinese demand (along with other factors, including accelerated growth in India, temporary shortages of shipping capacity, and instability in the Middle East, Nigeria, and Venezuela) produced a spike in global prices for crude oil, iron ore, and many other mineral products during 2004–5. Initial exports of China-made automobiles call attention to the anticipated impact of China-based producers (including both domestic and foreign-invested firms) on global markets for both cars and auto parts. Clearly this phenomenon will not be limited to the auto and auto parts sectors. Actual and proposed takeover of international companies by Chinese firms in the computer (Lenovo), energy (PetroKazakhstan), automotive (Ssangyong, MG-Rover), and machine tool (Ikegai) sectors, among others, prefigure a growing role of Chinese companies in the upper echelons of global commerce. And finally, current investment trends indicate a massive shift of semiconductor production to China, which housed fully one-third of all fabrication facilities under construction as of 2004.

During the half century since the Second World War, only America's national economic perturbations regularly translated into global economic fluctuations. We have now entered a new phase in which China's economy (and in ten years, perhaps India's as well) will be sufficiently large and open to permit domestic economic and political factors to spill over into a broad array of global markets. The resulting uncertainties and dislocations will create strong economic and political ripples in many regions. The impact of such reverberations on U.S. political life is particularly important because of the long-standing dependence of global trade liberalization on U.S. leadership.

Policy Considerations

The essays in this volume demonstrate the impact of China's long boom on Asia's political and economic circumstances. The changes are not simply responses to events in China, but rather broad realignments of economic, technological, and business structures as well as political and security relations. The response to China's ascent includes indirect consequences such as strengthening bilateral military ties between the United States and Japan, India, Singapore, and Indonesia, as well as growing interest in bilateral and multilateral free trade arrangements on the part of Japan, Korea, and India.

The wide-ranging discussions that produced this volume reveal that neither the Clinton nor the George W. Bush administrations have responded to these events in proportion to their size and significance. Perhaps the scale and permanence of China's new position was not yet sufficiently clear to elicit a sustained response from the Clinton policy team. Overwhelming focus on the twin issues of terrorism and Iraq may have diverted the Bush administration from rethinking Asian policy. Whatever the causes, recent U.S. administrations have not yet come to terms with the magnitude of economic and political change that must accompany the emergence of a new economic and political center of gravity in Asia. Republican and Democratic administrations alike have failed to initiate a comprehensive reevaluation of U.S. policy toward Asia that the broad impact of China's rise would appear to warrant. Such an assessment should surely become a top priority for President Bush's successor.

A full-scale reevaluation of the U.S.-China relationship should aim to develop a consistent, coordinated, comprehensive, and constructive foundation for future Asia policy to supplant the ad hoc and often inconsistent policies that have prevailed over the past fifteen years.[14] This is increasingly critical because Asia's influence on the U.S. economy and on the global market system has expanded massively and will continue to grow. Likely future trends, including the acceleration of India's growth, the revival of Japan's economy, and the growing scope and sophistication of Asian innovation systems will magnify this outcome by enhancing Asian economic and military strength relative to Europe and the United States.

Only an integrated policy can provide a consistent framework for resolving thorny issues and calibrating responses to new developments. The costs associated with ad hoc policy making have become painfully apparent in recent years. Do we welcome Chinese imports because they ameliorate inflationary pressures and raise real incomes, or do we attack them as harbingers of domestic unemployment? Do we welcome opportunities to sell computing and communications equipment to China or strengthen export controls in the hope of slowing China's military progress? Do we welcome Chinese participation in international capital markets or prevent Chinese firms from making overseas acquisitions in energy or other sensitive industries? Do we assign a central role to decrying China's limited progress in the human rights field or push these issues into the background, following the example of Washington's policy toward Russia, Israel, and Saudi Arabia? In the absence of serious and thoughtful policy guidelines, many current policy choices seem unduly influenced by the media and by the concerns of single-issue interest groups.

While Washington pursues a national security policy focused on the Middle East and the Islamic world and founded on the dual pillars of "promoting freedom, justice, and human dignity" and "leading a growing community of democracies,"[15] the Chinese focus on diplomacy is intended to configure relations in the Pacific basin in their own, apparently more pragmatic interests. Given the importance of the Asia-Pacific region to future peace and prosperity, the United States must develop a consistent and long-term policy toward Asia that emphasizes key commercial and military objectives and institutes a coordinated strategy to pursue them.

NOTES

Chapter 1: Asia's Shifting Strategic and Economic Landscape

1. For example, Beijing not only rejects U.S. criticism of its human rights record, but joins Singapore and other Asian nations in challenging American conceptions of human rights: see "Unprecedented Progress Made in 13 Years," *China Daily*, 3 April 2003; and "Guardian of 'Human Rights' Shows Its True Colour," *China Daily*, 10 March 2006.

2. William W. Keller and Richard J. Samuels, "Innovation and the Asian Economies," in *Crisis and Innovation in Asian Technology*, ed. Keller and Samuels (New York: Cambridge University Press, 2003), 230.

3. Data for United States trade with "Asia & Pacific" and "Europe" from United States Department of Commerce, Bureau of Economic Analysis. See http://www.bea.gov/bea/international/bp_web/tb_download.cfm?anon=71&table_id=10&area_id=26; http://www.bea.gov/bea/international/bp_web/tb_download.cfm?anon=71&table_id=10&area_id=34 (accessed 5 September 2006).

4. Figures are in constant 2000 U.S. dollars and are taken from International Institute for Strategic Studies, *The Military Balance 2002–2003* (Oxford: Oxford University Press, 2002), table 26, pp. 332–34.

5. All 2003 figures are in current U.S. dollars and are taken from International Institute for Strategic Studies, *The Military Balance 2004–2005* (Oxford: Oxford University Press, October 2004), table 38, pp. 353–55.

6. Jim Rohwer, *Asia Rising: Why America Will Prosper as Asia's Economies Boom* (New York: Simon & Schuster, 1995).

7. Alastair Iain Johnston, "Beijing's Security Behavior in the Asia-Pacific: Is China Dissatisfied Power?" in *Rethinking Security in East Asia: Identity, Power, and Efficiency*, ed. J. J. Suh, Peter J. Katzenstein, and Allen Carlson (Stanford, CA: Stanford University Press, 2004), 77.

8. See for example, Evan S. Medeiros et al., *A New Direction for China's Defense Industry*," prepared for the U.S. Air Force (Santa Monica, CA: RAND, 2005), xv–xvi; Neil King Jr., "Secret Weapon, Inside Pentagon, a Scholar Shapes View of China," *Wall Street Journal*, September 8, 2005; and United States Department of

Defense, *Annual Report to Congress: The Military Power of the People's Republic of China 2005* (Washington, DC: Department of Defense, 2005), 25–35.

9. Jonathan Pollack, "The Transformation of the Asian Security Order: Assessing China's Impact," in *Power Shift: China and Asia's New Dynamics*, ed. David Shambaugh (Berkeley: University of California Press, 2005), 335.

10. See, for example, Paul Bracken, *Fire in the East: The Rise of Asian Military Power and the Second Nuclear Age* (New York: Harper Collins, 1999); and Kent E. Calder, *Asia's Deadly Triangle: How Arms, Energy and Growth Threaten to Destabilize Asia-Pacific* (London: Nicholas Brealey Publishing, 1997).

11. United States, U.S.-China Economic and Security Review Commission, 2005 Report to Congress (Washington, DC: U.S. Government Printing Office, 2005), 1.

12. Ellen L. Frost, "Economic Integration: Implications of Regional Economic Integration," in *Fragility and Crisis: Strategic Asia 2003–2004* (Seattle: National Bureau of Asian Research, 2003).

13. For an overview of the divergence of political economy and security studies, see Michael Mastanduno, "Economics and Security in Statecraft and Scholarship," *International Organization* 52, no. 4 (Autumn 1998): 825–54; David Baldwin, "Security Studies and the End of the Cold War," *World Politics* 48, no. 1 (October 1995); Jonathan Kirshner, "Political Economy of Security Studies after the Cold War," *Review of International Political Economy* 5, no. 1 (1998): 64–91; Jean-Marc F. Blanchard, Edward D. Mansfield, and Norrin M. Ripsman, eds., *Power and the Purse: Economic Statecraft, Interdependence, and National Security* (London: Frank Cass, 2000); and Barry Buzan, "Rethinking Security after the Cold War," *Cooperation and Conflict* 32, no. 1 (1997): 5–28.

14. William W. Keller and Janne E. Nolan, "Proliferation of Advanced Weaponry: Threat to Stability," in *The Global Century*, ed. Richard L. Kugler and Ellen L. Frost (Washington, DC: National Defense University Press, 2001).

15. When President Clinton ordered U.S. carrier battle groups into the Taiwan Strait in 1996 to calm tensions between China and Taiwan, a serving officer commented that a potential Chinese attack had "zero" probability of inflicting major damage on a U.S. carrier. Would a future U.S. president repeat such action if the probable success of a hypothetical attack increased to 5 percent? Fifteen percent? Twenty-five percent?

16. Robert Novak, "Squeezing the U.S. Army," *Chicago Sun-Times*, 23 June 2003; see http://www.townhall.com/columnists/RobertDNovak/2003/06/23/squeezing_the_us_army, consulted 6 July 2003.

17. For example, World Bank, *China 2020: Development Challenges in the New Century* (Washington, DC: World Bank, 1997); Nicholas R. Lardy, *China's Unfinished Economic Revolution* (Washington, DC: Brookings, 1998); OECD, *China in the World Economy: Synthesis Report* (Paris: OECD, 2002); OECD, *Economic Surveys: China 2005* (Paris: OECD, 2005); Justin Yifu Lin, Fang Cai, and Zhou Li, *The China Miracle: Development Strategy and Economic Reform*, rev. ed. (Hong Kong: Chinese University Press, 2003).

18. Data for trade in goods only (excluding services) are from United States Census Bureau, Foreign Trade Statistics, Trade in Goods (Imports, Exports and Trade Balance) with China, and Trade in Goods (Imports, Exports and Trade Balance) with Japan. See http://www.census.gov/foreign-trade/balance/c5880.html; also http://www.census.gov/foreign-trade/balance/c5700.html (accessed 9 January 2007).

19. Thus "Indian manufacturers scratch their heads in bafflement at China's ability to undercut them." See "Two Systems, One Grand Rivalry," *Economist*, 21 June 2003, 23.

20. Figures provided by Loren Brandt based on FDI inflows to eight Asian countries: China, Indonesia, Japan, Malaysia, the Philippines, Singapore, Thailand, and South Korea.

21. China's National Bureau of Statistics, for example is proud to report that "over 400 of the world's 500 largest firms have made investments in China." See "Opportunities for China's Manufacturing Industry after Joining WTO and Relevant Suggestions," *Guoyou zichan guanli*, [Management of State Assets] no. 4 (2003): 4.

22. Thus Chinese premier Zhu Rongji, "addressing Indian IT leaders in the southern city of Bangalore [in January 2002], said that if Indian software was combined with Chinese hardware, it would lead the world." See http://news.bbc.co.uk/1/hi/world/south_asia/1765525.stm.

23. Soviet aid focused on 156 large-scale projects concentrated in steel, machine building, and related manufacturing sectors. In 1954, China reported 31,187 "large industrial establishments"; in 1957, total industrial employment amounted to 7.9 million. N. R. Chen, *Chinese Economic Statistics* (Chicago: Aldine, 1967), 182, 475. In 2005, industrial firms with partial or full offshore investment and with sales over RMB 5 million numbered over 106,000 and employed 19.9 million workers. *Zhongguo tongji nianjian 2006* [China Statistics Yearbook 2006] (Beijing: China Statistics Press, 2006), 505.

24. "Export Controls: Rapid Advances in China's Semiconductor Industry Underscore Need for Fundamental U.S. Policy Review," United States General Accounting Office, GAO-02-620, April 2002, 2–3.

25. See "Human Rights: Australia-China Human Rights Dialogue" at http://www.dfat.gov.au/hr/achrd/aus_proc_dialogue.html (accessed 5 September 2006).

26. While India may exhibit patterns of economic development similar to China's, we focus on the latter because the Chinese economy to date is far larger, more open, and competitive in a wider range of sectors, posing greater and more immediate challenges to the established global economic order.

Chapter 2: International Dimensions of China's Long Boom

The authors gratefully acknowledge research assistance from Elena Capatina, Tingting Huang, and Yifan Zhang along with comments, information, and advice from Ellen Frost, William Keller, Nicholas Lardy, Chang Kyu Lee, Françoise

Lemoine, Francis Ng, Nam Kyong Oh, Li Qi, Robert Ross, Wei Wang, Yuxin Zheng, and two reviewers.

1. Although specialists debate the accuracy of annual economic data (see Thomas G. Rawski, "What Is Happening to China's GDP Statistics?" *China Economic Review* 12 [2001]: 347–54; Nicholas R. Lardy, "Evaluating Economic Indicators in Post-WTO China," *Issues & Studies* 39 [2003]: 249–68), there is little disagreement about the magnitude of China's long-term growth. We regard standard official statistics as the best available guide to medium- and long-term economic trends, and therefore rely on data from official Chinese sources throughout this chapter.

2. Nicholas R. Lardy, *Foreign Trade and Economic Reform in China, 1978–1990* (Cambridge: Cambridge University Press, 1992).

3. Detailed accounts of this process include Lardy, *Foreign Trade and Economic Reform*; Nicholas R. Lardy, *Integrating China into the Global Economy* (Washington, DC: Brookings Institution Press, 2002); Australia, Department of Foreign Affairs and Trade, East Asia Analytical Unit, *China Embraces the Market: Achievements, Challenges and Opportunities* (Canberra: Department of Foreign Affairs and Trade, 1997); Barry Naughton, ed., *The China Circle: Economics and Electronics in the PRC, Taiwan, and Hong Kong* (Washington, DC: Brookings Institution Press, 1997); and Ippei Yamazawa and Ken-ichi Imai, eds., *China Enters WTO: Pursuing Symbiosis with the Global Economy* (Tokyo: Institute of Developing Economies, Japan External Trade Organization, 2001).

4. Lee Branstetter and Nicholas R. Lardy, "China's Embrace of Globalization," in *China's Great Economic Transformation*, ed. Loren Brandt and Thomas G. Rawski (Cambridge: Cambridge University Press, forthcoming).

5. Wu Yong and Fu Jing, "Foreign Investors Able to Buy Large SOEs," *China Daily*, 16 September 2005.

6. Huaichuan Rui, *Globalization, Transition and Development in China: The Case of the Coal Industry* (London: RoutledgeCurzon, 2005); Cao Desheng, "Private, Foreign Funds an Option to Plug Rail Funding Shortfall," *China Daily*, 6 June 2005.

7. Loren Brandt, "China's Foreign Trade since 1450," in *History of World Trade since 1450*, ed. John J. McCusker, (Farmington Hills, MI: Macmillan Reference USA, 2006); Andre Gunder Frank, *ReOrient: Global Economy in the Asian Age* (Berkeley: University of California Press, 1998).

8. Calculation based on data from United Nations Commodity Trade Statistics Database, http://comtrade.un.org/db/default.aspx (hereafter, UNCOM trade data).

9. Vera V. Achvarina provides a detailed analysis for aluminum in "Integration of the Chinese Aluminum Market into the Global Economy and the Efficiency of the Shanghai Futures Exchange: Empirical Study," MA thesis, University of Pittsburgh, 2003.

10. Peter Wonacott, "Gas Lines and Growing Pains: China's Fuel Shortages Add to Pressure to End Central Planning," *Wall Street Journal*, 16 August 2005; Zhan

Lisheng and Wang Ying, "Guangzhou Oil Supply 'Returning To Normal,'" *China Daily*, 24 September 2005.

11. Dwight H. Perkins and Moshe Syrquin, "Large Countries: The Influence of Size," in *Handbook of Development Economics*, ed. Hollis Chenery and T. N. Srinivasan, 2:1691–753 (Amsterdam and New York: North Holland, 1989).

12. The Chinese data record the geographic origin of exports and destination of imports rather than the port of entry or exit. Trade ratios for Chinese provinces are calculated from the national figure and from provincial shares in GDP (valued in renminbi) and in combined exports and imports (valued in U.S. dollars). See *Zhongguo tongji nianjian 2006* [China Statistics Yearbook 2006] (Beijing: Zhongguo tongji chubanshe, 2006), tables 3-1, 3-14, and 18-12. International data for 2003–5 are from country trade profiles posted by the World Trade Organization at http://stat.wto.org/CountryProfile (accessed 10 January 2007).

13. See "One-Stop Service," Chongqing New North Zone Web site, http://www.cnnz.gov.cn/en/top03_05.asp (for Chongqing) and http://h20331.www2.hp.com/enterprise/downloads/Wuhan_eGovernment_6.pdf (for Wuhan) (both accessed 12 February 2006).

14. John L. Davie, "China's International Trade and Finance," in *China's Economy Looks toward the Year 2000*, ed. Joint Economic Committee, United States Congress (Washington: U.S. Government Printing Office, 1986), 331.

15. Results based on authors' analysis of information from UNCOM trade data. The classification of imports is unavoidably arbitrary, so that findings reflect orders of magnitude only.

16. Naughton, *The China Circle*; Yun-wing Sung, *The Emergence of Greater China : The Economic Integration of Mainland China, Taiwan and Hong Kong* (Houndmills: Palgrave Macmillan, 2005).

17. Feng-Hwa Mah, "Foreign Trade," in *Economic Trends in Communist China*, ed. Alexander Eckstein, Walter Galenson, and Ta-chung Liu (Chicago: Aldine, 1968), 704–11.

18. Official data overstate the flow of external funds from Hong Kong. Sung indicates that funds sent out of China and repatriated to qualify for favorable tariff, tax, and regulatory treatment may account for 25–40 percent of reported FDI arriving from Hong Kong (*The Emergence of Greater China*, 16). Geng Xiao concludes that such funds may contribute 30–50 percent of China's recorded FDI. See *People's Republic of China's Round-Tripping FDI: Scale, Causes and Implications*, ADB Institute Discussion Paper No. 7 (Manila: Asian Development Bank, 2004), 23. We expect the share of "round-tripping" in measured FDI to decline because of the growing importance of retained earnings from China-based foreign-linked firms in measured FDI, and because the convergence of tax systems affecting foreign and domestic firms limits the incentive to conceal the origin of Chinese funds.

19. *Zhongguo tongji zhaiyao 2005* [China Statistical Abstract 2005] (Beijing: Zhongguo tongji chubanshe, 2005), 55.

20. *Zhongguo tongji nianjian 2005* [China Statistical Yearbook 2005] (Beijing: Zhongguo tongji chubanshe, 2005), 192.

21. *Zhongguo tongji zhaiyao 2005*, 170.

22. Calculated from data in Country Fact Sheets posted on the Web site of the United Nations Conference on Trade and Development (UNCTAD), http://www.unctad.org/Templates/Page.asp?intItemID=3198&lang=1 (accessed 9 January 2007).

23. Hiroshi Ohashi, "China's Regional Trade and Investment Profile" in *Power Shift: China and Asia's New Dynamics*, ed. David Shambaugh (Berkeley: University of California Press, 2005).

24. Xiaojuan Jiang, *FDI in China: Contributions to Growth, Restructuring, and Competitiveness* (New York: Nova Science Publishers, 2004).

25. This calculation uses China Industrial Microdata, a database compiled by China's National Bureau of Statistics, to calculate the weighted average ratio of pretax profits to total capital for firms with and without external investment in 2000 and 2003, using total capital as weights. This database includes all state-owned enterprises as well as firms outside the state sector with annual sales above RMB 5 million. Other information (*Zhongguo tongji nianjian 2005*, 493–94, 505–6) shows a much smaller gap between profits of FIEs and of industrial firms with no foreign investment.

26. Wu Yong, "Machine Tool Firm Recalls Products," *China Daily*, 11 August 2005.

27. Daniel H. Rosen, *Behind the Open Door: Foreign Enterprises in the Chinese Marketplace* (Washington, DC: Institute for International Economics, 1999), 70, 135.

28. John Sutton, "The Auto Component Supply Chain in China and India: A Benchmarking Study," 2003, http://personal.lse.ac.uk/sutton/auto_component_printroom_version3.pdf.

29. See Loren Brandt, Thomas G. Rawski, and John Sutton, "Industrial Development in China," in *China's Great Economic Transformation*, ed. Loren Brandt and Thomas G. Rawski (Cambridge: Cambridge University Press, forthcoming). Inconsistent classification methods prevent us from evaluating the entire spectrum of Chinese trade flows. Unpublished work by Peter K. Schott uses a different approach to study quality changes in China's commodity trade, and obtains similar results.

30. Nicholas Lardy informs us that China's Customs Administration tabulates imports on a CIF basis, meaning that the import totals include cost of insurance and freight. China's export data, by contrast, are tabulated FOB ("free on board"), that is, excluding insurance and freight charges. Treating exports and imports consistently would raise China's trade surplus.

31. K. C. Fung and Lawrence J. Lau, "Adjusted Estimates of United States–China Bilateral Trade Balances, 1995–2002," *Journal of Asian Economics* 14 (2003): 489–96.

32. Robert E. Scott, *U.S.-China Trade 1989–2003: Impact on Jobs and Industries.* Economic Policy Institute, 2005, http://www.uscc.gov/researchpapers/2005/05_02_07_epi_wp_rscott.pdf.

33. Barry Naughton, "China's Trade Regime at the End of the 1990s," in *China's Future: Constructive Partner Or Emerging Threat?* ed. T. G. Carpenter and J. A. Dorn (Washington: Cato Institute, 2000).

34. Hu Yuanyuan, "Insurer: Search for Investor Going Well," *China Daily*, 8 September 2005.

35. Jim Dai, Yuepeng Li, Xiutian Liu, Yang Wang, Nancy Wong, and Chen Zhou, *2004 China Road Transportation Enterprise Survey Report* (Northeastern University in China at Qinhuangdao, 2005), http://www.tliap.nus.edu.sg/tliap/Research_WhitePapers/China_Road_Transportation_Enterprise_Survey.pdf.

36. You Wan and Qi Jianguo, "China's Long-Term Development Trend and Environmental Economy," *Caimao jingji* [Finance and Trade Economics] 10 (2004): 13.

37. "China Pours More Money Overseas," posted by Embassy of the People's Republic of China in the United States of America, http://www.china-embassy.org/eng/xw/t166686.htm, dated 22 October 2004 (accessed 9 January 2007). Japan External Trade Organization reports Japan's outward FDI for 2005 as US$16.2 billion. See "Japan's Outward and Inward Foreign Direct Investment," http://www.jetro.go.jp/en/stats/statistics (accessed 17 January 2007).

38. Rosen, *Behind the Open Door*, 71–76.

39. Mark Landler and Keith Bradsher, "VW to Build Hybrid Minivan with Chinese," *New York Times*, 9 September 2005.

40. *Zhongguo qiche gongye nianjian 2005* [China Automotive Industry Yearbook 2005] (Beijing: Zhongguo qiche gongye nianjian bianjibu, 2005), 263.

41. Hu Meidong and Li Dapeng, "Fuyao Sees through Glass Sales to Audi," *China Daily*, 2 June 2005; Hu Meidong and Li Dapeng, "Fuyao Launches Three Glass Production Lines," *China Daily*, 25 June 2005.

42. Li Fangfang, "Youthful Mobility," *China Business Weekly*, 19–25 September 2005; Associated Press, "China's Automakers on Mission," *St. Petersburg Times*, 24 September 2005, http://www.sptimes.com/2005/07/19/news_pf/Business/China_s_automakers_on.shtml; Gong Zhengzheng, "Egypt to Make Brilliance Cars," *China Daily*, 24 September 2005, http://www.chinadaily.com.cn/english/doc/2005-04/15/content_434431.htm#; Qiao You, "Car Makers Move Production into Russia," *China Daily*, 5 July 2005.

43. Daniel H. Rosen, Scott Rozelle, and Jikun Huang, *Roots Of Competitiveness: China's Evolving Agriculture Interests*, Policy Analyses in International Economics 72 (Washington, DC: Institute for International Economics, 2004), 2–3.

44. Li Jing, "Top LNG Ship Takes Shape in Shanghai," *China Daily*, 18 July 2005.

45. Li Jing, "We're Not Building an Aircraft Carrier," *China Daily*, 17 June 2005.

46. Thomas G. Moore, *China in the World Market: Chinese Industry and International Sources of Reform in the Post-Mao Era* (Cambridge: Cambridge University Press, 2002); William P. Alford, "The More Law, the More. . . ?

Measuring Legal Reform in the People's Republic of China," in *How Far across the River*, ed. Nicholas C. Hope, Dennis Tao Yang, and Mu Yang Li (Stanford: Stanford University Press, 2003); Jiang, *FDI in China*; Mary E. Gallagher, *Contagious Capitalism: Globalization and the Politics of Labor in China* (Princeton, NJ: Princeton University Press, 2005).

47. Zhu Boru, "Growth Engine," *China Business Weekly*, 9–11 September 2005.

48. Albert G. Hu and Gary H. Jefferson, "A Great Wall of Patents: What Is Behind China's Recent Patent Explosion?" discussion paper, Brandeis University, 2005, http://people.brandeis.edu/~jefferso/res.html; World Intellectual Property Organization, "Record Number of International Patent Filings in 2004," press release PR/403/2005, Geneva, 9 March 2005, http://www.wipo.int/edocs/prdocs/en/2005/wipo_pr_2005_403.html#.

49. Scott Kennedy, *The Business of Lobbying in China* (Cambridge, MA: Harvard University Press, 2005), 3.

50. Zheng Bijian, "China's 'Peaceful Rise' to Great Power Status," *Foreign Affairs* 84 (September/October 2005): 18–24.

51. United States Department of Defense, *Annual Report to Congress: The Military Power of the People's Republic of China 2005* (Washington: Department of Defense, 2005); United States, U.S.-China Economic and Security Review Commission, *2004 Report to Congress* (Washington: U.S. Government Printing Office, 2004); Harold Brown, Joseph W. Prueher, and Adam Segal, *Chinese Military Power: Report of an Independent Task Force Sponsored by the Council on Foreign Relations* (New York: Council on Foreign Relations, 2003).

52. For a graphic summary of this recent trend, see Christopher M. Dent, "Taiwan and the New Regional Political Economy of East Asia," *China Quarterly* 182 (2005): 385–406.

53. David Shambaugh, "China Engages Asia: Reshaping the Regional Order," *International Security* 29, no. 3 (Winter 2004–2005): 64–99.

54. Li Jing, "Top LNG Ship Takes Shape in Shanghai," *China Daily*, 18 July 2005; Li Jing, "We're Not Building an Aircraft Carrier," *China Daily*, 17 June 2005.

55. Wen Jiabao, "Report of the Work of the Government" (Delivered at the Fourth Session of the Tenth National People's Congress on 5 March 2006), http://www.gov.cn/english/2006-03/14/content_227247.htm.

Chapter 3: Building a Technocracy in China

We are grateful for the support of the Matthew B. Ridgway Center for International Security Studies at the University of Pittsburgh, the Center for International Studies at the University of Toronto, the Canada Research Chair Program, and the Semiconductor Research Corporation (SRC), and especially to Larry Sumney and Dinesh Mehta of SRC who have supported our work on applied semiconductor research over the past decade. An early version of this chapter appeared in the working paper series of the Research Group in International Security (REGIS), Université de Montréal and McGill University. We thank

T. V. Paul and his colleagues and students for helpful comments. Fieldwork was undertaken in Washington, Silicon Valley, Hong Kong, Beijing, Shanghai, and Xi'an. Special thanks to the Faculties of Engineering at City University in Hong Kong, Tsinghua University in Beijing, and Fudan University in Shanghai. Logistical support and advice were provided by the Semiconductor Industry Association, the MIT International Science and Technology Initiatives, the North American Chinese Semiconductor Association, and the United States Information Technology Organization in Beijing. Noman Lateef and Adam Bowers provided research assistance.

1. This chapter follows earlier work on the semiconductor industry in Japan, Taiwan, and South Korea. See William W. Keller and Louis W. Pauly, "Crisis and Adaptation in Taiwan and Korea: The Political Economy of Semiconductors," in *Crisis and Innovation in Asian Technology*, ed. William W. Keller and Richard J. Samuels (Cambridge: Cambridge University Press, 2003), 137–59; and Keller and Pauly, "Crisis and Adaptation in East Asian Innovation Systems: The Case of the Semiconductor Industry in Taiwan and South Korea," *Business and Politics* 2, no. 3 (November 2000): 327–52. In the cases of Taiwan and South Korea, we documented both the rapidly developing success of university systems in training engineers and the ability of local industry to absorb and conduct high-quality applied research. On the Japanese case in closely related industries, see Paul N. Doremus, William W. Keller, Louis W. Pauly, and Simon Reich, *The Myth of the Global Corporation* (Princeton, NJ: Princeton University Press, 1998).

2. Mark R. Brawley, "The Political Economy of Balance of Power Theory," in *Balance of Power: Theory and Practice in the 21st Century*, ed. T. V. Paul, Jim Wirtz, and Michel Fortmann (Stanford, CA: Stanford University Press, 2004), 94.

3. Weifeng Liu, Michael Pecht, and Zhenya Huang, "China's Semiconductor Industry," in *China's Electronics Industries*, ed. Michael Pecht and Y. C. Chan (College Park, MD: CALCE EPSC Press, 2004), 79.

4. For an overview of the challenges China faces in its regional context, see Douglas B. Fuller, "Moving along the Electronics Value Chain: Taiwan in a Global Economy," in *Global Taiwan*, ed. Suzanne Berger and Richard K. Lester (Armonk, NY: M. E. Sharpe, 2005), 137–65; Dieter Ernst, "Pathways to Innovation in the Global Network Economy," *East-West Center Working Papers, Economics Series*, no. 58 (June 2003): especially pp. 29–33; Dieter Ernst, "Late Innovation Strategies in Asian Electronics Industries," *East-West Center Working Papers, Economics Series*, no. 66 (March 2004); and Dieter Ernst, "Internationalization of Innovation: Why Is Chip Design Moving to Asia?" *East-West Center Working Papers, Economics Series*, no. 64 (March 2004).

5. Michael Pecht and Y. C. Chan (eds.), *China's Electronics Industries* (College Park, MD: CALCE EPSC Press, 2004), 84–85.

6. For a thorough treatment of this issue, still relevant even after China agreed in 2004 to remove the VAT rebate system, see *China's Emerging Semiconductor Industry: The Impact of China's Preferential Value-Added Tax on Current*

Investment Trends (Washington, DC: Semiconductor Industry Association and Dewey Ballantine LLP, October 2003).

7. National Science Board, *Science and Engineering Indicators 2004*, Table 2.9, http://www.nsf.gov/statistics/seind04/c2/tt02-09.htm (accessed 21 January 2007).

8. Ibid.

9. General Accounting Office, "Export Controls: Rapid Advances in China's Semiconductor Industry Underscore Need for Fundamental U.S. Policy Review" (April 2002), GAO-02-620.

10. See United States, U.S.-China Economic and Security Review Commission, *2004 Report to Congress* (Washington, DC: Government Printing Office, June 2004).

11. Michael Pillsbury, "China's Military Strategy toward the U.S.: A View from Open Sources," background paper prepared for the U.S.-China Economic and Security Review Commission, *2004 Report to Congress.*

12. General Accounting Office, "Export Controls," 16–17.

13. Ibid., 17–18. Competitive pressures have increased ever since a famous case in 1998, where Emcore of the USA was denied permission to sell an advanced metal organic vapor deposition machine to Hebei Semiconductor Research Institute. The German toolmaker Aixtron immediately scooped up the contract and supplied a comparable machine. Strong diplomatic protests in this and subsequent cases have accomplished little.

14. Pecht and Chan, *China's Electronics Industries*, 85; and interviews.

15. Pecht and Chan, *China's Electronics Industries*, 86.

16. Ibid., 87.

17. See Richard P. Suttmeier and Xiangkui Yao, "China's Post-WTO Technology Policy: Standards, Software, and the Changing Nature of Technonationalism," NBR Special Report No. 7 (Seattle: National Bureau of Asian Research, May 2004). The authors see Chinese standards policy as motivated by "neo-technonationalism," in which technological development in support of national economic and security interests is pursued through leveraging the opportunities presented by globalization for national advantage. They depict a China that to this point in time has benefited in absolute terms from technology transfer into the country but is still losing out in relative terms. Paying substantial royalties to foreign corporations leaves it in a "patent trap" that it fully intends to escape, partly by designing its own technology standards.

18. For an excellent overview, see Deh-I Hsiung, "An Evaluation of China's Science and Technology System and Its Impact on the Research Community," Special Report for the Environment, Science and Technology Section, U.S. Embassy, Beijing, Summer 2002.

19. For relevant background, see Cong Cao and Richard P. Suttmeier, "China's New Scientific Elite: Distinguished Young Scientists, the Research Environment and the Hopes for Chinese Science," *China Quarterly* 168 (2001): 960–84.

20. Hsiung, "An Evaluation of China's Science and Technology System," 26.

21. China moved along this specialized lab route during the same era that the United States was burying the remains of its famous Bell Labs. It is, perhaps, no coincidence that President Bush's Council of Advisors on Science and Technology has recently raised the issue once more and called for the development of a substitute national organ. See The President's Council of Advisors on Science and Technology, *Sustaining the Nation's Innovation Ecosystems: Report on Information Technology Manufacturing and Competitiveness* (Washington, DC, January 2004), 25.

22. Hsiung, "An Evaluation of China's Science and Technology System," 29–30.

23. Gary Gereffi et al., "Framing the Outsourcing Engineering Debate: Placing the United States on a Level Playing Field with China and India," 5–6. http://memp.pratt.duke.edu/downloads/duke_outsourcing_2005.pdf (accessed on September 11, 2006).

24. *China Electronics Report*, 21 February 2005.

25. For relevant analysis of key dependencies that complicate the closing of such gaps, see Cong Cao, "Challenges for Technological Development in China's Industry," *China Perspectives* 54 (July–August 2004): 4–24.

26. Some 3,000 U.S. companies are currently being watched by the FBI, which suspects they are collecting information for China. See Brian Bennett, "China's Big Export," *Time*, 21 February 2005.

27. See Alberto Gabriele, "S & T Policies and Technical Progress in China's Industry," *Review of International Political Economy* 9, no. 2 (Summer 2002): 333–73.

28. On this theme, see Peter Hays Gries, *China's New Nationalism* (Berkeley: University of California Press, 2004), 137. For an opposing view emphasizing the dynamics of structural competition, see John Mearsheimer, *The Tragedy of Great Power Politics* (New York: W. W. Norton, 2003), 4.

29. Robert L. Paarlberg, "Knowledge as Power: Science, Military Dominance, and U.S. Security," *International Security* 29, no. 1 (Summer 2004): 122–51.

30. See Alastair Iaian Johnston, "Is China a Status Quo Power?" *International Security* 27, no. 4 (Spring 2003): 5–56; Thomas J. Christensen, "Posing Problems without Catching Up: China's Rise and Challenges for U.S. Security Policy," *International Security* 25, no. 4 (Spring 2001): 5–40; and Peter Hays Gries and Thomas J. Christensen, "Correspondence: Power and Resolve in U.S. China Policy," *International Security* 26, no. 2 (Fall 2001): 155–65.

Chapter 4: The Politics of Economic Liberalization

The author has benefited from the comments of Bill Keller, Tom Rawski, Ellen Frost, and Bruce Dickson. The errors that remain are, alas, those of the author.

1. Kenneth Jowitt, *Leninist Responses to National Dependency* (Berkeley: Institute of International Studies, University of California, 1978); and Jowitt, *New World Disorder: The Leninist Extinction* (Berkeley: University of California Press, 1992).

2. This was a major theme in Hu Yaobang's seminal speech, "The Radiance of the Great Truth of Marxism Lights Our Way Forward," Xinhua, 13 March 1983, in Foreign Broadcast Information Service (hereafter FBIS), 14 March 1983, K1–17.

3. Joseph Fewsmith, *Dilemmas of Reform: Political Conflict and Economic Debate* (Armonk, NY: M. E. Sharpe, 1994); and Barry Naughton, *Growing Out of the Plan: Chinese Economic Reform, 1978–1993* (Cambridge: Cambridge University Press, 1995).

4. Merle Goldman, *Sowing the Seeds of Democracy: Political Reform in the Deng Xiaoping Era* (Cambridge, MA: Harvard University Press, 1994).

5. For a more extended treatment, see Richard Baum, *Burying Mao* (Princeton, NJ: Princeton University Press, 1994).

6. Conservative arguments following Tiananmen are laid out in Joseph Fewsmith, *China since Tiananmen: The Politics of Transition* (Cambridge: Cambridge University Press, 2001), 21–43.

7. Gloria Davies, ed., *Voicing Concerns: Contemporary Chinese Critical Inquiry* (Lanham, MD: Rowman & Littlefield, 2001).

8. Fewsmith, *China since Tiananmen.*

9. Wu Guoguang, *Zhao Ziyang yu zhengzhi gaige* [Political Reform under Zhao Ziyang] (Hong Kong: Taipingyang shiji yanjiusuo, 1997).

10. Kang Xiaoguang, "Weilai 3–5 nian Zhongguo dalu zhengzhi wendingxing fenxi" [An Analysis of the Stability of Chinese Politics on the Chinese Mainland in the Coming 3–5 Years], *Zhanlue yu guanli* [Strategy and Management], no. 3 (2002).

11. *Zhongguo tongji nianjian* [China Statistical Yearbook], various years.

12. It should be noted that although this tax reform greatly increased the fiscal strength of the central state, it undermined local finances, particularly at the county and township levels. Many of the fiscal and political problems at the local level stem in part from this centralization of fiscal control.

13. Yunxiang Yan, "The Politics of Consumerism in Chinese Society," in *China Briefing 2000: The Continuing Transformation*, ed. Tyrenne White, 159–93 (Armonk, NY: M. E. Sharpe, 2000).

14. Tang Tsou, "Introduction," *The Cultural Revolution and Post-Mao Reforms: A Historical Interpretation* (Chicago: University of Chicago Press, 1986).

15. Gu Xin and David Kelly, "Realistic Responses and Strategic Options: An Alternative CCP Ideology and Its Critics," *Chinese Law and Government* 29, no. 2 (Spring–Summer 1996).

16. Suisheng Zhao, *A Nation-State by Construction: Dynamics of Modern Chinese Nationalism* (Stanford, CA: Stanford University Press, 2004), 218–27.

17. Song Qiang, Zhang Zangzang, and Qiao Bian, *Zhongguo keyi shuobu* [China Can Say No] (Beijing: Zhonghua gongshang lianhe chubanshe, 1996).

18. Fewsmith, *China since Tiananmen*, 75–100.

19. Sun Liping, "Pingmin zhuyi yu Zhongguo gaige" [Populism and China's Reform], *Zhanlue yu guanli* [Strategy and Management], no. 5 (October 1994):

1–10. See also Sun Liping, *Zhuanxing yu duanlie: gaige yilai Zhongguo shehui jiegou de bianhua* [Transition and Fracture: The Change in Social Structure since Reform] (Beijng: Qinghua daxue chubanshe, 2004); and Yu Peilin, Li Qiang, and Sun Liping, eds., *Zhongguo shehui fenceng* [Social Stratification in China] (Beijing: Shehui kexue wenxian chubanshe, 2004).

20. Zhang Jingping, *Quanbian: Cong guanyuan xiahai dao shangren congzheng* [Power Shift: From Officials Going into Business to Businessmen Going into Government] (Hangzhou: Zhejiang renmin chubanshe, 2004).

21. Li Changping, *Wo xiang zongli shuo shihua* [Speaking the Truth to the Premier] (Beijing: Guangming ribao chubanshe, 2002).

22. Zhao Shukai, "Xiangcun zhili: Zuzhi he chongtu" [Governance in Villages: Organization and Conflict], *Zhanlue yu guanli* [Strategy and Management] (November 2003) 1–8; and Yu Jianrong, "Nongcun hei'e shili he jiceng zhengquan tuihua: Xiangnan diaocha" [The Evil Forces in Rural Areas and the Deterioration of Grassroots Administration: A Survey of Southern Hunan], *Zhanlue yu guanli* [Strategy and Management] (September 2003): 1–14.

23. Wang Keqin and Qiao Guodong, "Investigation Report on 'The Strikes on Villagers' in Dingzhou, Hebei," *Zhongguo jingji shibao* [China Economic Times], 20 June 2005; and Leu Siew Ying, "Riot Police Seize Files Being Guarded by Protesting Villagers," *South China Morning Post*, 13 September 2005.

24. Bill Savadove, "Shanghai Reveals Surge in 'Mass Dispute' Court Cases," *South China Morning Post*, 27 July 2005.

25. Peng Guo, "Asymmetrical Information, Suboptimal Strategies, and Institutional Performance: The Paradox of the 1995 Regulations of China's Official Promotion System," PhD diss., Boston University, 2004.

26. Wen Shengtang, "2003 nian de fanfubai douzheng" [The Struggle against Corruption in 2003], in *2004 nian: Zhongguo shehui xingshi fenxi yu yuce* [The State of Chinese Society: Analysis and Forecast, 2004], ed. Ru Xin, Lu Xueyi, and Li Peilin (Beijing: Shehui kexue wenxian chubanshe, 2004), 162.

27. Joseph Fewsmith, "Taizhou Area Explores Ways to Improve Local Governance," *China Leadership Monitor*, no. 15 (Summer 2005), available at www.hoover.org/publications/clm.

28. Joseph Fewsmith, "Chambers of Commerce in Wenzhou and the Potential Limits of 'Civil Society' in China," *China Leadership Monitor*, no. 16 (Fall 2005), available at www.hoover.org/publications/clm.

29. Bruce Gilley, *China's Democratic Future* (New York: Columbia University Press, 2004).

30. Joseph Fewsmith, "Continuing Pressure on Social Order," *China Leadership Monitor*, no. 10 (Spring 2004), http://media.hoover.org/documents/clm10_jf.pdf.

31. Hu Angang, Wang Shaoguang, and Ding Yuanzhu, "Jingji fanrong beihou de shehui bu wending" [The Social Instability behind Economic Prosperity], *Zhanlue yu guanli* [Strategy and Management] (June 2002): 26–33.

32. Dali L. Yang, *Remaking the Chinese Leviathan: Market Transition and the Politics of Governance in China* (Stanford, CA: Stanford University Press, 2004).

33. An early expression of this argument, albeit from a leftist perspective, was Luo yi ning ge er, *Disanzhi yanjing kan Zhongguo* [Looking at China Through a Third Eye] (Taiyuan: Shanxi renmin chubanshe, 1994).

34. Joseph Fewsmith, "China under Hu Jintao," *China Leadership Monitor*, no. 14 (Spring 2005), available at www.hoover.org/publications.clm.

35. Qin Chujun, "Former Kelon Chief Faces Court," *China Daily*, 3 August 2006; and Hu Yuanyuan, "Kelon Gets Fined for Accounting Fraud," *China Daily*, 6 July 2006.

36. "Hu Jintao, Wu Bangguo, Zeng Qinghong, and Jia Qinglin Participate in Deliberations and Discussions" [in Chinese], *Renmin ribao*, March 7, 2006.

37. China Central Television, 14 March 2006, trans. Open Source Center CPP20060314070001.

38. "Hu Jintao's Talk to Fourth Plenum Exposed: He Sharply Attacks Liberalization Saying Methods Must Not Be Lax" [in Chinese], *Kaifang* [Openness], December 2004, http://www.open.com.hk/2003_12news1.htm

39. Fewsmith, "China under Hu Jintao."

40. "Further Develop and Bring about Flourishing Philosophy and Social Sciences," *Qiushi* [Seek Truth], no. 4 (16 February 2004): 1–4.

41. Li Ruiying: "Make New Contributions to Upholding and Developing Marxism—An Interview with Leng Rong, Permanent Vice President of the Chinese Academy of Social Sciences and Concurrently Director of Research Academy on Marxism," *Guangming ribao*, 28 December 2005.

42. Lu Xueyi, ed., *Dangdai Zhongguo shehui liudong* [Social Mobility in Contemporary China] (Beijing: Shehui kexue wenxian chubanshe, 2004).

43. Wu Jinglian, "Gezhong shehui liliang duidai gaige de butong taidu" [The Different Attitudes of Various Social Forces toward Reform], *Dangdai Zhongguo jingji gaige* [Contemporary Chinese Economic Reform], 421–26, excerpted in *Shisan nianlai yingxiang zhongyang gaoceng jingji juece de lundian huibian* [Compilation of Points of View that have Influenced the High-Level Economic Decision Making of the Center over the Past Thirteen Years] (Beijing: n.p., 2003).

44. For a recent report detailing this tightening control over media, see Ashley Esarey, "Speak No Evil: Mass Media Control in Contemporary China." A Freedom House special report, February 2006.

45. Huang Ping and Cui Zhiyuan, eds., *Zhongguo yu quanqiuhua: Huashengdun gongshi haishi Beijing gongshi?* [China and Globalization: Washington Consensus or Beijing Consensus?] (Beijing: Shehui kexue wenxian chubanshe, 2005).

46. On the state's continuing efforts to support SOEs, see Yasheng Huang, *Selling China: Foreign Direct Investment during the Reform Era* (Cambridge: Cambridge University Press, 2003).

Chapter 5: China's Commercial Diplomacy in Asia

I am grateful to Dr. Phillip C. Saunders of the Institute for National Strategic Studies, National Defense University, for his comments and insights.

1. This definition is adapted from the Web page of the Institute for Trade & Commercial Diplomacy, Inc., http://www.commercialdiplomacy.org. The institute was founded by trade expert Geza Feketekuty, longtime employee of the Office of the U.S. Trade Representative and former chairman of the OECD Trade Committee.

2. See Martin W. Lewis and Karen E. Wigen, *The Myth of Continents: A Critique of Metageography* (Berkeley: University of California Press, 1997); Gungwu Wang, *The Chinese Overseas: From Earthbound China to the Quest for Autonomy* (Cambridge, MA: Harvard University Press, 2000); and Grant Evans, Christopher Hutton, and Kuah Khun Eng, *Where China Meets Southeast Asia: Social and Cultural Change in the Border Regions* (Bangkok: White Lotus; and Singapore: Institute for Southeast Asian Studies, 2000).

3. "ASEAN + 3" refers to the ten members of the Association of Southeast Asian Nations (ASEAN) plus China, Japan, and South Korea.

4. For a schematic map detailing the multitude of actual and proposed agreements, see T. J. Pempel, "Introduction," in *Remapping East Asia: The Construction of a Region*, ed. T. J. Pempel (Ithaca, NY: Cornell University Press, 2005), fig. 1.4, p. 17.

5. These impressions are based on the author's firsthand observations while working in the Office of the United States Trade Representative in 1993–95.

6. For some modeling results, see Robert Scollay and John P. Gilbert, *New Trading Arrangements in the Western Pacific?* (Washington, DC: Institute for International Economics, 2001), 57–58, 149; and Dean DeRosa, "Gravity Model Calculations of the Trade Impacts of U.S. Free Trade Agreements," a paper prepared for the Conference on Free Trade Agreements and U.S. Policy, Institute for International Economics, Washington, DC, 7–8 May 2003, p. 35. For a critique of economic regionalism in Asia, see Edward J. Lincoln, *East Asian Economic Regionalism* (New York; Council on Foreign Relations; Washington, DC: Brookings Institution Press, 2004).

7. It was in preparation for the first ASEM meeting that the selected Asian countries came to be known as "ASEAN + 3."

8. For more on ASEM and Asia-Europe relations, see Council for Asia-Europe Cooperation, *The Rationale and Common Agenda for Asia-Europe Cooperation* (Tokyo: Japan Center for International Exchange; London: International Institute of Strategic Studies, 1997); and Suthiphand Chirathivat, Franz Knipping, Poul Henrik Lassen, and Chia Siow Yue, eds., *Asia-Europe on the Eve of the 21st Century* (Bangkok: Centre for European Studies at Chulalongkorn University; Singapore: Institute of Southeast Asian Studies, 2001).

9. The China-ASEAN FTA is under negotiation, but there are no concrete plans for an ASEAN + 3 FTA.

10. For a thoughtful overview of the nongovernmental process, see Paul Evans, "Between Regionalism and Regionalization: Policy Networks and the Nascent East Asian Institutional Identity," in Pempel, *Remapping East Asia*, 195–215.

11. Mahathir proposed an "East Asian Economic Group" (subsequently renamed a "caucus") that included Japan but excluded Australia and New Zealand. On the quest for an Asian or East Asian identity, see the recent writings of Amitav Acharya. For visions of an East Asian community, see the East Asia Vision Group report, "Towards an East Asian Community: Region of Peace, Prosperity and Progress," 2001, http://www.mofa.go.jp/region/asia-paci/report2001.pdf; and "Charting East Asia's Milestones," Keynote Address by Prime Minister Abdullah Ahmad Badawi at the Second East Asia Forum, 7 December 2004, mimeograph.

12. See, for example, Yue Xiaoyong, "A Chinese Perspective on Strengthening Stability and Security in East Asia," presentation at the Wilton Park Conference on Reducing Tension in North East Asia, 6 October 2004. See also Zheng Bijian, "China's 'Peaceful Rise' to Great-Power Status," *Foreign Affairs* 84, no. 5 (September/October 2005): 18–24; and Wang Jisi, "China's Search for Stability with America," *Foreign Affairs* 84, no. 5 (September/October 2005): 39–48.

13. Eswar Prasad, ed., "China's Growth and Integration into the World Economy: Prospects and Challenges," *Occasional Paper 232*, International Monetary Fund, 2004, p. 1, available at http://www.imf.org/external/pubs/cat/longres.cfm?sk=17305.0.

14. Robert J. Samuelson, "The China Riddle," *Washington Post*, 30 January 2004.

15. Jeffrey Ng, "UPS Says It Has Big Plans for China," *Washington Post*, 27 February 2005.

16. David Murphy, "Europe, Here We Come," *Far Eastern Economic Review*, 26 February 2004, 42.

17. Prasad, "China's Growth and Integration," table 2.2, p. 6.

18. Ibid., 8.

19. "Koreans Look to China, Seeing a Market and a Monster," *New York Times*, 10 February 2003.

20. Kevin G. Cai, "The ASEAN-China Free Trade Agreement and East Asian Regional Grouping," *Contemporary Southeast Asia* 25, no. 3 (2003): 401.

21. Kazuko Hamada, "The Impact of China's Economic Integration: The Implications of China's Role in the Asian Production Network for the Global Economic System," unpublished paper, 7 February 2005.

22. "FTWorld's Most Respected Companies," *Financial Times*, Special Report, 20 January 2004, 2; and David Murphy, "State Giants Still Dominate," *Far Eastern Economic Review*, 25 December 2003, 56.

23. Richard E. Baldwin, "The Spoke Trap: Hub and Spoke Bilateralism in East Asia," unpublished paper written for the Korean Institute for International Economic Policy, 2003, unnumbered page.

24. In "China Engages Asia: Reshaping the Regional Order," David Shambaugh

makes a well-documented case that China's altered behavior, sometimes labeled "charm diplomacy," represents a strategic change in mind-set rather than a tactical shift. *International Security* 29, no. 3 (Winter 2004/2005): 64–99.

25. For China's participation in post-crisis financial diplomacy, see C. Randall Henning, *East Asian Financial Cooperation*, Policy Analysis 68 (Washington, DC: Institute for International Economics, 2002).

26. I am grateful to METI official Naoko Munakata for much of the information in this paragraph.

27. The 1997–98 Asian financial crisis makes it difficult to determine to what extent investment in Southeast Asia was in fact diverted to China. From 1996 to 1999, the inflow of foreign direct investment in China increased from US$27 billion to US$45 billion, while that into ASEAN dropped from US$28 billion to US$11 billion. Without the crisis, both areas might have continued to attract substantial investment.

28. Since Japanese agriculture is highly protected, Japan prefers to negotiate "economic partnership agreements" (EPAs) because they are more flexible and more sensitive to political realities. Makio Miyagawa, director of the Japan Institute of International Affairs, makes the case for EPAs in "Integrating Asia through Free Trade," *Far Eastern Economic Review*, July–August 2005, 45–49.

29. David Pilling and Bayan Rahman, "Japanese Trade Breakthrough with Mexico Points Way to Asia Deals," *Financial Times*, 11 March 2004.

30. David Pilling, "Japanese Soft Loans Pour into Indian Projects," *Financial Times*, 12 March 2004.

31. See, for example, the keynote address given by a Japanese Finance Ministry official to a high-level ASEAN + 3 seminar on the Asian Bond Market Initiative, at http://www.mof.go.jp/english/if/hls20030301b.htm.

32. Oral presentation by Shigeki Kimura, director, Research Division, International Bureau, Ministry of Finance, to a Japan Chair Forum on the Asian Bond Markets Initiative, Center for Strategic and International Affairs, Washington, DC, 14 September 2005.

33. Wang Jisi, "Geostrategic Trends in Asia: A Chinese View," conference paper presented at the Regional Outlook Forum, Institute of Southeast Asian Studies, Singapore, 6 January 2005. Wang is dean of the School of International Studies at Peking University and director of the Institute of International Strategic Studies at the Central Party School of the Communist Party of China.

34. For an analysis of Asia's energy needs from a strategic perspective, see Mikkal E. Herberg, "Asia's Energy Insecurity: Cooperation or Conflict?" in *Strategic Asia 2004–05: Confronting Terrorism in the Pursuit of Power*, ed. Ashley J. Tellis and Michael Wills, 338–77 (Seattle: National Bureau of Asian Research, 2004).

35. United States, U.S.-China Economic and Security Review Commission, *The National Security Implications of the Economic Relationship between the United States and China*, Report to Congress of the U.S.-China Security Review

Commission, Washington, DC, July 2002, 117. For a critique, see the dissenting comments by William A. Reinsch, 206–7.

36. David Kang, "Getting Asia Wrong: The Need for New Analytical Frameworks," *International Security* 27, no. 4 (Spring 2003): 71. For an argument against Kang's thesis, see Amitav Acharya, "Will Asia's Past Be Its Future?" *International Security* 28, no. 3 (Winter 2003–2004): 149–64. Kang's rebuttal, entitled "Hierarchy, Balancing, and Empirical Puzzles in Asian International Relations," appears in the same issue, pp. 165–80.

37. Peter Reuter and Edwin M. Truman, *Chasing Dirty Money: The Fight against Money Laundering* (Washington, DC: Institute for International Economics, 2004), 42, tables 3.1, 3.3.

38. James Politi and Doug Cameron, "Unocal Suitors Wary of Beijing," *Financial Times*, 4 March 2005, 15.

39. The White House, "Fact Sheet: Enterprise for ASEAN Initiative," http://www.whitehouse.gov/news/releases/2002/10/20021026-7.html. Candidate countries must be WTO members and must have signed a Trade and Investment Framework Agreement (TIFA), which sets up a nonbinding consultative mechanism to discuss bilateral issues of interest. Singapore and Thailand signed on to this offer and subsequently negotiated free trade agreements with the United States, while the Philippines and Indonesia hung back. Mahathir's Malaysia rejected the whole U.S. initiative, but after his departure Malaysia signed a TIFA and agreed to begin negotiations for a U.S.-Malaysian FTA.

40. U.S. Department of State, "An Overview of U.S.-East Asia Policy," Testimony by James A. Kelly, Assistant Secretary of State for East Asian and Pacific Affairs, before the House International Relations Committee, Washington, DC, 2 June 2004, p. 2.

41. "Joint Statement between the United States of America and the Republic of Indonesia," White House press release, 25 May 2005, emphasis added

42. The White House, "Joint Vision Statement on the ASEAN-U.S. Enhanced Partnership," 17 November 2005, http://www.whitehouse.gov/news/releases/2005/11/20051117-4.html.

43. U.S. Department of State, "The ASEAN-U.S. Enhanced Partnership," 17 November 2006, http://www.state.gov/r/pa/prs/ps/2006/76231.htm.

44. Sensitive to the Myanmar problem, ASEAN members persuaded the regime in Yangon (formerly Rangoon) to postpone assuming the chairmanship of ASEAN in 2006, even though it was its turn to do so.

Chapter 6: Balance of Power Politics and the Rise of China

A more theoretical version of this chapter appeared as Robert S. Ross, "Balance of Power Politics and the Rise of China: Accommodation and Balancing in East Asia," *Security Studies* 15, no. 3 (Fall 2006).

1. Traditional realists argue that international politics and conflict reflect the state's intrinsic drive for power, whereas neorealists argue that anarchy compels

states to seek security. The classic statement of traditional realism and the balance of power is Hans J. Morgenthau, *Politics among Nations: The Struggle for Power and Peace*, 5th ed. (New York: Alfred A. Knopf, 1978), chap. 12. For a traditional realist perspective on secondary state behavior, see Robert L. Rothstein, *Alliances and Small Powers* (New York: Columbia University Press, 1968). The classic statement of neorealism and balance of power politics is Kenneth N. Waltz, *Theory of International Relations* (Reading, MA: Addison-Wesley, 1979), chap. 6.

2. Stephen M. Walt, *The Origins of Alliances* (Ithaca, NY: Cornell University Press, 1987), 29–31.

3. Albert O. Hirschman, *National Power and the Structure of Foreign Trade* (Berkeley: University of California Press, 1980); Rawi Abdelal and Jonathan Kirshner, "Strategy, Economic Relations, and the Definition of National Interests," *Security Studies* 9, nos. 1/2 (Autumn 1999–Winter 2000): 119–56; Klaus Knorr, *The Power of Nations: The Political Economy of International Relations* (New York: Basic Books, 1975), chap. 6.

4. Samuel P. Huntington, *The Clash of Civilizations and the Remaking of World Order* (New York: Simon & Schuster, 1996).

5. David C. Kang, "Getting Asia Wrong: The Need for New Analytical Frameworks," *International Security* 27, no. 4 (Spring 2003): 57–85.

6. Richard K. Betts, "Wealth, Power and Instability: East Asia and the United States after the Cold War," *International Security* 18, no. 3 (Winter 1993–1994): 53–54; Aaron L. Friedberg, "The Struggle for Mastery in Asia," *Commentary* 110, no. 4 (November 2000): 17–26; James. F. Hoge Jr., "A Global Power Shift in the Making," *Foreign Affairs* 83, no. 4 (July–August 2004): 5.

7. Randall L. Schweller, "Bandwagoning for Profit: Bringing the Revisionist State Back In," *International Security* 19, no. 1 (Summer 1994): 80–81; Robert G. Kaufman, "To Balance or Bandwagon: Alignment Decisions in 1930s Europe," *Security Studies* 1, no. 3 (Spring 1992): 417–47.

8. Rothstein, *Alliances and Small Powers*, 29. Also see, for example, Edward Hallett Carr, *The Twenty Years Crisis, 1919–1939* (New York: Harper & Row, 1964), 103–5.

9. Rothstein, *Alliances and Small Powers*, 59, 62.

10. Morgenthau, *Politics among Nations*, chap. 12, 181–84.

11. George Liska, *Nations in Alliance: The Limits of Interdependence* (Baltimore, MD: Johns Hopkins University Press, 1968), 27.

12. Walt, *The Origins of Alliances*, 29–31.

13. Hirschman, *National Power and the Structure of Foreign Trade*, 16.

14. Ibid., 26–29. Also see Abdelal and Kirshner, "Strategy, Economic Relations, and the Definition of National Interests."

15. For a study of how economic interdependence among the great powers undermines timely balancing strategies, see Paul A. Papayoanou, "Economic Interdependence and the Balance of Power," *International Studies Quarterly* 41, no. 1 (March 1997): 113–40.

16. Hirschman, *National Power and the Structure of Foreign Trade*; Abdelal and Kirshner, "Strategy, Economic Relations, and the Definition of National Interests"; Knorr, *The Power of Nations*, chap. 6.

17. David Baldwin, "Power Analysis and World Politics: New Trends versus Old Tendencies," *World Politics*, 31, no. 2 (January 1979): 161–94.

18. Walt, in *Origins of Alliances*, uses alliances, formal and informal, as indicators of secondary state alignment. Given his empirical focus on the polarized Middle East during the Cold War, this is an effective measure.

19. Such indicators of secondary state alignment parallel Robert L. Jervis's discussions of the indices of great power commitment to defend secondary states. See *Logic of Images in International Relations* (New York: Columbia University Press, 1989).

20. On the sources of soft power, see Joseph S. Nye, *Soft Power: The Means to Success in World Politics* (New York: Public Affairs, 2004), chap. 1.

21. For a discussion of Sino-Russian strategic balance in Central Asia, see Stephen J. Blank, "Who's Minding the Store? The Failure of Russian Security Policy," *Problems of Post-Communism* 45, no. 2 (March–April 1998): 3–11.

22. For a comprehensive discussion of Chinese ground force modernization, see Dennis J. Blasko, *The Chinese Army Today* (New York: Routledge, 2004). Also see Dennis J. Blasko, "The New PLA Force Structure," in *The People's Liberation Army in the Information Age*, ed. James C. Mulvenon and Richard H. Yang (Santa Monica, CA: Rand, 1999), 263–70; Dennis J. Blasko, "PLA Ground Forces: Moving toward a Smaller, More Rapidly Deployable, Modern Combined Arms Force," in *The People's Liberation Army as Organization*, ed. James C. Mulvenon and Andrew N. D. Yang (Santa Monica, CA: Rand, 2002), 315–22.

23. "C^4I" refers to command, control, computers, communication, and intelligence. See United States Department of Defense, *Annual Report to Congress: The Military Power of the People's Republic of China 2003* (Washington, DC: U.S. Department of Defense, 2003); Andrew N. D. Yang and Col. Milton Wen-Chung Liao (ret.), "PLA Rapid Reaction Forces: Concept, Training, and Preliminary Assessment," in *The People's Liberation Army in the Information Age*, ed. James C. Mulvenon and Richard H. Yang (Santa Monica, CA: Rand, 1999), 48–57; James Mulvenon, "The PLA Army's Struggle for Identity," in *The People's Liberation Army and China in Transition*, ed. Stephen J. Flanagan and Michael E. Marti (Washington, DC: Institute for National Strategic Studies, National Defense University, 2003), 116; Dennis J. Blasko, "PLA Ground Forces," 322–25.

24. Yang and Liao, "PLA Rapid Reaction Forces"; Mulvenon, "The PLA Army's Struggle for Identity," 116–17.

25. Lonnie Henley, "PLA Logistics and Doctrine Reform, 1999–2009," in *The People's Liberation Army after Next*, ed. Susan M. Puska (Carlisle, PA: Strategic Studies Institute, U.S. Army War College, 2000), 72–73.

26. Susan M. Puska, "Rough but Ready Force Projection: An Assessment of Recent PLA Training," in *China's Growing Military Power: Perspectives on Security,*

Ballistic Missiles, and Conventional Capabilities, ed. Andrew J. Scobel and Larry M. Wortzel (Carlisle, PA: Strategic Studies Institute, U.S. Army War College, 2002), 223, 244–45.

27. Taeho Kim, "Korean Perspectives on PLA Modernization and the Future East Asian Security Environment," in *In China's Shadow: Regional Perspectives on Chinese Foreign Policy and Military Development*, ed. Jonathan D. Pollack and Richard H. Yang (Santa Monica, CA: Rand, 1998), 51, 54, 62.

28. United States Department of Defense, *Annual Report to Congress: The Military Power of the People's Republic of China 2003* (Washington, DC: U.S. Department of Defense, 2003), 5.

29. United States Department of Defense, *Annual Report to Congress: The Military Power of the People's Republic of China 2005* (Washington, DC: U.S. Department of Defense, 2005), 4; testimony of Richard P. Lawless, Deputy Undersecretary of Defense, International Security Affairs-Asia Pacific, to the Senate Foreign Relations Committee, Subcommittee on East Asian and Pacific Affairs, 22 April 2004. On the DF-15, also see Shirley A. Kan, *China: Ballistic and Cruise Missiles, CRS Report for Congress* (97–391 F) (Washington, DC: Congressional Research Service, Library of Congress, 2000), 11–12. On the survivability of PRC missile launchers, see Alan Vick, Richard Moore, Bruce Pirnie, and John Stillion, *Aerospace Operations against Elusive Ground Targets* (Santa Monica, CA: Rand, 2001).

30. See United States Department of Defense, *Annual Report to Congress: The Military Power of the People's Republic of China 2004* (Washington, DC: U.S. Department of Defense, 2004).

31. For a comprehensive assessment of Taiwan's vulnerability to mainland capabilities, see Bernard D. Cole, *Taiwan's Security: History and Prospects* (New York: Routledge, 2006).

32. On China's protracted discussion of whether to build a carrier, see Ian Storey and You Ji, "China's Aircraft Carrier Ambitions: Seeking Truth from Rumors," *Naval War College Review* 57, no. 1 (Winter 2004): 77–93.

33. Bernard D. Cole, *The Great Wall at Sea: China's Navy Enters the Twenty-First Century* (Annapolis, MD: Naval Institute Press, 2001), 97–99, chap. 8; Bernard D. Cole, "The PLA and 'Active Defense,'" in *The People's Liberation Army and China in Transition*, ed. Stephen J. Flanagan and Michael Marti (Washington, DC: National Defense University, 2003), 136; Bernard D. Cole, "China's Maritime Strategy," in Puska, *The People's Liberation Army after Next*, 305, 309; Lyle Goldstein and William Murray, "Undersea Dragons: China's Maturing Submarine Force," *International Security* 28, no. 4 (Spring 2004): 161–96.

34. "China Emerges as Biggest Export Market of South Korea," *People's Daily*, 14 November 2002 (internet version), http://english.peopledaily.com.cn/200211/14/eng20021114_106796.shtml. Also see James Brooke, "Korea Feeling Pressure as China Grows," *New York Times*, 8 January 2003.

35. Yonhap, 27 July 2000, in Foreign Broadcast Information Service (FBIS),

KPP20000727000014. The best treatment of this incident is Jae Ho Chung, "From a Special Relationship to a Normal Partnership: Interpreting the 'Garlic Battle,'" *Pacific Affairs* 76, no. 4 (Winter 2003–2004): 549–68.

36. "China Becomes South Korea's Number One Investment Target," *China Daily*, 2 February 2002.

37. So Chi-un, "Nation Braces for Industrial Hollowing Out," *Korea Herald*, 12 January 2004, in FBIS, KPP20040112000037; Yonhap, 29 January 2004, in FBIS, KPP20040129000060. On the trade figures, see the Republic of Korea customs figures at http://english.customs.go.kr/; Yonhap, 29 April 2004, in FBIS, KPP20040429000044; Xinhua, 19 May 2004, in FBIS, CPP20040519000077.

38. The 2002 trade statistics are from the Taiwan Board of Foreign Trade; Central News Agency, 15 September 2002, FBIS, CPP20020915000025; Central News Agency, 28 September 2002, FBIS, CPP20020928000044; Central News Agency, 7 August 2002, FBIS, CPP20020807000167; *Financial Times Global Newswire*, February 23, 2004, http://web.lexis-nexis.com/universe/. The investment statistics are in Central News Agency, 7 August 2002, FBIS, CPP20020807000167; Central News Agency, 21 October 2002, FBIS, CPP20021022000004; Liu Yusheng, "Wang Zaixi States that Stopping 'Taiwan Independence' is a Current Urgent Task for All Sons and Daughters of China," Zhongguo Xinwenshe, 3 January 2004, FBIS, CPP20040103000056.

39. See the analysis in U.S. International Trade Commission, *U.S.-Taiwan FTA: Likely Economic Impact of a Free Trade Agreement between the United States and Taiwan* (Washington, DC: International Trade Commission of the United States, 2002), http://www.usitc.gov/publications/abstract_3548.htm.

40. Editorial, *Taipei Times*, 13 June 2004, 8, http://www.taipeitimes.com/News/editorials/archives/2004/06/13/2003174891; Central News Agency, 7 August 2002, FBIS, CPP20020807000167; Central News Agency, 21 October 2002, FBIS, CPP20021022000004; Zhongguo Xinwenshe, 3 January 2004, FBIS, CPP20040103000056; "Government Approves TSMC's Wafer Project," *China Post*, 1 May 2004; Zhongguo Xinwenshe, 18 February 2004, FBIS, CPP20040228000102; *Renmin ribao*, 26 December 2004, in FBIS, CPP20031226000049; *Taipei Times*, 6 January 2004, in FBIS, CPP20040106000145.

41. On Taiwan's "no haste, be patient" and "go south" policies, see T. Y. Wang, "Lifting the 'No Haste, Be Patient' Policy: Implications for Cross-Strait Relations," *Cambridge Review of International Affairs* 15, no. 1 (2002): 131–39; Sheng Lijun, *China and Taiwan: Cross-Strait Relations under Chen Shui-bian* (Singapore: Institute of Southeast Asian Relations, 2002). For a Taiwan government discussion of the growing danger of dependence, see, for example, Central News Agency, 13 January 2004, in FBIS, CPP20040112000209.

42. World Bank Group, *World Development Indicators*, WDI Online.

43. For an early Chinese assessment of Japan's enduring economic and societal problems, see Liu Xiaofeng and Zhang Yulin, *Riben de weiji* [Japan's Crisis] (Beijing: Renmin chubanshe, 2001).

44. The figures are from the Japanese Customs Agency, http://www.customs.go.jp/toukei/srch/indexe.htm. Ken Belson, "Japanese Capital and Jobs Flowing to China," *New York Times*, 17 February 2004.

45. Ken Hijino, "China-Japan Trade Deepens," *Financial Times*, 15 December 2001; James Kynge, "Japan, China in 11th-hour Trade Deal," *Financial Times*, 22 December 2001; James J. Przystup, "Japan-China Relations: From Precipice to Promise," *Comparative Connections* 3, no. 4 (October–December 2001): 89, http://www.csis.org/media/csis/pubs/0104q.pdf.

46. David Ibison, "Koizumi Visits to War Shrine Attacked," *Financial Times*, 26 November 2004; "Great Wall: Yasukuni Issue Dashes Hopes for Improvement of Japan-China," *Asahi Shimbun* (English edition), 2 October 2004.

47. The figures are from the Japanese Ministry of Finance, http://www.mof.go.jp/english/.

48. For a Chinese discussion of the importance of the Chinese market to the ASEAN countries, see Zhang Yunling, *Weilai 10–15 nian Zhongguo zai Taipingyang diqu mianlin de guoji huanjing* [The International Environment China Faces in the Asia-Pacific in the Next 10–15 Years] (Beijing: Zhongguo shehui kexue chubanshe, 2003), 299–319.

49. Alice D. Ba, "China and ASEAN; Reinvigorating Relations for a 21st Century Asia," *Asian Survey* 43, no. 4 (July–August 2003): 638–44; Xinhua, 8 February 2004, FBIS, CPP20040208000018; Peter S. Goodman, "Made in China—With Neighbors' Imports," *Washington Post*, 5 February 2004; Brad Grosserman, "China's Influence in Asia Soars," *Japan Times*, 17 May 2004. For Singapore statistics, see Singapore Department of Statistics, Government of Singapore, http://www.singstat.gov.sg/keystats/mqstats/ess/aesa63.pdf. Philippine statistics are from Department of Trade and Industry, the Philippines, at http://tradelinephil.dti.gov.ph/betp/trade_stat.expcod_sumprod.

50. Edward J. Lincoln, *East Asian Economic Regionalism* (Washington, DC: Brookings Institution Press, 2004), 45–48, 55–56.

51. See also Peter Drysdale and Xinpeng Xu, "Taiwan's Role in the Economic Architecture of East Asia and the Pacific," in *Economic Reform and Cross-Strait Relations: Taiwan and China in the WTO*, ed. Julian Chang and Steven M. Goldstein (New Jersey: World Scientific, 2007). On the 2004 agreement, see Jane Perlez, "Chinese Premier Signs Trade Pact at Southeast Asian Summit," *New York Times*, 30 November 2004.

52. On the 1994 crisis, see Joel S. Wit, Daniel B. Poneman, and Robert L. Gallucci, *Going Critical: The First North Korean Nuclear Crisis* (Washington, DC: Brookings Institution Press, 2004), 196–200.

53. Doug Struck, "Observers See Rising Risk of U.S.–N. Korea Conflict," *Washington Post*, 28 February 2003; Bradley Graham and Doug Struck, "U.S. Officials Anticipate More Provocations by North Korea," *Washington Post*, 3 March 2003; Doug Struck, "War Games on Korean Peninsula Upset North," *Washington Post*, 23 March 2003; Korean Central News Agency, 1 April 2003, in

FBIS, KPP20030401000074; Bradley Graham and Doug Struck, "U.S., Asian Allies Face Tough Choices," *Washington Post*, 25 April 2003.

54. Agence France Presse, 31 May 2003, in FBIS, JPP20030531000047; Yonhap, 31 May 2003, in FBIS, AFS KPP20030531000068; Yonhap, 7 August 2003, in FBIS, AFS KPP20030807000014; Yonhap, 31 May 2003, in FBIS, AFS KPP20030531000020.

55. James Brooke, "Threats and Responses: Weapons; South Opposes Pressuring North Korea, Which Hints It Will Scrap Nuclear Pact," *New York Times*, 1 January 2003.

56. "Roh Says No to Greater USFK Role in Northeast Asia," *Chosun Ilbo*, 8 March 2005, at http://english.chosun.com/w21data/html/news/200503/200503080028.html.

57. William H. Gleystein Jr., *Massive Entanglement, Marginal Influence: Carter and Korea in Crisis* (Washington, DC: Brookings Institution Press, 1999), 2–3, 12–13, 40–50.

58. "U.S. Considers Cuts to Forces in Korea," *New York Times*, 7 March 2003; James Brooke, "Musings on an Exodus of G.I.'s, South Korea Hails U.S. Presence," *New York Times*, 8 March 2003; Thom Shanker, "Rumsfeld Reassures Seoul on Regrouping G.I.'s," *New York Times*, 18 November 2003; Thom Shanker, "Pentagon Weighs Transferring 4,000 G.I.'s in Korea to Iraq," *New York Times*, 17 May 2004; James Brooke and Thom Shanker, "U.S. Plans to Cut Third of Troops in South Korea," *New York Times*, 8 June 2004; Thom Shanker and David E. Sanger, "U.S. Defends Plan to Reduce Forces in South Korea," *New York Times*, 9 June 2004.

59. Jung Sung-ki, "'Balancer' Theory Faces Criticism," *Korea Times*, 7 April 2005, at http://search.hankooki.com/times/times_view.php?terms=%22yoon+code%3A+kt&path=hankooki3%2Ftimes%2Flpage%2F200504%2Fkt2005040716314810230.htm.

60. Ryu Jin, "Seoul Taps Tokyo over Missile Response," *Korea Times*, 11 June 2006, http://search.hankooki.com/times/times_view.php?term=raps++&path=hankooki3/times/lpage/200607/kt2006071117210310440.htm&media=kt.

61. James Brooke, "Courtship of Beijing and Seoul: A New Twist for an Old Bond," *New York Times*, 26 February 2004; Choson Ilbo, 6 February 2004, in FBIS, KPP20040206000110; Xinhua, 8 July 2003, in FBIS, CPP20030708000197.

62. Eric V. Larson, Norman D. Levin, Seonhae Baik, and Bogdan Savych, *Ambivalent Allies? A Study of South Korean Attitudes toward the U.S.* (Santa Monica, CA: Rand, 2004), 62–64.

63. See Wit, Poneman, and Gallucci, *Going Critical*, 198–99; Don Oberdorfer, *The Two Koreas: A Contemporary History* (New York: Basic Books, 1997), 320–21.

64. Yonhap, 4 June 2003, in FBIS, KPP20030604000001. On the oil shipments, see, for example, Chiu Chen-hai, "US-PRC-DPRK Talks: Russia Has Trump Card to Play," 25 April 2003, in FBIS, CPP20030425000041; David E. Sanger, "A Nation at War: The Asian Front; North Koreans and U.S. Plan Talks in Beijing," *New York Times*, 16 April 2003; Burt Herman, "China Reduces Oil Shipment to North

Korea," Associated Press, 26 August 2006; "China Reduces Its Crude Oil Support to North Korea by a Sizable Quantity," Chosun Ilbo, 30 August 2006, in FBIS, 200608301477.1_9a0d0073b439d116. On counterfeiting, see Joong Ang Ilbo, 26 July 2006, in FBIS, KPP20060727971191.

65. Shen Jiru, "Weihu dongbei ya anquan de dangwu zhi ji" [The Pressing Matter of Protecting Northeast Asian Security], in *Shijie jingji yu zhengzhi* [World Economics and Politics], no. 9 (2003). Reports indicate that China may have directly suggested to North Korea that the two sides should renegotiate their defense treaty. See, for example, James Brooke, "North Korea Lashes Out at Neighbors and U.S.," *New York Times*, 19 August 2003.

66. "FBIS Report," 26 September 2004, in FBIS, CPP20040926000026; Lilian Wu, "63% Favor Cross-Strait Peace Agreement," Central News Agency, 22 July 2004, http://web.lexis-nexis.com/universe .

67. *Taiwan News*, "MND Report Says PRC Would Most Likely Invade Taiwan in 2010," 23 September 2004, in FBIS, CPP20040923000195.

68. On the defense budgets, see Central News Agency, 2 November 2003, in FBIS, CPP20041102000130; "FBIS Report," 22 October 2004, in FBIS, CPP20041022000164; Brian Hsu, "Military Spending," *Taipei Times*, 4 September 2002, http://taipeitimes.com/news/2002/09/04/print/0000166702; "FBIS Report," in FBIS, 22 October 2004, CPP20041022000164. For an analysis of the trends in Taiwan defense spending, see Cole, *Taiwan's Security*, 155–61, 172–75.

69. For assessments of Chinese military capability, see Michael O'Hanlon, "Why China Cannot Conquer Taiwan," *International Security* 25, no. 2 (Fall 2000): 51–86; Michael A. Glosny, "Strangulation from the Sea? A PRC Submarine Blockade of Taiwan," *International Security* 28, no. 4 (Spring 2004): 125–60.

70. Edward Gargan, "Long-Term Forecast for Taiwan Remains Upbeat," *New York Times*, 22 March 1996; Sheila Tefft, "Taiwan Moves to Restore Shaken Investor Confidence," *Christian Science Monitor*, 1 April 1996; Steven Mufson, "China-Taiwan Conflict 'In Remission, Not Resolved,'" *Washington Post*, 22 April 1996.

71. See the Taiwan Mainland Affairs Council's line graph of public opinion trends at http://www.mac.gov.tw/english/english/pos/9211/9211e_1.gif; Melody Chen, "Polls Indicate Few Want Cross-Strait Status Quo Changed," *Taipei Times*, 10 February 2004, FBIS, CPP20040210000187; Lilian Wu, "63% Favor Cross-Strait Peace Agreement," Central News Agency, 22 July 2004.

72. Associated Press, 15 December, 2003; "FBIS Report," 16 January 2004, in FBIS, CPP20040116000193; Agence France Presse, 18 January 2004, in FBIS, CPP20040118000010; "FBIS Report," 2 February 2004, in FBIS, CPP20040202000013; "FBIS Report," 10 February 2004, in FBIS, CPP20040217000222; interviews with DPP and Taiwan government officials, January 2004; "Constitution Rewrite Delay Urged," *Taipei Times*, 12 May 2004, in FBIS, CPP20040512000167; Central News Agency, 12 May 2004, in FBIS, CPP20040512000186.

73. See the post-election poll results in Central News Agency, 7 May 2004, in FBIS, CPP20040507000051.

74. "Pro-Independence Parties Defeated in Taiwan," *New York Times*, 11 December 2004. The vote tally is reported in "FBIS Report," 11 December 2004, in FBIS, CPP20041211000110.

75. Interview by author with DPP legislators and government officials, Taipei, January 2004 and January 2005; "Business Leaders 'Hold the Key to President's Fate,'" *South China Morning Post*, 10 February 2004; Jacky Hsu, "Taiwan's Tycoons Stay Clear of Politics," *South China Morning Post*, 27 May 2004; report on Taiwan media reports in FBIS, CPP20060531326001.

76. Ong Hwee Hwee, "China, Taiwan Boost Air Link," *The Straits Times*, 15 June 2006, http://web.lexis-nexis.com/universe.

77. Zhongguo Xinwenshe, 3 January 2004, in FBIS, CPP20040103000056; interview by author with official from Taiwan's Mainland Affairs Council, Taipei, January 2004; Mark Magnier, "Unions across a Divide," *Los Angeles Times*, 22 November 2004; Xinhua, 9 February 2004, in FBIS, CPP20040209000131; Zhongguo xinwen she, 28 February 2004, in FBIS, CPP20040228000102; Xinhua, 28 February 2004, in FBIS, CPP2003022800083.

78. Chu Yun-han, "Taiwan's National Identity Politics and the Prospect of Cross-Strait Relations," *Asian Survey* 44, no. 4 (July/August 2004): 484–512; G. Andy Chang and T. Y. Wang, "Taiwanese or Chinese? Independence or Unification? An Analysis of Generational Differences in Taiwan," *Journal of Asian and African Studies*, 40, no. 1–2 (April 2005): 29–49.

79. The best discussion of the transformation in Japanese defense policy is Christopher Hughes, *Japan's Re-emergence as a "Normal" Military Power*, Adelphi Papers no. 368–69 (Oxford: Oxford University Press for the International Institute of Strategic Studies, 2004).

80. See Paul S. Giarra and Akisha Nagashima, "Managing the New U.S.-Japan Security Alliance: Enhancing Structures and Mechanisms to Address Post–Cold War Requirements," in *The U.S.-Japan Alliance: Past, Future and Present*, ed. Michael J. Green and Patrick M. Cronin (New York: Council on Foreign Relations, 1999).

81. Norimitsu Onishi, "Japan Support of Missile Shield Could Tilt Asia Balance of Power," *New York Times*, 3 April 2004.

82. Amb. J. Thomas Shieffer, "Nuclear-Powered Carrier to Replace Kitty Hawk," 28 October 2005, http://tokyo.usembassy.gov/e/p/tp-20051028-77.htm; "Japan, U.S. Troops Hold 1st Joint Exercise for Island Defense," Kyodo, 13 January 2006, http://web.lexis-nexis.com/universe.

83. "Joint Statement of the U.S.-Japan Consultative Committee," 19 February 2005, http://www.state.gov/r/pa/prs/ps/2005/42490.htm.

84. James Dao, "Coalition Widens Its Ocean Manhunt," *New York Times*, 17 March 2002; Norimitsu Onishi, "Japan Heads to Iraq, Haunted by Taboo Bred in Another War," *New York Times*, 19 November 2003. Also see Michael H.

Armacost, "Tilting Closer to Washington," in *Strategic Asia 2003–04: Fragility and Crisis*, ed. Richard J. Ellings and Aaron L. Friedberg, 81–107 (Seattle, WA: National Bureau of Asian Research, 2004).

85. Bennett Richardson, "Japan Beefs Up Its Defense Stance," *Christian Science Monitor*, 10 December 2004, 6; Reuters, 22 December 2005.

86. Kyodo, 7 November 2004, in FBIS, JPP20041107000035; Agence France Presse, 2 December 2005, in FBIS, JPP20051202064005; "Agency Plans Long-range Missile," *Daily Yomiuri*, 3 December 2004; Associated Press, 28 March 2005, http://web.lexis-nexis.com/universe; Bruce Wallace, "Japan to Pursue Drilling in Disputed Area," *Los Angeles Times*, 13 April 2005.

87. David Pilling, "Comments and Analysis," *Financial Times*, 14 April 2004; Anthony Faiola, "Japan's Draft Charter Redefines Military," *Washington Post*, 23 November 2005, 16.

88. David Pilling, "Comments and Analysis," *Financial Times*, 14 April 2004; Howard W. French, "Can Japan Change?" *New York Times*, 22 July 2003; Howard W. French, "Taboo against Nuclear Weapons Is Being Challenged in Japan," *New York Times*, 9 June 2002. See also, for example, Kan Ito, "China's Nuclear Power Will Control the World by 2020," *Tokyo Shokun*, 1 January 2006, in FBIS, JPP20051205016001.

89. Ming Wan, "Tensions in Recent Sino-Japanese Relations: The May 2002 Shenyang Incident," *Asian Survey*, 43, no. 5 (September/October 2003): 840–42.

90. "Koizumi Fears Backlash over Yasukuni Ire," *Japan Times*, 24 March 2004, http://search.japantimes.co.jp/cgi-bin/nn20040316a2.html; "Fukuda Gets Testy over Yasukuni Shrine Questions," *Japan Times*, 16 March 2004, http://search.japantimes.co.jp/cgi-bin/nn20040324b4.html; Howard W, French, "Can Japan Change?" *New York Times*, 22 July 2003; "ODA for China to Fall Below ¥100 Billion," *Sankei Shimbun*, in FBIS, JPP20041130000029; "ODA Strategy Enters New Era," *Daily Yomiuri*, 1 April 2004. On public attitudes toward leadership visits to the Yasukuni Shrine, see David Pilling, "Japanese Support Leader's War Shrine Visits," *Financial Times*, 14 December 2004. For trends in Japan's China policy, including policy on development assistance and the Yasukuni Shrine, see Lam Peng Er, "Japan's Deteriorating Ties with China: The Koizumi Factor," *China: An International Journal* 3, no. 2 (September 2005): 275–91; Ming Wan, *Sino-Japanese Relations: Interaction, Logic, and Transformation* (Stanford, CA: Stanford University Press, 2006).

91. Although Indonesian acquiescence to U.S. interests is not an example of "balancing," it underscores the impact of superior great power capabilities on secondary state alignment. For coverage of U.S. and allied deployments, see Geoff Spencer, "First International Combat Troops Land in East Timor," Associated Press, 20 September 1999, http://web.lexis-nexis.com/universe/; David Briscoe, "U.S. Force of 200 Expected in Australia for East Timor," Associated Press, 22 September 1999, http://web.lexis-nexis.com/universe/; Charles Miranda, "U.S. Spy Plane Tracks Militia, Indon Army," *Northern Territory News*, 29 September 1999,

http://web.lexis-nexis.com/universe/; "Navy Eye on Timor," *Sunday Telegraph*, 1 August 1999, http://web.lexis-nexis.com/universe/; Agence France Presse, 29 September 1999, http://web.lexis-nexis.com/universe/.

92. Indonesia National News Agency, 21 April 2004, http://web.lexis-nexis.com/universe/; *The Jakarta Post*, 18 May 2001; Agence France Presse, 16 May 2001, FBIS, SEP20010516000031; "Indonesia Requests US Technical Support to Secure Malacca Strait," Antara, 23 January 2006, in FBIS, 200607121477.1_3380004e8a7dbe5b; "R.I., U.S. Navies Conclude Joint Exercise Aimed at Fighting Terrorism," *Jakarta Post*, 21 March 2006, in FBIS, 200603211477.1_f53d0027841bc9e0.

93. Ian Storey, *Malaysia and the United States 2004–2005: The Best of Times?* (Honolulu, HI: Asia-Pacific Center for Security Studies, 2005), 5; Ng Eng Kiat and Selvam Arjunan, "New US Aircraft Carrier on First Malaysian Visit," Malaysiakini, 5 June 2006, in FBIS, 200606051477.1_c1bf005f528d30b4.

94. Kay Min Chan, "High-Tech 'Stars' at New Naval Base," *Straits Times*, 11 March 2001. On Cobra Gold, see Edward Tang, "S'pore to Join Cobra Gold This Year," *Straits Times*, 14 January 2000.

95. Anthony L. Smith, *Singapore and the United States 2004–2005: Steadfast Friends* (Honolulu, HI: Asia-Pacific Center for Security Studies, 2005), 4–5; Jim Garamone, "Singapore, U.S. Reaffirm, Strengthen Relationship," American Forces Press Service, 12 July 2005, http://www.defenselink.mil/news/Jul2005/20050712_2040.html.

96. Robert Karniol, "U.S. Doubles Personnel for 'Balikatan 2004,'" *New York Times*, 3 March 2004; *Jane's Defence Weekly*, http://web.lexis-nexis.com/universe/; Richard Halloran, "U.S. Forces Prepare for Surprises in Asia," *Japan Times*, 29 March 2004; Agence France Presse, "Malampaya Defense 'Incidental' to War Games," *Business World*, 25 February 2004. See also Ronald A. Rodriguez, "Conduct Unbecoming in the South China Sea?" *PacNet*, no. 22A, 21 May 2004; "RP-US Military Exercise," *Business World*, 16 November 2004, http://web.lexis-nexis.com/universe/.

97. "RP Now Biggest Recipient of US Military Aid in East Asia," *Manila Standard*, 6 March 2004; "More Jets for AFP Modernization," *Manila Standard*, 9 January 2004.

98. For a full development of this argument, see Robert S. Ross, "Explaining Taiwan's Revisionist Diplomacy," *Journal of Contemporary China* 15, no. 48 (August 2006): 443–58.

99. "Memorandum of Conversation, by the Secretary of State," January 5, 1950, U.S. Department of State, *Foreign Relations of the United States* 1950, no. 6 (Washington, DC: Government Printing Office, 1976), 260–61; and "Memorandum of Conversation, by the Secretary of State," December 29, 1949, *Foreign Relations of the United States* 1949, no. 9 (Washington, DC: Government Printing Office, 1974), 467. See also Thomas J. Christensen, *Useful Adversaries: Grand Strategy, Domestic Mobilization, and Sino-American Conflict, 1947–1958* (Princeton, NJ: Princeton University Press, 1996), 106.

100. See, for example, Storey and You, "China's Aircraft Carrier Ambitions." Also see Cole, *The Great Wall at Sea*. On the technological limitations of the PLA, see Bernard D. Cole and Paul H. B. Godwin, "Advanced Military Technology and the PLA: Priorities and Capabilities in the 21st Century," in *The Chinese Armed Forces in the 21st Century*, ed. Larry M. Wortzel (Carlisle, PA: Strategic Studies Institute, U.S. Army War College, 1999).

Chapter 7: Chinese Economic Statecraft

1. U.S.-China Business Council, "Foreign Investment in China: 2005," available at http://www.uschina.org/statistics/2005foreigninvestment_2.html.

2. Prepared statement of Paul Sarbanes to U.S.-China Security Review Commission, 14 June 2001.

3. Edward Cody, "China's Quiet Rise Casts Wide Shadow," *Washington Post*, 26 February 2006.

4. See for example, Mike M. Mochizuki, "Security and Economic Interdependence in Northeast Asia," Asia Pacific Research Center, 1998; available at http://aparc.stanford.edu/publications/10089/.

5. David Baldwin, *Economic Statecraft* (Princeton, NJ: Princeton University Press, 1985).

6. Jonathan Kirshner, "The Political Economy of Realism," in *Unipolar Politics: Realism and State Strategies after the Cold War*, ed. Ethan B. Kapstein and Michael Mastanduno, 69–102 (New York: Columbia University Press, 1999).

7. Paul Papayoanou and Scott Kastner, "Sleeping with the (Potential) Enemy: Assessing the US Policy of Engagement with China," in *Power and the Purse: Economic Statecraft, Interdependence, and National Security*, ed. Jean-Marc F. Blanchard, Edward D. Mansfield, and Norrin M. Ripsman, 157–87 (London: Frank Cass, 2000).

8. Albert O. Hirschman, *National Power and the Structure of Foreign Trade*, expanded ed. (Berkeley: University of California Press, 1980).

9. Ibid.

10. Rawi Abdelal and Jonathan Kirshner, "Strategy, Economic Relations, and the Definition of National Interests," *Security Studies* 9 (Autumn 1999–Winter 2000): 119–56.

11. Michael Mastanduno, "Economic Engagement Strategies: Theory and Practice," in *Economic Interdependence and Conflict: New Perspectives on an Enduring Debate*, ed. Edward Mansfield and Brian Pollins, 175–88 (Ann Arbor: University of Michigan Press, 2003).

12. Taiwan export data are taken from the Republic of China National Statistics Bureau's Statistical Database. Taiwan total FDI statistics are from the Statistical Yearbook of Commerce and External Trade 2004. Both sources available at http://eng.stat.gov.tw/mp.asp?mp=5.

13. The "three no's"—no contact, no negotiation, and no compromise between Taiwan and China—was a KMT policy. Kao Chang, *Dalu jingji yu liangan jingmao*

guanxi [Mainland Economic Reform and Cross-Strait Relations] (Taipei: Wu Nan, 1994). Quoted in Tung Chen-yuan, "China's Economic Leverage and Taiwan's Security Concerns with Respect to Cross-Strait Economic Relations," PhD diss., Johns Hopkins University, May 2002.

14. Mainland Affairs Council, *Dalu gongzuo cankao ziliao* [Reference Documents on Mainland Work]. Quoted in Tung, "China's Economic Leverage and Taiwan's Security Concerns."

15. Chiu Yu-tzu, "Technology Law to Guard Valued Assets," *Taipei Times*, 17 April 2002; Lawrence Chung, "Taiwan Woos Its Companies Back," *Straits Times*, 12 December 2002.

16. "President Chen Calls for Taiwan-US-Japan Free Trade Agreement," *Chinese Economic News Service*, 12 April 2002.

17. Lin Chieh-yu, "Nation Must 'Go its Own Way': Chen," *Taipei Times*, 30 July 2002.

18. "China Invites Taiwan Businessmen for Talks," *BBC Online*, 22 May 2002, http://news.bbc.co.uk/2/hi/asia-pacific/2002237.stm

19. "Chen Shui-bian Again Provokes the Mainland." *Hong Kong Ta Kung Pao*, 30 July 2002, in FBIS-China.

20. Quoted in Tung Chen-yuan, "China's Economic Leverage and Taiwan's Security Concerns," 222.

21. Quoted in Tung Chen-yuan, "China's Economic Leverage and Taiwan's Security Concerns," 240

22. "China Will Not Yield on a Matter of Principle," Xinhua, 8 April 2000.

23. Mure Dickie and James Kynge, "Business in Taiwan Heeds Warning on Independence," *Financial Times*, 11 March 2000.

24. Craig Addison, *Silicon Shield: Taiwan's Protection against Chinese Attack* (Irvington, TX: Fusion Press, 2001), 203. See also "Presidential Office Cautions Mainland over Chi Mei Plant," *China Post*, 12 March 2001.

25. Mark O'Neill, "Shi Underlines Risk of Packing Politics in Business Briefcase," *South China Morning Post*, 19 March 2001.

26. "Qian Qichen Inspects Guangdong, Holds Discussion with Taiwan Businessmen," Xinhua, 8 December 2002, in FBIS-China.

27. Joanne Gowa, *Allies, Adversaries, and International Trade* (Princeton, NJ: Princeton University Press, 1994).

28. Quoted in Edward Cody, "China's Quiet Rise Casts Wide Shadow," *Washington Post*, 26 February 2005

29. Baldwin, *Economic Statecraft*.

30. Avery Goldstein, "An Emerging China's Emerging Grand Strategy: A Neo-Bismarckian Turn?" in *International Relations Theory and the Asia-Pacific*, ed. G. J. Ikenberry and M. Mastanduno (New York: Columbia University Press, 2003).

31. Jonathan Kirshner, "States, Markets, and Great Power Relations in the Pacific: Some Realist Expectations," in *International Relations Theory and the*

Asia-Pacific, ed. G. J. Ikenberry and M. Mastanduno (New York: Columbia University Press, 2003).

32. Elizabeth Economy and Adam Segal, "China's Luster Fades," *Los Angeles Times*, 30 December 2004.

33. James Przystup, "A Volatile Mix: Natural Gas, a Submarine, a Shrine, and a Visa. Japan-China Relations," *Comparative Connections* 6, no. 3 (October–December 2004), http://www.csis.org/pacfor/cc/0404Qjapan_china.html.

34. Erica Strecker Downs and Phillip Saunders, "Legitimacy and the Limits of Nationalism: China and the Diaoyu Islands," *International Security* 23, no. 3 (Winter 1998/99): 114–46.

35. Mure Dickie and David Pilling, "Unbowed: Koizumi's Assertive Japan is Standing Up Increasingly to China," *Financial Times*, 14 February 2005.

36. Andrew Ward, "Ties between China and South Korea Blossom," *Financial Times*, 18 February 2002

37. Scott Snyder, "Waiting Game: China-Korea Relations," *Comparative Connections*, October–December 2004, http://www.csis.org/pacfor/cc/0404Qchina_skorea.html (accessed February 2006).

38. Ralph Clough, *Reaching across the Taiwan Strait: People-to-People Diplomacy* (San Francisco: Westview Press, 1993), 93–95.

39. For example, Wang Yung-ching, CEO of Formosa Plastics Group, stated on 19 June 2001: "If there is parity between the two sides, 'One China' is not wrong, is it? Taiwan's people should calmly accept the 'one China' principle and from this position of equality both sides can cooperate to enjoy long-lasting mutual benefits." Richard Dobson, "Formosa's Wang Says 'One China' Must Be Accepted," *Taipei Times*, 20 June 2001.

40. Ming-Chi Chen, "Sinicization and Its Discontents: Cross-Strait Integration and Taiwan's 2004 Presidential Election," *Issues & Studies* 40, no. 3–4 (September 2004): 334–41.

41. Harold Brown, Joseph Prueher, and Adam Segal, *Chinese Military Power: Report of an Independent Task Force* (New York: Council on Foreign Relations, 2003).

42. Mu Lu, "Sino-U.S. Relations: A Century of Strategic Cooperation and Competition," *China Strategy* 3 (July 2004) (Center for Strategic and International Studies), http://www.csis.org/isp/csn/040720.pdf (accessed February 2005).

43. Yan Xuetong, "Origins of the Policy to 'Pay Any Price to Contain Taiwan's Independence,'" *China Strategy* 3 (Center for Strategic and International Studies), http://www.csis.org/isp/csn/040720.pdf (accessed February 2005).

44. Evan S. Medeiros and M. Taylor Fravel, "China's New Diplomacy," *Foreign Affairs*, November/December 2003.

45. See for example Evan Feigenbaum, "China's Challenge to Pax," *Washington Quarterly* 24, no. 3 (Summer 2001); Denny Roy, "Hegemon on the Horizon?" *International Security* 19, no. 1 (Summer 1994): 149–68; and Bates Gill,

"Contrasting Visions: China, the United States, and the World Order," remarks to the U.S.-China Security Review Comission, Washington, DC, 3 August 2001.

46. Amitav Acharya, "Will Asia's Past Be Its Future?" *International Security* 28, no. 3 (Winter 2003–2004): 149–64.

47. Lyall Breckon, "A New Strategic Relationship Is Declared: ASEAN-China Relations," *Comparative Connections*, October–December 2003, http://www.ciaonet.org/olj/cpc/cpc_jan04/cpc_jan04g.pdf.

48. Ellen Frost, "Economic Integration: Implications of Regional Economic Integration," in *Fragility and Crisis: Strategic Asia 2003–2004* (Seattle: National Bureau of Asian Research, 2003).

49. Alastair Iain Johnston, "Is China a Status Quo Power?" *International Security* 27, no. 4 (Spring 2003): 38.

50. Undersecretary of Defense (Policy), "Summer Study Final Report: Asia 2025," (1999), referenced in Robert Kaiser, "2020 Vision: A China Bent on Asian Dominance," *Washington Post*, 17 March 2000.

51. Thomas Christensen, "China," in *Strategic Asia 2001–2002* (National Bureau of Asian Research, 2001), 28.

52. Breckon, "A New Strategic Relationship."

53. George Gilboy and Eric Heginbotham, "U.S. Asia (and China) Policy Reconceived," *National Interest*, no. 69 (Fall 2002): 99–109.

Chapter 8: China's "Peaceful Development" and Southeast Asia

1. *China Online*, 14 November 2002, quoted in Busakorn Chantasasawat et al., *International Competition for Foreign Direct Investment: The Case of China*, paper presented at the Hitotsubashi Conference on International Trade and FDI, Tokyo, December 2003. Mr. Lee succeeded Goh Chok Tong as Singapore's prime minister in August 2004. The term "peaceful development" (*heping fazhan*) has increasingly been preferred in China's official statements to the term "peaceful rise" (*heping jueqi*); the use of the latter term had the (presumably) unintended consequence of further unsettling rather than reassuring China's neighbors.

2. The most recent calculations by World Bank staff are included in Elena Ianchovichina, Sethaput Suthiwart-Narueput, and Min Zhao, "Regional Impact of China's WTO Accession," in *East Asia Integrates: A Trade Policy Agenda for Shared Growth*, ed. K. L. Krumm and H. J. Kharas, 57–78 (New York: World Bank, 2004); and Elena Ianchovichina and Terrie Louise Walmsley, *The Impact of China's WTO Accession on East Asia*, Policy Research Working Paper 3109 (Washington, DC: World Bank Poverty Reduction and Economic Management Network Economic Policy Division, August 2003), http://econ.worldbank.org/resource.php?type=5. Earlier work is reported in Will Martin and Elena Ianchovichina, "Implications of China's Accession to the World Trade Organization for China and the WTO," *World Economy* 24 (2001): 1205–19. For similar conclusions drawn from market share analysis rather than a computable general equilibrium approach, see John Weiss and Shanwen Gao, *People's Republic of China's Export Threat to ASEAN:*

Competition in the US and Japanese Markets, ADB Institute Discussion Paper 2 (Manila: Asian Development Bank, January 2003); and John Weiss, *People's Republic of China and Its Neighbors: Partners or Competitors for Trade and Investment?* ADB Institute Discussion Paper 13 (Manila: Asian Development Bank, August 2004). Lall and Albaladejo present a less alarmist scenario: Sanjaya Lall and Manuel Albaladejo, "China's Competitive Performance: A Threat to East Asian Manufactured Exports?" *World Development* 32 (2004): 1441–66. Eichengreen, Rhee, and Tong, using a gravity model, reach conclusions broadly similar to those of the World Bank, namely that China's growth will have a negative impact on low-income countries that export consumer goods but a positive impact on higher-income Asian exporters of capital goods. Barry Eichengreen, Yeongseop Rhee, and Hui Tong, "The Impact of China on the Exports of Other Asian Countries" (mimeograph, University of California, Berkeley, September 2004).

3. John Wong and Sarah Chan, "China-ASEAN Free Trade Agreement: Shaping Future Economic Relations," *Asian Survey* 43 (2003): 523.

4. Data in this section are for the six largest ASEAN economies: Indonesia, Malaysia, Philippines, Singapore, Thailand, and Vietnam. Unless otherwise noted, data are from United Nations Conference on Trade and Development (UNCTAD), *World Investment Report*, http://unctad.org/Templates/Page.asp?intItemID=1465&lang=1.

5. Geng Xiao, *People's Republic of China's Round-Tripping FDI: Scale, Causes and Implications*, ADB Institute Discussion Paper No. 7 (Manila: Asian Development Bank, July 2004).

6. See Dieter Ernst, "Global Production Networks in East Asia's Electronics Industry and Upgrading Perspectives in Malaysia," *East-West Center Working Papers, Economics Series*, no. 44 (Honolulu, HI: East-West Center, 2002).

7. See UNCTAD's annual *World Investment Report*.

8. The International Monetary Fund (IMF) provides guidelines to member governments for the compilation of balance of payments and international investment position statistics. FDI, according to the IMF, consists of three components: equity capital; borrowings from the parent company; and reinvested earnings. These data therefore exclude investment funds that a subsidiary raises from sources other than the parent company, e.g., from borrowings from minority investors in the subsidiary, or from loans from local or international banks. Moreover, while reinvested earnings are part of the IMF's definition of FDI flows, a number of countries, including Thailand, do not include them as part of their reporting of investment data to the IMF. According to the ASEAN Secretariat, reinvested earnings constituted 37 percent of FDI flows to the ASEAN region between 1995 and 2002. "Seventh ASEAN Investment Area (AIA) Council Meeting, Joint Media Statement" (Jakarta, 2 September 2004), http://www.aseansec.org/16347.htm.

9. Graham cites U.S. government data that suggest foreign direct investment each year financed between one-half and two-thirds of the capital expenditures by

foreign subsidiaries of U.S. companies in the period from 1973 to 1992. Edward M. Graham, "Foreign Direct Investment in the World Economy," IMF Working Paper WP/95/59 (Washington, DC: International Monetary Fund, June 1995), chart 1.

10. Xiao, *People's Republic of China's Round-Tripping FDI*, 17.

11. Ibid., 9.

12. Ibid., 11.

13. Of course, some of this money may have originated in the Triad and reflects investments by Hong Kong–based subsidiaries of Triad multinational corporations.

14. Peter Harrold and Rajiv Lall, "China: Reform and Development in 1992–93," Discussion Paper 215 (Washington, DC: World Bank, August 1993), 24; cited in Nicholas R. Lardy, "The Role of Foreign Trade and Investment in China's Economic Transformation," *China Quarterly* 144 (1995): 1067.

15. World Bank, *Global Development Finance* (Washington, DC: World Bank, 2002).

16. Xiao, *People's Republic of China's Round-Tripping FDI.*

17. Frank R. Gunter, "Capital Flight from China: 1984–2001," *China Economic Review* 15 (2004): 63–85.

18. Before 2005, that is, when a huge outflow of U.S. FDI from Singapore (in excess of US$10 billion) distorted the figures.

19. They note, however, that the "China effect" is not the most important determinant of FDI flows to these other economies; of far greater significance are market size and policy and institutional variables including levels of corporate taxation, degrees of economic openness, and the extent of corruption. See Busakorn Chantasasawat et al., "International Competition for Foreign Direct Investment: The Case of China," paper presented at the Hitotsubashi Conference on International Trade and FDI, Tokyo, December 2003; Busakorn Chantasasawat et al., "Foreign Direct Investment in China and East Asia" (paper presented at the Third Annual Conference on China Economic Policy Reform, Stanford Center for International Development, 12 November 2004); Busakorn Chantasasawat et al., *Foreign Direct Investment in East Asia and Latin America: Is There a People's Republic of China Effect?* ADB Institute Discussion Paper 17 (Manila: Asian Development Bank, November 2004).

20. They find no significant association before 1992 between FDI into China and that into Southeast Asia. Their study uses a most unorthodox definition of "Southeast Asia," however, that includes both the Republic of Korea and Taiwan. See Yuping Zhou and Sanjaya Lall, "The Impact of China's FDI Surge on FDI in South-East Asia: Panel Data Analysis for 1986–2001," *Transnational Corporations* 14 (2005): 41–65.

21. Barry Eichengreen and Hui Tong, "Is China's FDI Coming at the Expense of Other Countries?" (Cambridge, MA: National Bureau of Economic Research, Working Paper 11335, May 2005), http://www.nber.org/papers/w11335.

22. All of these graphs record data drawn from the UN's COMTRADE

database. In all cases, the columns on the graph represent the absolute value of imports from ASEAN, China, and the world, with the value measured on the left vertical axis. The lines on the graph represent the shares of ASEAN and China in total imports, with the percentage share measured on the right vertical axis. For the purposes of the analysis of trade data, the ASEAN grouping is taken as the five original members: Indonesia, Malaysia, the Philippines, Singapore, and Thailand.

23. David Roland Holst and John Weiss, "ASEAN and China: Export Rivals or Partners in Regional Growth?" *World Economy* 27 (2004): 1255–74. More sophisticated methods used to examine the impact of China's WTO accession on its neighbors have their own problems. Computable general equilibrium models make a variety of assumptions regarding elasticities of supply and demand, technological shifts, factor movements, etc., that may have little foundation in the real world, and they have no way of factoring in the decisions that multinationals make on where to locate particular segments of a production chain. See, for instance, Sanjaya Lall and Manuel Albaladejo, "China's Competitive Performance: A Threat to East Asian Manufactured Exports?" *World Development* 32 (2004): 1441–66.

24. Holst and Weiss, "ASEAN and China." Compare Alan G. Ahearne, John G. Fernald, Prakash Loungani, and John W. Schindler, "China and Emerging Asia: Comrades or Competitors?" International Finance Discussion Paper No. 789 (Washington, DC: Federal Reserve, December 2003).

25. Edward J. Lincoln, *East Asian Economic Regionalism* (New York: Council on Foreign Relations; Washington, DC: Brookings Institution Press, 2004).

26. Peter Drysdale, *International Economic Pluralism: Economic Policy in East Asia and the Pacific* (Sydney: Allen and Unwin, 1988).

27. Wong and Chan, "China-ASEAN Free Trade Agreement," 508n4, 517, 519, 525.

28. Mitchell Bernard and John Ravenhill, "Beyond Product Cycles and Flying Geese: Regionalization, Hierarchy, and the Industrialization of East Asia," *World Politics* 45 (1995): 179–210; Michael Borrus, Dieter Ernst, and Stephan Haggard, eds. *International Production Networks in Asia: Rivalry or Riches?* (London: Routledge, 2000); David McKendrick, Richard F. Doner, and Stephan Haggard, *From Silicon Valley to Singapore: Location and Competitive Advantage in the Hard Disk Drive Industry* (Stanford, CA: Stanford University Press, 2000). Recognition of the significance of such networks in the study of economics has come somewhat late. See, for instance, Sven W. Arndt and Henryk Kierzkowski, eds., *Fragmentation: New Production Patterns in the World Economy* (Oxford: Oxford University Press, 2001); Francis Ng and Alexander J. Yeats, *Production Sharing in East Asia: Who Does What for Whom and Why*, Policy Research Working Paper 2197 (Washington, DC: World Bank Development Research Group Trade, 1 October 1999), http://econ.worldbank.org/docs/921.pdf.

29. Harm Zebregs, "Intraregional Trade in Emerging Asia" (Washington, DC: IMF Policy Discussion Paper, PDP/04/1, April 2004), 9.

30. Monetary Authority of Singapore, "Assessing the Support from Regional Domestic Demand," *Macroeconomic Review* 2, no. 1 (January 2003): 60–70.

31. Guillaume Gaulier, Françoise Lemoine, and Deniz Ünal-Kesenci, *China's Integration in Asian Production Networks and Its Implications* (Tokyo: Research Institute of Economy, Trade and Industry, Discussion Paper 04033, 2004), 13. http://www.rieti.go.jp/jp/publications/dp/04e033.pdf.

32. Prema-chandra Athukorala, "Product Fragmentation and Trade Patterns in East Asia," Division of Economics, Research School of Pacific and Asian Studies, Working Papers in Trade and Development 2003/21 (Canberra: Australian National University, 2003), table A2, p. 48.

33. Prema-chandra Athukorala, "Multinational Production Networks and the New Geo-Economic Division of Labor in the Pacific Rim," paper presented at the 31st Pacific Trade and Development Conference, Guadalajara, Mexico, 10–12 June 2006, p. 10.

34. The most recent data provide a more positive picture than that portrayed by earlier analysis. Holst and Weiss, for instance, estimate that the net gain to ASEAN from exports to China in the 1995–2000 period was equivalent to less than 20 percent of the value of the combined losses to China in the export markets of Japan and the United States in the same period ("ASEAN and China," 1263). As we have seen, increases in the value of sales to the Chinese market have more than offset losses in the Japanese and U.S. markets for the products reviewed in this chapter.

35. In 2004, Vietnam had the greatest dependence on the Chinese market, which accounted for 9.0 percent of its exports; the next highest dependence was that of Singapore at 8.6 percent.

Chapter 9: China's Peaceful Rise

1. The World Bank gives total output (GNI, gross national income) for 2003 in purchasing power parity terms as US$6,235 billion for China, US$3,641 billion for Japan, US$3,068 billion for India, and US$10,914 billion for the United States. (*World Development Report 2005*, 256–57).

2. Trade ratios for Chinese provinces are calculated from the national figure and from provincial shares in GDP (valued in renminbi) and in combined exports and imports (valued in U.S. dollars). See *Zhongguo tongji nianjian 2006* [China Statistics Yearbook 2006] (Beijing: Zhongguo tongji chubanshe, 2006), tables 3-1, 3-14, and 18-12. European data for 2003–5 are from Country Trade profiles posted by the World Trade Organization at http://stat.wto.org/ (accessed 10 January 2007).

3. Richard J. Samuels, *"Rich Nation, Strong Army": National Security and the Technological Transformation of Japan*. (Ithaca, NY: Cornell University Press, 1994).

4. See United States Department of Defense, *Annual Report to Congress: The Military Power of the People's Republic of China 2003* (Washington, DC: Department of Defense, 2003), Executive Summary, http://www.defenselink.mil/pubs/20030730chinaex.pdf.

5. United States Department of Defense, *Annual Report to Congress: The Military Power of the People's Republic of China 2006* (Washington, DC: Department of Defense, 2006), Executive Summary and pp. 1–6, http://www.defenselink.mil/pubs/pdfs/China%20Report%202006.pdf.

6. Michael A. Weinstein, "China's Geostrategy: Playing a Waiting Game," *Power and Interest News Report*, 7 January 2005, http://www.pinr.com/report.php?ac=view_report&report_id=253&language_id=1.

7. Information Office of the State Council, People's Republic of China, "China's National Defense in 2006," 29 December 2006, http://www.fas.org/nuke/guide/china/doctrine/wp2006.

8. In this context, note the concern expressed by prominent economist Liu Guoguang that China should curb the growth of foreign economic influence. "Views on Several Macroeconomic Issues," *Gaige* [Reform], no. 2 (2002): 5–9.

9. On 9 December 2003, with Premier Wen at his side, President Bush said, "We oppose any unilateral decision by either China or Taiwan to change the status quo. And the comments and actions made by the leader of Taiwan indicate that he may be willing to make decisions unilaterally to change the status quo, which we oppose." http://www.whitehouse.gov/news/releases/2003/12/20031209-2.html (accessed 2 July 2005).

10. President Franklin D. Roosevelt, in a letter to a friend, 1935. Quoted in Barbara Tuchman, *Stilwell and the American Experience in China, 1911-1945* (New York: Macmillan, 1970), 249.

11. For a comprehensive treatment of preventive military intervention, see William W. Keller and Gordon R. Mitchell, eds., *Hitting First: Preventive Force in U.S. Security Strategy* (Pittsburgh, PA: University of Pittsburgh Press, 2006).

12. John Steinbruner, *Principles of Global Security* (Washington, DC: Brookings Institution Press, 2000), 2.

13. Daniel Yergin, "Ensuring Energy Security," *Foreign Affairs* 85, no. 2 (2006): 72.

14. Lippencott provides extensive detail on the first Clinton administration's "confusing policy of mixed signals and misunderstanding." Brett C. Lippencott, "Ending the Confusion in U.S. China Policy" (Heritage Foundation, Asian Studies Backgrounder, 18 April 1994), www.heritage.org/Research/AsiaandthePacific/asb130.cfm?renderforprint=1 (accessed 19 March 2006). Subsequent policies remain open to similar criticism.

15. George W. Bush, "The National Security Strategy," 16 March 2006, http://www.whitehouse.gov/nsc/nss/2006/intro.html.

REFERENCES

Abdelal, Rawi, and Jonathan Kirshner. "Strategy, Economic Relations, and the Definition of National Interests." *Security Studies* 9 (Autumn 1999–Winter 2000): 119–56.

Acharya, Amitav. "Will Asia's Past Be Its Future?" *International Security* 28, no. 3 (Winter 2003/2004): 149–64.

Achvarina, Vera V. "Integration of the Chinese Aluminum Market into the Global Economy and the Efficiency of the Shanghai Futures Exchange: Empirical Study." Master's thesis, East Asian Languages and Literatures, University of Pittsburgh, Pittsburgh, 2003.

Addison, Craig. *Silicon Shield: Taiwan's Protection against Chinese Attack.* Irvington, TX: Fusion Press, 2001.

Agence France Presse. "Malampaya Defense 'Incidental' to War Games." *Business World*, 25 February 2004.

"Agency Plans Long-range Missile." *Daily Yomiuri*, 3 December 2004.

Ahearne, Alan G., John G. Fernald, Prakash Loungani, and John W. Schindler. "China and Emerging Asia: Comrades or Competitors?" Washington, DC: Federal Reserve, International Finance Discussion Paper Number 789, December 2003.

Alford, William P. "The More Law, the More . . . ? Measuring Legal Reform in the People's Republic of China." In *How Far across the River*, edited by Nicholas C. Hope, Dennis Tao Yang, and Mu Yang Li, 122–49. Stanford: Stanford University Press, 2003.

Armacost, Michael H. "Tilting Closer to Washington." In *Strategic Asia 2003–04: Fragility and Crisis*, edited by Richard J. Ellings and Aaron L. Friedberg, 81–107. Seattle: National Bureau of Asian Research, 2004.

Arndt, Sven W., and Henryk Kierzkowski, eds. *Fragmentation: New Production Patterns in the World Economy.* Oxford: Oxford University Press, 2001.

Associated Press. "China's Automakers on Mission." *St. Petersburg Times*, 19 July 2005. http://www.sptimes.com/2005/07/19/news_pf/Business/China_s_automakers_on.shtml.

Athukorala, Prema-chandra. "Multinational Production Networks and the New Geo-Economic Division of Labour in the Pacific Rim." Paper presented to the 31st Pacific Trade and Development Conference. Guadalajara, Mexico, 10–12 June 2006.

———. "Product Fragmentation and Trade Patterns in East Asia." Division of Economics, Research School of Pacific and Asian Studies, Working Papers in Trade and Development 2003/21. Canberra: Australian National University, 2003.

Australia. Department of Foreign Affairs and Trade. East Asia Analytical Unit. *China Embraces the Market: Achievements, Challenges and Opportunities.* Canberra: Department of Foreign Affairs and Trade, 1997.

Ba, Alice D. "China and ASEAN: Reinvigorating Relations for a 21st Century Asia." *Asian Survey* 43, no. 4 (July–August 2003): 638–44.

Baldwin, David. *Economic Statecraft.* Princeton, NJ: Princeton University Press, 1985.

———. "Power Analysis and World Politics: New Trends versus Old Tendencies." *World Politics* 31, no. 2 (January 1979): 161–94.

———. "Security Studies and the End of the Cold War." *World Politics* 48, no. 1 (October 1995): 117–41.

Baldwin, Richard E. "The Spoke Trap: Hub and Spoke Bilateralism in East Asia." Unpublished paper written for the Korean Institute for International Economic Policy, 8 December 2003.

Bank of Japan. *Hundred-Year Statistics of the Japanese Economy.* Tokyo: Bank of Japan, 1966.

Baum, Richard. *Burying Mao.* Princeton, NJ: Princeton University Press, 1994.

Belson, Ken. "Japanese Capital and Jobs Flowing to China." *New York Times,* 17 February 2004.

Bennett, Brian. "China's Big Export." *Time,* 21 February 2005.

Bernard, Mitchell, and John Ravenhill. "Beyond Product Cycles and Flying Geese: Regionalization, Hierarchy, and the Industrialization of East Asia." *World Politics* 45 (1995): 179–210.

Betts, Richard K. "Wealth, Power and Instability: East Asia and the United States after the Cold War." *International Security* 18, no. 3 (Winter 1993–1994): 34–77.

Blanchard, Jean-Marc F., Edward D. Mansfield, and Norrin M. Ripsman, eds. *Power and the Purse: Economic Statecraft, Interdependence, and National Security.* London: Frank Cass, 2000.

Blank, Stephen J. "Who's Minding the Store? The Failure of Russian Security Policy." *Problems of Post-Communism* 45, no. 2 (March–April 1998): 3–11.

Blasko, Dennis J. *The Chinese Army Today.* New York: Routledge, 2004.

———. "The New PLA Force Structure." In *The People's Liberation Army in the Information Age,* edited by James C. Mulvenon and Richard H. Yang, 263–70. Santa Monica, CA: Rand, 1999.

———. "PLA Ground Forces: Moving toward a Smaller, More Rapidly Deployable,

Modern Combined Arms Force." In *The People's Liberation Army as Organization*, edited by James C. Mulvenon and Andrew N. D. Yang, 315–22. Santa Monica, CA: Rand, 2002.

Borrus, Michael, Dieter Ernst, and Stephan Haggard, eds. *International Production Networks in Asia: Rivalry or Riches?* London: Routledge, 2000.

Bracken, Paul. *Fire in the East: The Rise of Asian Military Power and the Second Nuclear Age*. New York: Harper Collins, 1999.

Brandt, Loren. "China's Foreign Trade since 1450." In *History of World Trade since 1450*, edited by John J. McCusker. Farmington Hills, MI: Macmillan Reference USA, 2006.

Brandt, Loren, Thomas G. Rawski, and John Sutton. "Industrial Development in China." In *China's Great Economic Transformation*, edited by Loren Brandt and Thomas G. Rawski. Cambridge: Cambridge University Press, forthcoming.

Branstetter, Lee, and Nicholas R. Lardy. "China's Embrace of Globalization." In *China's Great Economic Transformation*, edited by Loren Brandt and Thomas G. Rawski. Cambridge: Cambridge University Press, forthcoming.

Brawley, Mark R. "The Political Economy of Balance of Power Theory." In *Balance of Power: Theory and Practice in the 21st Century*, edited by T. V. Paul, Jim Wirtz, and Michel Fortmann. Stanford: Stanford University Press, 2004.

Breckon, Lyall. "A New Strategic Relationship Is Declared: ASEAN-China Relations," *Comparative Connections* (October–December 2003). http://www.ciaonet.org/olj/cpc/cpc_jan04/cpc_jan04g.pdf.

Briscoe, David. "U.S. Force of 200 Expected in Austalia for East Timor." Associated Press, 22 September 1999. http://web.lexis-nexis.com/universe/.

Brooke, James. "Courtship of Beijing and Seoul: A New Twist for an Old Bond." *New York Times*, 26 February 2004.

———. "Korea Feeling Pressure as China Grows." *New York Times*, 8 January 2003.

———. "Musings on an Exodus of G.I.'s, South Korea Hails U.S. Presence." *New York Times*, 8 March 2003.

———. "North Korea Lashes Out at Neighbors and U.S." *New York Times*, 19 August 2003.

———. "Threats and Responses: Weapons; South Opposes Pressuring North Korea, Which Hints It Will Scrap Nuclear Pact." *New York Times*, 1 January 2003.

Brooke, James, and Thom Shanker. "U.S. Plans to Cut Third of Troops in South Korea." *New York Times*, 8 June 2004.

Brown, Harold, Joseph Prueher, and Adam Segal. *Chinese Military Power: Report of an Independent Task Force*. New York: Council on Foreign Relations, 2003.

Browne, Andrew. "China Drew Over $60 Billion in Foreign Investment in 2005." *Wall Street Journal*, 14–15 January 2006.

Bush, George W. "The National Security Strategy." The White House, 16 March 2006. http://www.whitehouse.gov/nsc/nss/2006/intro.html.

Buzan, Barry. "Rethinking Security after the Cold War." *Cooperation and Conflict* 32, no. 1 (1997): 5–28.

Cai, Kevin G. "The ASEAN-China Free Trade Agreement and East Asian Regional Grouping." *Contemporary Southeast Asia* 25, no. 3 (2003): 401.

Calder, Kent E. *Asia's Deadly Triangle: How Arms, Energy and Growth Threaten to Destabilize Asia-Pacific*. London: Nicholas Brealey Publishing, 1997.

Cao, Cong. "Challenges for Technological Development in China's Industry." *China Perspectives* 54 (July–August 2004): 4–24.

Cao, Cong, and Richard P. Suttmeier. "China's New Scientific Elite: Distinguished Young Scientists, the Research Environment and the Hopes for Chinese Science." *China Quarterly* 4 (2001): 960–84.

Cao Desheng. "Private, Foreign Funds an Option to Plug Rail Funding Shortfall." *China Daily*, 6 June 2005.

Carr, Edward Hallett. *The Twenty Years Crisis, 1919–1939*. New York: Harper & Row, 1964.

Chan Kay Min. "High-Tech 'Stars' at New Naval Base." *Straits Times*, 11 March 2001.

Chang, G. Andy, and T. Y. Wang. "Taiwanese or Chinese? Independence or Unification? An Analysis of Generational Differences in Taiwan." *Journal of Asian and African Studies* 40, no. 1/2 (April 2005): 29–49.

Chantasasawat, Busakorn, K. E. Fung, Hitomi Iazaka, and Alan Liu. "Foreign Direct Investment in China and East Asia." Paper presented at the Third Annual Conference on China Economic Policy Reform, Stanford Center for International Development, 12 November 2004.

———. *Foreign Direct Investment in East Asia and Latin America: Is There a People's Republic of China Effect?* ADB Institute Discussion Paper 17. Manila: Asian Development Bank, November 2004.

———. "International Competition for Foreign Direct Investment: The Case of China." Paper presented at the Hitotsubashi Conference on International Trade and FDI, Tokyo, December 2003.

Chen, Melody. "Polls Indicate Few Want Cross-Strait Status Quo Changed." *Taipei Times*, 10 February 2004.

Chen, Ming-Chi. "Sinicization and Its Discontents: Cross-Strait Integration and Taiwan's 2004 Presidential Election." *Issues & Studies* 40, no. 3–4 (September 2004): 334–41.

Chen, Nai Ruenn. *Chinese Economic Statistics*. Chicago: Aldine Publishing Company, 1967.

"Chen Shui-bian Again Provokes the Mainland." *Hong Kong ta kung pao*, in Foreign Broadcast Information Services-China, 30 July 2002.

"China Becomes South Korea's Number One Investment Target." *China Daily*, 2 February 2002. http://www1.chinadaily.com.cn/news/2002-02-05/55641.html.

"China Emerges as Biggest Export Market of South Korea." *People's Daily*, 14 November 2002. http://english.peopledaily.com.cn/200211/14/eng20021114_106796.shtml.

"China Invites Taiwan Businessmen for Talks." *BBC Online*, 22 May 2002.

"China Pours More Money Overseas." 22 October 2004. http://www.china-embassy.org/eng/xw/t166686.htm (accessed 9 January 2007).
"China Reduces Its Crude Oil Support to North Korea by a Sizable Quantity." Chosun Ilbo, 30 August 2006. In FBIS, 200608301477.1_9a0d0073b439d116.
"China Will Not Yield on a Matter of Principle." Xinhua, 8 April 2000.
China's Emerging Semiconductor Industry: The Impact of China's Preferential Value-Added Tax on Current Investment Trends. Washington, DC: Semiconductor Industry Association and Dewey Ballantine LLP, 2003.
Chirathivat, Suthiphand, Franz Knipping, Poul Henrik Lassen, and Chia Siow Yue, eds. *Asia-Europe on the Eve of the 21st Century.* Bangkok: Centre for European Studies at Chulalongkorn University; and Singapore: Institute of Southeast Asian Studies, 2001.
Chiu Yu-tzu. "Technology Law to Guard Valued Assets." *Taipei Times,* 17 April 2002.
Christensen, Thomas. "China." In *Strategic Asia 2001–2002.* National Bureau of Asian Research, 2001 (Online information shows the article was published in *Strategic Asia 2002–2003*).
———. "Posing Problems without Catching Up: China's Rise and Challenges for U.S. Security Policy." *International Security* 25, no. 4 (Spring 2001): 5–40.
———. *Useful Adversaries: Grand Strategy, Domestic Mobilization, and Sino-American Conflict, 1947–1958.* Princeton, NJ: Princeton University Press, 1996.
Chu Yun-han. "Taiwan's National Identity Politics and the Prospect of Cross-Strait Relations." *Asian Survey* 44, no. 4 (July/August 2004): 484–512.
Chung, Jae Ho. "From a Special Relationship to a Normal Partnership: Interpreting the 'Garlic Battle,'" *Pacific Affairs* 76, no. 4 (Winter 2003–2004): 549–68.
Chung, Lawrence. "Taiwan Woos Its Companies Back." *Straits Times,* 12 December 2002.
Clough, Ralph. *Reaching across the Taiwan Strait: People-to-People Diplomacy.* San Francisco: Westview Press, 1993.
Cody, Edward. "China's Quiet Rise Casts Wide Shadow." *Washington Post,* 26 February 2005.
Cole, Bernard D. "China's Maritime Strategy." In *The People's Liberation Army after Next,* edited by Susan M. Puska. Carlisle, PA: Strategic Studies Institute, U.S. Army War College, August 2000.
———. *The Great Wall at Sea: China's Navy Enters the Twenty-First Century.* Annapolis: Naval Institute Press, 2001.
———. "The PLA and 'Active Defense.'" In *The People's Liberation Army and China in Transition,* edited by Stephen J. Flanagan and Michael E. Martin, 129–38. Washington, DC: National Defense University, 2003.
———. *Taiwan's Security: History and Prospects.* New York: Routledge, 2006.
Cole, Bernard D., and Paul H. B. Godwin. "Advanced Military Technology and the PLA: Priorities and Capabilities in the 21st Century." In *The Chinese Armed*

Forces in the 21st Century, edited by Larry M. Wortzel, 159–215. Carlisle, PA: Strategic Studies Institute, U.S. Army War College, 1999.

Council for Asia-Europe Cooperation. *The Rationale and Common Agenda for Asia-Europe Cooperation*. Tokyo: Japan Center for International Exchange; and London: International Institute of Strategic Studies, 1997.

Dai, Jim, Yuepeng Li, Xiutian Liu, Yang Wang, Nancy Wong, and Chen Zhou. *2004 China Road Transportation Enterprise Survey Report*. Qinhuangdao: Northeastern University in China at Qinhuangdao, 2005.

Dao, James. "Coalition Widens Its Ocean Manhunt." *New York Times*, 17 March 2002.

Davie, John L. "China's International Trade and Finance." In *China's Economy Looks toward the Year* 2000, edited by Joint Economic Committee, United States Congress, 311–34. Washington, DC: U.S. Government Printing Office, 1986.

Davies, Gloria, ed. *Voicing Concerns: Contemporary Chinese Critical Inquiry*. Lanham, MD: Roman & Littlefield, 2001.

Dent, Christopher M. "Taiwan and the New Regional Political Economy of East Asia." *China Quarterly* 182 (2005): 385–406.

DeRosa, Dean. "Gravity Model Calculations of the Trade Impacts of U.S. Free Trade Agreements." Paper prepared for the Conference on Free Trade Agreements and U.S. Policy, Institute for International Economics, Washington, DC, 7–8 May 2003.

Dickie, Mure, and James Kynge. "Business in Taiwan Heeds Warning on Independence." *Financial Times*, 11 March 2000.

Dickie, Mure, and David Pilling, "Unbowed: Koizumi's Assertive Japan Is Standing Up Increasingly to China." *Financial Times*, 14 February 2005.

Dobson, Richard. "Formosa's Wang Says 'One China' Must Be Accepted." *Taipei Times*, 20 June 2001.

Doremus, Paul N., William W. Keller, Louis W. Pauly, and Simon Reich. *The Myth of the Global Corporation*. Princeton, NJ: Princeton University Press, 1998.

Downs, Erica Strecker, and Phillip Saunders. "Legitimacy and the Limits of Nationalism: China and the Diaoyu Islands." *International Security* 23, no. 3 (Winter 1998/99): 114–46.

Drysdale, Peter. *International Economic Pluralism: Economic Policy in East Asia and the Pacific*. Sydney: Allen and Unwin, 1988.

Drysdale, Peter, and Xinpeng Xu. "Taiwan's Role in the Economic Architecture of East Asia and the Pacific." In *Economic Reform and Cross-Strait Relations: Taiwan and China in the WTO*, edited by Julian Chang and Steven M. Goldstein. New Jersey: World Scientific, 2007.

East Asia Vision Group. "Towards an East Asian Community: Region of Peace, Prosperity and Progress." 2001. http://www.mofa.go.jp/region/asia-paci/report2001.pdf.

Economy, Elizabeth, and Adam Segal. "China's Luster Fades." *Los Angeles Times*, 30 December 2004.

Eichengreen, Barry, and Hui Tong. *Is China's FDI Coming at the Expense of Other Countries?* Cambridge, MA: National Bureau of Economic Research, Working Paper 11335, May 2005. http://www.nber.org/papers/w11335.

Eichengreen, Barry, Yeongseop Rhee, and Hui Tong. "The Impact of China on the Exports of Other Asian Countries." Mimeograph, University of California, Berkeley, September 2004.

Ernst, Dieter. "Global Production Networks in East Asia's Electronics Industry and Upgrading Perspectives in Malaysia." *East-West Center Working Papers, Economics Series*, no. 44. Honolulu, HI: East-West Center, 2002.

———. "Internationalization of Innovation: Why Is Chip Design Moving to Asia?" *East-West Center Working Papers, Economics Series*, no. 64. Honolulu, HI: East-West Center, 2004.

———. "Late Innovation Strategies in Asian Electronics Industries." *East-West Center Working Papers, Economics Series*, no. 66. Honolulu, HI: East-West Center, 2004.

———. "Pathways to Innovation in the Global Network Economy." *East-West Center Working Papers, Economics Series*, no. 58. Honolulu, HI: East-West Center, 2003.

Esarey, Ashley. "Speak No Evil: Mass Media Control in Contemporary China." *A Freedom House Special Report*, February 2006.

Estevadeordal, Antoni, Brian Franz, and Alan M. Taylor. "The Rise and Fall of World Trade, 1870–1939." Working Paper w9318. Cambridge, MA: National Bureau of Economic Research, November 2002.

Evans, Grant, Christopher Hutton, and Kuah Khun Eng. *Where China Meets Southeast Asia: Social and Cultural Change in the Border Regions*. Bangkok: White Lotus; and Singapore: Institute for Southeast Asian Studies, 2000.

Evans, Paul. "Between Regionalism and Regionalization: Policy Networks and the Nascent East Asian Institutional Identity." In *Remapping East Asia: The Construction of a Region*, edited by T. J. Pempel, 195–215. Ithaca, NY: Cornell University Press, 2005.

"Export Controls: Rapid Advances in China's Semiconductor Industry Underscore Need for Fundamental U.S. Policy Review." United States General Accounting Office, GAO-02-620, April 2002.

Faiola, Anthony. "Japan's Draft Charter Redefines Military." *Washington Post*, 23 November 2005.

Feigenbaum, Evan. "China's Challenge to Pax." *Washington Quarterly* 24, no. 3 (Summer 2001).

Fewsmith, Joseph. "Chambers of Commerce in Wenzhou and the Potential Limits of 'Civil Society' in China." *China Leadership Monitor*, no. 16 (Fall 2005). http://media.hoover.org/documents/clm16_jf.pdf.

———. *China since Tiananmen: The Politics of Transition*. Cambridge: Cambridge University Press, 2001.

———. "China under Hu Jintao." *China Leadership Monitor*, no. 14 (Spring 2005). http://media.hoover.org/documents/clm14_jf.pdf.

———. "Continuing Pressure on Social Order." *China Leadership Monitor*, no. 10 (Spring 2004). http://media.hoover.org/documents/clm10_jf.pdf.

———. *Dilemmas of Reform: Political Conflict and Economic Debate*. Armonk, NY: M. E. Sharpe, 1994.

———. "Taizhou Area Explores Ways to Improve Local Governance." *China Leadership Monitor*, no. 15 (Summer 2005). http://media.hoover.org/documents/clm15_jf.pdf.

Frank, Andre Gunder. *Reorient: Global Economy in the Asian Age*. Berkeley: University of California Press, 1998.

French, Howard W. "Can Japan Change?" *New York Times*, 22 July 2003.

———. "Taboo against Nuclear Weapons Is Being Challenged in Japan." *New York Times*, 9 June 2002.

Friedberg, Aaron L. "The Struggle for Mastery in Asia." *Commentary* 110, no. 4 (November 2000): 17–26.

Frost, Ellen. "Economic Integration: Implications of Regional Economic Integration." *Fragility and Crisis: Strategic Asia 2003–2004*. Seattle: National Bureau of Asian Research, 2003.

———. "Implications of Regional Economic Integration." In *Strategic Asia 2004–2005: Fragility and Crisis*. Seattle: National Bureau of Asian Research, 2003.

"FTWorld's Most Respected Companies." *Financial Times*, Special Report, 20 January 2004.

Fuller, Douglas B. "Moving along the Electronics Value Chain: Taiwan in a Global Economy." In *Global Taiwan*, edited by Suzanne Berger and Richard K. Lester, 137–65. Armonk, NY: M. E. Sharpe, 2005.

Fung, K. C., and Lawrence J. Lau. "Adjusted Estimates of United States–China Bilateral Trade Balances, 1995–2002." *Journal of Asian Economics* 14 (2003): 489–96.

"Further Develop and Bring About Flourishing Philosophy and Social Sciences." *Qiushi* [Seek Truth] 4 (16 February 2004): 1–4.

Gabriele, Alberto. "S & T Policies and Technical Progress in China's Industry." *Review of International Political Economy* 9, no. 2 (Summer 2002): 333–73.

Gallagher, Mary E. *Contagious Capitalism: Globalization and the Politics of Labor in China*. Princeton, NJ: Princeton University Press, 2005.

Garamone, Jim. "Singapore, U.S. Reaffirm, Strengthen Relationship." American Forces Press Service, 12 July 2005. http://www.defenselink.mil/news/Jul2005/20050712_2040.html.

Gargan, Edward. "Long-Term Forecast for Taiwan Remains Upbeat." *New York Times*, 22 March 1996.

Gaulier, Guillaume, Françoise Lemoine, and Deniz Ünal-Kesenci. *China's Integration in Asian Production Networks and Its Implications*. Tokyo: Research

Institute of Economy, Trade and Industry, Discussion Paper 04033, 2004. http://www.rieti.go.jp/jp/publications/dp/04e033.pdf.

General Accounting Office. "Export Controls: Rapid Advances in China's Semiconductor Industry Underscore Need for Fundamental U.S. Policy Review." April 2002. GAO-02-620.

Gereffi, Gary, et al. "Framing the Outsourcing Engineering Debate: Placing the United States on a Level Playing Field with China and India." http://memp.pratt.duke.edu/downloads/duke_outsourcing_2005.pdf.

Giarra, Paul S., and Akisha Nagashima. "Managing the New U.S.-Japan Security Alliance: Enhancing Structures and Mechanisms to Address Post–Cold War Requirements." In *The U.S.-Japan Alliance: Past, Future and Present*, edited by Michael J. Green and Patrick M. Cronin, 94–113. New York: Council on Foreign Relations, 1999.

Gilboy, George, and Eric Heginbotham. "U.S. Asia (and China) Policy Reconceived." *National Interest*, no. 69 (Fall 2002): 99–109.

Gill, Bates. "Contrasting Visions: China, the United States, and the World Order." Remarks to the U.S.-China Security Review Commission, Washington, DC, 3 August 2001.

Gilley, Bruce. *China's Democratic Future*. New York: Columbia University Press, 2004.

Gleystein, William H., Jr. *Massive Entanglement, Marginal Influence: Carter and Korea in Crisis*. Washington, DC: Brookings Institution Press, 1999.

Glosny, Michael A. "Strangulation from the Sea? A PRC Submarine Blockade of Taiwan." *International Security* 28, no. 4 (Spring 2004): 125–60.

Goldman, Merle. *Sowing the Seeds of Democracy: Political Reform in the Deng Xiaoping Era*. Cambridge, MA: Harvard University Press, 1994.

Goldstein, Avery. "An Emerging China's Emerging Grand Strategy: A Neo-Bismarckian Turn?" In *International Relations Theory and the Asia-Pacific*, edited by G. J. Ikenberry and M. Mastanduno, 57–106. New York: Columbia University Press, 2003.

Goldstein, Lyle, and William Murray. "Undersea Dragons: China's Maturing Submarine Force." *International Security* 28, no. 4 (Spring 2004): 161–96.

Gong Zhengzheng. "Egypt to Make Brilliance Cars." *China Daily*, 24 September 2005. http://www.chinadaily.com.cn/english/doc/2005-04/15/content_434431.htm#.

Goodman, Peter S. "Made in China—With Neighbors' Imports." *Washington Post*, 5 February 2004.

"Government Approves TSMC's Wafer Project." *China Post*, 1 May 2004.

Gowa, Joanne. *Allies, Adversaries, and International Trade*. Princeton, NJ: Princeton University Press, 1994.

Graham, Bradley, and Doug Struck. "U.S., Asian Allies Face Tough Choices." *Washington Post*, 25 April 2003.

——. "U.S. Officials Anticipate More Provocations by North Korea." *Washington Post*, 3 March 2003.
Graham, Edward M. "Foreign Direct Investment in the World Economy." IMF Working Paper, WP/95/59. Washington, DC: International Monetary Fund, June 1995.
Gries, Peter Hays. *China's New Nationalism*. Berkeley: University of California Press, 2004.
Gries, Peter Hays, and Thomas J. Christensen. "Correspondence: Power and Resolve in U.S. China Policy." *International Security* 26, no. 2 (Fall 2001): 155–65.
Grosserman, Brad. "China's Influence in Asia Soars." *Japan Times*, 17 May 2004.
"Guardian of 'Human Rights' Shows Its True Colour." *China Daily*, 10 March 2006.
Gunter, Frank R. "Capital Flight from China: 1984–2001." *China Economic Review*, 15 (2004): 63–85.
Guo, Peng. "Asymmetrical Information, Suboptimal Strategies, and Institutional Performance: The Paradox of the 1995 Regulations of China's Official Promotion System." PhD diss., Boston University, 2004.
Halloran, Richard. "U.S. Forces Prepare for Surprises in Asia." *Japan Times*, 29 March 2004.
Hamada, Kazuko. "The Impact of China's Economic Integration: The Implications of China's Role in the Asian Production Network for the Global Economic System." Unpublished manuscript, 7 February 2005.
Harrold, Peter, and Rajiv Lall. "China: Reform and Development in 1992–93." Washington, DC: World Bank Discussion Paper 215, August 1993.
Henley, Lonnie. "PLA Logistics and Doctrine Reform, 1999–2009." In *The People's Liberation Army after Next*, edited by Susan M. Puska. Carlisle, PA: Strategic Studies Institute, U.S. Army War College, 2000.
Henning, C. Randall. *East Asian Financial Cooperation*. Policy Analysis 68. Washington, DC: Institute for International Economics, 2002.
Herberg, Mikkal E. "Asia's Energy Insecurity: Cooperation or Conflict?" In *Strategic Asia 2004–05: Confronting Terrorism in the Pursuit of Power*, edited by Ashley J. Tellis and Michael Wills, 338–77. Seattle: National Bureau of Asian Research, 2004.
Herman, Burt. "China Reduces Oil Shipment to North Korea." Associated Press, 26 August 2006.
Hijino, Ken. "China-Japan Trade Deepens." *Financial Times*, 15 December 2001.
Hirschman, Albert O. *National Power and the Structure of Foreign Trade*. Expanded ed. Berkeley: University of California Press, 1980.
Hoge, James. F., Jr. "A Global Power Shift in the Making." *Foreign Affairs* 83, no. 4 (July–August 2004): 2–7.
Holst, David Roland, and John Weiss. "ASEAN and China: Export Rivals or Partners in Regional Growth?" *World Economy* 27 (2004): 1255–74.
Hsiao, Liang-lin. *China's Foreign Trade Statistics, 1964–1949*. Cambridge, MA: Harvard East Asian Monographs, 1974.

Hsiung, Deh-I. "An Evaluation of China's Science & Technology System and Its Impact on the Research Community." *Special Report for the Environment, Science & Technology Section*. U.S. Embassy, Beijing, Summer 2002.

Hsu, Jacky. "Taiwan's Tycoons Stay Clear of Politics." *South China Morning Post*, 27 May 2004.

Hu, Albert G., and Gary H. Jefferson. "A Great Wall of Patents: What Is Behind China's Recent Patent Explosion?" Discussion paper, Brandeis University, 2005. http://people.brandeis.edu/~jefferso/res.html.

Hu Angang, Wang Shaoguang, and Ding Yuanzhu. "The Social Instability behind Economic Prosperity." *Zhanlue yu guanli* [Strategy and Management] (June 2002): 26–33.

Hu Meidong and Li Dapeng. "Fuyao Sees Through Glass Sales to Audi." *China Daily*, 2 June 2005.

———. "Fuyao Launches Three Glass Production Lines." *China Daily*, 25 June 2005.

Hu Yaobang. "The Radiance of the Great Truth of Marxism Lights Our Way Forward." Speech, Xinhua, 13 March 1983.

Hu Yuanyuan. "Insurer: Search for Investor Going Well." *China Daily*, 8 September 2005.

Huang Ping and Cui Zhiyuan, eds. *Zhongguo yu quanqiuhua: Huashengtun gongshi haishi Beijing gongshi?* [China and Globalization: Washington Consensus or Beijing Consensus?]. Beijing: Shehui kexue wenxian chubanshe, 2005.

Huang, Yasheng. *Selling China: Foreign Direct Investment during the Reform Era*. Cambridge: Cambridge University Press, 2003.

Hughes, Christopher. *Japan's Re-emergence as a "Normal" Military Power.* Adelphi Papers no. 368–69. Oxford: Oxford University Press for the International Institute for Strategic Studies, 2004.

"Human Rights: Australia-China Human Rights Dialogue." http://www.dfat.gov.au/hr/achrd/aus_proc_dialogue.html.

Huntington, Samuel P. *The Clash of Civilizations and the Remaking of World Order.* New York: Simon & Schuster, 1996.

Ianchovichina, Elena, Sethaput Suthiwart-Narueput, and Min Zhao. "Regional Impact of China's WTO Accession." In *East Asia Integrates: A Trade Policy Agenda for Shared Growth*, edited by K. L. Krumm and H. J. Kharas, 57–78. New York: World Bank, 2004.

Ianchovichina, Elena, and Terrie Louise Walmsley. *The Impact of China's WTO Accession on East Asia*. Washington, DC: World Bank Poverty Reduction and Economic Management Network Economic Policy Division, Policy Research Working Paper 3109. August 2003. http://econ.worldbank.org/resource.php?type=5.

Ibison, David. "Koizumi Visits to War Shrine Attacked." *Financial Times*, 26 November 2004.

Information Office of the State Council, People's Republic of China. "China's

National Defense in 2006." 29 December 2006. http://www.fas.org/nuke/guide/china/doctrine/wp2006.
International Institute for Strategic Studies. *The Military Balance 2002–2003*. Oxford: Oxford University Press, 2002.
———. *The Military Balance 2004–2005*. Oxford: Oxford University Press, 2004.
Ito, Kan. "China's Nuclear Power Will Control the World by 2020." *Tokyo Shokun*, 1 January 2006, in FBIS, JPP20051205016001.
Jervis, Robert L. *Logic of Images in International Relations*. New York: Columbia University Press, 1989.
Jiang Wei. "Outbound FDI up 123 Percent in 2005." http://www.chinadaily.com.cn/bizchina/2006-09/05/content_681592.htm.
———. "Outward Investment Steady." *China Daily*, 24 January 2006.
Jiang, Xiaojuan. *FDI in China: Contributions to Growth, Restructuring, and Competitiveness*. New York: Nova Science Publishers, 2004.
Johnston, Alastair Iain. "Beijing's Security Behavior in the Asia-Pacific: Is China a Dissatisfied Power?" In *Rethinking Security in East Asia: Identity, Power, and Efficiency*, edited by J. J. Suh, Peter J. Katzenstein, and Allen Carlson. Stanford, CA: Stanford University Press, 2004.
———. "Is China a Status Quo Power?" *International Security* 27, no. 4 (Spring 2003): 5–56.
"Joint Statement of the U.S.-Japan Consultative Committee." 19 February 2005, http://www.state.gov/r/pa/prs/ps/2005/42490.htm.
Jowitt, Kenneth. *Leninist Responses to National Dependency*. Berkeley: Institute of International Studies, University of California, 1978.
———. *New World Disorder: The Leninist Extinction*. Berkeley and Los Angeles: University of California Press, 1992.
Kan, Shirley A. *China: Ballistic and Cruise Missiles. CRS Report for Congress* (97–391 F). Washington, DC: Congressional Research Service, Library of Congress, 2000.
Kang, David C. "Getting Asia Wrong: The Need for New Analytical Frameworks." *International Security* 27, no. 4 (Spring 2003): 57–85.
———. "Hierarchy, Balancing, and Empirical Puzzles in Asian International Relations." *International Security* 28, no. 3 (Winter 2003): 165–80.
Kang Xiaoguang. "Weilai 3–5 nian Zhongguo dalu zhengzhi wendingxing fenxi" [An Analysis of the Stability of Chinese Politics on the Chinese Mainlaind in the Coming 3–5 Years]. *Zhanlue yu guanli* [Strategy and Management] 3 (2002): 1–15.
Kao, Chang. *Dalu jingji yu liangan jingmao guanxi* [Mainland Economic Reform and Cross-Strait Relations]. Taipei: Wu Nan, 1994.
Karniol, Robert. "U.S. Doubles Personnel for 'Balikatan 2004.'" *New York Times*, 3 March 2004.
Kaufman, Robert G. "To Balance or Bandwagon: Alignment Decisions in 1930s Europe." *Security Studies* 1, no. 3 (Spring 1992): 417–47.

Keller, William W., and Gordon R. Mitchell, eds. *Hitting First: Preventive Force in U.S. Security Strategy*. Pittsburgh, PA: University of Pittsburgh Press, 2006.

Keller, William W., and Janne E. Nolan. "Proliferation of Advanced Weaponry: Threat to Stability." In *The Global Century*, edited by Richard L. Kugler and Ellen L. Frost, 785–808. Washington, DC: National Defense University Press, 2001.

Keller, William W., and Louis W. Pauly. "Crisis and Adaptation in East Asian Innovation Systems: The Case of the Semiconductor Industry in Taiwan and South Korea." *Business and Politics* 2, no. 3 (2000): 327–52.

———. "Crisis and Adaptation in Taiwan and Korea: The Political Economy of Semiconductors." In *Crisis and Innovation in Asian Technology*, edited by William W. Keller and Richard J. Samuels, 137–59. Cambridge: Cambridge University Press, 2003.

Keller, William W., and Richard J. Samuels. "Innovation and the Asian Economies." In *Crisis and Innovation in Asian Technology*, edited by William W. Keller and Richard J. Samuels, 9–12. New York: Cambridge University Press, 2003.

Kennedy, Scott. *The Business of Lobbying in China*. Cambridge, MA: Harvard University Press, 2005.

Kim, Taeho. "Korean Perspectives on PLA Modernization and the Future East Asian Security Environment." In *China's Shadow: Regional Perspectives on Chinese Foreign Policy and Military Development*, edited by Jonathan D. Pollack and Richard H. Yang. Santa Monica, CA: Rand, 1998.

King, Neil, Jr. "Secret Weapon, Inside Pentagon, a Scholar Shapes View of China." *Wall Street Journal*, 8 September 2005.

Kirshner, Jonathan. "The Political Economy of Realism." In *Unipolar Politics: Realism and State Strategies after the Cold War*, edited by Ethan B. Kapstein and Michael Mastanduno, 69–102. New York: Columbia University Press, 1999.

———. "Political Economy of Security Studies after the Cold War." *Review of International Political Economy* 5, no. 1 (1998): 64–91.

———. "States, Markets, and Great Power Relations in the Pacific: Some Realist Expectations." In *International Relations Theory and the Asia- Pacific*, edited by G. J. Ikenberry and M. Mastanduno, 273–98. New York: Columbia University Press, 2003.

Knorr, Klaus. *The Power of Nations: The Political Economy of International Relations*. New York: Basic Books, 1975.

"Koreans Look to China, Seeing a Market and a Monster." *New York Times*, 10 February 2003.

Kynge, James. "Japan, China in 11th-hour Trade Deal." *Financial Times*, 22 December 2001.

Lall, Sanjaya, and Manuel Albaladejo. "China's Competitive Performance: A Threat to East Asian Manufactured Exports?" *World Development* 32 (2004): 1441–66.

Lam Peng Er. "Japan's Deteriorating Ties with China: The Koizumi Factor." *China: An International Journal* 3, no. 2 (September 2005): 275–91.

Landler, Mark, and Keith Bradsher. "VW to Build Hybrid Minivan with Chinese." *New York Times*, 9 September 2005.
Lardy, Nicholas R. *China's Unfinished Economic Revolution*. Washington, DC: Brookings Institution Press, 1998.
———. "Evaluating Economic Indicators in Post-WTO China." *Issues & Studies* 39 (2003): 249–68.
———. *Foreign Trade and Economic Reform in China, 1978–1990*. Cambridge and New York: Cambridge University Press, 1992.
———. *Integrating China into the Global Economy*. Washington, DC: Brookings Institution Press, 2002.
———. "The Role of Foreign Trade and Investment in China's Economic Transformation." *China Quarterly* 144 (1995): 1065–82.
Larson, Eric V., Norman D. Levin, Seonhae Baik, and Bogdan Savych. *Ambivalent Allies? A Study of South Korean Attitudes toward the U.S.* Santa Monica, CA: Rand Corporation, 2004.
Lewis, Martin W., and Karen E. Wigen. *The Myth of Continents: A Critique of Metageography*. Berkeley: University of California Press, 1997.
Li Changping. *Wo xiang zongli shuo shihua* [Speaking the Truth to the Premier]. Beijing: Guangming ribao chubanshe, 2002.
Li Fangfang. "Youthful Mobility." *China Business Weekly*, 19–25 September 2005.
Li Jing. "Top LNG Ship Takes Shape in Shanghai." *China Daily*, 18 July 2005.
———. "We're Not Building an Aircraft Carrier." *China Daily*, 17 June 2005.
Li Ruiying. "Make New Contributions to Upholding and Developing Marxism—An Interview with Leng Rong, Permanent Vice President of the Chinese Academy of Social Sciences and Concurrently Director of Research Academy on Marxism." *Guangming ribao*, 28 December 2005.
Lin Chieh-yu. "Nation Must 'Go its Own Way': Chen." *Taipei Times*, 30 July 2002.
Lin, Justin Yifu, Fang Cai, and Zhou Li. *The China Miracle: Development Strategy and Economic Reform*, revised ed. Hong Kong: Chinese University Press, 2003.
Lincoln, Edward J. *East Asian Economic Regionalism*. Washington, DC: Brookings Institution Press, 2004.
Lippencott, Brett C. "Ending the Confusion in U.S. China Policy." Heritage Foundation, Asian Studies Backgrounder, 18 April 1994. www.heritage.org/Research/AsiaandthePacific/asb130.cfm?renderforprint=1
Liska, George. *Nations in Alliance: The Limits of Interdependence*. Baltimore, MD: Johns Hopkins University Press, 1968.
Liu Guoguang. "Views on Several Macroeconomic Issues." *Gaige* [Reform], no. 2 (2002): 5–9.
Liu, Weifeng, Michael Pecht, and Zhenya Huang. "China's Semiconductor Industry." In *China's Electronics Industries*, edited by Michael Pecht and Y. C. Chan. College Park, MD: CALCE EPSC Press, 2004.
Liu, Weiling. "Bad Medicine." *China Business Weekly*, 7–13 November 2005.
———. "Prince of Patents." *China Business Weekly*, 31 October–6 November. 2005.

Liu Xiaofeng and Zhang Yulin. *Riben de weiji* [Japan's Crisis]. Beijing: Renmin Chubanshe, 2001.

Lu, Mu. "Sino-U.S. Relations: A Century of Strategic Cooperation and Competition." *China Strategy*, 3 July 2004. Washington, DC: Center for Strategic and International Studies. http://www.csis.org/isp/csn/040720.pdf.

Lu Xueyi, ed. *Dangdai Zhongguo shehui liudong* [Social Mobility in Contemporary China]. Beijing: Shehui kexue wenxian chubanshe, 2004.

Luo yi ning ge er. *Disanzhi yanjing kan Zhongguo* [Looking at China through a Third Eye]. Taiyuan: Shanxi renmin chubanshe, 1994.

Magnier, Mark. "Unions across a Divide." *Los Angeles Times*, 22 November 2004.

Mah, Feng-Hwa. "Foreign Trade." In *Economic Trends in Communist China*, edited by Alexander Eckstein, Walter Galenson, and Ta-chung Liu, 671–738. Chicago: Aldine Publishing Company, 1968.

Mainland Affairs Council. *Dalu gongzuo cankao ziliao* [Reference Documents on Mainland Work]. Taipei, 1993.

Martin, Will, and Elena Ianchovichina. "Implications of China's Accession to the World Trade Organization for China and the WTO." *World Economy* 24 (2001): 1205–19.

Mastanduno, Michael. "Economic Engagement Strategies: Theory and Practice." In *Economic Interdependence and International Conflict: New Perspectives on an Enduring Debate*, edited by Edward Mansfield and Brian Pollins, 175–88. Ann Arbor: University of Michigan Press, 2003.

———. "Economics and Security in Statecraft and Scholarship." *International Organization* 52, no. 4 (Autumn 1998): 825–54.

McKendrick, David, Richard F. Doner, and Stephan Haggard. *From Silicon Valley to Singapore: Location and Competitive Advantage in the Hard Disk Drive Industry*. Stanford, CA: Stanford University Press, 2000.

Mearsheimer, John. *The Tragedy of Great Power Politics*. New York: W. W. Norton, 2003.

Medeiros, Evan S., et al. *A New Direction for China's Defense Industry*. Prepared for the U.S. Air Force. Santa Monica, CA: Rand, 2005.

Medeiros, Evan, and M. Taylor Fravel. "China's New Diplomacy." *Foreign Affairs*, November/December 2003.

"Memorandum of Conversation, by the Secretary of State." 29 December 1949. *Foreign Relations of the United States (FRUS)* 9 (1949): 467. Washington, DC: Government Printing Office, 1974.

"Memorandum of Conversation, by the Secretary of State." 5 January 1950. U.S. Department of State, *Foreign Relations of the United States (FRUS)* 6 (1950): 260–61. Washington, DC: Government Printing Office, 1976.

Miyagawa, Makio. "Integrating Asia through Free Trade." *Far Eastern Economic Review*, July–August 2005, 45–49.

Mochizuki, Mike M. "Security and Economic Interdependence in Northeast Asia." Asia Pacific Research Center, 1998. http://aparc.stanford.edu/publications/10089/.

Monetary Authority of Singapore. "Assessing the Support from Regional Domestic Demand." *Macroeconomic Review* II (January 2003): 60–70.

Moore, Thomas G. *China in the World Market: Chinese Industry and International Sources of Reform in the Post-Mao Era.* Cambridge: Cambridge University Press, 2002.

Morgenthau, Hans J. *Politics among Nations: The Struggle for Power and Peace.* 5th ed. New York: Alfred A. Knopf, 1978.

Mufson, Steven. "China-Taiwan Conflict 'In Remission, Not Resolved.'" *Washington Post*, 22 April 1996.

Mulvenon, James. "The PLA Army's Struggle for Identity." In *The People's Liberation Army and China in Transition*, edited by Stephen J. Flanagan and Michael E. Marti, 116. Washington, DC: Institute for National Strategic Studies, National Defense University, 2003.

Murphy, David. "Europe, Here We Come." *Far Eastern Economic Review*, 26 February 2004, 42.

———. "State Giants Still Dominate." *Far Eastern Economic Review*, 25 December 2003, 56.

Naughton, Barry, ed. *The China Circle : Economics and Electronics in the PRC, Taiwan, and Hong Kong.* Washington, DC: Brookings Institution Press, 1997.

———. "China's Trade Regime at the End of the 1990s." In *China's Future: Constructive Partner or Emerging Threat?* edited by T. G. Carpenter and J. A. Dorn, 235–60, Washington, DC: Cato Institute, 2000.

———. *Growing Out of the Plan: Chinese Economic Reform, 1978–1993.* Cambridge: Cambridge University Press, 1995.

Ng, Francis, and Alexander J. Yeats. *Production Sharing in East Asia: Who Does What for Whom and Why.* Washington, DC: World Bank Development Research Group Trade, Policy Research Working Paper 2197, 1 October 1999. http://econ.worldbank.org/docs/921.pdf

Ng, Jeffrey. "UPS Says It Has Big Plans for China." 27 February 2005. http://www.washingtonpost.com.

Novak, Robert. "Squeezing the U.S. Army." *Chicago Sun-Times*, 23 June 2003. http://www.townhall.com/columnists/RobertDNovak/2003/06/23/squeezing_the_us_army.

Nye, Joseph S. *Soft Power: The Means to Success in World Politics.* New York: Public Affairs, 2004.

Oberdorfer, Don. *The Two Koreas: A Contemporary History.* New York: Basic Books, 1997.

"ODA Strategy Enters New Era." *Daily Yomiuri*, 1 April 2004.

Odaka, Konosuke, ed. *The Long-Term Economic Statistics of Taiwan, 1905–1995: An International Workshop.* Tokyo: Institute of Economic Research, Hitotsubashi University, 1999.

Odaka, Konosuke, and Insang Hwang. *The Long-Term Economic Statistics of*

Korea, 1910–1990: An International Workshop. Tokyo: Institute of Economic Research, Hitotsubashi University, 2000.
OECD. *China in the World Economy: Synthesis Report.* Paris: OECD, 2002.
———. *Economic Surveys: China 2005.* Paris: OECD, 2005.
O'Hanlon, Michael. "Why China Cannot Conquer Taiwan." *International Security* 25 (Fall 2000): 51–86.
Ohashi, Hiroshi. "China's Regional Trade and Investment Profile." In *Power Shift: China and Asia's New Dynamics*, edited by David Shambaugh, 71–95. Berkeley: University of California Press, 2005.
Ohkawa, Kazushi, and Henry Rosovky. *Japanese Economic Growth: Trend Acceleration in the Twentieth Century.* Stanford, CA: Stanford University Press, 1973.
O'Neill, Mark. "Shi Underlines Risk of Packing Politics in Business Briefcase." *South China Morning Post*, 19 March 2001.
Onishi, Norimitsu. "Japan Heads to Iraq, Haunted by Taboo Bred in Another War." *New York Times*, 19 November 2003.
———. "Japan Support of Missile Shield Could Tilt Asia Balance of Power." *New York Times*, 3 April 2004.
"Opportunities for China's Manufacturing Industry after Joining WTO and Relevant Suggestions." *Guoyou zichan guanli* [Management of State Assets] 4 (2003): 4.
Paarlberg, Robert L. "Knowledge as Power: Science, Military Dominance, and U.S. Security." *International Security* 29, no. 1 (Summer 2004): 122–51.
Papayoanou, Paul A. "Economic Interdependence and the Balance of Power." *International Studies Quarterly* 41, no. 1 (March 1997): 113–40.
Papayoanou, Paul, and Scott Kastner. "Sleeping with the (Potential) Enemy: Assessing the US Policy of Engagement with China." In *Power and the Purse: Economic Statecraft, Interdependence, and National Security*, edited by Jean-Marc F. Blanchard, Edward D. Mansfield, and Norrin M. Ripsman, 157–87. London: Frank Cass, 2000.
Patent Filings. "Record Number of International Patent Filings in 2004." http://www.wipo.int/edocs/prdocs/en/2005/wipo_pr_2005_403.html#.
Paul, T. V., James J. Wirtz, and Michael Fortmann. *Balance of Power: Theory and Practice in the 21st Century.* Stanford, CA: Stanford University Press, 2004.
Pecht, Michael, and Y. C. Chan, eds. *China's Electronics Industries.* College Park, MD: CALCE EPSC Press, 2004.
Pempel, T. J. "Introduction." In *Remapping East Asia: The Construction of a Region*, edited by T. J. Pempel, 1–30. Ithaca, NY: Cornell University Press, 2005.
Perkins, Dwight H., and Moshe Syrquin. "Large Countries: The Influence of Size." In *Handbook of Development Economics*, edited by Hollis Chenery and T. N. Srinivasan, 2:1691–753. Amsterdam and New York: North Holland, 1989.
Perlez, Jane. "Chinese Premier Signs Trade Pact at Southeast Asian Summit." *New York Times*, 30 November, 2004.

Pilling, David. "Comments and Analysis." *Financial Times*, 14 April 2004.
———. "Japanese Soft Loans Pour into Indian Projects." *Financial Times*, 12 March 2004.
———. "Japanese Support Leader's War Shrine Visits." *Financial Times*, 14 December 2004.
Pilling, David, and Bayan Rahman. "Japanese Trade Breakthrough with Mexico Points Way to Asia Deals." *Financial Times*, 11 March 2004.
Pillsbury, Michael. "China's Military Strategy toward the U.S.: A View from Open Sources." Background paper prepared for the U.S.-China Economic and Security Review Commission on China. *2004 Report to Congress*.
Politi, James, and Doug Cameron. "Unocal Suitors Wary of Beijing." *Financial Times*, 4 March 2005.
Pollack, Jonathan. "The Transformation of the Asian Security Order: Assessing China's Impact." In *Power Shift: China and Asia's New Dynamics*, edited by David Shambaugh, 329–46. Berkeley: University of California Press, 2005.
Prasad, Eswar, ed. "China's Growth and Integration into the World Economy: Prospects and Challenges." *Occasional Paper* 232, International Monetary Fund, 2004. http://www.imf.org/external/pubs/cat/longres.cfm?sk=17305.0.
"President Chen Calls for Taiwan-US-Japan Free Trade Agreement." *Chinese Economic News Service*, 12 April 2002.
"Presidential Office Cautions Mainland over Chi Mei Plant." *China Post*, 12 March 2001.
President's Council of Advisors on Science and Technology. *Sustaining the Nation's Innovation Ecosystems: Report on Information Technology Manufacturing and Competitiveness*. Washington, DC, January 2004.
"Pro-Independence Parties Defeated in Taiwan." *New York Times*, 11 December 2004.
Przystup, James J. "Japan-China Relations: From Precipice to Promise." *Comparative Connections* 3, no. 4 (October–December 2001). http://www.csis.org/pacfor/cc/0104Qjapan_china.html.
———. "A Volatile Mix: Natural Gas, a Submarine, a Shrine, and a Visa: Japan-China Relations." *Comparative Connections* 6, no. 4 (October–December 2004). http://www.csis.org/pacfor/cc/0404Qjapan_china.html.
Puska, Susan M., ed. *The People's Liberation Army After Next*. Carlisle, PA: Strategic Studies Institute, U.S. Army War College, 2000.
———. "Rough but Ready Force Projection: An Assessment of Recent PLA Training." In *China's Growing Military Power: Perspectives on Security, Ballistic Missiles, and Conventional Capabilities*, edited by Andrew J. Scobel and Larry M. Wortzel, 223, 244–45. Carlisle, PA: Strategic Studies Institute, U.S. Army War College, 2002.
"Qian Qichen Inspects Guangdong, Holds Discussion with Taiwan Businessmen." Xinhua, Foreign Broadcast Information Service–China, 8 December 2002.
Qiao You. "Car Makers Move Production into Russia." *China Daily*, 5 July 2005.

Rawski, Thomas G. "What Is Happening to China's GDP Statistics?" *China Economic Review* 12 (2001): 347–54.
Reuter, Peter, and Edwin M. Truman. *Chasing Dirty Money: The Fight against Money Laundering.* Washington, DC: Institute for International Economics, 2004.
Richardson, Bennett. "Japan Beefs Up Its Defense Stance." *Christian Science Monitor,* 10 December 2004. http://www.csmonitor.com/2004/1210/p06s02-woap.html.
Rock, Stephen R. *Appeasement in International Politics.* Lexington: University Press of Kentucky, 2000.
Rodriguez, Ronald A. "Conduct Unbecoming in the South China Sea?" *PacNet,* no. 22A (21 May 2004).
Rohwer, Jim. *Asia Rising: Why America Will Prosper as Asia's Economies Boom.* New York: Simon & Schuster, 1995.
Rosen, Daniel H. *Behind the Open Door: Foreign Enterprises in the Chinese Marketplace.* Washington, DC: Institute for International Economics, 1999.
Rosen, Daniel H., Scott Rozelle, and Jikun Huang. *Roots Of Competitiveness: China's Evolving Agriculture Interests.* Policy Analyses in International Economics 72. Washington, DC: Institute for International Economics, 2004.
Ross, Robert S. "Balance of Power Politics and the Rise of China: Accommodation and Balancing in East Asia." *Security Studies* 15 (Fall 2006): 355–95.
———. "Explaining Taiwan's Revisionist Diplomacy." *Journal of Contemporary China* 15, no. 48 (August 2006): 443–58.
Rothstein, Robert L. *Alliances and Small Powers.* New York: Columbia University Press, 1968.
Roy, Denny. "Hegemon on the Horizon?" *International Security* 19, no. 1 (Summer 1994): 149–68.
"RP Now Biggest Recipient of US Military Aid in East Asia." *Manila Standard,* 6 March 2004.
Rui, Huaichuan. *Globalization, Transition and Development in China: The Case of the Coal Industry.* London: RoutledgeCurzon, 2005.
Samuels, Richard J. *"Rich Nation, Strong Army": National Security and the Technological Transformation of Japan.* Ithaca, NY: Cornell University Press, 1994.
Samuelson, Robert J. "The China Riddle." *Washington Post,* 30 January 2004.
Sanger, David E. "A Nation at War: The Asian Front; North Koreans and U.S. Plan Talks in Beijing." *New York Times,* 16 April 2003.
Savadove, Bill. "Shanghai Reveals Surge in 'Mass Dispute' Court Cases." *South China Morning Post,* 27 July 2005.
Schweller, Randall L. "Bandwagoning for Profit: Bringing the Revisionist State Back In." *International Security* 19, no. 1 (Summer 1994): 72–107.
———. *Unanswered Threats: Political Constraints on the Balance of Power.* Princeton, NJ: Princeton University Press, 2006.

Scollay, Robert, and John P. Gilbert. *New Trading Arrangements in the Western Pacific?* Washington, DC: Institute for International Economics, 2001.
Scott, Robert E. *U.S.-China Trade 1989–2003: Impact on Jobs and Industries.* Economic Policy Institute, 2005. http://www.uscc.gov/researchpapers/2005/05_02_07_epi_wp_rscott.pdf.
"Seventh ASEAN Investment Area (AIA) Council Meeting, Joint Media Statement." Jakarta, 2 September 2004. http://www.aseansec.org/16347.htm.
Shambaugh, David. "China Engages Asia: Reshaping the Regional Order." *International Security* 29, no. 3 (Winter 2004): 64–99.
Shanker, Thom. "Pentagon Weighs Transferring 4,000 G.I.'s in Korea to Iraq." *New York Times*, 17 May 2004.
———. "Rumsfeld Reassures Seoul on Regrouping G.I.'s." *New York Times*, 18 November 2003.
Shanker, Thom, and David E. Sanger. "U.S. Defends Plan to Reduce Forces in South Korea." *New York Times*, 9 June 2004.
Shen Jiru. "Weihu dongbei ya anquan de dangwu zhi ji" [The Pressing Matter of Protecting Northeast Asian Security]. *Shijie jingji yu zhengzhi* [World Economy and Politics] 9 (2003).
Sheng, Lijun. *China and Taiwan: Cross-Strait Relations under Chen Shui-bian.* Singapore: Institute of Southeast Asian Relations, 2002.
Smith, Anthony L. *Singapore and the United States 2004–2005: Steadfast Friends.* Honolulu, HI: Asia-Pacific Center for Security Studies, 2005.
Snyder, Scott. "China-Korea Relations: Waiting Game." *Comparative Connections*, October–December 2004. http://www.ciaonet.org/olj/cpc/cpc_jan05/cpc_jan05j.pdf.
Song Qiang, Zhang Zangzang, and Qiao Bian. *Zhongguo keyi shuobu* [China Can Say No]. Beijing: Zhonghua gongshang lianhe chubanshe, 1996.
Spencer, Geoff. "First International Combat Troops Land in East Timor." Associated Press, 20 September 1999. http://web.lexis-nexis.com/universe/.
Steinbruner, John. *Principles of Global Security.* Washington, DC: Brookings Institution Press, 2000.
Storey, Ian. *Malaysia and the United States 2004–2005: The Best of Times?* Honolulu, HI: Asia-Pacific Center for Security Studies, 2005.
Storey, Ian, and You Ji. "China's Aircraft Carrier Ambitions: Seeking Truth from Rumors." *Naval War College Review* 57, no. 1 (Winter 2004): 77–93.
Struck, Doug. "Observers See Rising Risk of U.S.–N. Korea Conflict." *Washington Post*, 28 February 2003.
———. "War Games on Korean Peninsula Upset North." *Washington Post*, 23 March 2003.
Sun, Liping. "Pingmin zhuyi yu Zhongguo gaige" [Populism and China's Reform]. *Zhanlue yu guanli* [Strategy and Management] 5 (October 1994): 1–10.
———. *Zhuanxing yu duanlie: gaige yilai Zhongguo shehui jiegou de bianhua*

[Transition and Fracture: The Change in Social Structure since Reform]. Beijing: Qinghua daxue chubanshe, 2004.
Sung, Yun-wing. *The Emergence of Greater China: The Economic Integration of Mainland China, Taiwan and Hong Kong.* Houndmills: Palgrave Macmillan, 2005.
Suttmeier, Richard P., and Xiangkui Yao. "China's Post-WTO Technology Policy: Standards, Software, and the Changing Nature of Technonationalism." NBR Special Report 7. Seattle: National Bureau of Asian Research, May 2004.
Sutton, John. "The Auto Component Supply Chain in China and India: A Benchmarking Study." 2003. http://personal.lse.ac.uk/sutton/auto_component_printroom_version3.pdf.
Tang, Edward. "S'pore to Join Cobra Gold This Year." *Straits Times*, 14 January 2000.
Tefft, Sheila. "Taiwan Moves to Restore Shaken Investor Confidence." *Christian Science Monitor*, 1 April 1996.
Treisman, Daniel. "Rational Appeasement." *International Organization* 58, no. 2 (Spring 2004): 345–75.
Tsou, Tang. *The Cultural Revolution and Post-Mao Reforms: A Historical Interpretation.* Chicago: University of Chicago Press, 1986.
Tuchman, Barbara. *Stilwell and the American Experience in China, 1911–1945.* New York: Macmillan, 1970.
Tung, Chen-yuan. "China's Economic Leverage and Taiwan's Security Concerns with Respect to Cross-Strait Economic Relations." PhD diss., Johns Hopkins University, May 2002.
"Two Systems, One Grand Rivalry." *Economist*, 21 June 2003.
United Nations Conference on Trade and Development (UNCTAD). *World Investment Report.* http://unctad.org/Templates/Page.asp?intItemID=1465&lang=1.
United States. Department of Defense. *Annual Report to Congress: The Military Power of the People's Republic of China 2003.* Washington, DC: Department of Defense, 2003.
———. *Annual Report to Congress: The Military Power of the People's Republic of China 2004.* Washington, DC: Department of Defense, 2004.
———. *Annual Report to Congress: The Military Power of the People's Republic of China 2005.* Washington, DC: Department of Defense, 2005.
———. *Annual Report to Congress: The Military Power of the People's Republic of China 2006.* Washington, DC: Department of Defense, 2006.
United States. Department of State. "An Overview of U.S.–East Asia Policy." Testimony by James A. Kelly, Assistant Secretary of State for East Asian and Pacific Affairs, before the House International Relations Committee, Washington, DC, 2 June 2004.
United States. International Trade Commission of the United States. *U.S.-Taiwan*

FTA: Likely Economic Impact of a Free Trade Agreement between the United States and Taiwan. Washington, DC: International Trade Commission of the United States, 2002. http://www.usitc.gov/publications/abstract_3548.htm.
United States. U.S.-China Economic and Security Review Commission. *The National Security Implications of the Economic Relationship between the United States and China.* 2002 Report to Congress. Washington, DC: U.S. Government Printing Office, July 2002.
———. *The National Security Implications of the Economic Relationship between the United States and China.* 2004 Report to Congress. Washington, DC: U.S. Government Printing Office, 2004.
———. *The National Security Implications of the Economic Relationship between the United States and China.* 2005 Report to Congress. Washington, DC: U.S. Government Printing Office, 2005.
United States. The White House. "Fact Sheet: Enterprise for ASEAN Initiative." http://www.whitehouse.gov/news/releases/2002/10/20021026-7.html.
———. "Joint Statement between the United States of America and the Republic of Indonesia." White House Press Release, 25 May 2005.
———. "Joint Vision Statement on the ASEAN-U.S. Enhanced Partnership." 17 November 2005. http://www.whitehouse.gov/news/releases/2005/11/20051117-4.html.
———. *The National Security Strategy of the United States of America.* 16 March 2006. http://www.whitehouse.gov/nsc/nss/2006/intro.html.
"Unprecedented Progress Made in 13 Years," *China Daily*, 3 April 2003
U.S.-China Business Council. "Foreign Investment in China: 2005." http://www.uschina.org/statistics/2005foreigninvestment_2.html.
"U.S. Considers Cuts to Forces in Korea." *New York Times*, 7 March 2003.
Vick, Alan, Richard Moore, Bruce Pirnie, and John Stillion. *Aerospace Operations Against Elusive Ground Targets.* Santa Monica, CA: Rand, 2001.
Walt, Stephen M. *The Origins of Alliances.* Ithaca, NY: Cornell University Press, 1987.
Waltz, Kenneth N. *Theory of International Relations.* Reading, MA: Addison-Wesley, 1979.
Wan, Ming. *Sino-Japanese Relations: Interaction, Logic, and Transformation.* Stanford, CA: Stanford University Press, 2006.
———. "Tensions in Recent Sino-Japanese Relations: The May 2002 Shenyang Incident." *Asian Survey* 43, no. 5 (September–October 2003): 826–44.
Wang Gungwu. *The Chinese Overseas: From Earthbound China to the Quest for Autonomy.* Cambridge, MA: Harvard University Press, 2000.
Wang Jisi. "China's Search for Stability with America." *Foreign Affairs* 84, no. 5 (September/October 2005): 39–48.
———. "Geostrategic Trends in Asia: A Chinese View." Conference paper presented at the Regional Outlook Forum, Institute of Southeast Asian Studies, Singapore, 6 January 2005.
Wang Keqin and Qiao Guodong. "Investigation Report on 'The Strikes on

Villagers' in Dingzhou, Hebei." *Zhongguo jingji shibao* [China Economic Times], 20 June 2005.

Wang, T. Y. "Lifting the 'No Haste, Be Patient' Policy: Implications for Cross-Strait Relations." *Cambridge Review of International Affairs* 15, no. 1 (2002): 131–39.

Ward, Andrew. "Ties between China and South Korea Blossom." *Financial Times*, 18 February 2002.

Weinstein, Michael A. "China's Geostrategy: Playing a Waiting Game." *Power and Interest News Report*, 7 January 2005. http://www.pinr.com/report.php?ac=view_report&report_id=253&language_id=1.

Weiss, John. *People's Republic of China and Its Neighbors: Partners or Competitors for Trade and Investment?* Manila: Asian Development Bank, ADB Institute Discussion Paper 13, August 2004.

Weiss, John, and Shanwen Gao. *People's Republic of China's Export Threat to ASEAN: Competition in the US and Japanese Markets.* Manila: Asian Development Bank, ADB Institute Discussion Paper 2, January 2003.

Wen Jiabao. "Report of the Work of the Government" (Delivered at the Fourth Session of the Tenth National People's Congress on 5 March 2006). http://www.gov.cn/english/2006-03/14/content_227247.htm.

Wen Shengtang. "2003 nian de fanfubai douzheng" [The Struggle against Corruption in 2003]. In *2004 nian: Zhongguo shehui xingshi fenxi yu yuce* [The State of Chinese Society: Analysis and Forecast 2004], edited by Ru Xin, Lu Xueyi, and Li Peilin. Beijing: Shehui kexue wenxian chubanshe, 2004.

Wit, Joel S., Daniel B. Poneman, and Robert L. Gallucci. *Going Critical: The First North Korean Nuclear Crisis.* Washington, DC: Brookings Institution Press, 2004.

Wonacott, Peter. "Gas Lines and Growing Pains: China's Fuel Shortages Add to Pressure to End Central Planning." *Wall Street Journal*, 16 August 2005.

Wong, John, and Sarah Chan. "China-ASEAN Free Trade Agreement: Shaping Future Economic Relations." *Asian Survey* 43 (2003): 507–26.

World Bank. *China 2020: Development Challenges in the New Century.* 7 vols. Washington, DC: World Bank, 1997.

———. *Global Development Finance, 2002.* Washington, DC: World Bank, 2002.

———. *World Development Report 2005: A Better Investment Climate for Everyone.* http://siteresources.worldbank.org/INTWDR2005/Resources/complete_report.pdf.

World Intellectual Property Organization. "Record Number of International Patent Filings in 2004." Press release PR/403/2005. Geneva, 9 March 2005. http://www.wipo.int/edocs/prdocs/en/2005/wipo_pr_2005_403.html#.

Wu Guoguang. *Zhao Ziyang yu zhengzhi gaige* [Political Reform under Zhao Ziyang]. Hong Kong: Taipingyang shiji yanjiusuo, 1997.

Wu Jinglian. "Gezhong shehui liliang duidai gaige de butong taidu" [The Different Attitudes of Various Social Forces toward Reform]. *Dangdai Zhongguo jingji gaige* [Contemporary Chinese Economic Reform], 421–26, excerpted in *Shisan nianlai yingxiang zhongyang gaoceng jingji juece de lundian huibian*

[Compilation of Points of View That Have Influenced the High-Level Economic Decision Making of the Center over the Past Thirteen Years]. Beijing: n.p., 2003.

Wu, Lilian. "63% Favor Cross-strait Peace Agreement." *Central News Agency*, 22 July 2004. http://web.lexis-nexis.com/universe/.

Wu Yong. "Machine Tool Firm Recalls Products." *China Daily*, 11 August 2005.

Wu Yong and Fu Jing. "Foreign Investors Able to Buy Large SOEs." *China Daily*, 16 September 2005.

Xiao, Geng. *People's Republic of China's Round-Tripping FDI: Scale, Causes and Implications*. Manila: Asian Development Bank, ADB Institute Discussion Paper No. 7, July 2004.

Xin, Gu, and David Kelly. "Realistic Responses and Strategic Options: An Alternative CCP Ideology and Its Critics." *Chinese Law and Government* 29, no. 2 (Spring–Summer 1996).

Yamazawa, Ippei, and Ken-ichi Imai. *China Enters WTO: Pursuing Symbiosis with the Global Economy*. Tokyo: Institute of Developing Economies, Japan External Trade Organization, 2001.

Yan Xuetong. "Origins of the Policy to Pay Any Price to Contain Taiwan's Independence." *China Strategy Newsletter* 3 (July 2004): 39–42.(Center for Strategic and International Studies). http://www.csis.org/isp/csn/040720.pdf.

Yan, Yunxiang. "The Politics of Consumerism in Chinese Society." In *China Briefing 2000: The Continuing Transformation*, edited by Tyrenne White, 159–93. Armonk, NY: M. E. Sharpe, 2000.

Yang, Andrew N. D., and Col. Milton Wen-Chung Liao (ret.). "PLA Rapid Reaction Forces: Concept, Training, and Preliminary Assessment." In *The People's Liberation Army in the Information Age*, edited by James C. Mulvenon and Richard H. Yang, 48–57. Santa Monica, CA: Rand, 1999.

Yang, Dali L. *Remaking the Chinese Leviathan: Market Transition and the Politics of Governance in China*. Stanford, CA: Stanford University Press, 2004.

Yergin, Daniel. "Ensuring Energy Security." *Foreign Affairs* 85, no. 2 (March/April 2006): 69–82.

Ying, Leu Siew. "Riot Police Seize Files Being Guarded by Protesting Villagers." *South China Morning Post*, 13 September 2005.

You Wan and Qi Jianguo. "China's Long Term Development Trend and Environmental Economy." *Caimao jingji* [Finance and Trade Economics] 10 (2004): 11–17.

Yu Jianrong. "The Evil Forces in Rural Areas and the Deterioration of Grassroots Administration—A Survey of Southern Hunan." *Zhanlue yu guanli* [Strategy and Management] (September 2003): 1–14.

Yu Peilin, Li Qiang, and Sun Liping, eds. *Zhongguo shehui fenceng* [Social Stratification in China]. Beijing: Shehui kexue wenxian chubanshe, 2004.

Yue Xiaoyong. "A Chinese Perspective on Strengthening Stability and Security in East Asia." Presentation at the Wilton Park Conference on Reducing Tension in North East Asia, 6 October 2004.

Zebregs, Harm. "Intraregional Trade in Emerging Asia." Washington, DC: IMF Policy Discussion Paper, PDP/04/1, April 2004.

Zhan Lisheng and Wang Ying. "Guangzhou Oil Supply 'Returning to Normal.'" *China Daily*, 24 September 2005. http://www.chinadaily.com.cn/english/doc/2005-08/19/content_470459_2.htm.

Zhang Jingping. *Quanbian: Cong guanyuan xiahai dao shangren congzheng* [Power Shift: From Officials Going into Business to Businessmen Going into Government]. Hangzhou: Zhejiang renmin chubanshe, 2004.

Zhang Yunling. *Weilai 10–15 nian Zhongguo zai Taipingyang diqu mianlin de guoji huanjing* [The International Environment China Faces in the Asia-Pacific in the Next 10–15 Years]. Beijing: Zhongguo shehui kexue chubanshe, 2003.

Zhao Shukai. "Xiangcun zhili: Zuzhi he chongtu" [Governance in Villages: Organization and Conflict]. *Zhanlue yu guanli* [Strategy and Management] (November 2003): 1–8.

Zhao, Suisheng. *A Nation-State by Construction: Dynamics of Modern Chinese Nationalism*. Stanford, CA: Stanford University Press, 2004.

Zheng Bijian. "China's 'Peaceful Rise' to Great Power Status." *Foreign Affairs* 84 (September/October 2005): 18–24.

Zhongguo duiwai jingji tongji nianjian 2004 [China External Economic Statistics Yearbook 2004]. Beijing: Zhongguo tongji chubanshe, 2004.

Zhongguo qiche gongye nianjian 2005 [China Automotive Industry Yearbook 2005]. Beijing: Zhongguo qiche gongye nianjian bianjibu, 2005.

Zhongguo tongji nianjian 2005 [China Statistics Yearbook 2005]. Beijing: Zhongguo tongji chubanshe, 2005.

Zhongguo tongji nianjian 2006 [China Statistics Yearbook 2006]. Beijing: Zhongguo tongji chubanshe, 2006.

Zhongguo tongji zhaiyao 2005 [China Statistical Abstract 2005]. Beijing: Zhongguo tongji chubanshe, 2005.

Zhongguo tongji zhaiyao 2006 [China Statistical Abstract 2006]. Beijing: Zhongguo tongji chubanshe, 2006.

Zhou, Yuping, and Sanjaya Lall. "The Impact of China's FDI Surge on FDI in South-East Asia: Panel Data Analysis for 1986–2001." *Transnational Corporations* 14 (2005): 41–65.

Zhu Boru. "Growth Engine." *China Business Weekly*, 9–11 September 2005.

CONTRIBUTORS

LOREN BRANDT is Professor of Economics at the University of Toronto, Toronto, Canada.

JOSEPH FEWSMITH is Professor of International Relations and Political Science and Director of the East Asian Studies Interdisciplinary Program at Boston University.

ELLEN L. FROST is Visiting Fellow, Peter G. Peterson Institute for International Economics, and Adjunct Research Fellow, Institute of National Strategic Studies, National Defense University, Washington, D.C.

WILLIAM W. KELLER is Wesley W. Posvar Professor of International Security Studies and Director of the Matthew B. Ridgway Center for International Security Studies at the University of Pittsburgh, Pittsburgh, Pennsylvania.

LOUIS W. PAULY is Professor of Political Science and Director of the Center for International Studies at the University of Toronto, Toronto, Canada.

JOHN RAVENHILL is Professor in the Department of International Relations, Research School of Pacific and Asian Studies at the Australian National University, Canberra, Australia.

THOMAS G. RAWSKI is Professor of Economics and History and UCIS Research Professor at the University of Pittsburgh, Pittsburgh, Pennsylvania.

ROBERT S. ROSS is Professor of Political Science at Boston College, and Research Associate, John King Fairbank Center for East Asian Research, Harvard University, Cambridge, Massachusetts.

Adam Segal is Maurice R. Greenberg Senior Fellow in China Studies at the Council on Foreign Relations, New York, New York.

Xiaodong Zhu is Professor of Economics at the University of Toronto, Toronto, Canada.

INDEX

Note: Page numbers followed by *f* or *t* refer to figures or tables, respectively.